A HANDBOOK
on
THE LETTER TO
THE HEBREWS

The Handbooks in the **UBS Handbook Series** are detailed commentaries providing valuable exegetical, historical, cultural, and linguistic information on the books of the Bible. They are prepared primarily to assist practicing Bible translators as they carry out the important task of putting God's Word into the many languages spoken in the world today. The text is discussed verse by verse and is accompanied by running text in at least one modern English translation.

Over the years church leaders and Bible readers have found the UBS Handbooks to be useful for their own study of the Scriptures. Many of the issues Bible translators must address when trying to communicate the Bible's message to modern readers are the ones Bible students must address when approaching the Bible text as part of their own private study and devotions.

The Handbooks will continue to be prepared primarily for translators, but we are confident that they will be useful to a wider audience, helping all who use them to gain a better understanding of the Bible message.

Helps for Translators

A HANDBOOK ON

The Letter to the Hebrews

by Paul Ellingworth
and Eugene A. Nida

UBS Handbook Series

United Bible Societies
New York

PRINTED IN THE UNITED STATES OF AMERICA

Books in the series of **Helps for Translators** may be ordered from a national Bible Society or from either of the following centers:

United Bible Societies
European Production Fund
P.O. Box 81 03 40
70520 Stuttgart
Germany

United Bible Societies
1865 Broadway
New York, NY 10023
U. S. A.

L. C. Cataloging-in-Publication Data

Ellingworth, Paul.
    [Translator's handbook on the Letter to the Hebrews]
    A handbook on the Letter to the Hebrews / by Paul Ellingworth and Eugene A. Nida.
        p. cm. — (UBS handbook series) (Helps for translators)
    Originally published: Translator's handbook on the Letter to the Hebrews. c1983.
    Includes bibliographical references and index.
    ISBN 0-8267-0169-8
    1. Bible. N.T. Hebrews—Translating. 2. Bible. N.T. Hebrews —Commentaries. I. Nida, Eugene Albert, 1914– . II. Title. III. Title: Letter to the Hebrews. IV. Series. V. Series: Helps for translators.
BS2775.2.E4415 1994
227'.8706—dc20
                                       94–18834
                                          CIP

ABS-10/94-300-3,350-CM-5-102767

Contents

[v]

Preface

A Translator's Handbook on the Letter to the Hebrews is a continuation of the series of Handbooks in the United Bible Societies' Helps for Translators series. Special attention has been given to the structure of the discourse so that the translator will be able to understand the movement and the logical progression of the sections of this letter and how they contribute to the message of the whole.

The Today's English Version (TEV) and Revised Standard Version (RSV) translations are shown at the beginning of each section. TEV is then reproduced again at the beginning of the discussion of each verse. When TEV is quoted in the discussion, the words are underlined, while quotation marks are used when other translations are quoted. In addition, words and phrases from TEV or RSV are set in bold face when discussed, so that the translator can more easily locate the comments on a particular expression.

As is true for both Handbooks and Guides in the series, this volume concentrates on exegetical matters that are of prime importance for translators, and it attempts to indicate possible solutions for translational and linguistic problems that may occur. Translators' Guides provide important information in a relatively condensed form, using a format that makes it possible to retrieve the information easily. Handbooks such as this volume are biblical commentaries that deal with the full range of information important to translators. However, the authors do not attempt to provide the kind of help not directly related to translating, which other scholars and theologians may be seeking, since much of that information is available elsewhere. A limited Bibliography is included for the benefit of those who are interested in further study. Details of interest to translators with advanced training in textual studies and exegesis are included in the footnotes.

A Glossary is provided that explains technical terms according to their usage in this volume. An Index gives the location by page number of some of the important words and subjects discussed in the Handbook, especially as help is provided the translator in rendering these concepts into the receptor language.

Abbreviations Used in This Volume

<u>Bible Texts, Versions and Other Works Cited</u> (for details see Bibliography, page 325)

BJ	Bible de Jérusalem
Brc	Barclay
CLT	Common Language Translation
DuCL	Dutch common language translation
FrCL	French common language translation
GeCL	German common language translation
ItCL	Italian common language translation
JB	Jerusalem Bible
KJV	King James Version
Lu	Luther, Revidierter Text
Mft	Moffatt, The Bible: A New Translation
NAB	New American Bible
NEB	New English Bible
NIV	New International Version
Phps	Phillips
PoCl	Portuguese common language translation
RSV	Revised Standard Version
Seg	Segond
SpCL	Spanish common language translation
Syn	Synodale
TEV	Today's English Version
TNT	Translator's New Testament
TOB	Traduction Oecuménique de la Bible
UBS	United Bible Societies
Zür	Zürcher Bibel

Books of the Bible

1,2 Chr	1,2 Chronicles	Isa	Isaiah
Col	Colossians	Jer	Jeremiah
1,2 Cor	1,2 Corinthians	1,2 Kgs	1,2 Kings
Dan	Daniel	Lev	Leviticus
Deut	Deuteronomy	Mal	Malachi
Eph	Ephesians	Matt	Matthew
Exo	Exodus	Num	Numbers
Ezek	Ezekiel	Prov	Proverbs
Gal	Galatians	Psa	Psalms
Gen	Genesis	Rev	Revelation
Hag	Haggai	Rom	Romans
Heb	Hebrews	1,2 Sam	1,2 Samuel
Hos	Hosea	1,2 Tim	1,2 Timothy

Translating the Letter to the Hebrews

We do not know who wrote the Letter to the Hebrews, and we know nothing else that the author wrote. This means that we cannot, as in the case of Paul, use other letters to discover more about how the author thinks and writes. We have to rely mainly on the letter itself, which is rather short—less than one-seventh as long as Luke's writings. The evidence of writings which seem to have a background similar to that of this letter can also be used to help us understand Hebrews, but this evidence is less direct and must be used with care. Scholars have seen similarities to other parts of the New Testament, especially Stephen's speech in Acts 7; also to the letter of Barnabas, written in the last quarter of the first century A.D.; and still more to the writings of Philo, the Greek-speaking Jew who lived from about 20 B.C. to about A.D. 50. Such similarities, however, are limited. Stephen, for example, does not mention Jesus until the very end of his sermon (Acts 7.56)!

Just as we do not know the name of the writer, so we do not know to whom he was writing. This is less of a problem for the translator than might at first appear. One of the major difficulties in translating 1-2 Corinthians, for example, is that Paul knew so much more than we do about his readers' situation. Hebrews, by contrast, though written to a specific community, does not discuss the readers' problems in great detail. It has even been suggested that Hebrews grew out of a collection of sermons preached to one group of Christians, and then sent to another church with a concluding note. This would explain why Hebrews ends like a letter, but does not begin like one.

Hebrews, perhaps more than any other New Testament writing, is steeped in the Old Testament, which the author cited on the basis of the Septuagint, a Greek translation made some two hundred years before Christ. The author's use of Old Testament texts and his method of argument owe much to the influence of Jewish rabbis.

One of the general translation problems which arises out of the writer's Jewish background is his reluctance to use the name of God, even in Greek. For example, it is used in the first verse of the letter, but not again (except in quotations from the Old Testament) until 2.4, although there are several verbs in the passage which have God as subject. In translation, it will often be necessary to insert the name "God" rather than using a pronoun such as "he," which may not be clear.

The translator must be careful not to change the cultural setting; that is, he must not replace references to Jewish culture by features drawn from the translator's own culture. If this is done on any large scale, the translator will find himself in serious difficulties. One apparently minor change (for example, the replacement of "shedding of blood" by "libation" in an African language) could involve more and more changes in a hopeless attempt at consistency. It is better to find the closest possible linguistic equivalent for the original cultural features, and then to give any necessary explanations in footnotes or a glossary.

Although the author was a Jewish Christian, it is clear that he had an excellent grasp of Greek language and style. This is one reason why Luther (Lu) and some modern commentators have thought he was the "eloquent speaker" Apollos (see Acts 18.24-28). It seems best to describe this writing as a letter, written to encourage a group of Christians to hold on to their faith under persecution. However, it is carefully planned and may have been originally given as one or more sermons.

The literary character of this letter has three practical consequences for the translator:

1. There are passages where the translator may wish to use a somewhat more literary level of language than, for example, in translating Mark or James. Even a common language translation should be flexible enough to reflect differences between the various biblical writers.

2. There are many points at which the author seems to use different expressions primarily for the sake of variety, rather than as a means of conveying precise differences of meaning. Each of these cases will be discussed on its own merits, but the translator should remember that the writer is a literary craftsman rather than a technician trying to write with scientific precision.

3. The author is very skillful in moving smoothly from one subject to another. His usual method is to introduce a subject in passing, and then to discuss it in detail later in the letter. For example, the theme of Jesus as Son of God is stated in 1.2 and is not expanded until 2.10-17. The comparison between Jesus and the angels is mentioned in 1.4 and then explored in detail in the rest of the chapter. This means that although the main divisions of the letter are fairly clear, there is considerable difference of opinion on smaller divisions, and even about the precise points of the major ones (New American Bible [NAB] and New English Bible [NEB], for example, make major breaks at 5.1 and 11.1 instead of at 5.11 and 10.19). The most detailed study of the literary structure of Hebrews is that of A. Vanhoye (see bibliography), whose divisions are summarized in Appendix A, together with his reasons for dividing the text in this way.

Chapter 1

Today's English Version   **1.1-3**   Revised Standard Version

God's Word through His Son

1 In the past God spoke to our ancestors many times and in many ways through the prophets, 2 but in these last days he has spoken to us through his Son. He is the one through whom God created the universe, the one whom God has chosen to possess all things at the end. 3 He reflects the brightness of God's glory and is the exact likeness of God's own being, sustaining the universe with his powerful word. After achieving forgiveness for the sins of mankind, he sat down in heaven at the right side of God, the Supreme Power.

1 In many and various ways God spoke of old to our fathers by the prophets; 2 but in these last days he has spoken to us by a Son, whom he appointed the heir of all things, through whom also he created the world. 3 He reflects the glory of God and bears the very stamp of his nature, upholding the universe by his word of power. When he had made purification for sins, he sat down at the right hand of the Majesty on high,

In Greek, as in the King James Version (KJV) and the Zürcher Bibel (Zür), verses 1-4 form a single sentence. Most translations, with the exception of the common language translations (CLTs), treat them as a separate paragraph or section. However, if a translation is not to be based on the grammatical structure of the Greek but on its meaning, the translator may treat verses 1-3 as a separate section. Verse 4 has a double function. It points backward: the emphatic **name,** the last word in this long sentence in the Greek, probably refers to **Son** in verse 2. But it also points forward to the comparison between the Son and the angels, 1.5-14.

Within verses 1-3 there is an important break at the end of verse 2, where KJV has a semicolon and Revised Standard Version (RSV) a full stop. Grammatically, the subject of the first two verses is God the Father, and these verses include the main verb **has spoken.** Verses 3-4, on the other hand, make various statements about the Son. However, from the point of view of meaning, the transition is more gradual. On the one hand, verse 2b speaks of what the Father has done through the Son, and this is reflected in the Today's English Version's (TEV's) **he** (the Son) **is the one through whom God created.** On the other hand, verse 3 emphasizes the close relationship and **likeness** between the Father and the Son. In translating verse 2b, and in deciding where to end this section, the translator must not be guided by grammar alone, but primarily by meaning.

[3]

Verses 1-2a, to **through his Son**, express a contrast between God's speaking through the prophets and through his Son. This contrast is not developed either here or later in the letter. The points of contrast are as follows:

1.	2.
(a) in the past	in these last days
(b) many times and in many ways	("once" is implied by the singular "a son" and emphasized later in 7.27; 9.12; 10.10)
(c) to our ancestors	to us
(d) through the prophets	through his Son

Item (b) is emphasized in the Greek by its position at the beginning of the sentence. Both parts of item (a) are also in an emphatic position, and so are both parts of item (d), which come at the end of their respective clauses. Item (c) is not particularly emphasized. Each language has its own way of showing emphasis. Sometimes this is done by placing an expression at the beginning or at the end of a sentence, sometimes by placing it in an unusual position, or sometimes by the use of unusual or emphatic words.

KJV, like Phillips (Phps), produces a majestic example of restructuring by beginning with "God," the word which unites both halves of the contrast. Unfortunately, most modern translators will need to divide the sentence in order to make its meaning clearer.

The TEV section heading **God's Word through His Son** must often be restructured as "God speaks through his Son" or "God reveals himself through his Son" or even "God speaks to people through his Son." (See the comments in verse 1 on God spoke and through the prophets.)

1.1   **In the past God spoke to our ancestors many times and in many ways through the prophets,**

In the past implies "long ago" (Barclay [Brc]; Knox "in old days"). At the time this letter was written, most Jews believed that the age of prophecy had ended centuries before. The early church had its prophets too (see Acts 11.27; 13.1; 15.32; 21.10), but the context, and the use of the Greek article translated **the**, show that the Old Testament prophets are meant.

The phrase **In the past** may be expressed in some languages by a remote past tense of the verb. It is important, however, that such a tense form of the verb should not reflect mythological or legendary information but should point to some event which took place many, many years before.

God spoke (compare verse 2 **he has spoken**). The tense of **spoke** and **has spoken** (verse 2) is the same in Greek and refers to an event completed in the past. It is more natural in English to say "has spoken" about a recent event such as the coming of Christ. The Greek verbs throughout verses 1-2 make it clear that the events are thought of as taking place at particular times; they are not a gradual process. In verse 3, the writer will change to present tense in order to describe the unchanging nature and work of the Son.

The expression **God spoke . . . through his prophets** must be treated as a causative in a number of languages: "God caused the prophets to speak on his behalf" or "God caused the prophets to speak for him."

To our ancestors is literally "to the fathers." "Fathers" was a common Jewish way of describing all ancestors, just as "son of David" could mean a descendant many generations after David. **Our** is not in the Greek and may have been omitted because not all the original readers were Jews. Similarly, most modern readers of Hebrews are not Jews. If **our** is added in translation, it is best to use the inclusive rather than the exclusive form, in the case of most languages which employ the so-called inclusive-exclusive distinction for the first person plural.

Many times and in many ways: some people take these expressions to mean the same thing and combine them in translation, for example, "many different glimpses of the truth" (Phps), "in many manners" (Dutch common language translation [DuCL]). The distinction between them should not be overemphasized, as Jerusalem Bible (JB) tends to do ("at various times in the past and in various different ways"), since the author may use two similar words for stylistic effect. If there is a distinction in meaning, it is that the word translated **many times** means "in many parts," that is, each prophet gave his own part of a message which has now been given completely through Christ (compare KJV). NEB's "in fragmentary . . . fashion" gives the meaning, though not in common language; the dictionary of the United Bible Societies' (UBS) Greek New Testament gives "little by little, many times."

Since the meaning of the expression **many times and in many ways** is essentially distributive, in the sense that certain parts of the revelation take place at different times, it is appropriate in a number of languages to translate this expression as "part then, part later" or "part part, then again." Such expressions are highly idiomatic, and have a distributive meaning by the repetition of the same or closely related expressions. If, however, one wishes to make a distinction in the meaning of the two Greek expressions, it is, of course, possible to translate **many times and in many ways** as "often and by means of many different persons."

Through the prophets balances **through his Son** in verse 2. The Greek is literally "in the prophets." It is unlikely that this means "in the person of the prophets" or "in what they said and did." More probably it means "in what the prophets wrote" (compare "in Isaiah the prophet," Mark 1.2), and it may be necessary to state this in translation. However, the more general meaning "by," "through," or "by means of the prophets" is also possible and makes a better parallel to "in a Son" in verse 2. The translation **through** is to be preferred, both in verse 1 and in verse 2, for three reasons: first, the Greek word is the same, and there is nothing to suggest that the meaning varies. Second, there is a close parallel in the context, which speaks of God using different means, **the prophets** and **the Son,** to achieve the same end. Third, in English and in many other languages, "God has spoken in his Son" is not natural and in any case does not convey anything more than "God has spoken through his Son."

As already noted in the discussion of the expression **God spoke,** the phrase **through the prophets** must be understood in most languages as being part of a causative construction, that is to say, "God caused his prophets to speak on his behalf," or even "what the prophets said was what God caused them to say."

Though it is true that the term **prophets** could be translated in this context as "those who foretell the future" or "those who speak about what is to happen," it seems better in general to use some such expression as "to speak on behalf of God" rather than to focus primarily upon foretelling. Throughout the Scriptures the emphasis of the role of the prophet is upon his speaking on behalf of God.

1.2 but in these last days he has spoken to us through his Son. He is the one through whom God created the universe, the one whom God has chosen to possess all things at the end.

TEV **but** expresses in a word the contrast which the original expresses in sentence structure, literally, "God having spoken . . . through the prophets . . . he has spoken to us through the Son." If **but** is used in translation, it is important to employ a term that will not suggest contradiction in content but merely contrast in the way in which this communication took place, that is, through the **Son** rather than merely through the **prophets.** It may even be necessary in some languages to translate "then it was through the prophets; now it is through his Son."

In these last days does not mean simply "these last few days," as in Luke 24.18, where the Greek is different. The writer means that the time had now come which the Old Testament had called "the last days," "the day of the Lord," or simply "that day" (for example, Num 24.14; Dan 10.14; compare Joel 3.1; Acts 2.17,20); "the last days" had become "these last days, in which we are living." JB gives the meaning "in our own time, the last days"; compare French common language translation (FrCL) "in these days which are the last." **In these last days** is a slightly awkward expression in English, and it was very unusual in Greek. Some translations replace "these" by its equivalent "now," to give "now, at the end of time" (for example, German common language translation [GeCL]; compare DuCL). The translator should in any case avoid translating "day" by a term which can only refer to a period of twelve or twenty-four hours.

The expression **in these last days** is extremely difficult to translate without being misleading, for the term **last** must be related to some other period of time or sequence if people are really to understand what is involved. In some languages the closest equivalent of **in these last days** is "now at the end of this age" or "now when we are living near the end of this age."

To us clearly includes both the writer and his readers, and probably others as well. For languages which make the distinction, an inclusive "we" must clearly be used.

Through his Son (see also notes on verse 1) is literally "through a Son," as in RSV. This is not a suggestion, despite 2.10, that Jesus was only one son among many sons of equal status. In writing "a Son" rather than "the Son," the author means **God has spoken to us through** one who is not merely a prophet but a **Son.**

Brc gives a good paraphrase: "he has spoken in one whose relation to himself is that of Son." However, in most languages the rendering of **his Son** by "a son" would be misleading, since the indefinite form would suggest any one of several sons. Since the reference is obviously to a particular son, it is essential in most languages to employ a definite marker, and in this instance the possessive pronoun **his** serves best to indicate specifically the person involved.

There is no distinction in Greek between "Son" and "son." Most European languages keep the form "Son" in referring to Christ, but there is a general tendency to use fewer capitals, and the translator must be guided by normal usage in his own language. The translator should also remember that the distinction between "Son" and "son" is lost when a text is read aloud; the distinction should thus be made clear in other ways, depending on the context.

The second half of verse 2 contains two statements about the Son: (a) God appointed him heir of all things; (b) through him God created the world. TEV and other CLTs reverse the order of these two statements, since the first points to the future and the second points to the past. Before coming to a decision about their relation to one another, it is useful to look in more detail at certain individual words.

The word translated **created** is a good example of the author's flexible use of words. A technical term for **created** exists in Greek, and the author uses the related noun in 4.13 and 9.11. In this verse, however, he uses the common word for "made" (KJV, Spanish common language translation [SpCL]), which in Greek occurs in different meanings in 3.2; 8.9; 10.9; and elsewhere. It is not advisable in translation to use a term for "create" in the sense of "to make out of nothing." In a number of languages there is no technical term for "create" which differs essentially in meaning from a more general term meaning "to make." There is certainly no necessity to use a phrase meaning "to make out of nothing" in order to represent what some persons might insist is a necessary component of "create."

The expression translated **the universe** can mean "the ages." La Bible de Jérusalem (BJ)—but not JB—misleadingly adopts this rendering here. In this verse, as always, words must be translated according to their context. With two exceptions the writer uses the word for "age" in the singular, or in set phrases meaning "forever." As to the two exceptions, 9.26 clearly refers to time and 11.3 to place. In 1.2 the writer is not thinking of time, but rather of the world and all it contains (compare **all things**, verse 2; **the universe**, verse 3).

In a number of languages the equivalent of **the universe** is "the sky and the earth." But in other languages it may be better to translate "everything there is" or "all that exists."

The word which RSV translates "**also**" is not essential to the structure of the Greek sentence. By including it, the author emphasizes the words "he made the world."

Chosen translates a common Greek word for "appointed"; appointment to an office implies a choice of the one appointed. **Chosen** does not imply "chosen among several sons." It is therefore better in most languages to use an expression which will emphasize the fact of "being appointed." This may be expressed in some languages by a word meaning essentially "designated" or "selected for the purpose of." Theologians discuss at what moment Jesus was appointed heir of all things. The translator is not concerned with this, but he should note that the verb refers to an event which occurred at some particular point of time. See the comment on God spoke in verse 1.

The one . . . to possess is literally "**heir**," as in RSV. "Heir" in English means someone who receives or is entitled to receive something when its previous owner dies. In biblical Greek, with its Hebrew background, this idea may sometimes be present (compare 9.16; Mark 12.7 and parallel passages). However, more often the main thought is that of taking possession of land or other property, whether or not the former owner has died. In the New Testament, believers are said to "inherit" the kingdom of God, that is, to share in God's reign or rule (for example Matt 25.34). They are also said to "inherit" or take possession of salvation (Heb 1.14), a blessing (1 Peter 3.9), glory (Rom 8.7-18), and incorruption (1 Cor 15.50); also "the promise" (Heb 6.12). The author is probably thinking of Old Testament stories about Israel taking possession of the Promised Land. In the New Testament, inheritance is often connected with gifts which can only be fully possessed in the future. This is the basis for TEV's **possess all things at the end.**

A literal rendering of the term "**heir**" (the expression found in many translations) can be misleading, as already noted, since one important component is the death of the individual who previously owned or possessed some object. The emphasis in the Bible is upon "coming to possess what is rightfully one's own," and therefore some such phrase as "to come to possess," or "to become the owner of," or "to become the one to whom all things belong" may be more satisfactory.

At the end is implied, but TEV and GeCL make it explicit. There may be complications involved in the phrase **at the end,** since it may be necessary in some languages to specify what has come to an end or the end of what. Sometimes this may be expressed more satisfactorily as "finally possess all things."

It is now easier to see the meaning of verse 2b as a whole. This may be expanded as follows: "By God's command and appointment, his Son is shortly to take possession of the entire universe. But in any case, the universe belongs by right to the Son, since it was through him that God made it and everything it contains." GeCL brings out the implied logical relation between the two statements: "Through him God created the world. Therefore God also decided that at the end, everything should belong to him." However, a slight weakness in both TEV and GeCL is that by making **at the end** explicit, they weaken to some extent the idea that "the end" has already begun (see comment on **in these last days**).

1.3   He reflects the brightness of God's glory and is the exact likeness of God's own being, sustaining the universe with his powerful word. After achieving forgiveness for the sins of mankind, he sat down in heaven at the right side of God, the Supreme Power.

This verse is full of picture language. Here, as in similar passages, the translator needs to ask a number of important questions: (a) How far was each metaphor still "live"[1] for the writer? (b) What is its literal meaning? (c) Does our language use the same metaphor with the same meaning? (d) If not, does it have a different metaphor with the same meaning? (e) If not, how can I translate the metaphor literally?

The brightness of God's glory was probably a live metaphor for the writer: **glory** is often associated with light and less often with weight. The word translated **brightness** may mean either "radiance" (Knox, Phps, Brc; compare KJV "brightness"; JB, NAB "radiant light"; NEB "effulgence"; Translator's New Testament [TNT] "radiates") or "reflection" (NAB; compare RSV). FrCL includes both meanings: "He reflects the splendor of the divine glory." The same word is used in Wisdom 7.26, where the same meanings are also possible (see NEB text and note).

In a number of languages it is difficult to speak about "reflecting the brightness of God's glory." In the first place "glory" is often related to "wonderfulness" and not to the concept of being "shiny" or of "brightness." As a result it is very difficult to use some term which is based upon the concept of light being "reflected." Therefore, it may be best to translate **He reflects the brightness of God's glory** as "He shows how wonderful God is" or "How wonderful God is can be seen in how wonderful he is."

The original meanings of the Greek word translated **exact likeness** included "engraving," "engraved sign," "imprint," and "reproduction." Brc paraphrases: "He is the exact impression of his being, just as the mark is the exact impression of the seal." However, by the time this letter was written, the term was becoming a dead metaphor meaning "essential nature" or "characteristic." The wider context stresses the Son's unity with God, and the way in which he shares in various aspects of God's work. Therefore in the first part of verse 3 it is better to stress the idea of the Son's **brightness** (compare GeCL "in the Son of God, the glory of God shines forth"). The idea of a "pale reflection" should in any case be avoided.

Is the exact likeness of God's own being may be expressed most satisfactorily in a number of languages as "is just like God," or "is the same as God," or "what God is like is what he is like," or "what is true about God is true about his Son."

As already noted, verse 3 does not begin a new sentence in Greek. The first part of the verse is literally "who being a brightness of glory and a character of nature his," "his" referring both to "brightness" and "character." Most translations begin a new sentence at this point and replace the participle "being" with a verb in the present tense, such as TEV's **He reflects.** This makes the passage easier to read. It also marks more clearly the difference between verses 1-2, which speak about particular acts of God, and verse 3, which describes what the Son is and has done.

---

[1] See J. de Waard, "Biblical Metaphors and their Translation" in Technical Papers for the Bible Translator, January 1974, pp. 107-116. In English, for example, "He was a lion in the fight" is a live metaphor, since the sentence makes one think of a lion. "He is an ace racing driver" is a dead metaphor, since the sentence does not usually make one think of an ace in a pack of playing cards.

The meaning of the Greek word translated **sustaining** is the common word for "bear" or "carry." Although it may also mean "bring into being," none of the translations consulted relate it to God's act of creation. It is difficult to find a translation which will convey the two ideas of support and movement, that is, of "upholding" and "carrying on or forward." Brc's expanded translation is better than most: "It is he who sustains all things by the dynamic power of his word." GeCL has "through his strong word he holds the universe together." In some languages, two verbs may be needed. The literal "word of power" is a common biblical way of saying "powerful word." We are not told what kind of a word it is; JB translates "his powerful command." "Word" in any case means "message" rather than a single word.

In a number of instances it may be preferable to render the participial phrase **sustaining the universe with his powerful word** as a separate sentence, but it may be extremely difficult to express in a succinct way the relation between **sustaining** and **his powerful word.** In some instances the closest equivalent may be "by his powerful command he causes the universe to function as it does" or "by his powerful words he causes all that exists to continue to exist" or ". . . he causes everything to continue to be as it is."

The second sentence of 1.3 in TEV makes two statements about God's Son: (a) he made people clean from their sins, and (b) he sat down at the right side of God. Both these statements refer to events which took place at particular points in time, "once and for all," as the writer will insist later in the letter (7.27; 9.12; 10.10). The Greek text makes the second statement depend on the first, and most translations, including TEV, keep this construction. However, this does not always mean that the second statement, containing the main verb, is the more important. In other words, making men clean from their sins is not just a preliminary to the main event of sitting down at the right side of God. DuCL uses two main verbs linked by "and": "He cleansed humanity from their sins, and afterward took his place at the right side of God's majesty in heaven."

After achieving forgiveness for the sins of mankind. The phrase **of mankind** is implied, as RSV shows. Some ancient manuscripts, followed by KJV, have "when he had by himself purged sins," but this is not the best text to be followed. **After achieving forgiveness** is literally "having made purification." In Hebrew (compare Job 7.21), Greek, English, and other languages, this is a natural metaphor for dealing with sin. The meaning is "forgave" or "set free from" (GeCL). **Achieving forgiveness for the sins of mankind** can be expressed as a causative: "causing people's sins to be forgiven" or "making it possible for people's sins to be forgiven."

In some languages there are two different words which are often translated as "sins," the first referring to specific events or deeds, and the second referring primarily to the resulting guilt. In such instances it is, of course, this second meaning which is in focus in this expression, since it is not the actual events that are forgiven but the resulting guilt.

Forgiveness is often expressed in rather idiomatic ways: "to blot out," "to wipe clean," "to throw behind one's back," "to throw away," or even "to determine to remember no more."

In some cases it may be necessary to indicate that God is the one who is ultimately the agent for the forgiveness of sins, and thus **achieving forgiveness for the sins of mankind** may be expressed as "making it possible for God to forgive people's sins" or "showing how God forgives people's sins."

In choosing an expression for **he sat down,** it is important to use a phrase which would imply sitting down in a position of authority. One would certainly want to avoid an expression which would suggest that Jesus sat down because he was exhausted from having procured the forgiveness of sins.

In many cultures, as in the Bible, **the right side** is the place of honor. Jesus is equal to God the Father, and so he is (figuratively) close to him, sharing fully in his power (see 1 Kgs 2.19; Acts 2.34; Eph 1.20; and especially Rev 3.21). On the other hand, in some cultures the left side is the place of honor, but it would not be appropriate to change throughout the Bible the metaphorical expressions of "right side" in order to read "left side." However, it may be necessary to employ some marginal note indicating that from the biblical viewpoint it is the right side which is the place of honor.

God is implied; literally "the greatness in the high (places)," a common way for Jews, and therefore Jewish Christians, to speak indirectly about God.

The Supreme Power may be expressed as "the one who is powerful above all," or "the one who alone has great power," or "the one who alone is able to do anything."

TEV	**1.4-14**	RSV

The Greatness of God's Son

4 The Son was made greater than the angels, just as the name that God gave him is greater than theirs. 5 For God never said to any of his angels,

    "You are my Son;
        today I have become your
        Father."

Nor did God say about any angel,

    "I will be his Father
        and he will be my Son."

6 But when God was about to send his first-born Son into the world, he said,

    "All of God's angels must worship
        him."

7 But about the angels God said,

    "God makes his angels winds,
        and his servants flames of
        fire."

8 About the Son, however, God said:

    "Your kingdom, O God, will last[a]
        forever and ever!

4 having become as much superior to angels as the name he has obtained is more excellent than theirs.

5 For to what angel did God ever say,

    "Thou art my Son,
        today I have begotten thee"?

Or again,

    "I will be to him a father,
        and he shall be to me a son"?

6 And again, when he brings the first-born into the world, he says,

    "Let all God's angels worship
        him."

7 Of the angels he says,

    "Who makes his angels winds,
        and his servants flames of fire."

8 But of the Son he says,

    "Thy throne, O God,[a] is for ever
        and ever,
        the righteous scepter is the

[11]

You rule over your[b] people
with justice.
9 You love what is right and
hate what is wrong.
That is why God, your God, has
chosen you
and has given you the joy of an
honor far greater
than he gave to your
companions."
10 He also said,
"You, Lord, in the beginning
created the earth,
and with your own hands
you made the heavens.
11 They will disappear, but you
will remain;
they will all wear out like
clothes.
12 You will fold them up like a
coat,
and they will be changed like
clothes.
But you are always the same
and your life never ends."
13 God never said to any of his angels:
"Sit here at my right side
until I put your enemies
as a footstool under your feet."
14 What are the angels, then? They
are spirits who serve God and are sent
by him to help those who are to receive
salvation.

[a] Your kingdom, O God, will last; or
God is your kingdom.
[b] your; some manuscripts have his.

scepter of thy[b] kingdom.
9 Thou hast loved righteousness
and hated lawlessness;
therefore God, thy God, has
anointed thee
with the oil of gladness beyond
thy comrades."
10 And,
"Thou, Lord, didst found the earth
in the beginning,
and the heavens are the work of
thy hands;
11 they will perish, but thou
remainest;
they will all grow old like a
garment,
12 like a mantle thou wilt roll
them up,
and they will be changed.[c]
But thou art the same,
and thy years will never end."
13 But to what angel has he ever said,
"Sit at my right hand,
till I make thy enemies
a stool for thy feet"?
14 Are they not all ministering spirits
sent forth to serve, for the sake of
those who are to obtain salvation?

[a] Or God is thy throne
[b] Other ancient authorities read his
[c] Other ancient authorities add like a
garment

The section heading **The Greatness of God's Son** must be rendered in some languages as "How great God's Son is" or "About how great God's Son is." In other languages it may be more appropriate to translate "God's Son is indeed great."

<u>**1.4**</u>   **The Son was made greater than the angels, just as the name that God gave him is greater than theirs.**

Verse 4 forms a bridge between the introductory statement of verses 1-3 about the greatness of the Son, and an extended comparison between the Son and angels, which goes on (with an interruption in 2.5-9) until the end of chapter 2. That is why some translations begin a new section here, as in TEV. The comparison is expressed as a proportion. A mathematical parallel would be "2 is to 4 as 3 is to 6." As RSV shows, this can produce a heavy and complicated sentence if translated literally, and TEV simplifies by using **just as.**

The word **Son** is not used in this verse in the Greek, but TEV supplies it from the context in order to have an explicit subject of the sentence. It is often impossible to speak about "the Son," since in many languages all terms which involve kinship must have some indication as to whom such an individual is related. In this case it may be necessary, therefore, to say "God's Son."

Was made is clearer than RSV's literal "**having become.**" Verse 5 states what verse 4 already implies, that it was by a specific act of the Father that Jesus became his Son. **Made** here has a meaning similar to **chosen** ("appointed") in verse 2; it does not have the meaning of **created** in verse 2. If one interprets **was made** in the sense of "became," it is possible to say "God's Son became greater than the angels"; but since the result derives from God's action, it may be appropriate to use a causative, for example, "God caused his Son to be greater than the angels." In this type of context **greater** must be understood in the sense of "more important," or "of higher rank," or "of greater authority."

In a number of languages **angels** is rendered as "messengers from heaven." It is far better to use such an expression than to employ some fanciful phrase such as "heavenly winged creatures" or "winged spirits."

In the Greek, the word **name** is in an emphatic position at the end of the sentence, and the context (especially verses 2 and 5) makes it probable that the **name** is that of the Son. DuCL translates "title," and this fits the immediate context well. In Hebrew thought, a name was not just a means of identification; it referred to someone's whole nature or personality. For example, when Jesus gives Simon the name Peter (Matt 16.18), he is declaring that Simon will **be** a rock; when God calls Jesus his Son, he **is** God's Son.

The name that God gave him is literally "he has inherited a name"; compare KJV "he hath by inheritance obtained a . . . name." The metaphor of inheritance was discussed in the comments on verse 2. Here the meaning is that the Son has received his name from God as a gift. The tense of the verb shows that the gift is a permanent possession.

In a number of languages it is difficult to speak of "giving a name to a person." Therefore it may be necessary to translate **the name that God gave him** as "the name that God assigned to him," or "the name by which God calls him," or "the name that God said belonged to him." By introducing an expression such as "belonged to," one can do justice to the underlying meaning of the Greek, in which "inheritance" involves the concept of "coming into one's rightful possession."

It may, however, be strange in some languages to speak of a "name" as being "greater" than that of someone else. In some instances, **is greater than theirs** may be rendered as "shows that he is greater than they are."

In a number of languages one must distinguish clearly between a personal name which identifies an individual, and a title indicating rank. In this context the emphasis is upon the title which was given to Jesus.

Verses 5-14 consist almost entirely of quotations from the Old Testament which are used to illustrate the fact that God has given the Son greater authority than the angels. The writer usually does not quote directly from the Hebrew but from the Septuagint, and often he does not quote the Septuagint exactly. This is the reason why the quotations in Hebrews are not always exactly as they appear in the Old Testament. In translating a quotation, the translator should respect its New Testament form and not try to harmonize the quotation with the Old Testament passage quoted.

1.5   **For God never said to any of his angels,**
            "You are my Son;
                today I have become your Father."
        Nor did God say about any angel,
            "I will be his Father
                and he will be my Son."

The quotations are (a) from Psalm 2.7 and (b) from 2 Samuel 7.14, which is narrated again in 1 Chronicles 17.13. Both TEV and RSV correctly make **God** explicit (KJV "he"). At the beginning of sections it is often good to replace pronouns by nouns, since public readings of Scriptures and published selections often omit the earlier verses.

In the original, as in RSV, this verse is a rhetorical question, that is, a question to which the answer is assumed. In this case, the only possible answer to the question "To which angel . . . ?" is "To no angel," so that the question is the equivalent of a strong negative statement. Knox modifies the question to make its rhetorical nature clearer: "Did God ever say to one of the angels . . . ?" Most common language translations, and other translations such as JB, NEB, and TNT, replace the question by a statement.

TEV's **For** translates a common Greek word which often indicates a general causal connection, and in some places it may be omitted in translation. Here, however, the word **For** has its full force and implies "The Son has been given by God a higher status than angels (verse 4), and this is confirmed by God speaking in Scripture as follows . . . ." It may therefore be better to expand **For;** for example, "That is why God never said to any of the angels . . . ."

TEV's **his** before **angels** is implicit, as RSV shows; SpCL has "God never said to any angel." **God never said to any of his angels** may be rendered as "God never said to any one of his messengers" or ". . . any one of his heavenly messengers."

In the first quotation, **you** and **Son** are emphasized.

I have become your Father avoids the metaphor "begotten," which could be misleading for various reasons: first, because the English word is archaic; second, because in English, as in some other languages, the verb "beget" is not often used as a metaphor; and third, because it could suggest that the Son did not exist until the moment at which God said "I have begotten you." As the wider context shows (especially 2.14-18), it is not Christ's existence which begins at this point, but the relationship between Father and Son which Hebrews links with the death and exaltation of Christ.

There are a number of problems in rendering **today I have become your Father**. Technically there should be no complication in this expression which denies God's relationship to an angel, but indirectly this statement is to be interpreted as the relation of God to his Son. In some languages to say "I have become your father" would mean either by adoption, or by recognition that someone actually was a son even though the relationship had been previously denied. Some translators have wanted to use some such expression as "from now on you are my Son," but this involves serious problems for the preincarnate state of Christ. One way to deal with this complex expression is to say "today I declare that you are my Son." In this way the focus, as in the Greek, is upon the relationship between the Father and the Son without introducing what may be extraneous and otherwise misleading implications. In some languages the translation of **you are my Son** and **I have become your Father** may have to be combined into a single statement.

Nor did God say about any angel: RSV's **"Or again"** (KJV more literally "and again"; compare 2.13; 4.5; 10.30) is a formula which simply serves to mark the beginning of a new quotation; it has the same function as closing and reopening quotation marks. TEV is followed rather closely by most other CLTs: FrCL "about an angel"; GeCL, SpCL "about any angel"; DuCL has simply "or," which is quite enough.

In the second quotation, the Greek for (I) **will be** and (he) **will be** are different forms of the same verb. In some languages, where the forms for the first and third person of the verb are the same, the sentence can be made more simple by omitting the second verb; compare DuCL "I will be his Father, and he my Son." In some languages it may be necessary to render **will be** as "will become" since there is an implied change of state or relationship; for example, "I will become his Father, and he will become my Son."

1.6   **But when God was about to send his first-born Son into the world, he said,**
          "All of God's angels must worship him."

The quotation probably comes from the Septuagint of Deuteronomy 32.43, but the author may also have had Psalm 96.7 in mind.

The introduction to the quotation raises several problems for the translator.

The word **But** makes a contrast with what verse 5 has said about angels. GeCL first edition expressed this contrast even more clearly: "But of the Son he said, when he sent . . . ." The Greek adds "also" to "he said," but only to show that another quotation is about to open. However, "also" can be omitted, especially in translations which use quotation marks.

The Greek word for RSV's **"And again"** probably introduces a new quotation, as in verse 5b. If so, the phrase may be omitted in any translation which uses other ways to mark quotations, for example, with quotation marks. Some scholars see here a reference to the return or second coming of Christ, and therefore translate "When God brings again his first-born Son into the world . . ." (similarly Knox), but the clause more probably refers to Christ's becoming man.

[15]

RSV's **"when he brings"** may refer (a) to an indefinite time; (b) to something which had not happened when Deuteronomy was written, but which had happened when Hebrews was written; for example, the birth of Jesus, or his earthly life as a whole, or his exaltation; (c) to something which had not yet happened when Hebrews was written. Many translations and commentaries, including TEV, choose (b), **when God was about to send**, referring to the birth of Jesus, or his coming into the world. However, the context, especially verses 1-4 and 13, is more concerned with Christ's enthronement or ascension. This too is a past event which may be referred to in translation by a past tense.

The Greek verb may mean either **send** or **"bring"** (RSV). If verse 6a is understood, as in TEV, to refer to the incarnation, **send** is right; God in heaven is sending his Son to earth. If verse 6a refers to Christ's enthronement, RSV's **"bring"** is correct, indicating movement toward God in heaven.

His first-born Son: literally **"the first-born"** (RSV). In view of 2.10-15, TEV is probably correct, though **his** and **Son** are not explicit in the Greek. GeCL has "with the right of the first-born," emphasizing the supreme status of the Son, not his coming first in time. In Old Testament times the eldest son was considered the most important. He was given special privileges (see Gen 25.5-6; 27.35-36; 37.21-24). It was therefore natural for Christians to think of Jesus, the Messiah, as God's first-born Son (see Col 1.15-17,18; Rom 8.29; Rev 1.5). Chapter 2 states that there are other sons after the **first-born**, namely "believers," but this is not emphasized at this point.

In a number of languages there may be complications involved in attempting to render literally "first-born." In the first place, a term meaning "born" may refer primarily to the activity of a mother in giving birth rather than to the relationship of a father to a son. It may therefore be better to render **his first-born** as simply "his first son."

When God was about to send his first-born Son into the world may be more satisfactorily rendered in some languages as "just before God sent his first Son into the world." The expression **send . . . into the world** presupposes a type of preexistence.

The Greek word for **world** may mean (a) the present inhabited earth (like **world** in Heb 4.3; 9.26, though the Greek word there is different); or (b) the future or heavenly world (as 2.5 makes clear).

TEV chooses (a) and is supported by Brc: "When he leads his firstborn Son on to the stage of world history." This brings out the human element in **the world**, though perhaps "world history" is too modern a concept for Hebrews.

The context is generally concerned with Christ's enthronement and therefore favors (b). If this is chosen, some such phrase as "the heavenly world" may be needed.

If verse 1.6a is understood in this second way, TEV's **he said** is still clearer than RSV's literal **"he says."** The author probably means "What is written in Deuteronomy 32.43 is what God said when he brought his Son back to heaven to sit at his right side."

Verse 6a may thus be translated: "When God brought his first-born Son back into the heavenly world, he said . . . ."

KJV's "And" before "let all the angels of God worship him" is included in the Greek text as part of the quotation, but it interrupts the flow of the sentence and adds nothing to the meaning. It is best omitted in translation.

The Greek word for **worship** originally implied bowing low before someone and kissing the ground before his feet: GeCL "All God's angels shall throw themselves down before him."

In some languages it may be more natural for God to speak of "my angels" rather than **God's angels,** as in the verse quoted from the Old Testament.

In some languages it may be rather strange to say as in TEV, **he said, "All of God's angels must worship him,"** since in so many instances it is important to have with a verb such as **said** an indication of precisely to whom such a command is addressed. Therefore it may be far more natural and meaningful to say "he said to all of his angels, You must worship him." Though in some languages worship is expressed in terms of "bowing before" or "prostrating oneself on the ground before," in a number of languages the act of worship is expressed as "giving honor to" or "recognizing as divine."

1.7   But about the angels God said,
        "God makes his angels winds,
          and his servants flames of fire."

This verse begins another contrast: verse 7 refers to the angels, and verses 8-12 to the Son. The "And" with which the verse opens (KJV) should therefore be omitted, so as to make a clean break. **But** in TEV suggests a contrast with verse 6, and TEV therefore uses **however** in verse 8 for variety. However, in the Greek the major contrast is clearly between verses 7 and 8. Earlier editions of TEV left the minor contrast between verses 6 and 7 implicit by beginning verse 7 This is what God said about the angels.

About the angels God said may be expressed as "God spoke about his angels" or "in speaking about his angels, God said."

God, at the beginning of the quotation, is implied, but RSV shows how confusing a translation can be if this is not made explicit. On a first reading, it is not at all clear to whom RSV's **"Who"** refers.

The quotation is an example of parallelism, a common device of Hebrew poetry. As in this verse, the two halves of the statement often mean essentially the same. For stylistic reasons it may be necessary to use two different words for **angels** and **servants,** but there is no difference in meaning in this context. In English and some other languages, the **and** can be omitted before **his servants** to make it clear that the second line of the quotation largely repeats the first.

In order to understand the first line of the quotation, it is necessary to realize that Greek has the same word for **wind** and "spirit." (The same play on words is made in John 3.8.) Since the second line of the quotation mentions **flames of fire,** it is best to translate **winds** in the first line. However, since the same Greek word is used in verse 14 with the meaning spirits, it may be helpful to add a footnote to verse 7; for example, "The same Greek word means 'wind' and 'spirit.' "

[17]

What is the exact relationship between **angels** and **servants** on the one hand, and **winds** and **flames of fire** on the other hand? In other words, what is the meaning of the word translated **makes**? The Hebrew text of Psalm 104.4 may mean either (a) God makes winds and flames into his messengers and servants; or (b) God turns his servants into winds and flames. The Greek text can mean only (b). Moffatt (Mft) translates "turns his angels into winds, his servants into flames of fire."

A strictly literal rendering of **God makes his angels winds, and his servants flames of fire** would imply that God was actually changing his angels into wind and changing his servants into flames of fire, as some kind of miraculous change of real substance. Obviously the emphasis here is upon the contrast between the functions and roles of the angels and of the servants of God. It is sometimes said that Hebrews wishes to emphasize the changeable nature of angels, in contrast with the eternal nature of the Son (verse 8). However, there is little or no evidence that "wind" and "fire" suggest weakness or changeableness in the Bible. The contrast between verses 7 and 8-10 is between angels as subordinate, created beings, and the Son as creator and Lord. It may thus be necessary in some languages to employ a simile rather than a metaphor. Hence, one may translate "God makes his angels to be like wind, and he causes his servants to be like flames of fire" or ". . . fiery flames."

1.8   About the Son, however, God said:
          "Your kingdom, O God, will last^a forever and ever!
          You rule over your^b people with justice.

^{a} Your kingdom, O God, will last; *or* God is your kingdom.
^{b} your; *some manuscripts have* his.

The word translated **About** in verses 7 and 8 more commonly means "To." **About** fits the context better in verse 7, where God is not speaking to the angels, but "To" is more suitable here in verse 8, because God is speaking to the Son. GeCL makes this distinction. **About the Son, however, God said** may therefore be rendered in a number of languages as "But God said to his Son." Alternatively, in some languages it may be possible to find a general expression meaning "with reference to," which may be used in both verses 7 and 8.

Verses 8-9 quote Psalm 45.6-7. The quotation is full of figures of speech. The way in which these are translated will depend largely on the culture of the people for whom the translation is being made. For example, in some areas "stool" is a better symbol of kingly power than "**throne**" (RSV), and TEV omits "**scepter**" (RSV) because it is a sign of authority which is no longer used in many cultures. There is a close parallel between "**throne**" and **kingdom** (in the sense of "kingly power").

There are two ways of punctuating the first line of the quotation. TEV's **Your kingdom, O God,** is the punctuation adopted by most translations. The alternative, "God is thy throne" (RSV footnote) is awkward, and nowhere else does the Bible use such language. At the end of the verse, as stated in the TEV note, a few good Greek manuscripts have "his God" instead of **your God**, and this is so difficult that it is probably the correct reading.

Therefore the meaning is probably:

> To the Son, however, God said:
> "Your kingdom, O God, will last forever and ever";
> and about him God said:
> "He rules over his kingdom with justice."

However, in translation it is simpler to follow early scribes in changing "his" to "your." No change of meaning is involved, since the subject in any case is Christ. TEV thus offers a good model of translation, except that, as already stated, "To" is better than **About** at the beginning of verse 8.

O God in English and some other languages is a little old-fashioned. The Traduction Oecuménique de la Bible (TOB) omits "O," and GeCL first edition turned the phrase into a separate statement: "You are God, your throne remains . . . ." However, the writer of Hebrews is not arguing, or trying to prove, that Christ is God. He assumes that Old Testament writers speak of Christ and sometimes call him "God."

Forever and ever is an English idiom equivalent to DuCL "in eternity"; FrCL, SpCL "for always"; GeCL "for all times."

It may seem very strange for God to address the Son as "God," and such an expression may even mislead a reader to think that God is addressing some other god. Therefore it may be far better to begin the quotation as "You are God and your kingdom will last forever and ever," or "You are God and you will always reign" or ". . . there will never be a time when you will not be reigning." **You rule over your people** may be simply rendered as "You govern your people."

The phrase **with justice** may require some expansion. For example, "Whenever you make decisions you do so justly" or "You are just in the way in which you rule your people."

1.9   **You love what is right and hate what is wrong.**
That is why God, your God, has chosen you
    and has given you the joy of an honor far greater
    than he gave to your companions."

This whole quotation, in its present context, is a favorable judgment given by God the Father on the total life and work of his Son. For this reason it is perhaps unnecessary to change the past tenses "loved" and "hated" into the present, as done in TEV and FrCL but not in other CLTs.

In rendering **You love what is right and hate what is wrong**, it may be necessary to specify who is related to what is right and what is wrong; for example, "You love to see people do what is right, and you hate to see people do what is wrong" or "You love what people do which is right, and you hate what people do which is wrong." This is probably what the verse means in its Old Testament setting. On the other hand, the relationship may be to the activity of the Son himself; therefore "You love to do what is right, and you hate to do what is wrong." This is probably what the verse means in Hebrews (compare 10.5-10).

In a number of languages it would be strange and even misleading to have a reference to **God, your God** in a place where God is already the speaker (see the beginnng of verse 8). Therefore it may be necessary to restructure the corresponding sentence as "That is why I your God have chosen you." It is also important to note that in some languages one cannot speak of **your God** in the sense of possessing God. One may, however, use a phrase such as "the God whom you worship" or "the God to whom you belong." Note that with this shift of **God, your God** to "I your God" it is also necessary to introduce the first person singular in the latter part of verse 9; for example, "far greater than I have given to your companions."

Anointing with oil is associated in the Old Testament with happiness (compare Isa 61.3), and especially with the coronation of a king. Oil is not used in this way in most cultures, and a glossary note on "anoint" may be needed as in TEV. GeCL brings out the meaning: "therefore has the Lord, your God, chosen you and given greater honor and joy to you than to all who belong to you." **Has given you the joy of an honor** is in many languages expressed only as a type of causative expression. For example, "I have given you honor which causes you joy" or "I have caused you to have joy because of an honor" or ". . . by means of an honor," or ". . . joy because I have honored you."

Your companions implies sharing rather than dependence. The writer does not say who are the **companions** of the Son, and so the translator does not need to make it explicit at this point, but the same word in Hebrews 3.1,14 (partners) refers to believers in Christ. **Companions** may be rendered as "those who are with you," but it can also be understood in the sense of "your friends" or "your colleagues."

Verses 10-12 are a quotation of Psalm 102.25-27, introduced simply by "**And**" (RSV), which TEV expands into **He also said.**

1.10   He also said,
        "You, Lord, in the beginning created the earth,
         and with your own hands you made the heavens.

The two halves of this quotation are parallel, so **and** may be omitted. "And," in English and other languages, leads the receptor to expect new information, not something largely equivalent to what has gone before. However, in Hebrew poetry "and" often introduces the second part of a parallelism. In such cases literal translation may be misleading, and the word "and" is best omitted.

The whole verse is introduced by an emphatic **You.** The writer is not saying that God began by creating the earth and went on to make the heavens. He is saying that, at the beginning of time, it was God who laid the foundations of the earth and at the same time made the heavens with his own hands.

In the Old Testament text, "the Lord" meant God. In Hebrews, as in Paul's letters, "the Lord" usually means the Son, and that is the probable meaning in this instance. In this context it is important to use for **Lord** the same term which is applied to Jesus in the Gospels, when he is addressed as "Lord." In some languages it is necessary to make a clear distinction between (a) "Lord" as it occurs in the New Testament in reference to Jesus Christ and (b) "Lord" in the Old Testament when it refers to God. In general, however, it is advisable to use precisely the same expression despite the ambiguity or obscurity.

In the beginning is a very difficult expression to render literally in some languages, since one must always specify what is involved in such a beginning. A more appropriate equivalent may be "before there was anything" or "before anything existed."

With your own hands is a poetic way of indicating direct involvement, but a literal rendering of such an expression might seem contradictory to those statements in Genesis which indicate that creation took place by the word of God (Gen 1.3,6,9). Other statements show that direct involvement without mentioning "hands" (Gen 2.7,8,19,22), though they may be implied. Therefore it may be better in some languages to translate **created the earth, and with your own hands you made the heavens** as "you, yourself, created the earth and the sky."

1.11　　　　**They will disappear, but you will remain;**
　　　　　　　　they will all wear out like clothes.

The main point of this verse is the contrast between the Lord, who will always remain in existence, and the world he has made, which will not.

The word for **disappear** is often used in the Bible in contexts which speak of violent destruction; therefore Brc and TNT translate "be destroyed." However, the idea of destruction is not present in the second half of the verse, which simply speaks of growing old. **They will disappear** may be rendered as "They will no longer be seen," or "They will no longer exist," or "There will be a time when they will no longer be."

The Greek verb for **remain,** as written in the oldest manuscripts, may mean either "you remain" (compare RSV) or **you will remain.** Most early translations have the future tense. The immediate context (**They will disappear, they will . . . wear out**) suggests the future, but **you are** (verse 12) is a present tense in the Greek. Whether present or future is chosen, the meaning is much the same, since **remain** suggests a permanent state, including both present and future. Therefore it is important in rendering **remain** to indicate continued existence rather than merely remaining in a place. Hence, **you will remain** may be rendered as "you will always exist."

It may be somewhat difficult to speak of the earth and the sky as "wearing out like clothes," but sometimes one may speak of such a process as "they will become useless like old clothes."

1.12   **You will fold them up like a coat,**
          and they will be changed like clothes.
      But you are always the same,
          and your life never ends."

Fold and **coat** suggest western clothing, whereas the Greek refers to rolling up a cloak or a wrap. TEV is able to make this slight change for readers of English, since it does not affect the rest of the passage nor alter the meaning of the comparison.

You will fold them up like a coat must be rendered in such a way as to suggest the useless nature of the worn-out garment; for example, "you will roll them up like a worn-out coat."

The writer repeats **like clothes** from verse 11. The word is singular in Greek, but **clothes** has no singular in English, and "a garment" is not common language. By introducing this repetition, which is not in the Old Testament text,[2] the writer somewhat alters the meaning. In Greek as in English, the word translated **be changed** can mean "be made different," or it can be used of taking off old or dirty clothes and then putting on others. The writer may be combining both meanings. If a translation is being made into a language which uses different words for "change" in general and "change clothes," the more general meaning should be chosen if possible.

In view of the difficulty of understanding the clause **and they will be changed like clothes,** it is probably best to choose a rather general rendering; for example, "they will be changed like old clothes."

You are always the same may be better expressed in some languages as "you never change."

Your life never ends: literally, "your years do not fail"; GeCL "your years do not end"; DuCL ". . . give out." This clause may be expressed as "you never die" or "you always keep on living."

1.13   **God never said to any of his angels:**
          "Sit here at my right side
             until I put your enemies
             as a footstool under your feet."

The last quotation in this chapter, like the first, is introduced by a rhetorical question which is equal to a strong negative statement. The quotation is from Psalm 110.1, the Old Testament text most often quoted in the New Testament. Translators may wish to check the other places where this text is quoted (see Psa 110.1 reference footnote in TEV) and avoid variations not made necessary by the

---

[2] The words meaning "as a garment" are repeated in the UBS Greek New Testament. Many manuscripts, followed by KJV, wrongly omit the words in verse 12, following Psalm 102.26.

[22]

context in which it is quoted. The first readers of Hebrews would remember that in the psalm, the verse begins "The Lord [God] said to my Lord [understood as Christ]." The rhetorical question therefore calls for the answer "To Christ, not to any angel."

The literal translation is clumsy in most languages: "Sit on my right, until I put your enemies (as) a footstool of your feet."

My right side: as in verse 3, it may be necessary again to indicate by some marginal note that the right side was a position of honor and dignity.

Sit here at my right side must be expressed in some languages as "Sit here beside me at my right side," since the emphasis is upon both the association and the honor.

Until I put: it is not certain whether the writer of Hebrews thinks of Christ as continuing to "sit" even after God has conquered his enemies. The Hebrew leaves this possiblility open, as in Isaiah 42.4, quoted in Matthew 12.10. However, this is not the most natural meaning of the Greek, and it is possible that the writer of Hebrews thought of Christ as having a further period of activity in the last days (see 10.13, where sit is replaced by waits; also 9.28).

Some translations avoid the repetition **footstool . . . feet** by using a word like "stool" which is not related to **feet,** although the Greek words are related; for example FrCL, GeCL, RSV. Other translations remove the first part of the metaphor and translate "until I put your enemies under your feet" (DuCL, SpCL). The metaphor is based on an old custom: there are ancient pictures of kings with their feet resting on the heads or necks of conquered enemies.

In some languages it may seem rather strange that God would say to anyone that he should sit at the right side, while God went about putting enemies as a footstool under someone's feet. The relationship, of course, is not that of a direct agent but that of a causative agent. Therefore one may render **until I put your enemies as a footstool under your feet** as "until I cause your enemies to become, as it were, a footstool beneath your feet."

In some cultures people normally sit on an object which is formally more or less equivalent to what is in the western world regarded as a footstool. A functional equivalent of a footstool in such a culture is therefore often spoken of as a "foot stick" or "a footboard," a low-lying object made of wood which keeps a person's feet off what is frequently the cold, damp floor.

1.14   **What are the angels, then? They are spirits who serve God and are sent by him to help those who are to receive salvation.**

Verse 14, like verse 4, has two functions: it sums up the message of the previous passage, and it prepares for what is to come. Looking back, **spirits who serve God** recalls the reference to angels in verse 7. Winds (verse 7) and **spirits** translate the same Greek word. Looking forward, the words **those who are to receive salvation** show that the writer is moving on to the consequences for the human race of what Christ has done. This theme was suggested in 1.3, forgiveness for the sins of mankind, but in 2.1-4 it will become central for the first time.

In its form, verse 14 is another rhetorical question, which in RSV expects the answer "Yes, they are ministering spirits." Some translations replace the question by a strong statement (Phps "surely"; Brc "clearly"; JB "the truth is"). TEV introduces the statement with a short nonrhetorical question, **What are the angels, then?**

Though the question **What are the angels, then?** is a reference to their function, it may be necessary in a number of languages to translate this as "Who, then, are the angels?" However, since the function is an important element in the response, it may be more appropriate to render the question as "What, then, do the angels do?" or "What, then, is the purpose of the angels?"

To translate the term **spirits,** it is important to use essentially the same expression which is used in the expression "Holy Spirit." However, in a number of languages the term for "Holy Spirit" is so closely related to the personality of God (for example, "the breath of God") that one cannot employ the same terminology. Therefore it may be necessary to translate "spirits" as "beings." In some languages it may even be necessary to translate **They are the spirits who serve God** as "They are those who serve God" or simply "They serve God."

TEV distinguishes more clearly than RSV between the two "serving" functions of the angels, which are expressed in Greek by two different terms: (a) they serve God, and (b) God sends them to help human beings. The word translated **serve** may be translated "worship," as in verse 6. In other contexts it can mean "serve the community."

A change of emphasis is reflected by the writer's use of the Greek word translated **receive** (NEB "inherit") in a new way, by comparison with verses 2 and 4. The meaning of the verb is basically to receive something as a gift from God. Here, however, it is no longer the Son but believers who **receive.** The meaning "inherit" is not yet explicit, as it will be in 9.15-20, but **are to receive** suggests that it may already be in the writer's mind, and NEB, Phps, and other modern translations, as well as KJV, use "heirs" or "inherit." See the discussion on verse 2.

Salvation is a fairly common term in this letter. It normally includes the idea of escaping from some danger (2.3), whether destruction (6.9; compare 6.8; 11.7), death (5.9; compare 5.7), or sin and judgment (9.28; compare 9.26,27; 7.25). Translators may wish to avoid words such as **salvation** if they are used only or mainly in "church language."

Receive salvation is a kind of substitute passive. That is to say, these are "persons who are to be saved" or, in the active form, "those whom God will save."

Chapter 2

The Great Salvation

1 That is why we must hold on all the more firmly to the truths we have heard, so that we will not be carried away. 2 The message given to our ancestors by the angels was shown to be true, and anyone who did not follow it or obey it received the punishment he deserved. 3 How, then, shall we escape if we pay no attention to such a great salvation? The Lord himself first announced this salvation, and those who heard him proved to us that it is true. 4 At the same time God added his witness to theirs by performing all kinds of miracles and wonders and by distributing the gifts of the Holy Spirit according to his will.

1 Therefore we must pay the closer attention to what we have heard, lest we drift away from it. 2 For if the message declared by angels was valid and every transgression or disobedience received a just retribution, 3 how shall we escape if we neglect such a great salvation? It was declared at first by the Lord, and it was attested to us by those who heard him, 4 while God also bore witness by signs and wonders and various miracles and by gifts of the Holy Spirit distributed according to his own will.

Throughout this letter, teaching about God and Christ alternates with appeals to the readers for action. This section is the first appeal for action. It is closely linked with the teaching of chapter 1, both by its opening words (**That is why . . .**) and by the contrast in verses 2-3 between **angels** and **the Lord.**

The TEV section heading, **The Great Salvation**, may be expressed in some languages as "God did something great in rescuing us" or "God's rescuing us is indeed wonderful." Vanhoye's section heading, "Recognize God's Authority" (see Appendix A), if used here, must be rendered in a number of languages as "You should recognize God's authority" or "You should realize that what God has said is true."

<u>2.1</u>   **That is why we must hold on all the more firmly to the truths we have heard, so that we will not be carried away.**

That is why (NAB "In view of this"; TNT "For this reason"; NEB, DuCL "Thus"; TOB "It follows"): these words connect verses 1-4 with the whole argument of chapter 1. **We** includes both the author and his readers.

It may be necessary in some instances to make somewhat more specific the transitional reference in the expression **That is why** or "In view of this" or "For this reason." In some instance a clause may be necessary, for example, "In view of what God has done" or "Because all this is true."

All the more firmly is a very strong comparative which raises the question "More firmly than what?" There are three possibilities. (a) "More firmly than we are doing now" (compare JB "more attentively than before"). This is probably what the word means in 13.19, but nothing in the context supports this meaning here. This meaning would be more likely if the text had "you" instead of "we." (b) "More firmly than we should do if the Christian message had been given merely by angels" fits the context well, and is the basis for TEV and many other translations. (c) It is also possible to translate "pay particular attention," the comparative being used for additional emphasis. This is the basis of GeCL's "Therefore must we first hold firm . . ." and perhaps DuCL's ". . . (pay) more than usual attention." On the whole, however, meaning (b) is to be preferred.

Hold on combines the ideas of paying close attention to something and putting it into practice; see Acts 8.6,10; 16.14.

It may be extremely difficult, if not impossible, to speak of "holding on more firmly to truth," since in some languages truth is something one does not "hold onto." It is, however, often possible to speak of "paying close attention to truth" or idiomatically "to listen with one's heart to the truth." In other instances, the concept of holding onto the truth must be expressed in terms of belief, for example, "we must believe even more the truths."

The truths we have heard (**truths** is implied): the writer never uses the Greek word for "Good News" or "Gospel," but this phrase is probably his way of saying the same thing.[1] The tense of the verb indicates that the **truths** have been **heard** at a particular point in time, but since the time is not stated, Knox's "which have now come to our hearing" is too specific.

Many languages do not use a noun for expressing the concept of truth. Rather, they use some type of qualifying adjective, so that **the truths we have heard** may be expressed as "that which we have heard which is true" or "the true words which we have heard." In some instances "truth" must be expressed in terms of that in which one may have confidence: "that which we have heard which can be believed" or ". . . which can be trusted."

So that we will not be carried away is not a statement about what will or will not happen. **So that** means "in order that," expressing purpose. Negative purpose must sometimes be expressed in terms of a condition; for example, "if we do that, we will not be . . . ." In some instances the purpose must be very plainly indicated as "the reason for our doing this is so that we will not be . . . ."

Be carried away translates a word which is used only once in the New Testament. It is the negative of what **hold on** has expressed positively (see Prov

---

[1] It has been suggested that the truths we have heard refers to readings from the Old Testament, but a reference to Christian teaching handed down from Jesus himself fits the context better (see verse 3, and compare 1 Cor 15.1-2).

3.21 where the Septuagint uses the same verb). In secular Greek it is sometimes used to describe a ship drifting away; thus Brc, "Otherwise, we may well be like a ship which drifts past the harbour to shipwreck."

A literal rendering of **be carried away** can be quite misleading since it might suggest that someone actually carried persons away. It may therefore be better to use an expression such as "pass by" or "drift by" (if the figurative language of the motion of a ship can be implied). In some cases the equivalent of **be carried away** may be expressed in terms of failure to reach one's intended destination; for example, "so as not to arrive at one's goal."

Verses 2-4 form a single sentence in Greek. They present a comparison between the Old Testament Law and the Christian message, followed by two conclusions. This structure may be outlined as follows:

A. The Old Testament Law   B. The Christian message of salvation

1. The Law, given through angels, was true (verse 2a)   1. was announced by the Lord (verse 3b)

2. As a result, acts of disobedience were punished (verse 2b)   2. was attested by witnesses (verse 3c)

                                            3. was confirmed by miracles and wonders by the Holy Spirit (verse 4)

therefore

C.   The Christian message is more important than the Old Testament Law (implied)

therefore

D.   Conclusion: we cannot be saved if we ignore the Christian message (verse 3a)

Notice that the logical order is not the same as the grammatical order, which is followed by most translations, including TEV. The difficulty in following the logical order is the length and subdivisions of point B (verses 3b-4). The logical solution would be to transfer verse 3a (point D: How, then, shall we escape. . . ?) to the end of verse 4. However, it is doubtful whether the author intended to adopt a strictly logical presentation. He is more concerned to persuade than to prove a point. Therefore in this passage the translator should take careful note of the underlying logical structure, though he need not necessarily follow it in translation. But he should be ready, as a matter of principle, to divide long sentences, and also to leave logical relations unexpressed if it is natural to do so in his language.[2]

---

[2] Languages differ greatly in the extent to which logical relations need to be expressed. For example, New Testament Greek used words to express such relations more freely than does modern English.

2.2 **The message given to our ancestors by the angels was shown to be true, and anyone who did not follow it or obey it received the punishment he deserved.**

Message is better in this context than KJV's and NEB's "word." **The message given . . . by the angels** is the Law of Moses. Jews believed that the Law had been given by God to Moses through angels. The writer is not referring to an individual word or even to a particular statement, but he is comparing the Old Testament Law and the Christian message. Most modern readers will not know this unless they are Jews, so some translations refer explicitly to the Law: Knox "The old law, which only had angels as its spokesmen"; TNT "the word of the Law, spoken through angels." If it is necessary to indicate the nature of this message, one can speak of "The message of how we are saved" or ". . . of how we are to live."

To our ancestors is not in the Greek, in earlier editions of TEV, or in other CLTs. The writer of Hebrews avoids expressions which suggest that all his readers were Jews, perhaps because they were in fact a mixed community. However, in some languages it may be essential to state to whom the message was proclaimed. Futhermore, in some languages it may be important to change the passive expression **The message given to our ancestors by the angels** into an active one; for example, "The angels proclaimed the message to our ancestors." An expression for **ancestors** is often literally "our grandfathers," but in some instances the reference is primarily one of time, not of family or racial relationship, for example, "those who lived long ago," though in some cases an idiomatic expression may be employed: "those who are our roots" or "those who traveled here ahead of us."

True: GeCL "reliable"; Phps "authentic"; TOB "came into effect." Some translations link this word with what follows, making explicit a relation of reason and result (see introduction to this section): JB "so true that every infringement and disobedience brought its proper punishment"; TNT "so binding that anyone who broke it or disobeyed it was duly punished."

Though many languages speak of **true** as "that which really is," the concept of "being true" is more often expressed in terms of that which can be relied upon or trusted. Accordingly, **was shown to be true** may be expressed as "proved to be what people can trust" or ". . . what we can trust."

Follow it and **obey it** have practically the same meaning, as TEV's **or** suggests. TEV and RSV are therefore right to avoid the literal translation "and." Two equivalent words are used in Greek, perhaps for emphasis. GeCL combines them: "whoever did not follow it received the deserved punishment." Quite frequently it is possible to use a figurative meaning of **follow** in a sense of adhering to or being loyal to a person, but it is difficult to speak of "not following a message." It is usually possible to say "did not do what they were told," but this is simply another way of saying "did not obey what they were told." Therefore in some instances the meaning of **follow it** and **obey it** can perhaps best be combined into a single expression, namely, "did not at all do what they were told" or ". . . what the message said they should do."

The rare word translated **punishment** sometimes has the positive meaning "reward" (as in 10.35; 11.26), but the context here demands a negative meaning. (Compare the expression "he got what he deserved," which may take on positive or negative overtones, depending on the context.) The expression **received the punishment** is a type of substitute passive, for the subject of such an expression is the goal of the action, while the one who punishes is left implicit. The equivalent may be expressed in some languages as "they were punished" or "God punished them," and the qualification of the punishment, namely, "what they deserved" may be rendered as "as they should have been" or "as was right because of what they did."

2.3   **How, then, shall we escape if we pay no attention to such a great salvation? The Lord himself first announced this salvation, and those who heard him proved to us that it is true.**

How . . . shall we escape? refers to a real future event, that is, the last judgment, and so Brc's "how can we escape?" (compare TNT) is too weak.

How, then, shall we escape must be amplified in some instances to indicate from what one is to escape. Furthermore, the meaning of **escape** in this context is not that of "escaping from prison" or "getting out of confinement" but rather "avoidance." Accordingly, **How, then, shall we escape** may be rendered as "How, then, can we possibly avoid being punished?"

Such a great salvation: great is explicit in the text; Knox's "such a message of salvation . . ." is weaker. **Pay no attention to . . . salvation** and also **a . . . salvation** are stylistically awkward, at least in English. "Pay no attention to the news of such great salvation" is smoother and is what the text means. Several translations make explicit the implied contrast between two **messages,** the law and the gospel: Knox "a message of salvation"; Brc "a way to salvation"; TNT "an offer of salvation."

It may be necessary to make specific the relationship of persons to **such a great salvation,** that is to say, attention should not be paid to the fact of someone else being saved but to the possibility of the people themselves being saved. Therefore **if we pay no attention to such a great salvation** may be rendered "if we pay no attention to how God wants to save us in such a wonderful way."

The Lord in this context must mean Jesus, since God is mentioned separately in verse 4. **The Lord** was a common title of God in the Old Testament, and the writer of Hebrews has previously shown no hesitation in applying to Jesus Old Testament texts which he believed called Jesus "Lord" and "God" (1.8,10). However, the writer often uses the name "Jesus" without any title (2.9; 3.1; 6.20; 7.22; 10.19; 12.2,24; 13.12), so the translator should not replace **The Lord** by "Jesus" in this passage. If there is any real danger of misunderstanding, "The Lord Jesus" may be used. The emphatic expression **Lord himself** may be expressed as "It was the Lord who" or "It was indeed the Lord who."

The Greek word for **announced** is usually used of speech rather than writing; KJV "spoken."

The adverb **first,** though related to the verb **announced,** must in some languages be related to the subject, since the Lord was the first one to make such

2.3

an announcement. Therefore, **The Lord himself first announced** must be rendered as "The Lord was the first one to announce." Otherwise a literal translation of **The Lord himself first announced** might mean that the first among many statements which the Lord made was a statement about salvation.

Again, the expression **this salvation** must be expressed in some instances as "this way in which God saves."

Him after **heard** is implied, but Brc's "those who actually heard it from his own lips" seems too strong. The context distinguishes between (a) those who heard Jesus directly, and (b) those who handed on the message to the writer and his readers. The two groups are distinguished but not sharply contrasted; both those who heard Jesus with their own ears, and those who heard the message indirectly, are said to "hear" (see verse 1).

Proved: Mft, Knox, JB, Brc "guaranteed"; Phps, NEB, TNT "confirmed." This verb corresponds to the adjective translated true in verse 2. It is important in selecting a rendering of **proved** to avoid any implication of "argument" or "reasoned discussion." Here the meaning is "to demonstrate clearly," and obviously this was by experience. Accordingly, **proved to us that it is true** may be rendered as "showed clearly to us that it is true" or ". . . to be trusted."

2.4   **At the same time God added his witness to theirs by performing all kinds of miracles and wonders and by distributing the gifts of the Holy Spirit according to his will.**

This verse confirms that the writer is more concerned with the continuity between the first Christians and his readers than with any contrast between them. How did God add **his witness** to those of earlier Christians? Verse 4 gives four answers (although TEV combines the first two into one): (a) by signs, (b) by **wonders,** (c) by all kinds of powerful acts, and (d) **by distributing the gifts of the Holy Spirit.** When the first three terms are used separately, (a) emphasizes the significance of the events, (b) their effect in astonishing those who see them, and (c) the power behind them. However, in this verse, as often in the New Testament (for example, Mark 13.22; John 4.48; Acts 4.30; 15.12), (a) and (b) are closely connected and similar in meaning, and so TEV is right to combine them and even link **all kinds of** with (a) and (b), as well as with (c).

At the same time may be expressed by a clause, "While this was happening."

Added his witness translates a Greek present participle implying continuous action: "went on adding his witness." The translation of **added his witness to theirs** must be rendered in such a way as to reflect the previous rendering of proved to us. For example, if proved to us is rendered "showed to us" or "made it clear to us," then **added his witness** may be expressed as "also made it clear to us" or "also showed clearly to us."

By performing all kinds of miracles and wonders may be expressed as "by doing all kinds of miracles and wonders." In some languages miracles are spoken of simply as "great deeds" or "unusual deeds," but sometimes more idiomatic

[30]

expressions are used, for example, "open-mouth things" (something which is so astonishing that people open their mouths in wonder) or even "long-necked things" (events that are so marvelous that people stretch their necks in order to see). In order to suggest something of the meaning of the Greek, which clearly indicates the power which is necessary in the performing of such unusual deeds, one may speak of "powerful deeds" or "deeds which show God's power."

It is not clear whether **according to his will** is linked only with **distributing the gifts of the Holy Spirit** or with the whole of (a)-(d). 1 Corinthians 12.11 similarly speaks of the one Holy Spirit "distributing" different gifts **as he wishes**, suggesting that **according to his will** may relate to (d) alone. The parallel with 1 Corinthians 12.11 also suggests that **his will** may mean "the Holy Spirit's" rather than "God's" will, but this is not certain. Many cases will be noted in this *Handbook* where the writer of Hebrews does not clearly state whether "his" and similar pronouns refer to God, Jesus, or the Holy Spirit.

Most translations, like TEV, refer to **gifts of the Holy Spirit** although **gifts** is implicit; literally, "distributions of the Holy Spirit" (compare Mft "distributing the holy Spirit as it pleased him"; DuCL "Moreover he dealt out the Holy Spirit as he wished"; SpCL ". . . by means of the Holy Spirit which he has given us in different ways, according to his will"). Stress is on the origin of the gifts (the Spirit) rather than on the individual gifts themselves.

By distributing the gifts of the Holy Spirit may be expressed as a type of causative, since the distribution is basically causative while **the gifts** are that which comes from the Holy Spirit. Therefore **by distributing the gifts of the Holy Spirit** may be expressed as "by causing people to have what the Holy Spirit gives."

Will implies a settled purpose rather than a series of separate decisions. It is generally impossible to preserve the ambiguity in the phrase **according to his will**, and the translator will have to specify whether this is a reference to the will of the Holy Spirit or to the will of God. In the first case one may translate **the gifts of the Holy Spirit according to his will** as "what the Holy Spirit gives as he wants to." In the second case the translation would be "the gifts which the Holy Spirit gives according to what God desires." If, however, one wishes to emphasize that it is not the gifts which come from the Holy Spirit but the Holy Spirit who is the gift, it may be necessary to translate "by God distributing or giving to people the Holy Spirit according as he wanted to."

TEV	**2.5-10**	RSV

The One Who Leads Us to Salvation

5 God has not placed the angels as rulers over the new world to come—the world of which we speak. 6 Instead, as it is said somewhere in the Scriptures:
"What is man, O God, that
 you should think of him;

5 For it was not to angels that God subjected the world to come, of which we are speaking. 6 It has been testified somewhere,
"What is man that thou art
 mindful of him,

mere man, that you should
care for him?
7 You made him for a little while
lower than the angels;
you crowned him with glory
and honor,[c]
8 and made him ruler over all
things."
It says that God made man "ruler over
all things"; this clearly includes everything. We do not, however, see man
ruling over all things now. 9 But we do
see Jesus, who for a little while was
made lower than the angels, so that
through God's grace he should die for
everyone. We see him now crowned
with glory and honor because of the
death he suffered. 10 It was only right
that God, who creates and preserves all
things, should make Jesus perfect
through suffering, in order to bring
many sons to share his glory. For Jesus
is the one who leads them to salvation.

[c] *Many manuscripts add:* you made him
ruler over everything you made *(see Ps
8.6).*

or the son of man, that thou
carest for him?
7 Thou didst make him for a little
while lower than the
angels,
thou hast crowned him with glory
and honor,[d]
8 putting everything in subjection
under his feet."
Now in putting everything in subjection
to him, he left nothing outside his
control. As it is, we do not yet see
everything in subjection to him. 9 But
we see Jesus, who for a little while was
made lower than the angels, crowned
with glory and honor because of the
suffering of death, so that by the grace
of God he might taste death for every
one.

10 For it was fitting that he, for
whom and by whom all things exist, in
bringing many sons to glory, should
make the pioneer of their salvation
perfect through suffering.

[d] Other ancient authorities insert *and
didst set him over the works of thy
hands*

The larger section, verses 5-18, has several things in common with 1.4-14.
It is based on Old Testament texts, though less heavily than 1.4-14. Like 1.4-14,
but unlike 2.1-4, it consists of doctrinal teaching. It develops the contrast between the angels and the Son, Jesus. It shows the same tendency as 1.4-14 to
speak in greater detail about the person and work of Christ than about the angels.

The key word in verses 5-9, and in the quotations from Psalm 8.4-6 which
the passage contains, is "subjected." TEV turns the original text around. Instead
of saying that God "subjected" the world to man, not to angels, TEV says that God
placed man, not angels, over the world. The meaning is the same, and TEV rightly
gives greater emphasis to man and angels than to the world.

The section heading of the TEV text, namely, **The One Who Leads Us to
Salvation,** may be readily rendered as "He who causes us to be saved" or ". . .
shows us how to be saved."

<u>2.5</u>   **God has not placed the angels as rulers over the new world
to come—the world of which we speak.**

RSV's "**For**" can be omitted in translation; like the beginning of a new
paragraph, it serves only to mark the beginning of a new stage in the discussion.

God has not placed the angels as rulers may be rendered as "God has not made the angels rulers" or "God has not caused the angels to rule." **God** is understood; pronouns are often best replaced by nouns at the beginning of a section.

The new world to come is an improvement on earlier editions of TEV, which had the unusual translation the world he was about to create, and is supported by GeCL and FrCL. **World,** as in 1.6, means "the inhabited world"; Phps "future world of men"; DuCL "the dwelling-city of the future." The writer is thinking of human society, not of a particular place. In all other passages in which Hebrews uses this Greek verb "about-to-be," there is some reference to the renewal of this world through Christ, never to its creation.

The phrase **the new world to come** may be especially difficult to render, since a more or less literal rendering of **world** is likely to be understood in the sense of "earth." In some cases it may be necessary to translate **the new world to come** as "the new way in which people are going to live." The focus here is far more upon the culture than upon any kind of physical earth.

The phrase **the world of which we speak** may be rendered as "this is what I am talking about" or "this new kind of life is what I am talking about." However, in some languages one cannot use a term such as "speak," since in reality the author of Hebrews is communicating in writing. Therefore one must render **the world of which we speak** as "the kind of life which I am writing about."

It is not until 13.19 that the writer uses a verb form that calls for the pronoun I when translated. Elsewhere, as in the present verse, he uses forms that call for the pronoun we. There is, however, no evidence that Hebrews was written jointly by more than one author, and it was common in ancient times for writers to refer to themselves as "we." In languages and cultures where this is not natural, "we" should be translated as "I."

For **speak,** see discussion on 1.1-2. Since the author is in fact writing, not speaking, it may be better in some languages to translate "write."

2.6   **Instead, as it is said somewhere in the Scriptures:**
          "What is man, O God, that you should think of him;
          mere man, that you should care for him?

Instead (literally "but") strongly marks the contrast with verse 5.

As it is said somewhere in the Scriptures is literally "affirms somewhere someone saying." This clause is a curiously vague way of introducing a psalm attributed to David. **In the Scriptures** is clearly implied. "Affirms" is related to the Greek word translated as added his witness in verse 4. The writer is continuing to pile up evidence for the supremacy of Christ.

As it is said somewhere in the Scriptures must be rendered in some languages as "as it is written somewhere in the Scriptures," since "saying" can only be related directly to speech, and anything involved in writing must be mentioned as such. However, the passive expression **it is said** must often be made active; for example, "as someone has written somewhere in the holy writings."

[33]

It is rare that one can use for **Scriptures** merely an expression "writings," for the reference is unlikely to be clear. For that reason the expression "holy writings" is often necessary.

The first two lines of the quotation are in close parallel (see discussion on 1.7). **Man** and **mere man** (literally "son of man") mean the same, and the Greek expressions for **think of** (literally "remember") and **care for** are closer to each other than are their English equivalents. In biblical thought, when God "remembered" or thought of someone, something happened to that person; that is, God's thought always resulted in action. The problem for the translator is to make it clear that the two lines mean the same, but to do so without using monotonous repetition. GeCL chooses the radical solution, adopted in many places in TEV Old Testament, of combining the two lines: "What is man, that you ask about him?" In any language which does not use poetic parallelism, translators should consider whether the two lines can be combined without loss of meaning

In the psalm, as in Ezekiel 2.1, "man" and "son of man" mean the same thing. However, in the Gospels Jesus often uses the phrase "Son of man" as an indirect way of speaking of himself. Hebrews does not use "son of man" except in this quotation. The question as to whether the author understands "son of man" in the quotation to refer to Christ is dealt with in the discussion of "to him" in verses 8-9 (see below).

In a number of languages it is impossible to introduce the expression **O God** in the position which it has in TEV, namely, **What is man, O God, that you should think of him**. A direct vocative such as **O God** must generally occur first in a sentence, or occur next to the word for **you;** for example, "God, what is man that you should think of him?" or "What is man that you, God, should think of him?"

In this context **man** refers to human beings in general—certainly not to any particular male—and therefore it may be far more satisfactory in many languages to translate "What are people that you, God, should think of them" or ". . . pay attention to them" or ". . . be concerned with them."

It may be even necessary to indicate something of the significance of the question by amplifying the implication of the interrogative pronoun **What;** for example, "How important are people that you, God, should be concerned with them?"

It may be important in some languages to make clear the nature of this rhetorical question. This may be done by employing the phrase **mere man** as a kind of response to the double question; for example, "What are people that you, God, should be concerned with them or should take care of them? They are nothing more than people."

2.7   **You made him for a little while lower than the angels;**
               you crowned him with glory and honor,[c]

   [c] *Many manuscripts add:* you made him ruler over everything
you made *(see Ps 8.6).*

For a little while lower may also mean "a little lower" in place or in status, as in KJV, Knox, Phps. This is certainly what the phrase means in the psalm. However, verses 8-9 strongly suggest that the writer of Hebrews is more interested here in time than place: (a) for a little while in the past, Jesus was made lower than the angels; (b) now . . . we see Jesus crowned with glory and honor; (c) in the future, we shall see Jesus (or man; see discussion on verses 8-9) as ruler over all things. There is thus a contrast between 7a and 7b. GeCL brings out the meaning of the passage as the writer of Hebrews understands it: "You lowered him for a short time, made him lower than the angels; but then you gave him fame and honor. . . ." GeCL first edition also replaced the metaphor **crowned** by a simile: "like a king."

As in verse 6, it may be necessary to translate "him" as "people," since this is a reference to mankind and not to one specific individual. **Lower than the angels** must often be expressed as "less important than the angels" or "with less power than the angels." In some cases the hierarchical nature of man's position may be expressed in terms of authority; for example, "with less authority than the angels."

You crowned him with glory and honor must often be recast, since the concept of "crowning" may be relatively meaningless. **You crowned him with glory** may be expressed as "you made him wonderful" or more literally "you gave him glory." **And honor** must often be expressed as a verb; for example, "you caused him to have honor" or ". . . be honored."

2.8   **and made him ruler over all things."**
         It says that God made man "ruler over all things"; this clearly
         includes everything. We do not, however, see man ruling over
         all things now.

As the footnotes to verse 7 in TEV and RSV show, many Greek manuscripts continue the quotation to the end of Psalm 8.6, but the shorter text is more likely to be correct.[3] The last line of the quotation includes picture language ("**under his feet**") which RSV keeps, but which TEV, FrCL, GeCL replace by a nonfigurative expression, **ruler over all things.** See note on 1.13.

And made him ruler over all things may be rendered as "and gave him authority to control everything" or "caused him to rule over everything that exists" or ". . . everything in the world."

It is important to note that the word **man** is not in the Greek text of verse 8. A closer and also fuller translation than either TEV or RSV would be "when this quotation speaks about 'subjecting all things (to him),' it means that God left

---

3 There are various reasons for this. (a) Generally speaking, scribes added words more often than they omitted them. (b) The quotation most naturally ends with the line in which the key word "subjected" occurs (see introduction to this section). (c) Everything you (that is, God) made, Psalm 8.6, would weaken what the writer has said in 1.2,10 about Christ's role in creation.

nothing that is not subjected to him."[4] So, what does "to him" mean? (a) "To man," as in the psalm, or (b) "to Jesus"?

(a) If TEV and RSV are right in understanding that "to him" means "to man," the line of thought in verses 8b-9 is as follows: The last line of the quotation means what it says: God has made man ruler over absolutely everything (verse 8b). But this contradicts our present experience; we do not yet see this happening (verse 8c). The contradiction disappears if we remember that Jesus, the perfect man of whom Psalm 8 is really speaking, has been crowned with glory and honor (verse 9).

(b) If "to him" means "to Jesus," this needs to be stated in the translation of verse 8. In this case, the thought would be: Jesus has not yet fulfilled the last line of the quotation; all things are not yet under his feet. But he has died, and God has now crowned him with glory and honor. This interpretation would fit in excellently with the previous quotation in 1.13: Jesus is already sitting at God's right hand, but his enemies have not yet been put as a footstool under his feet (compare 10.12-13).

Most commentators, and most translations which make a clear choice, prefer (a), but (b) is possible, especially in a passage which says more about the close relationship between Christ and believers than about any contrast between them.

It says must be rendered in some instances as "In that passage one may read" or "Those words mean that." It is clear that in the expression **God made man "ruler over all things"** it will be necessary to adjust the translation to what has been employed in verses 7 and 8a; for example, "God made people to rule over everything."

This clearly includes everything may be rendered as "these words clearly speak about everything" or "this means that nothing is excluded" or ". . . that everything is involved."

The adversative adverb **however** is strong and in many languages should be placed at the beginning of the clause. Likewise, the temporal adverb **now** is extremely important because of the contrast which follows. This means that in many languages the last sentence of verse 8 should be rendered as "However, now we do not see people ruling over all things."

2.9 **But we do see Jesus, who for a little while was made lower than the angels, so that through God's grace he should die for everyone. We see him now crowned with glory and honor because of the death he suffered.**

---

[4] The first "to him" is in parentheses because it is omitted in some manuscripts, but this does not affect the meaning, since the second "to him" is certainly part of the text.

The adversative conjunction **But** at the beginning of verse 9 is particularly important, and it may be necessary in some instances to employ a phrase such as "But in contrast" or "But different from this."

Different Greek words for **see** are used in verses 8c and 9, but there is no difference in meaning. In other contexts, the **see** of verse 9 can mean literally "look at," but here the writer seems concerned simply to avoid repetition. It may not be possible to translate literally **we do see Jesus,** since this might imply actual visual perception. A more satisfactory rendering may be "But we do know about Jesus."

Who for a little while was made lower than the angels must be rendered in a form parallel to what has been employed in verse 7 in speaking of mankind, but it may be necessary to indicate clearly the agent of the passive expression **was made lower,** for this could be interpreted by some as a reference to the humiliation of Jesus by his enemies. The reference, however, seems to be clearly to the incarnation, and therefore one may translate "for a little while God made him lower than the angels," with the implication of "lower in rank" or "lower in status," in view of his human nature.

The purpose expressed in the conjunctive phrase **so that** must be made quite clear, and in some instances one may translate "the purpose of what God did" or "this happened in order that."

A comparison of TEV and RSV shows how extensively TEV has rearranged the rest of the verse. There are two main difficulties, one related to the text, and the other to the structure of the sentence.

Instead of **through God's grace,** which is the reading of most good manuscripts, some manuscripts have "apart from God" (NEB note); however, this is a difficult phrase which is not usually adopted by editions or translations of the New Testament.[5] **Through God's grace** is expressed in a number of languages as "because God loved us." **Grace,** however, may be expressed in some languages as "love in action" or "love leading to kindness." In other instance, **grace** is expressed essentially in terms of "undeserved mercy." The preposition **through** in this

---

[5] The text which means "apart from God" is so difficult that it is difficult to know how it arose, if it is not original. One explanation is that a scribe added the words "apart from God" in the margin, as a comment on ruler over all things in verse 8, that this was then recopied by mistake as part of verse 9, and changed to an expression meaning through God's grace in an attempt to make sense of the phrase. All extant manuscripts, however, have either through God's grace or "apart from God."

If the author of Hebrews wrote "apart from God," he may have been thinking of Jesus' cry My God, my God, why did you abandon me? (Mark 15.34; Matt 27.46). This is a quotation from Psalm 22, from which Hebrews also quotes a few verses later (2.12). This interpretation is followed by most ancient and modern commentators, and by most translations which make the meaning of "to him" clear. The strongest argument in taking "to him" to mean "to men" is the emphatic Jesus in verse 9, which suggests a contrast with "man," implied in verse 8. However, it should not be assumed that because Psalm 8 speaks of man, Hebrews must do so also when it quotes the Psalm.

context does not express primarily means but indicates underlying circumstances which prompt or make possible some event.

It is virtually impossible to link "**crowned with glory and honor because of the suffering of death**" (RSV) with "**so that by the grace of God he might taste death for everyone**" (RSV). It therefore seems best to follow TEV in adopting for translation the order that revises RSV: 9a, 9c, 9b. A possible expanded translation would be:

> What we do see is Jesus. For a short time he "was brought lower than the angels" (9a). God's gracious purpose in doing this was that Jesus should die for everyone (9c). But the other part of Psalm 8.6 also applies to Jesus: he has been, and still is [perfect tense], "crowned with glory and honor," and this is precisely because of the death which he suffered (9b).

He should die for everyone involves a number of subtle problems in translation, since a literal rendering might imply "he should die because of everyone," suggesting that everyone caused him to die. The relation between the death and those who are to be benefited by the death must be made explicit in some languages; for example, "he died in order to benefit everyone" or "he died in order to help everyone."

Since the adverb **now** in the expression **We see him now crowned with glory and honor** is contrastive, it may be important to place it at the beginning of the sentence; for example, "But now we see him crowned with glory and honor." The rendering of the expression **crowned with glory and honor** must, of course, parallel what has been implied in the previous rendering of this expression in verse 7. Again, however, it may be necessary to translate **see** as "But now we know that he is glorious and has been honored."

"Taste death" is one translation of a common Hebrew metaphor for **die**, and should be replaced by **die** in languages which do not have either this metaphor, or another metaphor with the same meaning. The misunderstanding "he only tasted death, but did not experience it fully" must be avoided. **Because of the death he suffered** must often be expressed as "because of the way in which he suffered and died" or "because of the extent to which he suffered by dying."

2.10   **It was only right that God, who creates and preserves all things, should make Jesus perfect through suffering, in order to bring many sons to share his glory. For Jesus is the one who leads them to salvation.**

The emphasis in verses 10-18 is no longer on the comparison between angels and the Son, but on the unity between Jesus and believers. Angels are mentioned in verse 16, but they are no longer at the center of the writer's thought, as they were in chapters 1 and 2.5-9. In chapter 3 the writer returns to the subject of the supremacy of Jesus over Old Testament traditions, but in quite different terms.

RSV's "**For**," omitted in TEV, links this sentence with verse 9, which also refers to the suffering of Jesus **for everyone** as part of God's plan. The links between verses 9 and 10 are so close that in some languages it will be necessary to make this connection explicit, as in RSV.

Transitions in Hebrews are usually smooth and gradual. Verse 10 forms such a transition. Most translations make it the last verse of the previous paragraph; GeCL makes it the first verse of a new paragraph, verses 10-13. It would even be possible to print it as a separate paragraph on its own.

The first words in TEV raise the question, what was **only right** or "**fitting**"? Most translations follow the grammar of the Greek sentence in understanding the words "make the pioneer of their salvation perfect through suffering" as the main statement, and "bringing many sons to glory" as a less important statement. But, as was stated in the comments on 1.3, grammar is not always a clear guide to meaning. What the author intends to describe as **only right** or "**fitting**" may not be "**suffering**" but "**bringing many sons to glory**." This would produce the translation "It was only right that God, who creates and preserves all things, should bring many sons to glory. He did this by making Jeus perfect through suffering, who leads them to salvation."

It was only right is not a strong expression in Greek. It does not suggest that God was compelled to do anything, but simply that what he did was fitting or appropriate. There may be some complication involved in using the past tense **was** in reference to what God did in making Jesus perfect through suffering, and the adverb **only** may simply be emphatic. Therefore one may render the first part of verse 10 as "It is indeed fitting that God . . . should have made Jesus perfect."

God is implied (see RSV). In translation it is good to state the subject of the sentence, since "Jesus" becomes the subject in verse 11. RSV does not make this clear.

Translations give various equivalents for RSV's "**for whom and by whom**," which refers to God. RSV gives the most common meanings of the two expressions when they occur separately in other passages. The expression translated "**for whom**" most often gives the reason why something happens, or the person for whose sake something is done. The expression translated "**by whom**" generally indicates the cause of something, that is, either its origin or the means by which something happens. Here the two expressions overlap, and the writer may have been using them together for emphasis.

In order to indicate that the process of creation and preservation of all things has taken place in the past as well as in the present, it may be important to translate **who creates and preserves all things** as "who has created and has continued to preserve all things." The concept of **preserves** may be expressed as "has caused to function" or "causes things to do what they do."

Make . . . perfect is often used to refer to the ordination or consecration of Old Testament priests (for example, Lev 4.5; 8.33 Septuagint). **Make . . . perfect** translates the same verb used in John 19.30 for It is finished, and in both passages the idea of death is either expressed or implied. The writer is not separating suffering from death, but probably wrote "**suffering**" here as a stylistic change from death in verse 9.

As the context shows, **through suffering** does not mean that the suffering was a mere stage on the way to glory, but that it contributed to the fulfillment or "making perfect" of Jesus. Mft makes this clear in his "by suffering."

The expression **make Jesus perfect through suffering** is extremely difficult to translate adequately. A literal translation could suggest that by suffering, Jesus was able to atone for his own sins. Perhaps the most effective way of communicating this concept in some languages is "to cause Jesus to be what he should be by means of what he suffered." But since the Greek text suggests the exaltation of Jesus, it may be better to translate "cause Jesus to have the position that was rightly his because of the way in which he suffered."

The Greek word for **bring** does not indicate the direction of movement; it may also mean "take." Here, however, **bring** is correct; God is bringing men, through Jesus, to a place where he is at present.

Many sons, in biblical Greek, does not imply "many but not all"; compare for everyone in verse 9; see also Mark 10.45; 14.24. It means simply "a great number of sons" (DuCL "so many sons"; SpCL "all his sons").

A literal rendering of **in order to bring many sons to share his glory** can be misunderstood as a reference to Jesus' own sons. Accordingly, in some languages the equivalent meaning is expressed by "in order to cause many followers to share his glory" or ". . . to be wonderful even as he is wonderful."

To share his glory (that is, God's glory) slightly expands RSV's literal translation, **"to glory,"** but this is quite justified, since the biblical word for **"glory"** is usually associated with God.

For Jesus is the one who leads them to salvation brings out the meaning of the phrase which RSV translates literally **"pioneer of their salvation."** Elsewhere the Greek word for **"pioneer"** may describe the founder of a town or its great hero. This meaning may be present in Acts 3.15; 5.31. It can also mean "cause," "author" (see 12.2), or more generally "chief." In the Greek Old Testament, the word is used of Moses and other leaders of Israel (for example, in Num 14.4). In Hebrews it includes the meaning of "forerunner" (6.20 RSV) and is close in meaning to source (5.9), though different Greek words are used. "Leading" means more than giving an example; it includes the idea of opening up a path which was not open before, as in TOB "initiator." The phrase **make Jesus perfect** does not imply that he was imperfect, in the sense of sinful, before his suffering and death, but that by these experiences he became fully mature, fully adequate, or completely effective, and thus equipped to lead others to salvation. Knox has "crown with suffering," but this is a weak translation; TOB "lead to accomplishment."

GeCL restructures verse 10 as follows: "God is the goal of all things, and they also came into being through him. Because he wanted many children of God to be brought into his glorious kingdom, he brought the one who was to lead them there through suffering to perfection."

The one who leads probably implies "who has begun to lead." This phrase may refer either to God (as RSV implies) or to Jesus (as TEV states).

The one who leads them may be expressed as "the one who shows them the way." But it may be more accurately rendered as "the one who goes ahead of others to show them the way." This may be expressed idiomatically in some languages as "one who is the thorn-treader," that is to say, the one who goes ahead down the path and thus is the one who treads on any thorns.

On **salvation**, see comment on 1.14. **To salvation** may be expressed as "to the point of being saved," but it may be combined with the previous expression of **leads**, so as to express result; for example, "leads them so that as a result they are saved" or ". . . God saves them."

	TEV	2.11-13	RSV

11 He purifies people from their sins, and both he and those who are made pure all have the same Father. That is why Jesus is not ashamed to call them his brothers. 12 He says to God,
"I will tell my brothers what
you have done;
I will praise you in their
meeting."
13 He also says, "I will put my trust in God." And he also says, "Here I am with the children that God has given me."

11 For he who sanctifies and those who are sanctified have all one origin. That is why he is not ashamed to call them brethren, 12 saying,
"I will proclaim thy name to my
brethren,
in the midst of the congregation I
will praise thee."
13 And again,
"I will put my trust in him."
And again,
"Here am I, and the children God
has given me."

2.11   **He purifies people from their sins, and both he and those who are made pure all have the same Father. That is why Jesus is not ashamed to call them his brothers.**

Since verse 11 may begin a new paragraph, it may be useful to introduce the subject as "Jesus," for example, "Jesus purifies people from their sins."

There is nothing in the Greek corresponding to **He purifies people from their sins,** and no CLT other than TEV sees the need to add this clause. TEV does so in order to make a rather sudden transition more smooth. The transition is from God to Jesus as the subject and the central person in the sentence, and from the language of salvation or rescue to the language of sanctification. However, the change is not completely unprepared. Both "make perfect" in verse 10 and "purifies" here refer to the work of a priest.

Purifies people from their sins must in a number of languages be expressed as a causative, for example, "causes people to no longer have sin" or ". . . guilt." In some instances it may be necessary to express in figurative language the means by which sins are removed; for example, "He causes people's sins to be blotted out" or ". . . wiped away." In other instances it may be the attribution of guilt which is involved; for example, "He causes people no longer to be guilty."

The rendering of **those who are made pure** will depend on the manner in which the first clause has been translated, namely, **He purifies people from their sins.**

[41]

GeCL follows a different interpretation which may fit the context better. It notes (a) that **sins** are not mentioned in this section until verse 17 (compare 1.3), and (b) that the basic meaning of "to make holy" or "sanctify" is "to claim as God's possession." GeCL therefore continues the thought of verse 10 by translating "The one who leads men to God and those who are led by him to God are all descended from the same Father." This has the additional advantage of making a general statement such as is perhaps more natural at the beginning of a new paragraph, Brc has "For the consecrating priest and the consecrated people have one Father"; similarly NEB.

Have the same Father is literally "(are) all from one," and "one" may be either masculine or neuter. (a) If it is neuter, the meaning will be **"one origin,"** as in RSV, BJ, TOB. (b) If it is masculine, the most likely meaning is that given by TEV, other CLTs, and TNT. (c) Some translations give the masculine a more general meaning, such as "one stock" (NEB) or "common humanity" (Phps). (d) Older translations (KJV, Segond [Seg], Luther [Lu], Zür) translate ambiguously, unclearly, and unnaturally "from one." Meaning (b) fits much better than (a) in the wider context, which speaks of personal relationships between Father (1.5), Son (1.5,8), brothers (2.11-12), and children (2.13). However, (c) is possible and would fit in well with verse 14.

The mere use of capitalization with the term **Father** may not be satisfactory in some languages for showing that God is meant, especially since many more people hear the Scriptures read than read them for themselves. Therefore it may be appropriate to translate **have the same Father** as "have God as their Father" or "have the same one, namely, God, as their Father."

Ashamed is often used to describe the "loss of face" felt by someone who is treated without respect for his position or status. The meaning is that although Jesus is supreme, he nevertheless has so much in common with men that he can call them **his brothers** without any risk of losing his status. In some languages it may be necessary to replace **is not ashamed** by a positive expression. If so, "is happy" or "is content" may be used; "is proud" would be too strong.

Jesus is not ashamed to call them his brothers may be expressed as "Jesus does not feel bad when he calls them his brothers." But it is often better to render this statement as "Jesus does not hesitate to call them his brothers" or even "Jesus is ready to call them his brothers." Sometimes shame is expressed as a reaction to ridicule. For example, "Jesus is not worried if he is laughed at, when he calls them his brothers."

2.12 **He says to God,**
> **"I will tell my brothers what you have done;**
> **I will praise you in their meeting."**

The writer begins a series of three quotations. **He says:** the writer thinks of the Old Testament words (Psa 22.22) as spoken by Jesus. Jesus remains the subject of the verb. **To God** is not in the Greek but is implied. SpCL weakens the meaning by translating "as scripture says."

In order to indicate clearly that the following statement is a quotation from Scripture, it would be possible to translate **He says to God** as "He says to God by using words from the holy writings." However, the reference system may itself be sufficient to indicate to readers that the words are a quotation.

A literal rendering of **I will tell my brothers what you have done** could be a reference only to Jesus' own kin. It may therefore be necessary to translate "I will tell my followers what you have done." Though the term **brothers** in a number of biblical contexts can be translated as "fellow believers," such an expresion would not be appropriate in this context.

The two halves of this quotation are parallel; see the discussion on parallelism in 1.7. In an Old Testament setting, **my brothers . . . in their meeting** means fellow members of the people of God (Israel) gathered for worship in the Temple. For the writer of Hebrews, it means Jesus' followers gathered in worship.

Tell. . . what you have done is literally "proclaim your name," "tell people what you are like," for the "name" and the person are one (see comment on 1.4).

The Greek word for **meeting** became in New Testament times the common term for describing Christians meeting for worship, and only later became the specifically Christian word "church" (KJV). **I will praise you in their meeting** may be expressed as "I will praise you when they gather for worship" or "when they gather to worship you, I will praise you."

In some languages it is necessary to indicate praise by suggesting something of the content. For example, **I will praise you** may be expressed as "I will say how wonderful you are." Sometimes even direct discourse is required; for example, **I will praise you** may be rendered as "I will say to them, 'You are truly great.' "

2.13　　He also says, "I will put my trust in God." And he also says, "Here I am with the children that God has given me."

He also says, twice repeated, makes two separate quotations out of successive sentences of Isaiah 8.17-18 (the first quotation is similar to 2 Sam 22.3 and Isa 12.2). The writer does this because he is making two distinct points. First, the words **I will put my trust in God** (the **I** is emphasized) show that Jesus, like his **brothers**, depends on his Father. The key word of the second quotation is **children.** There is no distinction in meaning between <u>sons</u> in verse 10 and **children** here. Neither daughters nor adults are excluded; what matters is the relationship of dependence.

I will put my trust in God may be expressed merely as "I will trust God." But this type of confidence in God is often expressed idiomatically; for example, "I will lean my weight upon God" or "I will put myself in the hands of God."

A literal translation of **the children that God has given me** may be understood incorrectly as a reference to Jesus' children in a physical sense. It may therefore be better to translate the second part of verse 13 as "Here I am with the people whom God has given to me" or ". . . whom God has caused to belong to me." On the other hand, it may be useful to retain the figure of speech in **the children,** but to indicate that this is a simile; for example, "Here I am with the

[43]

people that God has given to me; these are like children." In this way one may anticipate the further extension of this figure of speech as it occurs in verse 14.

TEV	2.14-18	RSV

14 Since the children, as he calls them, are people of flesh and blood, Jesus himself became like them and shared their human nature. He did this so that through his death he might destroy the Devil, who has the power over death, 15 and in this way set free those who were slaves all their lives because of their fear of death. 16 For it is clear that it is not the angels that he helps. Instead, as the scripture says, "He helps the descendants of Abraham." 17 This means that he had to become like his brothers in every way, in order to be their faithful and merciful High Priest in his service to God, so that the people's sins would be forgiven. 18 And now he can help those who are tempted, because he himself was tempted and suffered.

14 Since therefore the children share in flesh and blood, he himself likewise partook of the same nature, that through death he might destroy him who has the power of death, that is, the devil, 15 and deliver all those who through fear of death were subject to lifelong bondage. 16 For surely it is not with angels that he is concerned but with the descendants of Abraham. 17 Therefore he had to be made like his brethren in every respect, so that he might become a merciful and faithful high priest in the service of God, to make expiation for the sins of the people. 18 For because he himself has suffered and been tempted, he is able to help those who are tempted.

2.14 Since the children, as he calls them, are people of flesh and blood, Jesus himself became like them and shared their human nature. He did this so that through his death he might destroy the Devil, who has the power over death,

Verses 14-15 form a single sentence in the Greek. Verse 14 partly overlaps in meaning with verse 10, and partly sums up what was said in verses 11-13.

RSV's **"therefore"** refers back to verse 11a, which this verse repeats in other words and then somewhat expands. TEV omits "therefore," perhaps because the connection with verse 11a is too far away to be seen by most readers, and because there is no direct link with the end of verse 13.

The first part of the sentence contains two statements: (a) the **children** share a common human nature with one another, and (b) Jesus shared this nature with them. **The children: the** is necessary because **the children** have just been mentioned in verse 13: TEV, FrCL brings this out by adding **as he calls them**. NEB, SpCL "The children of a family . . ." is less definite than the Greek. **The children** may be expressed as "these children," especially if a reference to "the children" has been made in the previous verse. The phrase **as he calls them** may be expressed parenthetically as "that's what he calls them."

[44]

Flesh and blood (literally "blood and flesh") is a common way of describing human nature, especially in its weakness. The expression **of flesh and blood** can rarely be translated literally, since people obviously consist of more than flesh and blood. Accordingly, **people of flesh and blood** may be rendered as "people like all other kinds of people" or "people in every sense of the word."

Like them is emphatic; Brc "in exactly the same way." TEV reproduces this emphasis by expansion, for there is nothing in the Greek which literally corresponds to **became like them and.** This phrase is presupposed by **shared their human nature** (literally "shared them," that is, shared their **flesh and blood**).

Became like them may be rendered as "became a person like they are persons" or "became a human being like them" or ". . . even as they are." It may, however, be extremely difficult to render the expression "shared their human nature," since a literal rendering would assume that in some way Jesus took from them part of their human nature, since the concept of "sharing" so frequently suggests dividing up something. Therefore, **shared their human nature** may be expressed as "was a human being just like they are." In fact **became like them and shared their human nature** must often be combined in a single expression such as "came to be just like all other human beings."

The phrase about Jesus' human nature is the focal point of the sentence, both in grammar and in meaning. The writer then goes on to describe the purpose of Christ's sharing human nature. Brc and TNT think the writer is referring to the result of this event, but this interpretation suits the structure less well.

He did this must be rendered in some languages as "He became like this" or even more specifically "He became a person."

Through his death may be expressed "by his dying" or "by means of his giving his life."

Destroy does not always imply that the thing destroyed no longer exists. The first meaning of the Greek is "render ineffective" (see 1 Cor 15.26, where TEV translates "defeated"). Here Mft has "crush"; Seg, JB "take away all the power of"; NAB "rob . . . of his power"; Knox, TNT "depose"; BJ, TOB "reduce to impotence." The point is that the Devil is so utterly defeated that he is no longer able to do anything, and is thus like the pagan gods mentioned in Isaiah 44.9-20.

A literal rendering of **might destroy the Devil** might appear to be contradictory to other passages of Scripture, especially those references in the book of Revelation. Therefore it may be important to use some such expression as "take away completely the power of the Devil" rather than to use a literal rendering of "destroy," which would mean annihilation.

TEV simplifies the structure by putting **the Devil** before the phrase which describes him, **who has the power over death.** The idea is that the Devil has both control over death and the power to inflict death. **Who has the power over death** may be rendered as "who is able to kill" or "who is able to cause people to die."

2.15   **and in this way set free those who were slaves all their lives because of their fear of death.**

This verse describes the second part of the purpose of Jesus in taking human nature. Logically it depends on the first: the Devil, as prince of death, has been utterly defeated, and **in this way** people are set free from fear of death. GeCL, however, understands this verse not as an expression of purpose but of result. This is possible and produces a clear translation: "In this way he has freed men who had been slaves . . . ."

Most translators and commentators agree generally with TEV and RSV, but it is also possible to translate ". . . and deliver from bondage all those who were subject to lifelong fear of death." This construction is the basis for Mft, and the Greek of Galatians 5.1 is similar. However, the construction represented by RSV is generally more probable and gives a meaning similar to that of Romans 8.21.

A literal rendering of TEV may lead to considerable misunderstanding, since the subject of the preceding clause is the Devil. Those who hear the scripture read might assume that the Devil is likewise the subject of the expression **set free**. It may therefore be better to begin a new sentence at the beginning of verse 15, or at least to introduce Jesus as the subject; for example, "and in this way Jesus set free those who were slaves."

In this way is an expression of means and may be rendered as "by means of what he did."

Set free may be expressed as "cause to be free" or "cause to no longer be enslaved."

Some translations make it clear that the slavery is figurative, not literal. Brc has "a kind of slavery"; FrCL, SpCL replace the metaphor by a simile, "were like slaves." In order to indicate clearly that the slaves in question are moral rather than physical slaves, the use of some term which will indicate the figurative nature of the expression is important; for example, "were like slaves" or "who were, as it were, slaves."

All their lives may be expressed as "during all the time they lived." It is important, however, that the order of elements be carefully noted in the latter part of verse 15; for example, "Those who during all the time they lived were just like slaves because they were afraid of dying."

2.16   **For it is clear that it is not the angels that he helps. Instead, as the scripture says, "He helps the descendants of Abraham."**

This verse, together with verse 17, marks a new step in the argument; verse 16 is a statement from which verse 17 draws a conclusion.

It is clear: compare Knox "After all," introducing the statement of something which almost goes without saying; GeCL omits this. **It is clear that it is not the angels** may be expressed as "it is obviously not the angels," or "it is indeed not the angels," or "one can readily see that it is not the angels."

A rather literal translation is given by KJV, "he took not on him the nature of angels," except that "the nature of" is not expressed in the Greek. The meaning of the word, twice repeated, which TEV translated **helps** has been the subject of furious argument for centuries, and the problem is not yet entirely solved. The first sentence may be understood in two main ways.

(a) It has often been understood to refer to God "taking on" human nature when Christ became man. This interpretation is followed by KJV and is suggested by NEB's "takes to himself"; compare JB, Phps, Lu, Zür. However, the translator must always beware of forcing biblical texts into the mold of later theological ideas.

(b) Most modern translations, though of various Christian traditions, essentially agree with TEV's **helps** (other CLTs, NAB, Brc, TNT; Mft has "succours"; Knox "make himself the angels' champion"). **"Be concerned with"** (RSV) is also possible, though rather weak. TEV and RSV both give an unusual meaning for a word which is not very common, but literal meanings such as "grasp" are impossible. In Sirach 4.11, NEB translates "cares for."

As the scripture says (compare FrCL, GeCL) is not in the text but is added to show that the following words are an allusion—in this case, to Isaiah 41.8-9. As elsewhere, the phrase **as the scripture says** must be rendered "as one may read in the holy writings" or "as in the words of the holy writings."

Descendants of Abraham: literally "seed of Abraham," that is, Israel. **Descendants of Abraham** may be expressed as "those in the lineage of Abraham" or "those who claim Abraham as a forefather."

2.17   This means that he had to become like his brothers in every way, in order to be their faithful and merciful High Priest in his service to God, so that the people's sins would be forgiven.

It is rare that one can translate literally **This means,** for the pronoun **This** refers to the arguments which have immediately preceded, and **means** is a reference to a logical result. Accordingly, **This means** must in some instances be rendered as "All this results in the fact that," or "Because of all this," or "If we understand what has just been said, then we know that."

Had to is stronger than It was only right in verse 10; it suggests that inner compulsion was needed (that is, "ought") if Jesus' purpose was to be fulfilled. **He had to** must be rendered in some languages as "it was necessary that he" or "there was no other way but that he."

To become like is literally "to be made like," but the idea of God's activity in all this has been strongly expressed in verse 10 and is not emphasized here.

His brothers does not refer only to other children of Joseph, or of Joseph and Mary. As in verses 11-12, it means all members of God's people, whose life Jesus shared (Hebrews does not usually distinguish between God's people in Old Testament and New Testament times).

To become like his brothers in every way may be rendered as "to become like other people in every way," or "to become just like any human being," or "to become exactly like all other human beings."

Beginning with **in order to be . . . ,** the second half of the verse introduces an idea which will become more and more important, especially in chapters 4—5 and 7—9. Here it is mentioned only briefly, in passing. This is the idea of Jesus as

High Priest, a title which is not given to Jesus anywhere else in the Bible. GeCL
marks this development by beginning a new sentence: "In this way he was able to
be their ... High Priest." The writer of Hebrews is mainly concerned with the
High Priest's function in leading Temple worship, especially on the annual Day of
Atonement, a festival concerned with the forgiveness of sins and the purification
of sinners.

Faithful here implies "faithful to God." The idea is not merely that Jesus is
generally reliable, but that God has placed him in a particular position of trust,
and that he has proved worthy of it (see also 3.1-6).

Faithful and merciful may be rendered as "one who is to be trusted and who
shows mercy." In some instances "to show mercy" is equivalent to "to be kind to
those in need."

High Priest should normally not be translated literally, since it would
indicate merely elevation of a priest in space. What is important here is the
position of the priest above other priests, and therefore a normal equivalent is
"the most important priest" or "the priest above all other priests." In many languages it is impossible to distinguish readily between "High Priest" and "chief
priest," and such a distinction is not relevant in the book of Hebrews.

In his service to God is slightly more literal than RSV "in the service of
God." The phrase **in his service to God** may be rendered as "in the way in which he
serves God" or "in the way in which he is God's helper."

The people, implying "God's people," is a favorite expression in which the
writer includes both Israel and the church, without any distinction between Jewish
and Gentile Christians. **The people** is thus the same as **his brothers** earlier in the
verse.

RSV's **"expiation"** translates a Greek word which refers to the removal of a
barrier between men and God. In pagan writings, it was often used of making the
gods favorable to the worshiper. In Luke 18.13 (the only other place in the New
Testament where this word is used) the object is the worshiper; TEV translates
have pity on me. In the Old Testament it sometimes refers to the blotting out or
"covering" of sins (not "covering up" with the idea of deceit!). This is the idea
here. There is no question of offering sacrifices to an angry God so that he will
stop being angry. It is not God who is being dealt with in this verse, but sins, and
they are "forgiven" (see Brc), "taken away" (see TNT), or wiped away.

The passive clause **so that the people's sins would be forgiven** may be made
active by introducing God as the agent; for example, "so that God would forgive
people's sins."

2.18   **And now he can help those who are tempted, because he himself was tempted and suffered.**

Now should be understood in a temporal sense; it is not a conjunction to
show some kind of connection in thought.

Help is not the same word as in verse 14, but the meaning is the same.

The temptations of Jesus are mentioned here for the first time and then
emphasized later. The same Greek word means both "tempt" (encourage to do

[48]

wrong) and "test." The first meaning is appropriate here, as it is in 4.15; the second is appropriate in 3.8-9 and in 11.17. The relation between tempting and suffering in this verse is not clear; the literal translation is "suffered, having been tempted (over a period)." Brc takes the two closely together ("went through the ordeal of suffering"; TNT "tested by suffering"), but not all of Jesus' temptations or testings were linked with suffering. TEV is therefore probably right to join **tempted** and **suffered,** in that order, by **and.** GeCL "what was demanded of him" tries to bring out the full meaning of "tempted-tested" in nonchurch language, although by whom is not expressed.

It is rare that one can combine in a single word the meaning of both "tempted" and "tested." It is possible to translate **those who are tempted** as "those who are encouraged to do wrong" or, in the active form, "those whom the Devil encourages to do wrong."

He himself was tempted may be expressed as "he himself was encouraged to do wrong," but it is probaby better to use a specific reference to the temptation of Jesus by the Devil. Therefore, "the Devil himself tried to get Jesus to do wrong." In reference to the tempation of Jesus it is probably better to use an expression such as "tried to," in order to indicate clearly that the Devil did not succeed in causing Jesus to sin.

Chapter 3

Jesus Is Greater than Moses

1 My Christian brothers, who also have been called by God! Think of Jesus, whom God sent to be the High Priest of the faith we profess. 2 He was faithful to God, who chose him to do this work, just as Moses was faithful in his work in God's house. 3 A man who builds a house receives more honor than the house itself. In the same way Jesus is worthy of much greater honor than Moses. 4 Every house, of course, is built by someone—and God is the one who has built all things. 5 Moses was faithful in God's house as a servant, and he spoke of the things that God would say in the future. 6 But Christ is faithful as the Son in charge of God's house. We are his house if we keep up our courage and our confidence in what we hope for.

1 Therefore, holy brethren, who share in a heavenly call, consider Jesus, the apostle and high priest of our confession. 2 He was faithful to him who appointed him, just as Moses also was faithful in^e God's house. 3 Yet Jesus has been counted worthy of as much more glory than Moses as the builder of a house has more honor than the house. 4 (For every house is built by some one, but the builder of all things is God.) 5 Now Moses was faithful in all God's house as a servant, to testify to the things that were to be spoken later, 6 but Christ was faithful over God's^f house as a son. And we are his house if we hold fast our confidence and pride in our hope.^{g}

^{e} Other ancient authorities insert *all*
^{f} Greek *his*
^{g} Other ancient authorities insert *firm to the end*

The section heading in TEV, **Jesus Is Greater than Moses**, may be rendered as "Jesus is more important than Moses" or, as in some languages, "Jesus stands greater than Moses" or "Jesus is in front of Moses."

Despite the repetition of **High Priest** from 2.17, the writer does not immediately go on to compare Jesus with either Aaron (5.4), Melchizedek (7.1-15), or any other high priest. Instead, he begins a comparison between Jesus, and Aaron's greater brother Moses. This comparison is introduced in verse 1; verse 2 states what Moses and Jesus had in common; verses 3-4 and 5-6a point out two ways in which Jesus is greater than Moses. Verse 6b begins another call for action (compare 2.1-4), which extends with little interruption to the end of chapter 4.

Verses 1-2 do not mark a completely new beginning, and FrCL does not follow TEV in omitting RSV's "**Therefore**," which is quite a strong word in the

Greek. There may be a distinct advantage in introducing some kind of transitional expression to reflect what in Greek is a relevant connective, meaning essentially "in view of what has been said" or "therefore." In some languages this may be expressed as "as a result of all this" or "because this is indeed true." Points of contact with the earlier part of the letter are (a) "share," compare 2.14; (b) **High Priest,** compare 2.17; (c) "faithful," compare 2.17. An important new stage in the argument is, however, marked by (a) addressing the readers as **My Christian brothers;** (b) the use of **called** (meaning invited, as distinct from "named" in 2.11); (c) the unique use of "**apostle**" (RSV); and (d) the new key word **house.**

3.1   **My Christian brothers, who also have been called by God! Think of Jesus, whom God sent to be the High Priest of the faith we profess.**

My Christian brothers is literally "holy brothers" (see RSV). The Greek word for "holy" describes either God himself or any person or thing that belongs to him in a special way (compare discussion of pure, purifies in 2.11). In English and in some other languages, "holy" and "saint" belong so much to church language that many modern translations avoid them; DuCL has "Brothers, you are called by God and belong to him"; GeCL "My brothers, you belong to God, for he has called you into his heavenly world"; TNT "my brothers, whom God has set apart for himself and called to share the life of heaven." TEV gives essentially the same sense, but **My** is not explicit (nothing until 13.19 shows whether the letter comes from an individual or a group).

The Greek expression of direct address, literally "holy brothers," is rather unusual. But as in so many contexts of the New Testament, the Greek term traditionally translated as "saints" is frequently better rendered as "people of God." In this type of context TEV has understandably used **Christian.** In a number of languages, however, it may be difficult, if not impossible, to use a word meaning "brothers." Therefore the TEV phrase **My Christian brothers** may be rendered as "My fellow believers in Jesus" or "My fellow Christians." In some languages the closest equivalent is simply "You who also believe in Christ."

Also is not in the text. It is implied by "**share**" (RSV) and means "as well as me."

RSV's "**share in a heavenly call**" is a very compact expression which can be understood in several slightly different ways:

(a) "**Share**" and "**call**" almost certainly go together, but it is not clear whether the writer means that they share their call with one another, or with God who called them, or with Christ (as in 1.9, where the same Greek word was translated companions). In view of the term "brothers," it is likely that "to share" refers to what is shared among fellow believers. "You who share the heavenly calling" may therefore be rendered as "you who are also called by God" or "you whom God has also called."

(b) "**Heavenly call**" may mean "call from God" or "call to heaven." The first possibility may suit verses 7-10 and 5.4 rather better, but GeCL follows the second, which is taken up in chapter 4 and in 12.1-2. If one assumes that the Greek phrase "heavenly calling" refers to "a call from God to go to heaven," it will be necessary to make the relation rather explicit; for example, "God's call to you to be those who will go to heaven." But this interpretation seems to be rather unlikely.

Think is less strong than keep our eyes fixed on Jesus in 12.2; compare **Think** in 12.3, where a different Greek word is used. KJV's "Christ" before "Jesus" is probably not part of the original text. The admonition to "keep Jesus in mind" is not simply a matter of "thinking about Jesus" or "meditating upon him." An equivalent in some languages is "consider how Jesus was the Apostle and High Priest of our faith." It might also be possible to translate the Greek term as "reckon with the fact that."

Whom God sent is literally "apostle." Both "apostle" and "angel" mean "someone who is sent." In secular language an "apostle" is an ambassador. In the New Testament it is usually someone sent by Jesus. Nowhere else in the New Testament is Jesus himself called an apostle. Perhaps the comparison with angels, last mentioned in 2.16, is still in the writer's mind; a translation such as **whom God sent** allows for this without emphasizing it. GeCL translates "apostle" in the secular meaning as "plenipotentiary," an ambassador with full powers, which makes good sense, though "plenipotentiary" would not be common language in English. Some of the meaning of the Greek term traditionally rendered "apostle" may be expressed as "God's messenger" or "God's ambassador." In some languages this is expressed literally as "one who speaks God's words" or "one who announces what God has said."

High Priest (see 2.17).

The faith we profess: TEV makes it clear that the word which RSV translates "**confession**" is confession of faith, not confession of sin. What is meant is not the act of confessing but what is confessed; SpCL "our religion." **The faith we profess** may be rendered as "what we believe" or perhaps better "what we say we believe."

In some languages there may be a problem involved in relating **High Priest** to **the faith we profess.** Sometimes this may be expressed as "High Priest in relation to what we say we believe" or "High Priest to assist us in everything relating to what we say we believe." It is often obscure and even misleading to say only "High Priest of the faith we profess" or even "High Priest of our religion."

3.2   He was faithful to God, who chose him to do this work, just as Moses was faithful in his work in God's house.

Many translations replace **He** by "Jesus" at the beginning of the verse, to make the sentence absolutely clear.

He was faithful to God may be expressed as "He did everything that God told him to do." In some languages this can be best expressed as "God could trust him completely." The context shows that the writer is thinking especially of Christ's performance of the tasks God gave him as High Priest.

Chose is a common language equivalent for "appointed." The same word is used about Jesus choosing the twelve disciples in Mark 3.14. It is the usual word for "made," but cannot have that meaning here. As so often in this letter, **God** is implied. So is **to do this work,** which explains the purpose of "choosing." **Who chose him to do this work** may be expressed as "who designated him to do what he did" or even "who said to him, 'This is what you must do.' "

The second half of the verse contains a key quotation which becomes the text for this whole section. It is taken from Numbers 12.7, where TEV translates "house" (RSV) as people. In Hebrews, however, the translation **house** is required for the play on words in verses 3-4. GeCL underlines the importance of this quotation and makes it clear that it is a quotation: "He was just as true to the one who had appointed him as Moses, of whom it was said: 'He was true to God in his whole house.' " This is one of the rare cases in which a word-for-word translation of a key term is essential to the meaning, since the argument turns on a literal understanding of the word "in."[1]

In God's house: God makes explicit the antecedent of the Greek pronoun meaning "his." In the Old Testament passage, God is speaking and says "my house." Some manuscripts have "whole house" instead of "house."

The same word for **house** is used six times in the Greek in five verses. The difficulty for the translator in most languages is that the meaning varies between (a) a building and (b) a household, family, or nation. Both meanings are possible in Greek as in Hebrew, depending on the context. The first meaning is clearest in verse 4 (built), the second in verse 6 (We are his house). The other references in this section combine both meanings in various ways. Translators into languages which do not use the same term for "house" and "family" have three main choices: (a) To use "house" (or some equivalent indicating a building) throughout, leaving We are his house in verse 6 as a striking metaphor. (b) To use "people," "household," or some other word indicating a kinship group, throughout; for example, using "founded" for "built." (c) To alternate between "house" and "household" according to the context, using related words if possible. The first choice, made by TEV and other CLTs, and also by RSV, is the simplest. **God's house** could be understood as the Temple, but this is at most only part of the meaning.

There are relatively few languages in which the play on words between the meaning of "house" and "household" (or "family") can be maintained. In general, it is better to make sense of the passage, so that it can be meaningful when heard. The basis for the underlying play on words can then be explained in a footnote.

The expression **Moses was faithful** must be rendered in a manner parallel to the way in which Jesus' faithfulness to God is expressed in the first part of this verse. But a literal rendering of **in God's house** will be understood by most persons to refer only to the Temple. This immediately suggests an anachronism, since the Temple was built only in the time of Solomon. Accordingly, **in his work in God's house** may be rendered in some languages as "what he did in leading God's people" or ". . . helping God's people."

---

[1] A similar case is Galatians 3.16, where the plural "seeds" is unnatural but essential to this type of argument, a type which was common in Jewish tradition.

3.3-4　**A man who builds a house receives more honor than the house itself. In the same way Jesus is worthy of much greater honor than Moses. 4 Every house, of course, is built by someone—and God is the one who has built all things.**

These verses introduce the first point of contrast between Moses and Jesus. TEV makes the comparison clearer by reversing the two halves of verse 3, so that the general statement of principle comes first, and the application to Moses and Jesus afterward. This order is more logical and also makes the sentence easier to follow, as a comparison with RSV shows. Verse 4, which several translations put in round brackets (parentheses), explains the background of the argument in verse 3, and so it is possible to adopt the order 4, 3b, 3a. Verse 4 in TEV would follow smoothly after verse 2, and it would only be necessary to add a "now," corresponding to RSV's "**For,**" at the beginning of verse 3, to mark the transition. Verse 5 in any case marks a new beginning. The result would be to reverse TEV's verses 4 and 3. In the following discussion, however, the order of TEV will be followed.

In reversing the two halves of verse 3, TEV divides them. In the original, we have an expression of proportion, of the kind

3 is to 2	as	6 is to 4
builder is to house	as	Jesus is to Moses.

In one sense, Moses could be considered as the "founder" of the nation of Israel. However, this does not fit the context here. As Numbers 12.7 implies, Moses is part of the **house,** that is, the people, that God has made. Jesus, on the other hand, is closely associated with God in building the house.

The word for **builds,** repeated three times in verses 3-4, may also include the meaning "equip, fit out." This meaning is probably present in 9.6 (arranged), and possibly in 9.2 (put up) as well as in 11.7 (built). Here, however, building rather than equipping is suggested by the context.

After having introduced a more or less literal translation of **A man who builds a house,** it may be important to introduce a marginal note indicating clearly that the term **house** at this point is the same Greek term which has been translated as "household" or "family" or even "people" in the preceding verse.

Honor in 3a and 3b translates two different Greek words, usually translated "glory" and "honor," but they have a similar meaning. Earlier editions of TEV had more glory than Moses. The writer uses the word for **honor** in 5.4 in speaking about men, and the word for glory in 1.3 and 13.21 in speaking of God or Christ. However, the two words are used together in 2.7 (quoting Psa 8.5) and 2.9, and there is no sharp distinction between them there or here in verse 3. He probably uses another word for the sake of variety. In its latest edition, TEV is therefore justified in using the same word **honor** in both sentences. In English, "glory" is more often used in church language than in common language.

Receives more honor is a kind of substitute passive and may be translated "is more honored." If an active expression is required, one may say "people honor more a man who builds a house than they honor the house itself." In some languages a term such as **honor** must be expressed in the form of direct discourse; for example, **receives more honor** may be rendered as "they say of him, 'He is greater.' "

The transitional phrase **In the same way** may be rendered in some languages as "Therefore." In other instances, one may use a clause such as "Since this is true."

Jesus is understood; literally "this one" (masculine), referring back to Jesus in verse 1. Yet **Jesus** is preferable to Phps "this Man," since at the moment the writer is not emphasizing that Jesus is a man, but as in 1.2, that he cooperated closely with God in the founding of God's people.

As "**has been counted worthy**" in RSV shows, **is worthy** translates a passive verb. The writer probably suggests that God has counted Jesus worthy of **much greater honor than Moses.** JB expresses this by saying "he has been found to deserve a greater glory than Moses"; similarly Mft. "Even greater honor" would be a possible translation. This verse presupposes that Moses has some glory; Numbers 12 narrates a glorious appearance of God to Moses in the pillar of cloud, and it is clear that God has set Moses apart from all other human beings.

Jesus is worthy of much greater honor may be expressed as "people ought to honor Jesus even more." One of the most difficult terms to render satisfactorily in some languages is the expression of "worthiness" or "that which is deserved." All such expressions, however, imply some kind of obligation of the basis of what is right and fitting, and therefore the meaning may be frequently conveyed by a modal verb or adverb meaning "ought to," or "deserves," or "should."

In some languages the expression of comparison is particularly difficult, and instead of using an expression such as "**more . . . than**" (RSV), a positive-negative is employed; for example, "they should honor Jesus, they should not honor Moses." However, this kind of positive-negative construction does not mean literally what it says. It does not refer to a positive in contrast with a completely negative statement as to what should or should not take place, but to a comparative degree. In a number of other languages, comparison is often expressed by a verb meaning "to surpass"; for example, "in honoring Jesus they should surpass the way they honor Moses."

Every house, of course, is built by someone must be expressed in some languages as an active construction, and this may be done by saying "There is, of course, always someone to build every house" or "If there is a house, then certainly someone has built it." If, however, a translator can employ a word meaning "household" or "family," it would be possible to say "there is always someone who has caused a family to be what it is." In a similar manner the final clause of verse 4 may be rendered as "and God is the one who has called all things to be what they are."

3.5-6a   Moses was faithful in God's house as a servant, and he spoke of the things that God would say in the future. 6 But Christ is faithful as the Son in charge of God's house.

As RSV's **"Now"** shows, these verses take up a second point of contrast between Moses and Jesus. Moses is a **servant**, that is, a house-servant or attendent, not a slave; but Christ is a **Son**. God often speaks of "my servant Moses," for example, in Numbers 12.7-8.

God's house: the Greek has "God's whole house" here, though probably not in verse 2, where earlier editions of TEV included the word whole. There is little difference of meaning, but it is probably best to follow the Greek in using the more emphatic expression "God's whole house" in verse 5. "God's whole house" is also the more exact quotation from Numbers 12. RSV translates the Hebrew of Numbers 12.7 as "entrusted with all my house." TEV fourth edition is almost certainly wrong in omitting "all" before **God's house.** The first through third editions of TEV had God's whole house. GeCL puts "in his whole house" in quotation marks. If quotation marks are used here, they should also enclose **faithful in.** On the meaning of **faithful,** see the discussion on 2.17. The main idea is that of doing reliably the tasks associated with an office or title.

A strictly literal translation of **Moses was faithful in God's house as a servant** can be misunderstood, since it would imply that Moses was simply a Levite in the Temple. It may also be necessary in some languages to indicate clearly the fact that Moses was "a servant of God" in the sense of "one who helped God" or "one who served God." Therefore some restructuring of the first part of verse 5 may be required; for example, "As one who served God in helping God's people, Moses was to be trusted" or ". . . Moses was a person whom God could trust."

And he spoke of the things that God would say in the future is literally "as a witness of things to be spoken." TEV is certainly right in seeing here one of the writer's typical indirect references to God, as in 1.1-2; 2.10.

It is less certain that Moses' "witness" consisted of "speaking" (though this may be suggested by Num 12.2). (The "tent of meeting" in Num 12, RSV, is called in the Greek Bible the "tent of witness.") The writer more probably means that Moses' whole work, especially the way in which he showed himself trustworthy as the leader of God's people, pointed ahead to greater things which God was to **say in the future** through the Son (Brc "His function was to point to the things which God was going to say in the future"; TNT "Moses was faithful in all God's household, and so bore witness to what God would say in the future"; see also Phps. However, "witness" in the Bible usually involves speaking, and therefore **spoke** is possible).

One may render **he spoke of the things that God would say in the future** as "he spoke about what God was going to say later" or even ". . . many years later." But, as already noted, it is possible that the reference is to what Moses did, and therefore one may translate "what Moses did pointed to what God was going to say later on."

Servant is emphasized as the point of the contrast with **Son** (verse 6): "It was as a servant that Moses was faithful . . . ." The author of Hebrews rearranges the quotation from Numbers 12.7 in order to bring this out, and if possible, translators should follow his example.

Son (verse 6) is the other point of the contrast: "Christ as Son (is faithful) over his (that is, God's) house." **In charge of** is literally "over." Phps emphasizes

"Son" by expanding: "In the household of . . . his own Father." **Son** has no "the" in Greek; as one having the title and status of Son, he is in charge of God's house, that is, of God's people, including both Israel and the church (see comments on 1.7). In 1.2 and here, RSV has "a Son" or "**a son**," but there is no suggestion of any other sons in this passage; 2.10 is the only place where the writer speaks of "sons" of God in the plural.

The phrase **as the Son** may be made emphatic and indicate significant contrast by placing it at the beginning of verse 6. In many languages it is necessary to indicate the relationship of the Son to God; therefore, "But as God's Son."

The expression **Christ is faithful** must be expressed in essentially the same manner as at the beginning of verse 2.

In charge of God's house, if retained in a relatively literal form, might seem to refer to Christ's activity as the head of the Temple ritual in his day. This would be quite misleading. Therefore **in charge of God's house** must often be expressed as "as one who had responsibility for God's people" or "as one whose job it was to care for God's people." TEV is almost certainly right in taking "his house" to mean **God's house,** in the light of verse 4b.

3.6b   We are his house if we keep up our courage and our confidence in what we hope for.

This sentence contains two textual problems. (a) Some manuscripts, followed by Mft, Knox, Phps, NAB, have "this" or "that house" instead of "whose house." "Whose house" is more likely to be what the author wrote, and this text is followed by most translations. (b) Some manuscripts, followed by KJV, DuCL, SpCL, add "firm to the end" at the end of the verse; RSV mentions the longer text in a note. These words were probably copied from 3.14.

Most translations begin a new sentence or even a new paragraph (Mft) with verse 6b. Translators must decide whether it is more natural in their language to place such transitional statements at the beginning of a new paragraph or at the end of the previous paragraph.

Note the present tense **We are.** According to the shorter and better text, the writer is not saying here, as he will say in 3.14, that he and his readers will become **partners with Christ** if they remain faithful to the end. He is saying that they **are** God's house or people if they are now holding with a firm grasp the gifts of **courage** and **confidence.**

We are his house is best rendered in many languages as "We are God's people." This takes up the meaning of the preceding phrase God's house.

If we keep up is often expressed as a continuous aspect of a verb; for example, "if we continue to." In some instances, however, a negative of this may be even stronger; for example, "if we do not diminish in" or "if we not fail to."

Courage and **confidence** are related first to God and then to other people. **Courage** is first the openness and freedom with which believers approach God in prayer and worship (4.16; 10.19), and next the consequent fearlessness with which they approach even enemies (10.35; Acts 4.13,29,31). Perhaps **courage** expresses fearlessness before other people more strongly than openness to God. Several modern translations and KJV have "confidence" for the term which TEV translates **courage**. The two words overlap in meaning. BJ, TOB have "assurance."

Confidence is related to God by the following words **in what we hope for**, since the Christian hope is clearly centered in God. However, the word also suggests speaking boldly and confidently to others. Sometimes it means "boasting," but this can have a negative meaning which is out of the question here. Mft, Knox use "proud" or "pride."

Several translations link not only **confidence** but also **courage** with hope; for example, Mft "if we will only hold on, confident and proud of our hope"; GeCL. Since the meaning of the two terms is so similar, it is quite possible to take **hope** with them both and omit **our** before **confidence**.

In a number of languages **courage** and **confidence** are best expressed as verbs rather than as nouns. A more or less literal rendering would be "if we continue to be courageous and trust."

In a number of languages **courage** is expressed idiomatically; for example, "to have a hard heart" (in contrast to "having a soft heart," which would mean "to be fearful") or "to not turn away," or even "to never say, 'I surrender.' "

In what we hope for may often be expressed as "in what we look forward to with patience." The essential components of **hope** are (a) expectancy (b) of something good (c) in the future and (d) patient confidence that what one expects will certainly take place. Sometimes hope may be expressed idiomatically as "what we see in our hearts" or "what our thoughts see in front of us."

| TEV | **3.7-11** | RSV |

A Rest for God's People

7 So then, as the Holy Spirit says, "If you hear God's voice today,	7 Therefore, as the Holy Spirit says,
8 do not be stubborn, as your ancestors were when they rebelled against God, as they were that day in the desert when they put him to the test.	"Today, when you hear his voice, 8 do not harden your hearts as in the rebellion, on the day of testing in the wilderness,
9 There they put me to the test and tried me, says God, although they had seen what I did for forty years.	9 where your fathers put me to the test and saw my works for forty years.
10 And so I was angry with those people and said, 'They are always disloyal and refuse to obey my commands.'	10 Therefore I was provoked with that generation, and said, 'They always go astray in their hearts; they have not known my ways.'
11 I was angry and made a solemn promise:	11 As I swore in my wrath, 'They shall never enter my rest.' "

'They will never enter the land
where I would have given
them rest!' "

A long section begins here, 3.7—4.13. Like 2.1-4, it is less concerned with teaching about God or Christ than with moving the readers to action. In these parts of the letter, the writer is more concerned with strengthening his readers' faith than with deepening their understanding.

These verses are marked off as a separate section by being mainly an exposition of Psalm 95.7-11. Some people think that this section was originally preached as a separate sermon.[2] Subdivisions within the section are difficult to establish, though My fellow believers, be careful (3.12) and Let us take care, then (4.1) seem to mark new steps forward in the writer's appeal to his readers or hearers.

The section heading in TEV, **A Rest for God's People**, covers the whole of 3.7—4.13. It reflects essentially the wording of 4.9 and a good deal of the discussion from 3.18 through 4.11. The section heading may be translated in many instances as "God's people will rest."

The quotation is from Psalm 95.7-11. The main difficulty in translating it is the change from third person ("his voice") in verses 7b-8 to first person (**put me to the test**) in verses 9-11. This type of change is common in Old Testament poetry. There are two ways in which the translator can make the meaning clearer for the modern reader. (a) As in TEV, the translator can insert **says God** in verse 9a. (b) As in GeCL, the pronouns in verses 7b-8 can be put into the first person ("today, if you hear my voice"). This adds clarity and continuity and does not distort the meaning in any way. (TEV does this in many Old Testament passages.) It is possible, however, that for the writer of Hebrews, though not for the psalmist, "his voice" (RSV) in verse 7 meant, not **God's voice**, but "Christ's voice." Christ ... the Son was mentioned in verse 6. If the translator thinks "his voice" means "Christ's voice," he should say so explicitly. **Against God** in verse 8 could then become "against me," and **says God** in verse 9 could be omitted.

3.7   **So then, as the Holy Spirit says,**
          "If you hear God's voice today,

So then links the quotation in a general way with what has gone before: "You are God's people, if you keep up your courage. **So then,** listen when God (or Christ) speaks to you in this psalm." It is grammatically possible to link So then with particular verbs, either (a) do not be stubborn in verse 8, or even (b) be careful in verse 12. Choice (b) would in effect put the entire quotation in parentheses and is very artificial. TEV's general **So then,** indicating a new step in the argument, is probably best. An equivalent of **So then** may be a phrase meaning "Therefore," or "In view of all this," or even "As a result of what has been said."

---

[2] See Appendix A.

[59]

Mention of **the Holy Spirit** would lead the original readers of Hebrews to expect a quotation from Scripture; ancient Jewish teachers often introduced quotations from the Old Testament in this way. However, modern readers may need to be told more clearly that a quotation is about to begin (SpCL "as the Holy Spirit says in Scripture"), or even that the Holy Spirit is God's Spirit (GeCL first edition "God says through his Spirit").

Is the correct translation **If** or "**when**" (Mft, RSV)? The Greek word usually means **If**, but sometimes, as in John 12.32; 14.3; 1 John 2.28, it is virtually equal to "when." Here the question is not whether people will **hear God's voice** (since God is speaking or is about to speak in this very passage), but whether, when people have heard his voice, they will obey it. NAB's "if you should hear his voice" is too indefinite, and "when" is more likely in this context. Some translations (Brc, TNT; compare JB) omit both "if" and "when," and translate **hear** as "listen to." **Hear** can mean "listen to," as it usually does in commands. Here Brc has "Today I plead with you, listen to his voice." TEV's construction is better, since it throws weight onto the first main verb of the quotation, do not be stubborn.

To speak about "hearing someone's voice" may be heavy or repetitive in some languages. JB has simply "listen to him." Another possibility is "when you hear me speaking (to you)."

A literal rendering of **If you hear God's voice today** could mean merely hearing the voice of God but not hearing the message that is actually said. It may be better, therefore, to translate the conditional clause as "When you hear what God is saying today."

3.8   do not be stubborn, as your ancestors were when they
              rebelled against God,
         as they were that day in the desert when they put him
              to the test.

RSV's literal "**harden your hearts**" suggests a cruel or unfeeling attitude, since in modern English the heart is associated with the emotions. For Hebrew thought, and generally in the New Testament, the heart was the center of the whole personality, including the intellect and will. Therefore "to harden one's heart" is to refuse to listen to or understand what someone is saying. This is the basis for **stubborn** in TEV; similarly GeCL, Brc, TNT. **Do not be stubborn** is often rendered idiomatically; for example, "do not stop up your ears," or "do not shout 'No' to what is said," or "do not close the door of your mind."

TEV fourth edition makes it clear from this verse that it is not the present generation of Israelites who rebelled against God, but **your ancestors**, as verse 9 implies. Earlier editions of TEV had simply "you." The psalmist assumes in verse 8 that the people of Israel are one group of people, disregarding the birth and death of individuals from generation to generation, and so he addresses them as "you." However, since his message, like that of Hebrews, is that the present generation should behave differently from its **ancestors**, TEV fourth edition brings out the meaning more clearly.

As your ancestors were may be rendered as "that is what your ancestors did."

The rest of this verse can scarcely be understood, however clear the translation, without references and notes. The Hebrew of Psalm 95.8 refers to Meribah and Massah, which footnotes in NEB translate as "Dispute" and "Challenge," and in JB "dispute" and "temptation." The Septuagint replaced the names Meribah and Massah by common nouns having a similar meaning. TEV replaces these nouns by verbal expressions. The reference is to Exodus 17.7, where, during the journey from Egypt to the promised land, the Israelites grumbled about Moses' leadership and provoked or tested God by asking "Is the Lord with us or not?"

They rebelled against God may be rendered as "they refused to do what God had told them to do," or "they refused to be led by God," or "they refused to listen to God."

That day . . . when they put him to the test is literally "on the day of testing in the wilderness." In the light of this verse and also Exodus 17.1-7, it is clear that "testing," not "tempting" (see KJV), is intended.

In some languages it may be better to employ a phrase such as "that time" or "on that occasion," rather than merely **that day**, since a reference to **day** might imply merely one particular occasion of 24 hours.

Desert is rough scrubland on which little or nothing will grow, rather than an expanse of sand.

They put him to the test may be rendered as "they decided to see what God would do." In some instances the concept of "putting to the test" is expressed idiomatically: "they pushed God hard" or even "they tried to make God fall."

3.9   **There they put me to the test and tried me, says God,**
        although they had seen what I did for forty years.

There are problems involved in the punctuation of verses 9-11, since these are stated as the direct words of God rather than what the Holy Spirit says (as in the introduction to verse 7). For this reason it may be necessary to make a shift in pronouns, and it may also be important to introduce a new set of quotation marks beginning with verse 9 and ending with verse 11. It may also be useful to shift the order of **says God** and place it at the beginning of verse 9. A shift in the tense may also be required; for example, "God said . . . ."

The writer rearranges the text of Psalm 95 slightly in order to make his point with greater emphasis. The changes, following RSV, are as follows: (a) "Therefore" is added at the beginning of verse 10. (b) "**For forty years,**" verse 9, is joined to "saw my works" and not joined with "I was provoked," verse 10, as in both the Hebrew and the Greek of Psalm 95. (Verse 17, however, follows the Septuagint text.) (c) "That generation" becomes "this generation" (despite RSV, NEB). The writer of Hebrews may already be thinking of the relevance of the psalm to his readers' own situation.

The first part of verse 9 makes it clear that the Greek word here means **test**, not "tempt"; literally, "where your fathers tested in testing" (using two different Greek words for "test"). TEV, **put me to the test and tried me,** translates both verbs. This is not essential, since they mean the same, and repetition in some languages does not increase emphasis but makes the sentence more complex. Mft has "put me to the proof"; compare RSV.

The rendering of **they put me to the test and tried me** will depend upon the manner in which a similar expression has been translated at the end of verse 8. In some languages this may be expressed effectively as "they opposed me strongly to see what I would do."

RSV's literal translation of verse 9b, "and (they) **saw my works for forty years,**" may be understood either as (a) "although they had seen the good I had done for them for forty years past" or as (b) "and they saw the harm I did to them for the next forty years."

TEV, and most other translations which make a clear choice, take it to mean (a): "The Israelites had experienced God's goodness for forty years, and were still so ungrateful as to put him to the test" (compare GeCL). It is also possible, and perhaps simpler, to take the text to mean (b): "The Israelites put God to the test, and as a result God punished them for forty years." Not only verse 17 (With whom was God angry for forty years?), but also Numbers 14, which tells the story to which Psalm 95 refers, supports (b); see especially Numbers 14.33-35, part of which Hebrews quotes in 3.17. If (b) is followed, verse 9b may be translated "and saw what I did to them for forty years."

The traditional system of verse numbering places "for forty years" in verse 10. But many editions of the Greek New Testament, as well as JB, TOB, Zür, make it clear by the arrangement of the poetic lines that the phrase is linked with the preceding clause in verse 9 and should be followed by a full stop. TEV simply includes the phrase in verse 9, ignoring the tradition in order to retain clarity. Most translators may wish to follow TEV.

It is unusual for a rendering of **although they had seen what I did for forty years** to be completely neutral, that is to say, ambiguous as to whether God's actions were helpful or harmful to the people in question. Therefore it may be necessary to select one or the other meaning involved and to translate either as "although they had seen how I helped them for forty years" or "although they had seen how I had punished them for forty years." Whichever interpretation is followed, the alternative should be placed in a marginal note.

3.10   **And so I was angry with those people and said,**
         'They are always disloyal
         and refuse to obey my commands.'

And so is the same word in the Greek as So then in verse 7. It is not strictly part of the quotation but is added by the writer of Hebrews, perhaps to draw attention to the following words.

TEV's **those people** corresponds to RSV's "that generation." Since the writer of Hebrews has changed the text of the quotation from "those" to "these," it is better to keep "these" in translation. The original context of Psalm 95 clearly refers to a "generation" in the strict sense, that is, those who were alive at the time of the rebellion in the desert (see Num 14.29-32). However, the word for "generation" can have the wider meaning of "descendants" or simply "people" of any group or type. The writer of Hebrews is not concerned only with Moses' generation. For this reason, most CLTs translate **people;** note GeCL "Therefore I was angry with them."

In choosing a term for **angry** it is important to select one which will suggest justified anger rather than merely intemperate peevishness or irritability.

And said must be rendered in such a way as not to suggest that what was said was communicated directly to the people in question. Otherwise it would be necessary to change the following **They** to "You." It may therefore be important to translate **And said** as "And said to himself" or even "And thought."

RSV's **"go astray in their hearts"** does not mean that their affections are turned in another direction, but that their minds and wills are directed away from God's will, hence, are **disloyal.** The term **disloyal** may be expressed as "they refuse to follow me," or "they refuse to acknowledge me as their leader," or "they have rejected me."

Refuse to obey my commands repeats the same message in different words: they "have not known my ways," that is, they have not understood or put into effect the behavior which God taught them; Knox they "have never learned my lessons." **Refuse to obey my commands** may be rendered as "refuse to do what I have commanded them to do." In some languages, however, direct discourse may be required; for example, "they say, 'We will not do what you command.' "

3.11   **I was angry and made a solemn promise:
'They will never enter the land where I would have
given them rest!' "**

Solemn promise (TEV first edition vow) avoids the misunderstanding of "swear" as "curse," but **promise** usually has a positive meaning, while in this context the meaning is negative. Since the expression **solemn promise** in English suggests something positive rather than negative, it is essential to avoid the wrong kind of connotation. It would be possible to say "I solemnly promised myself," but in general it is usually far more satisfactory to say "I declared."

In a number of languages the usual term for "vow" or "oath" is "to make a declaration in the presence of God" or ". . . with God witnessing." However, since it is God himself who makes the vow in this context, such a normal expression cannot be employed. In some languages the concept of "vow" may be expressed as "I said with strong words" or "I declared with unchangeable words."

The second half of the verse gives the content of the vow or **promise** and introduces a key word of chapter 4, **rest.** Translators generally deal with the word **rest** in one of three ways: (a) they translate it literally, raising the problems (i) what does it mean to "enter" a "rest"? and (ii) how can one enter anyone else's rest? (b) They replace the noun **rest** by a verbal expression, as early editions of TEV did with come in and rest with me. This is excellent in this verse but is difficult to do consistently throughout chapter 4. (c) TEV fourth edition, JB, DuCL consistently translate **land where I would have given them rest**, taking **rest** to mean "place of rest" or "resting place." In this way they can speak quite naturally of "entering," and later of a resting place "remaining" in existence even when no one is yet occupying it (4.1). There is strong evidence that both the Septuagint and the Hebrew Old Testament used words for "rest" in the sense of "resting place."

They will never enter: in Greek this has the form of a conditional sentence but the meaning of a strong negative statement, "They will certainly not enter."

In many languages it is impossible to speak of "giving no rest to someone." The more normal expression is a causative one; for example, "I would have caused them to rest." In choosing a word for **rest** it is important to avoid the concept of "lying down." The emphasis should be upon recuperating strength or relaxing after hardship, or finding peace and prosperity after a period of difficult trial and testing.

TEV	3.12-14	RSV
12 My fellow believers, be careful that no one among you has a heart so evil and unbelieving that he will turn away from the living God. 13 Instead, in order that none of you be deceived by sin and become stubborn, you must help one another every day, as long as the word "Today" in the scripture applies to us. 14 For we are all partners with Christ if we hold firmly to the end the confidence we had at the beginning.		12 Take care, brethren, lest there be in any of you an evil, unbelieving heart, leading you to fall away from the living God. 13 But exhort one another every day, as long as it is called "today," that none of you may be hardened by the deceitfulness of sin. 14 For we share in Christ, if only we hold our first confidence firm to the end,

3.12   **My fellow believers, be careful that no one among you has a heart so evil and unbelieving that he will turn away from the living God.**

After the Old Testament text comes the explanation of it. A new step forward is marked by an imperative, **be careful**, and the address to the readers, **fellow believers** (**my** is implied; see comment on 3.1). The emotive level is raised by the use of such words as **evil**, **unbelieving**, and **living** (compare 4.12).

My fellow believers may be rendered as "You who believe even as I do" or "You who together with me believe in Christ."

A literal rendering of **be careful** could suggest a positive content rather than a negative one. Therefore it may be necessary to use some such expression as "beware that you do not" or "watch out so that you will not."

No one among you makes it clear that at this point the writer is not afraid that the whole community to which he is writing will lose its faith, but that some individuals within it may do so.

KJV's literal translation "an evil heart of unbelief" represents a phrase which would be more natural in Hebrew than in Greek. (a) "Heart of unbelief" means **"unbelieving heart,"** as in RSV. (b) On **heart,** see discussion on 3.8. (c) "Unbelief" in the Old Testament was not just an attitude of mind but a motive for action, as the rest of the verse shows. The two Greek nouns which TEV translates **unbelieving** here and did not believe in 4.6 are similar in meaning, and both are stronger and less passive than TEV suggests. Here the idea is that of refusing to believe (GeCL translates "disobedient"); in 4.6, that of refusing to obey (GeCL "disobedience"). In 3.18 TEV excellently translates the second word as rebelled.

In a number of languages it may be necessary to change or drop the figure of **heart,** since in biblical language the heart stands for the will and purpose of the individual. Therefore one may translate "beware that no one among you is so evil and so unbelieving that . . . ." But in this context **unbelieving** may be better rendered as "rebellious" or "so opposed to God," or even "so disobedient."

RSV translates the metaphor for **"fall away"** literally. TEV's **turn away** revises it slightly, since **"fall away"** has become a technical expression in English church language for "apostatize" or "stop believing." NEB uses the stronger but more literary expression "a deserter from the living God." Any idea of a mere turning back to the past should in any case be avoided. In a number of languages **turn away** may be rendered "to turn one's back on" or "to reject," or possibly "to refuse to follow."

Most modern translations, including TEV, keep the traditional expression **the living God.** A comparison with similar expression such as living messages (Acts 7.38), the living . . . word of God (1 Peter 1.23; compare Hebrews 4.12), a living way (10.20), a living hope (1 Peter 1.3), living bread (John 6.51), and living stone (1 Peter 2.4) suggests that **the living God** is not only "the God who is alive" (in contrast to idols) but also "the God who gives life." That is how GeCL first edition translated **living God** in this verse.

Some of the force of the phrase **the living God** may be lost in the use of **living** as a kind of adjectival qualifier. However, in a nonrestrictive modifying clause the emphasis may be more satisfactorily reflected; for example, "to turn one's back on God, who is indeed alive" or ". . . away from God; he lives." If, however, one adopts the interpretation "who gives life," a causative must be employed; for example, "the one who causes people to live."

3.13   **Instead, in order that none of you be deceived by sin and become stubborn, you must help one another every day, as long as the word "Today" in the scripture applies to us.**

The word translated **Instead** or "But" (RSV) may also mean "What is more." The problem for the translator is to decide which meaning suits the context better. If the more common meaning **Instead** is chosen, this will emphasize the contrast between turn away from the living God and **help one another.** It may be helpful to use some such introductory clause as "You shouldn't do that but you should do this," or "Rather than turning away from God, you should . . . ."

However, in the somewhat wider context the alternative meaning "What is more" perhaps makes better sense. The two main imperatives of verses 12 and 13 are be careful and **help** (or "encourage"). The writer is advising negative action in verse 12 and positive action in verse 13, but both are directed to the same end. This meaning may be brought out by some such expression as "Indeed, in order that none of you be deceived by sin and become stubborn, you must do more . . . ."

None, like no one in the previous verse, means "no individual within the Christian community."

On **stubborn,** see discussion on verse 8. The close relation between **de-ceived by sin** and **stubborn** may be made clear by some such translation as "in order that no one among you be made stubborn by the deceit of sin."

Help in this context is a common language equivalent for "encourage," though practical help is not excluded from the meaning here. There is a play on words in the Greek between the word translated **help** and the word for **"called"** (RSV), but this has no importance for the meaning and should not influence the translation.

One another is literally "yourselves," and some older commentators have thought that this emphasized the unity existing between members of the church; but this is rather speculative, and virtually all translations have **one another.**

As long as the word "Today" in the scripture applies to us states clearly, and more concisely than some modern translations, the most likely sense of a rather concentrated expression. It was common to refer to biblical passages by key words, as in Mark 12.26, "the bush," meaning the passage about the burning bush. Here the writer probably means "as long as we hear the word 'Today' spoken in its context in Psalm 95." The psalm was probably used in Christian worship, as it is now. This interpretation is more likely than such translations as Knox "while the word To-day still has a meaning"; JB "as long as this 'today' lasts." The ex-pression **applies to us** may be rendered as "refers to us," or "includes us," or "is speaking to us."

In some languages, the purpose clause **in order that none of you be deceived by sin and become stubborn** must be shifted in order, so as to follow the main clause. If this is done, some adjustment needs to be introduced at the beginning of verse 14 in order to make the causal relationship clear.

In some languages it may be difficult to speak of "being deceived by sin." The closest equivalent may be "become deceived by the sins that you commit" or "you sin and thus believe a lie." **And become stubborn** may be rendered as "and thus become stubborn" in the sense of "and thus refuse to obey God."

3.14 **For we are all partners with Christ if we hold firmly to the end the confidence we had at the beginning.**

The word for **are** refers to an indefinite period including past, present, and in this context, future. It is not the simple present tense of 3.6, so the writer can include a reference to **the end** without inconsistency. Otherwise, this verse has much in common with 3.6.

Partners is one of the writer's favorite words (see 1.9; 3.1; 6.4; 12.8). It is used literally of fishermen in Luke 5.7. **We are all partners with Christ** may be rendered as "we work together with Christ" or "we join with Christ in working together."

If we hold firmly is best treated as an emphatic expression of continuation; for example, "if we continue steadfastly" or "if we continue not moving at all."

Modern translations adopt **confidence.** Some commentaries note that the Greek word also has a philosophical meaning, "real being," as in 1.3, but this is irrelevant here and should be ignored.

The confidence we had at the beginning may be expressed as "the trust which we showed when we began to believe" or even "the strong trust which we showed when we first believed."

In a number of languages one cannot say **to the end,** since it is necessary to specify what end is involved. Probably the most satisfactory rendering is "to the end of our lives" or "as long as we live."

	TEV	**3.15-19**	RSV

15 This is what the scripture says:
  "If you hear God's voice today,
    do not be stubborn, as your
      ancestors were
    when they rebelled against
      God."
16 Who were the people who heard God's voice and rebelled against him? All those who were led out of Egypt by Moses. 17 With whom was God angry for forty years? With the people who sinned, who fell down dead in the desert. 18 When God made his solemn promise, "They will never enter the land where I would have given them rest"—of whom was he speaking? Of those who rebelled. 19 We see, then, that they were not able to enter the land, because they did not believe.

15 while it is said,
  "Today, when you hear his voice,
    do not harden your hearts as in
      the rebellion."
16 Who were they that heard and yet were rebellious? Was it not all those who left Egypt under the leadership of Moses? 17 And with whom was he provoked forty years? Was it not with those who sinned, whose bodies fell in the wilderness? 18 And to whom did he swear that they should never enter his rest, but to those who were disobedient? 19 So we see that they were unable to enter because of unbelief.

3.15   **This is what the scripture says:**
      "If you hear God's voice today,
        do not be stubborn, as your ancestors were
        when they rebelled against God."

It is difficult to see exactly how this verse is related to its context. The possibilities are as follows:

(a) TEV and other CLTs solve the problem by making it a separate sentence, unrelated to anything else. This is the simplest practical solution and probably the best.

(b) Put verse 14 in round brackets (parentheses) and thus link **"while it is said"** (RSV) with verse 13. This raises almost as many problems as it solves.

(c) Link **"while it is said"** with hold firmly to the end (verse 14) is a rather awkward way of introducing a repetition of the quotation; compare Mft "this word ever sounding in our ears, To-day . . ."; TOB. This is the construction and punctuation chosen by the UBS Greek New Testament, first to third editions.

(d) Some editions of the Greek text, followed by Knox, JB, NAB, link verses 15 and 16. NAB has "When Scripture says, 'Today, if you should hear his voice, harden not your hearts as at the revolt,' 16 who were those that revolted when they heard that voice?" This translation rightly assumes that the writer of Hebrews goes on quoting the psalm until he reaches the word "rebel," because he wishes to comment on that word.

This is what the scripture says must often be restructured, as in other instances, as "This is what one may read in the Scriptures" or ". . . at one place in the holy writings."

The content of this passage should be translated in essentially the same manner as these words are rendered in 7b-8a.

<u>**3.16**</u>   **Who were the people who heard God's voice and rebelled against him? All those who were led out of Egypt by Moses.**

KJV, Knox, and JB (but not BJ) are in a minority in taking 16a to be a statement; Knox "those who provoked him." It is much more likely to be the first of three questions, continuing into verses 17-18, to which the writer immediately gives the answers. <u>Rebelled</u> (see discussion on verse 12) here refers back to rebelled in verse 8a.

KJV's "For" is rightly omitted except by Phps; it is the weakest kind of transition. RSV's **"yet"** marks the implied contrast between hearing and rebelling, but in a way which misleadingly emphasizes the contrast rather than the fact that they heard and then revolted (as in JB, BJ, Seg, Synodale [Syn]).

Who heard God's voice and rebelled against him is literally "having heard, they rebelled." "But" would bring the meaning out even more clearly than **and**; compare RSV's **"and yet."** Some contrasting conjunction is important in the first part of verse 16, so that **and rebelled against him** may be rendered as "and nevertheless they refused to follow him" or "and despite all of that they turned against him."

As RSV shows, the writer responds to one question with another, as Jesus often does; for example, see in Luke 17.7-8. TEV simplifies this by turning the second question into a statement, since interrogative-negative questions (such as "Was it not . . .?"), especially rhetorical ones, have little place in common language; they are in fact the equivalent of strong statements.

In providing the answer to the rhetorical question, it may be important to make the response somewhat more specific; for example, "the people were all those who were led out of Egypt by Moses." The relative clause in this instance may be made active by translating "whom Moses led out of Egypt."

3.17   With whom was God angry for forty years? With the people who sinned, who fell down dead in the desert.

In order to anticipate more clearly the response to the rhetorical question in verse 17, it may be useful to employ "Who were the people with whom God was angry for forty years?" There are, however, serious difficulties involved in the rhetorical questions found in verses 16, 17, and 18, for obviously the writer is not asking for information but is making emphatic statements by means of these rhetorical questions. In languages which do not employ such rhetorical questions, it may be necessary to use emphatic statements. For example, verse 17 may be rendered as "For forty years God was indeed angry with the people who sinned and who fell down dead in the desert." Similar adaptations may be made in verses 16 and 18.

In quoting Psalm 95 in verses 9-10 (see discussion), the writer has separated for forty years from I was angry. Now, as he comments on the psalm, he brings them together and adds in support a quotation from Numbers 14.29. This shows that he has in mind not only Psalm 95 but also the Old Testament story to which it refers.

Who fell down dead brings out the meaning more clearly than RSV's literal translation. "Fall" does not mean merely "fall over"; destruction or death is implied, as in KJV's "whose carcasses fell." On **desert**, see discussion on verse 8.

3.18   When God made his solemn promise, "They will never enter the land where I would have given them rest"—of whom was he speaking? Of those who rebelled.

The first part of verse 18 must be translated in a way which reflects the rendering of verse 11. But as already noted, it may be necessary to eliminate the rhetorical question and make an emphatic statement; for example, "When God solemnly declared, 'They will never enter the land where I would have given them rest,' he was indeed speaking about those who rebelled" or ". . . refused to follow him."

Rebelled translates a different Greek word from the one used in verse 16 (compare verses 8,15) but one related to that used in 4.6. The meaning in this verse is "disobeyed," but since a particular act of disobedience is intended, the two Greek words mean much the same. Different terms are used only to give variety.

3.19   We see, then, that they were not able to enter the land, because they did not believe.

Verse 19 is a simple summary of the previous argument. The conjunction **then** does not refer to time but to the sequence of argument and may be rendered by forms equivalent to "accordingly" or "therefore."

In place of the expression **We see**, it may be necessary to use some such expression as "We realize" or "We have come to know," since in reality there was no direct visual perception but simply understanding.

The final, emphatic word "unbelief" recalls verse 12 (see the discussion). "Unbelief" includes an element of rebellion, and GeCL translates "So we see why they did not reach the goal: (it was) because they did not remain true."

In order to emphasize the opposition implied in "not believing," it may be best to translate the causal clause as "because they refused to believe."

Chapter 4

1 Now, God has offered us the promise that we may receive that rest he spoke about. Let us take care, then, that none of you will be found to have failed to receive that promised rest. 2 For we have heard the Good News, just as they did. They heard the message, but it did them no good, because when they heard it, they did not accept it with faith. 3 We who believe, then, do receive that rest which God promised. It is just as he said,

> "I was angry and made a solemn promise:
> 'They will never enter the land where I would have given them rest!' "

He said this even though his work had been finished from the time he created the world.

1 Therefore, while the promise of entering his rest remains, let us fear lest any of you be judged to have failed to reach it. 2 For good news came to us just as to them; but the message which they heard did not benefit them, because it did not meet with faith in the hearers.[h] 3 For we who have believed enter that rest, as he has said,

> "As I swore in my wrath,
> 'They shall never enter my rest,' "

although his works were finished from the foundation of the world.

[h] Other manuscripts read *they were not united in faith with the hearers*

Verse 1 sums up the argument of 3.7-19 and also begins a new appeal to the readers on the basis of Psalm 95.7-11. The argument runs as follows: God's promise still applies to us (3.13-14). Those to whom the promise was first made rebelled and were punished (3.15-19). Therefore, let us be warned by their example (4.1-11).

The structure of the argument has important consequences for the translation, as TEV shows. The words which RSV translates "**while the promise of entering his rest remains**" are brought to the beginning of the verse in TEV and made into a separate statement. In the Greek it is a subordinate clause grammatically, but it forms the starting point of the argument.

The key word in this new stage in the interpretation of Psalm 95.7-11 is **rest**, found in the last line of the quotation. This line is quoted in 3.11, repeated for emphasis in 4.3,5, and linked in 4.4 with Genesis 2.2, which also speaks of God's **rest**.[1]

---

[1] The words for rest in Psalm 95 and Genesis 2.2 are quite different in Hebrew, but this does not matter to the writer of Hebrews, since his argument is based on the Septuagint, which uses related Greek words.

Verse 1 contains several echoes of 3.12-13: (1) **Take care** recalls be careful in 3.12. The word translated we see in 3.19 is the same verb translated be careful; so in verse 1, for reasons of style, the writer chooses another verb meaning **take care.** (2) **That none of you will be found** recalls 3.12: that no one among you. The writer is not saying that his readers will fail; he is warning them to "fear" or **take care.** (3) **None,** as in 3.12, means "no one individual." (4) **God has offered us the promise** recalls the promise of 3.11, as interpreted in 3.13. The following verses will show that even the condemnation of 3.11 (Psalm 95.11) contains a **promise** for the readers.

4.1   **Now, God has offered us the promise that we may receive that rest he spoke about. Let us take care, then, that none of you will be found to have failed to receive that promised rest.**

The adverb **Now** does not translate a specific word in the Greek text, but contrasts the past failure of the Jewish people to enter into God's rest (3.19) with the fact that such a rest is still promised to those who believe in Christ.

God has offered us the promise: the word **us** in TEV identifies the people to whom God makes the promise. The Greek does not state this explicitly until at least verse 3. **God has offered us the promise** must be expressed in some languages as "God has promised us" or "God has said that we could." In some languages the equivalent of **promise** is "to say strongly."

In a number of languages it is impossible to say "that we may receive that rest," since rest is not something which is received in the sense of receiving some object as a gift. In fact, **receive that rest** is essentially a kind of substitute passive, and therefore in many languages it is best translated as "that we may rest" or "that we may be permitted to rest."

Then, here and in verse 11, translates a Greek word meaning "therefore." In these two cases, **then** is not an expression of time. Possible equivalents of **then** are "as a result of this" or "because of all this."

Let us take care includes both the writer and his readers, but probably no one else, as **you** later in the verse shows. It may be difficult to state clearly the relationship between **Let us take care** and **that none of you will be found to have failed.** In reality, the phrase **Let us take care** is directed to the persons who are admonished not to fail. One might translate "We should all be concerned that not one of you will be found to have failed," in which case the form "We" should be inclusive. But it may be more appropriate to say "All of you must be watchful in order that not one of you will be found to have failed."

Will be found to have failed presents two problems. The first problem is whether **will be found** implies a judgment by God. The Greek term may mean (a) "be judged," though it is not the most common term for "judge," (b) "think," or (c) "seem." Meaning (a) is more likely to imply a judgment by God. Compare the English expression "he was found guilty," that is, by a judge or jury. This meaning is chosen by RSV, "**be judged**," and by TEV, **be found.** Meaning (b) is chosen by JB, TNT text, "think." Phps adopts (c), "that none of us even looks like failing . . . ," as do other CLTs and BJ. A comparison with 3.12 suggests the first meaning: the writer is not concerned with what seems to be, or with what people think, but with their real condition (their heart, 3.12), and with what will really happen to them, as the following verses show.

A literal translation of **that none of you will be found to have failed** can be misleading, since **found** might suggest "to have been discovered accidentally." The passive construction can also be misleading, if an active form is more natural or even required. Therefore it may be better to introduce God as the ultimate agent; for example, "so that God will not judge any of you to have failed."

The second problem, which is linked with the first, concerns the meaning of the words translated **to have failed.** Greek dictionaries give "to come too late" as the so-called root meaning of this verb. This produces the translation "none of you must think that he has come too late for it," that is, for what God promised (JB), or "be convinced of being left behind" (TOB, similarly DuCL). This meaning fits the context well here, and there are parallels outside the New Testament, but it is difficult to find this meaning in any other New Testament passage.[2] A more common meaning of the Greek verb translated **failed** is "to miss," "to fail to reach a goal," and this meaning is given by CLTs and most other modern translations.

To have failed to receive is equivalent in many languages to "to not receive," so that the clause **that none of you will be found to have failed to receive** may be expressed as "so that God will not judge any of you as not having received." However, it is usually better to keep explicit the idea of failure on the part of the people. In some instances it may be better to express the concept of "receiving" by direct discourse; for example, "so that God will not judge any of you by saying, 'You have failed to receive the promised rest.' " If direct discourse is used, the phrase **that promised rest** may be translated as "that rest that I have promised" or "the fact that I have promised to cause you to rest."

For **rest**, see comments on 3.11. JB, DuCL translate correctly "place of rest."

4.2   **For we have heard the Good News, just as they did. They heard the message, but it did them no good, because when they heard it, they did not accept it with faith.**

The first part of this verse emphasizes the comparison made in verse 1 between the readers and the Israelites at the time of the Exodus. This is the point of **For.** The conjunction **For** indicates a rather loose causal relationship. It would be wrong to translate **For** in such a way as to suggest that the first sentence of verse 2 is linked directly with the last clause of verse 1. In fact, it was not because believers heard the Good News that they failed to receive the promised rest. It may therefore be necessary to drop the causal conjunction.

---

[2] Seg "let us fear then . . . , lest anyone among you seem to have come too late" is almost the opposite of what the writer means, since the readers cannot control the time of their birth, and the writer means to encourage them.

We have heard the Good News is literally "we have been evangelized," "we have had the Good News preached to us" (see 2.1). The tense of the Greek verb implies that the effects of hearing the Good News are lasting. GeCL suggests that the writer means specifically "this piece of good news about the rest," and this makes good sense. Other translations suggest he means the Christian message in general.[3] There may be advantages in rendering **we have heard the Good News** in such a way as to specify the particular aspect of the Good News, namely, the promise of rest. Otherwise this expression could be interpreted to mean that the Good News as preached by Jesus Christ was also preached to the Jewish people as they left Egypt. The comparison may then be translated as "we heard the Good News about this rest in the same way that they heard about it."

Just as they did is emphatic. **They** are all the people who were led out of Egypt (3.16), whom the writer identifies with the people who sinned (3.17). GeCL makes this explicit: "just like the people in the wilderness" (compare Num 14.29).

It did them no good may be expressed as "having heard about it was no benefit to them" or "they did not profit from having heard about the rest."

The Greek which TEV translates **they did not accept it with faith** contains a difficult textual problem. A literal translation would be "not having been joined in faith with those who heard." "Not having been joined" suggests a continuing state; "those who heard" suggests a single past event. The main textual problem is to know whether "not having been joined" is singular, referring to **the message,** or plural, referring to the mass of the Israelites at the time of the Exodus (the people who sinned, 3.17; compare 3.16,18). TEV, RSV, and most other translations prefer the singular, but the UBS Greek text has the plural, and this is followed by JB, BJ, which translate "they did not share the faith of those who listened." In the setting of Numbers 14, this would mean that the whole community of Israel (verse 10) did not share the faith and loyalty of Caleb and Joshua (verses 6-9,24); compare Hebrews 4.8.

The translation of **with faith** varies, partly according to the text chosen. If a text making "not having been joined" singular is used, the meaning is that the "message" was not mixed or united with faith on the part of those who heard it. In other words, they did not respond positively by accepting and believing the message. If a text using the plural is chosen, the meaning is that those who heard the message but did not believe it were not united in faith (or, less probably, "by faith") with those who both heard and believed the message.

They did not accept it with faith may be expressed idiomatically in some languages as "they did not receive the message in their hearts," or "they did not trust what was said about the rest which God had promised," or "they did not have confidence in their hearts that God would give them rest."

---

[3] It is a point in favor of GeCL that the same verb for "to tell the good news" is used in verse 6 about the Israelites, where it can scarcely mean "the Christian message," unless, as a few scholars have thought, Christ is thought of as speaking Psalm 95 to Israel before his incarnation (see comments on 3.7).

4.3   **We who believe, then, do receive that rest which God promised. It is just as he said,**
> **"I was angry and made a solemn promise:**
>   **'They will never enter the land where I would have**
>   **given them rest!'"**

**He said this even though his work had been finished from the
time he created the world.**

Instead of RSV's **"For,"** some manuscripts have a stronger word, "There-fore," but this is less likely to be original. It would be wrong, however, to trans-late the Greek word as being an explicit or immediate causal conjunction, since the first clause of verse 3 is not the cause for the last part of verse 2. The Greek word in question may be translated by some such term as **then** (as in TEV).

Who believe is emphasized in the Greek text, and TEV expresses this by beginning the sentence **We who believe.** It may be possible to express this even more clearly: "(So) it is we who believe who do enter a resting place" (compare NEB); similarly JB "We, however, who have faith, shall reach a place of rest." **We who believe** may be rendered as "we who do trust God" or ". . . trust what God has said."

In Greek as in English, the expression meaning **We . . . do receive that rest** is a present tense in grammar, but it refers to a future event, as FrCL's "we are going to enter" shows. It may be essential to show that the receiving of rest is a future event, not something that has already taken place. Hence, **do receive that rest which God promised** may be rendered as "will rest even as God has promised us."

"We . . . enter" (RSV) is almost certain to be the correct text, rather than "let us enter," as in a few manuscripts. Both TEV and RSV have **that rest,** mean-ing "the rest referred to" (NEB); literally "the rest." Some important manuscripts, however, have simply "rest," which may mean "a rest" or "a resting place," like "a day" in verse 7.

As in 3.15, where a different Greek verb is used, the meanings **he said** and "it (scripture) says" are both grammatically possible. **He said** fits the context better, since God is the speaker in the quotation. The tense suggests a permanent record, which survives from the past into the present. However, here, as in 1.13; 10.9; 13.5 (compare 10.15), **he said** is probably the best translation, since God is the speaker in the quotation which follows. In 4.4, on the other hand, the same word translated there as <u>this is said</u> probably implies <u>in the Scriptures,</u> though it may mean "he says" or "he said." Each case must be decided in the light of the context.

It is just as he said may be somewhat misleading if rendered literally, since **It** must refer back to the content of verse 18. It may therefore be more satisfac-tory to translate **It is just as he said** as "As God had said."

The quotation in the second part of verse 3 should be translated as in 3.11, since the Greek text is the same.

The last clause, **his work had been finished from the time he created the world,** involves a number of complications, both linguistic and theological. The term **work** (which in Greek is plural) implies a whole series of activities and not merely something which was done once and for all at the time of creation. This may be translated "all God made," but not "all God did," since this would wrongly suggest that God had done nothing since creation. In GeCL the final part of verse 3 is rendered as a question, "Are not all of God's works already ready since the creation of the world?" By introducing a question one can recognize more readily the reason for the writer of Hebrews having introduced such a statement, especially in view of the content of the preceding direct quotation, which suggests God's having altered his plan. Since it is God's plan for action which was ready from the foundation of the world, it may be advisable to render the last sentence of verse 3 as "God said this even though his plans for what he would do were complete from the time he created the world."

TEV	**4.4-11** RSV

4 For somewhere in the Scriptures this is said about the seventh day: "God rested on the seventh day from all his work." 5 This same matter is spoken of again: "They will never enter that land where I would have given them rest." 6 Those who first heard the Good News did not receive that rest, because they did not believe. There are, then, others who are allowed to receive it. 7 This is shown by the fact that God sets another day, which is called "Today." Many years later he spoke of it through David in the scripture already quoted:
"If you hear God's voice today,
do not be stubborn."

8 If Joshua had given the people the rest that God had promised, God would not have spoken later about another day. 9 As it is, however, there still remains for God's people a rest like God's resting on the seventh day. 10 For whoever receives that rest which God promised will rest from his own work, just as God rested from his. 11 Let us, then, do our best to receive that rest, so that no one of us will fail as they did because of their lack of faith.

4 For he has somewhere spoken of the seventh day in this way, "And God rested on the seventh day from all his works." 5 And again in this place he said,
"They shall never enter my rest."
6 Since therefore it remains for some to enter it, and those who formerly received the good news failed to enter because of disobedience, 7 again he sets a certain day, "Today," saying through David so long afterward, in the words already quoted,
"Today, when you hear his voice,
do not harden your hearts."
8 For if Joshua had given them rest, God[i] would not speak later of another day. 9 So then, there remains a sabbath rest for the people of God; 10 for whoever enters God's rest also ceases from his labors as God did from his.
11 Let us therefore strive to enter that rest, that no one fall by the same sort of disobedience.

[i] Greek he

These verses express increasing emotion. Although grammatically divided into four sentences in the Greek, they can only be understood if they are read as a whole. The line of thought is as follows:

Old Testament texts about God's "rest" or "resting place" cannot simply refer to the seventh day of creation, for that was long ago. Nor was the promise ever fulfilled in Old Testament times, because God's people were punished for their disobedience. The resting place is meant for us who believe, so the rest which God enjoyed on the seventh day is open to us.

Verse 9 expresses this conclusion most clearly, but it is anticipated in verse 6, **There are, then, others who are allowed to receive it,** and even in verse 3a. Verse 10 explains verse 9, and verse 11 draws consequences for the readers' way of life.

GeCL makes the connections in verses 3b-9 particularly clear, and it is therefore worth quoting in full, with the more important connecting expressions underlined:

God, it is true, has said:
"I swore in my anger:
I will never take them into my rest."
But are not all God's works finished since the making of the world? 4 It is indeed written about the seventh day of creation: "On the seventh day God rested from all his work." 5 And it is also written in the same text: "Never will I take them into my rest." 6 So there must still be people who will be taken in, after the others, who first heard what God promised them, remain shut out through their disobedience. 7 For this reason God again fixes a day. It is the day called "Today" [but see comment on 3.13], of which David long afterward says:
"Do not be so stubborn today, if (when) you hear his voice."
8 If Joshua had led the people into rest, there would have been no talk later of another day. 9 So the time of rest for God's people must still be to come.

Even though in verse 3 is difficult to understand. It implies that the rest is not only the seventh day in the story of creation. Compare JB "God's work was undoubtedly all finished"; Phps "not because the rest was not prepared—it had been ready since the work of creation was completed." The expression translated created the world is used again in 9.26. RSV's "his works" often means "what he had made"; compare Phps "work of creation." However, the contrast with rest makes **work** or "labours" (Knox) a suitable translation here.

4.4   **For somewhere in the Scriptures this is said about the seventh day: "God rested on the seventh day from all his work."**

The conjunction **For** is a loose causal conjunction and should not link the first clause of verse 4 immediately with the final statement in verse 3.

Somewhere: in the Scriptures is implied. See discussion on 4.3. **Somewhere** is a vague reference, like that in 2.6, to Genesis 2.2. The expression **somewhere in the Scriptures this is said** may be rendered as "somewhere in the holy writings one may read."

It may be necessary to specify that **the seventh day** refers to "the seventh day of the week" or "the seventh day of making the universe," for it is not merely any seventh day.

In a number of languages temporal expressions may need to occur first in the sentence, especially if the temporal setting is emphasized. It may therefore be wise to restructure the direct quotation as "On the seventh day God rested from all that he had done" or, to make the activity more explicit, ". . . what he had done in creating the world."

4.5   **This same matter is spoken of again: "They will never enter that land where I would have given them rest."**

This same matter is literally "in this." It may also mean "in the text we are considering" (so JB; compare Phps, NAB, NEB). If this translation is chosen, it will be necessary to find in verse 7 a different expression which means the same thing. NEB, for example, has "the passage above" in verse 5 and "the words already quoted" in verse 7. RSV's "**again**" is a common way of introducing a second or later quotation, as RSV does in 1.5; 2.13.

Alternatively, **This same matter** may refer to something which the two Old Testament quotations in verses 4 and 5 have in common. This can only be God's "rest" or "resting place," by which the author means the state into which God entered on the seventh day of creation, which he says is the same state or "place" which God intends his people to occupy. It may be possible, therefore, to translate **This same matter is spoken of again** as "This matter about rest is spoken of in another place in the holy writings" or "God speaks in another place in the holy writings about experiencing rest."

They will never enter that land where I would have given them rest must be translated as in 3.11.

4.6   **Those who first heard the Good News did not receive that rest, because they did not believe. There are, then, others who are allowed to receive it.**

As a comparison with RSV shows, TEV follows the logical order rather than the grammatical order of the Greek sentence. Two thoughts run through the whole of verses 5-8. They are: (a) God promised a place of rest to his people in Old Testament times, but later, when they disobeyed him, he shut them out from it. (b) This place of rest remains available for God's people now. Yet the two ideas should not be separated. Both are rooted in the quotation from Psalm 95.11 and are thus closely related to one another.

The Good News in TEV usually means "the Christian message." This expression is strange here, in a verse which speaks of Old Testament times. GeCL solves the problem by translating "the message of God's rest" (verse 2) and "what God had promised them" (verse 6).

Those who first heard the Good News may be best rendered as "Those who heard the Good News about rest" or even ". . . the message about being able to rest."

Did not receive that rest may be rendered as in other verses as "were not allowed to rest" or "were not privileged to rest." RSV's "it" in "to enter it" refers back to "my rest" in verse 5.

RSV's "disobedience" is a more literal translation of the text than did not believe; it is also stronger. Belief and action are closely linked in biblical thought, and so are unbelief and disobedience (see also 3.12).

Because they did not believe may be rendered as "because they did not trust what God had said" or "because they refused to believe what God had said."

TEV's others does not contradict RSV's more literal "some." The Greek means simply "some people."

The passive expression who are allowed to receive it can often be best expressed in an active form with God being the one who permits the event to take place; for example, "others whom God allows to receive that rest" or "those whom God permits to rest."

<u>4.7</u>   This is shown by the fact that God sets another day, which is called "Today." Many years later he spoke of it through David in the scripture already quoted:
    "If you hear God's voice today,
        do not be stubborn."

The Greek which RSV translates "again" is not used here to introduce a quotation, as it is in verse 5, but has its usual meaning "once more" (compare 5.12; 6.1,6). This is shown by the reference to <u>another day</u> in verse 8.

This refers to the statement in verse 6 that <u>others . . . are allowed to receive</u> this rest. It may be necessary to specify what This refers to by introducing an entire clause; for example, "That others are allowed to receive this rest is shown by the fact . . . ."

Is shown by the fact may be expressed actively as "we know because of the fact that."

The literal "sets again a day" is translated more naturally by sets another day. God sets another day must be rendered in some languages as "God decides upon another day" or "God designates another day." In a number of languages a perfect form of a verb must be employed, since this is evidently something which took place in the past but which is still relevant; therefore, "God has designated another day."

The first "Today" can be related to the rest of the sentence in two ways: (a) as immediately interrupting the quotation (so Mft "To-day—as he says in

'David' . . ."; similarly NEB), or (b) as if the "certain day" which God sets is identified by the name "Today" (so CLTs; compare 3.13).

Which is called "Today" may be rendered as "which is spoken of in the holy writings as Today" or "which God speaks of as Today."

Many years later is literally "After such a long time."

Through David in TEV fourth edition is better style than earlier editions' "by means of David." As in through the prophets (1.1), where the literal "in the prophets" may also mean "in the writings of the prophets," so also in 4.7, "in David" would mean "in the Psalms" (so Mft, TNT). **He spoke of it through David** may be expressed as a causative; for example, "he caused David to speak of it" or "he used David to speak about it."

In the scripture already quoted is literally "as it has been said before," which may mean "as David said before" or "as God said before." However, this is less likely, since the contrast is between the seventh day of creation and the "today" of Psalm 95.7, not between two situations in which Psalm 95.7 is applied. Psalm 95.7 was not fulfilled in the Old Testament, but it is to be fulfilled for Christians for the first time.

In the scripture already quoted may be expressed as "in that part of the holy writings already spoken about" or ". . . which I have already mentioned" or ". . . which I have already written about."

Each time this verse is quoted, different words in it are emphasized. In 3.8 the key words are do not be stubborn (compare 3.12); in 3.15 the key word is rebelled (compare 3.16); here the key word is **today.**

Do not be stubborn may need to be related specifically to this particular context. Therefore one may translate "do not refuse to obey what God says."

4.8   **If Joshua had given the people the rest that God had promised, God would not have spoken later about another day.**

"Jesus" is the same name in Greek as the Hebrew name "Joshua." In this verse KJV's "Jesus" is corrected by all modern translations to **Joshua.** The meaning is clear if this is done. There is no need to add a note saying that "Joshua" and "Jesus" are the same in Greek.

If Joshua had given the people the rest may be expressed as "If Joshua had been able to cause the people to rest." If the noun **rest** is rendered as a verb, "to rest," then **that God had promised** may be translated as "in the way in which God had promised them."

The people is implicit here in the Greek, but it is expressed in verse 9. **God** is also implicit, but is more probable here than "David," especially if "David" in verse 7 is taken to mean the book of Psalms. In any case, God is the speaker in at least the later verses of this quotation (see introductory discussion on 3.7-11).

The verse clearly implies that Joshua did not give the people a place of rest. In some languages it is unnatural or impossible to speak in this way of conditions contrary to fact. If so, the condition in this sentence may be restructured as "Joshua was not able to cause people to rest as God had promised; therefore God had to speak later about another day."

4.9   **As it is, however, there still remains for God's people a rest**
like God's resting on the seventh day.

As RSV's **"So then"** shows, this is the statement to which the whole argument of verses 3-8 has led up. TEV's **As it is, however,** should not be misunderstood as indicating a contrast only with verse 8. In order to indicate a result, one
may employ some such expression as "As a result of all this" or "Therefore."

In place of the English construction which employs **there** in the subject
position and retains for the predicate position the so-called "new information,"
many languages use quite a different construction; for example, "God's people will
still be able to rest" or "it is still possible for God's people to rest."

Still is implied in the Greek. FrCL has "a rest . . . remains offered to the
people of God."

The simile **a rest like God's resting on the seventh day** is literally "a sabbath rest," a word which the author may have invented but whose meaning is clear
from verse 4. The two problems for the translator are (a) whether a note on
"sabbath" is needed (GeCL has simply "time of rest") and (b) whether the "rest" of
God's people is simply compared (TEV **like**) to God's resting on the seventh day, or
whether the two are identified. The references to the passage of time in verses 3
and 7 suggest that different "Todays" are involved, but that God's resting place
remains the same. If so, this would imply the translation "the resting place God
used on the seventh day is still available to his people."

Like God's resting on the seventh day may be combined with the previous
statement, "for God's people to rest in the way similar to the manner in which God
rested on the seventh day." In some instances, however, the particular seventh
day must be stated: "on the seventh day after he began to create the world."

4.10   **For whoever receives that rest which God promised will rest**
from his own work, just as God rested from his.

The causal conjunction **For** indicates a rather loose relationship. It does
not imply that the first clause of verse 10 is the specific cause for the last clause
of verse 9.

In a number of languages the indefinite relative clause beginning **whoever** is
better rendered as a conditional; for example, "if a person receives the rest . . . ."

This verse compares a past event (God resting from his work of creation)
with an event whose time is not specified (people entering God's "resting place").
Both these events are expressed by past tenses in Greek, but modern translations
are right to use a variety of tenses: **receives that rest** (literally "rests"), **will rest,**
rested. "God's rest" (RSV) is literally "his rest," and it is better to make the referent clear. This verse and verse 11 contain a good deal of repetition, perhaps for
emphasis.

Receives that rest may need to be expressed as a causative with God as the
agent; for example, "if God gives that person the opportunity to rest" or "if God
causes that person to rest." The clause of promise may then be expressed as "in
the way in which God promised" or "just as God had promised."

[81]

It may be difficult to speak of "resting from one's own work," for the relationship is temporal and based upon a completed activity. Therefore **will rest from his own work** must be translated in some languages as "will rest after having completed his own work" or ". . . after having done what he should have done." Similarly, **God rested from his** may be expressed as "God rested after he had completed his work." The final **his** is rather emphatic in the Greek, where it means "God's own work."

As noted on verses 3-4, **work** fits this context better than "works." This passage has nothing to do with Paul's discussion of salvation by works.

4.11   **Let us, then, do our best to receive that rest, so that no one of us will fail as they did because of their lack of faith.**

This verse forms a transition to verses 12-13, which conclude the section. Many translations agree with RSV in beginning a new paragraph here because of the exhortation, rather than at verse 12.

Then (literally "therefore") often begins a new paragraph (compare verses 1,14). Verse 11 marks a new appeal to the readers. RSV's "For" in verse 12 links that verse with verse 11. On the other hand, verse 11 concludes the discussion of the **rest** and contains the last reference to the events of Numbers 14. **Then** does not refer to time; it expresses a conclusion or result, rendered often as "therefore" or "as a result of all this."

Do our best: the Greek verb can mean "hurry" as in TOB (Mft, Phps "be eager"). However, verse 1 did not suggest the readers' being "too late" to enter God's rest. The idea is rather that of enthusiastic effort; NAB "strive"; Brc "make every effort"; TNT "do our utmost." Verses 12-13 emphasize the element of effort in Christian living.

Let us . . . do our best is not a request for permission but an exhortation and may often be rendered as "we should do our best" or "we should try very hard."

Fail is weaker than RSV's literal **"falls."** However, TEV avoids "fall" here, as in 3.12, where the meaning is the same, perhaps because in church language it means "lose one's faith." In this verse the writer is probably still thinking of those who fell down dead in the desert (3.17).

In a great many languages it is necessary to have some type of complement for the verb **fail**. **So that no one of us will fail** must then be rendered as "so that no one of us will fail to rest" or ". . . fail to receive the promise of being able to rest."

TEV, unlike RSV, completes the comparison by adding **as they did**. This refers back to Those who first heard the Good News in verse 6. Other CLTs have "the people in the desert" (compare 3.17; Num 14.22). The reference to **they** may be made in terms of the historical event, for example, "those who lived long ago."

Fail as they did is literally "in the same sort of disobedience." The Greek word means "example," but if a similar word is used in translation, as in KJV, JB, NEB, it should be made clear that a bad example is meant. Here, as in verse 6, translations are about equally divided between the related ideas of disobedience (for example, GeCL, Mft, JB) and unbelief (for example KJV, NEB). Numbers 14, especially verse 41, why are you disobeying the LORD now? suggests not only general unbelief but also specific acts of disobedience.

TEV   4.12-13   RSV

12 The word of God is alive and active, sharper than any double-edged sword. It cuts all the way through, to where soul and spirit meet, to where joints and marrow come together. It judges the desires and thoughts of man's heart. 13 There is nothing that can be hid from God; everything in all creation is exposed and lies open before his eyes. And it is to him that we must all give an account of ourselves.

12 For the word of God is living and active, sharper than any two-edged sword, piercing to the division of soul and spirit, of joints and marrow, and discerning the thoughts and intentions of the heart. 13 And before him no creature is hidden, but all are open and laid bare to the eyes of him with whom we have to do.

These verses are the climax of the whole section 3.7—4.13. They contain much repetition for the sake of emphasis. In verse 12 positive statements are repeated. In verse 13 a negative statement is followed by the same idea expressed in positive terms. It is not necessary for the translator to find an equal number of expressions, each one exactly parallel to one word or phrase of the text. What matters is that the full meaning should be forcefully expressed. RSV's "**For**," omitted by TEV, links these verses to verse 11. They give the motive for the attitude recommended in verse 11.

4.12   **The word of God is alive and active, sharper than any double-edged sword. It cuts all the way through, to where soul and spirit meet, to where joints and marrow come together. It judges the desires and thoughts of man's heart.**

Verses 12-13 are a single complex sentence in Greek and bring the section 3.7—4.13 to a moving climax. Translators will probably divide the sentence but should find other ways of expressing emotion.

What is the **word of God** in this context? The only other place where the writer uses this phrase, 13.7, shows that it can be either a written message or a spoken message. It is God speaking (Phps "the Word that God speaks"; TNT "God's message"), both through the Old Testament and in Christ (1.1-2).

The Old Testament often speaks of a message (especially a message from God, Isa 55.11) taking on a life of its own. When a prophet spoke in God's name, something happened as a result. Indeed, God's speech was itself an event. This is what is meant by saying that God's word is **alive**. The writer confirms this by adding **active** (SpCL "lives and has power"). Older French translations have "effective," and this is to be preferred to TOB's "energetic" (Knox "full of energy"), which describes the word rather than indicating the results it achieves. A literal rendering of **The word of God** may be misunderstood to refer only to the Scriptures. Therefore, it may be better to speak of "What God has said" or "What God has declared."

The bold figure of speech, namely, **The word of God is alive,** is sometimes difficult to render literally, since an adjective such as **alive** may refer only to animate beings, that is, people or animals. It may be possible, however, to use this figurative expression if one employs a simile; for example, "What God has said is, as it were, alive" or ". . . is as though it were alive." The expression **active** may be expressed as "has power," or "can do things," or "accomplishes whatever it is intended to accomplish."

JB translates the Greek adjective for **sharper** by a verbal expression: "it cuts better."

In New Testament times, the Greek word for **sword** could also mean "dagger," and this may be its meaning here. The tongue was compared to a dagger because they look similar (see also Prov 5.4). It may be more natural to translate **sharper than any double-edged sword** as a simile; for example, "it is even sharper, as it were, than any double-edged sword." However, in some languages the phrase **double-edged sword** may be a figure of speech referring to a liar or a hypocrite. If so, a different metaphor or simile may be used to express the meaning more clearly, provided the adjustment will fit in well with the rest of verse 12. In some cases it may even be necessary to use a marginal note to explain the basis for the biblical expression.

The pronoun **It** may need to be identified as "the word of God" or "what God says," in either one or both places where it occurs.

It is difficult to be sure exactly what the next figure of speech means. **Cuts all the way through** may imply piercing with the point of a sword or dagger, but more probably it means cutting with a blade. The verb can refer to going right through fortifications or armor so as to come out on the other side; but the rest of the verse suggests cutting into the middle of a body.

Joints and marrow is a figurative expression meaning the same thing as **soul and spirit;** GeCL first edition made this clear with "where marrow and bone, that is, soul and spirit, meet." **Come together** is literally "dividing" (see RSV). Biblical thought, in both the Old and the New Testament, thinks of the human being as a unity; it does not usually distinguish precisely between spirit, soul, or even body. However, **come together** would be an unusual meaning of the Greek. The meaning is more probably that God's word cuts through and separates soul from spirit and joints from marrow.

The statement which characterizes the word of God as being like a double-edged sword and thus being able to cut through **to where soul and spirit meet, to where joints and marrow come together** is extremely difficult. In fact, the joints and marrow do not come together. **Joints** refers to the place where the bones meet, while **marrow** is the portion which is in the center of the bone itself. Similarly, there is no particular place in the body where the **soul** and the **spirit** join together. What is intended by this figure of speech is to emphasize that the word of God penetrates deeply, so that there is nothing in the total personality which

[84]

can possibly be hidden from the revealing nature of what God says. If necessary, one may translate the second sentence of verse 12 in a strictly literal fashion, and then explain briefly in a marginal note that this is a reference to the extent to which the word of God penetrates to the very interior of a person. But it may also be possible to render the last part of this sentence as "to where the soul and spirit are and to where the joints and marrow are."

The terms for **soul** and **spirit** are even more difficult to translate. In some languages **soul** is equivalent to "that which causes life," and in many instances one may render **soul** as "life itself." In some languages the closest equivalent of **soul** is "breath," since breath is associated with life. If possible, the term for **spirit** should be the same as that which is used in speaking of God's Spirit. It is important to avoid a term for **spirit** which will suggest some disembodied spirit or ghost. An appropriate term for the spirit of a person should be that particular aspect of man which can respond to God's Spirit. In some instances **soul** is simply "that which causes life" and **spirit** is "that which reaches out to God."

To say that the **word of God . . . judges** is to say that God judges, and it may be necessary to make this explicit. GeCL translates "calls to account," but there is no suggestion that this judgment is limited to the last days (see also discussion on give an account in verse 13).

Judges may need to be expressed in this context as "determines what is good or bad about." This is not the use of **judges** in a sense of "to condemn," nor is there any suggestion of courtroom procedure. The idea is that the word of God reveals the true nature of people's desires and thoughts.

The words for **desires** and **thoughts** suggest their hidden nature; GeCL "the most secret desire and thoughts of men." On **heart**, see 3.12 and discussion on 3.8.

The desires and thoughts of man's heart may be expressed as "what people think and what they want."

4.13   **There is nothing that can be hid from God; everything in all creation is exposed and lies open before his eyes. And it is to him that we must all give an account of ourselves.**

This verse is divided into three unequal parts. The first two, beginning **There is nothing** and **everything,** balance one another. The subject being discussed is no longer the word of God, as in verse 12, but God himself. It may be more natural in translation to put the positive statement, beginning **everything,** first. The contrast between these first two parts of the verse is indicated in Greek by a "but" which, like the "and" at the beginning of the verse, is omitted in most modern translations.

In place of the so-called anticipatory expletive **there** followed by the real subject appearing in the predicate of the clause, **is nothing . . . ,** most languages employ some such expression as "nothing can be hidden from God," or "nothing exists which people can hide from God," or ". . . can keep God from seeing," or ". . . can keep God from knowing about."

Nothing is literally "no creature," that is, nothing which God has made. TEV transfers the idea of "**creature**" (RSV) to the second part.

From God could grammatically be "from it" (that is, "God's word"), and **his eyes** could be "its eye," but the context makes this practically impossible.

Everything in all creation is literally "all things." TEV keeps the weightier expression until last by expressing the idea of "creature, created thing" (RSV) in the second part instead of in the first.

Exposed and lies open: literally, "naked and exposed." SpCL, like KJV, avoids speaking of God's "eyes," and therefore translates "open to (his) view." It may be awkward in some languages to speak of everything "exposed and lying open before God's eyes." A more natural expression may be "he sees everything in all creation just as it really is."

The third part of the sentence, beginning **And it is to him,** may mean (a) "with whom we have to do," as in KJV, RSV, Phps; (b) "to whom we must give account," "with whom we have to reckon" (NEB); (c) "of whom we speak" (Zür); or (d) "before whom we speak." Meaning (c) would be a very weak ending to such an emphatic sentence. Meaning (b) may fit the context best, in which case judges in verse 12 could refer to the final judgment. However, since both present and future aspects of judgment are probably included, the more general rendering of NEB is probably best.

It would be possible to render **And it is to him that we must all give an account of ourselves** as "And he is the one who will judge us." But this seems to be inadequate, for the Greek text focuses upon some kind of "reckoning." The interpretation followed in TEV may be rendered in some languages as "we must explain to God all that we have done," or "we must justify to God what we have done," or "God is the one to whom we must defend the reasons for what we have done."

TEV	**4.14-16**	RSV

Jesus the Great High Priest

14 Let us, then, hold firmly to the faith we profess. For we have a great High Priest who has gone into the very presence of God—Jesus, the Son of God. 15 Our High Priest is not one who cannot feel sympathy for our weaknesses. On the contrary, we have a High Priest who was tempted in every way that we are, but did not sin. 16 Let us have confidence, then, and approach God's throne, where there is grace. There we will receive mercy and find grace to help us just when we need it.

14 Since then we have a great high priest who has passed through the heavens, Jesus, the Son of God, let us hold fast our confession. 15 For we have not a high priest who is unable to sympathize with our weaknesses, but one who in every respect has been tempted as we are, yet without sin. 16 Let us then with confidence draw near to the throne of grace, that we may receive mercy and find grace to help in time of need.

For the first time since 3.6, in 4.14—5.10 the writer turns from an appeal to his readers to the teaching about who Christ is and what he does. In 5.11—6.12 will come further appeals for action, and after that a more detailed discussion on the meaning of Priesthood. This is a subject which the writer begins to explore in the present section.

4.14—5.10 as a whole has strong links with 3.1-6. It is almost as if all of 3.7—4.13 were in parentheses, and the writer were now coming back to his main theme. Jesus is greater than Moses (3.1-6); he is also a high priest, like Moses' brother Aaron (5.4), indeed more than a high priest like Aaron. 3.1-6 and 4.14—5.10 also use similar language. In 3.1 Jesus was called the High Priest of the faith we profess, and what this means is explored more fully here and in 7.26—8.3. In 3.6, soon after calling Jesus the High Priest, he calls him the Son; the same two titles are linked in 5.5-6. In 3.6 the readers were told to keep up their courage and . . . confidence; a similar thought is expressed in different words in 4.14. In both passages, what the readers are told to hold firmly is the faith we profess.

Nevertheless, this section is also related to the one before, 3.7—4.13. The pattern is the same. Up to a certain point, the traditions of Israel can be compared with what Christ has done. Beyond that point they must be contrasted, because Jesus goes beyond the Old Testament traditions. Jesus gives God's people a rest which they never found in Old Testament times (3.7—4.13). He cares for God's people like an Old Testament High Priest (4.14—5.10), but he is of higher status and can therefore deal better with sin than any Old Testament priest (6.13—10.18).

Within this wider pattern, the theme of faith and obedience, contrasted with unbelief and rebellion, appears both in 3.7—4.13 (especially 3.15-19) and in 4.14—5.10 (especially 5.8-9). Here, though, the obedience of Christ himself is more emphasized than the obedience of Christians. 5.2-3 also recalls what was said in Numbers 15.22-31 about unintentional breaking of the Law. This follows Numbers 14, which was the background of the last section.

The heading of this section in TEV and in the UBS Greek New Testament is taken from 4.14: **Jesus the Great High Priest.** However, this is perhaps a little misleading when compared with the heading of chapter 8, Jesus Our High Priest, since in fact chapter 8 makes greater claims for Jesus than the present section. GeCL has "Jesus pleads (as an advocate) for us" as a heading for the present section and "Jesus our highest priest" for chapter 8. The GeCL section heading may be expressed as "Jesus goes before God on our behalf." If, however, one follows TEV, one may translate "Jesus is the important High Priest" or even "Jesus is a High Priest for us."

4.14   **Let us, then, hold firmly to the faith we profess. For we have a great High Priest who has gone into the very presence of God—Jesus, the Son of God.**

TEV reverses the two parts of this verse (contrast RSV) and divides the sentence into two. **We have a great High Priest** should not, however, be emphasized in translation. It is not new information; it is repeated from 2.17. RSV's

"Therefore," a stronger word than **then,** draws a conclusion from this and marks a return to the teaching of chapters 1—2.

The translation of **High Priest** raises several problems.

(a) Many cultures have priests, but their work and their place in society vary greatly. They are sometimes different from those of the Old Testament High Priest. His qualifications are described in Leviticus 21.10-15, and what he did on the Day of Atonement is described in Leviticus 16.6-17, where "Aaron" means any High Priest. CLTs and some other translations give additional information in a glossary note.

(b) The common words for "priest" may be used to describe ministers of a particular denomination. If so, it may be necessary to choose another word to translate **High Priest;** for example, "chief sacrificer," as in some French translations. But in most instances a term used for "priest" in major Christian churches is quite satisfactory when used in referring to the role of Jesus Christ. In some languages, however, there may be more than one term for priest, and these terms may differ significantly in connotation. Therefore one must make certain that a term used in referring to Jesus Christ is one which has acceptable connotations; that is to say, it should be a term which does not suggest a hypocritical or exploitive role, or have any other negative features.

(c) Except at 9.7, the writer does not lay much stress on the distinction between priest and High Priest. "High Priest" is one word in Greek, so in some languages it may be necessary to translate **great High Priest** as "great priest" or "highest priest" (GeCL), omitting **great** to avoid repetition.

Here and in the following verses, the writer continues to link himself with his readers. For example, he writes **Let us . . . hold firmly,** not "you must hold firmly." **Let us** is not a request for permission but an exhortation, equivalent to "We should continue strongly to," often expressed negatively as "we should not for a moment cease to."

The faith we profess, literally **"our confession"** (RSV), may mean either the act of stating publicly what one believes, or the words in which one's faith is expressed. Similar language is used in 3.1 and 10.23. By the time Hebrews was written, more or less fixed summaries of Christian belief were probably being used. **The faith we profess** may be expressed as "what we say we believe" or "how we declare that we trust Christ."

It may seem strange to say **we have a great High Priest,** for the High Priest is not possessed by people. He acts on behalf of people, and therefore it may be more natural and correct to say "he is a great High Priest for us."

TEV reverses the order of the Greek, beginning with an appeal which rounds off the previous section, and then introducing the theme of the High Priest. **Gone into the very presence of God** is literally "having gone through the heavens." "Heaven" was often used in order to avoid speaking directly of God. Perhaps the writer is already thinking of Jesus passing through several heavens, as the High Priest on the Day of Atonement passed through the veils of the Temple in Jerusalem (9.3). For the idea of several heavens, see 2 Corinthians 12.2. But the plural **"heavens"** (RSV) has no special significance here. The corresponding Hebrew word is dual in form but singular in meaning, and this fact probably influenced biblical Greek. It is impossible to make a precise distinction between the use of "heaven" (9.24) and "heavens" (9.23) in the Greek. Matthew uses the phrase "kingdom of the heavens" instead of "kingdom of God," with no difference of meaning.

Who has gone into the very presence of God may be rendered as "who has gone before God himself" or "who has entered where God is."

The apposition marked by the dash, and introducing **Jesus, the Son of God,** can rarely be translated literally, at least in the sequence which occurs in TEV, since it would imply that **Jesus, the Son of God** is in apposition to **God.** It may be more appropriate in some languages to translate "this High Priest is Jesus, who is the Son of God."

4.15 **Our High Priest is not one who cannot feel sympathy for our weaknesses. On the contrary, we have a High Priest who was tempted in every way that we are, but did not sin.**

The possessive relationship in the phrase **Our High Priest** may have to be expressed differently in some languages; for example, "The High Priest on our behalf" or "He who serves as High Priest for us."

The Greek contains a double negative: "we do *not* have a high priest who is *not* able to sympathize. . . ." Most translations simplify this by making it into an emphatic positive statement. This may be expressed as "Our High Priest is one who completely sympathizes with our weaknesses" or ". . . is one who understands well our weaknesses."

A literal translation along the lines of RSV could be misunderstood in some languages as a contradiction: "**We have a great high priest** (verse 14) . . . . **We have not a high priest . . . .**" The meaning is "Our High Priest is not one who cannot sympathize . . . ."

In this verse a comparison begins between Jesus and the Old Testament priest, who offered sacrifices on behalf of those who had disobeyed the Law without intending to do so (Num 15.22-29). The comparison will be developed in 5.2-3. This is the point of the reference to **our weaknesses,** and translators should avoid any term which could include deliberate sin. The writer believes there are other sins so serious that they cannot be forgiven or wiped out (10.26; compare Num 15.30-31). **Our weaknesses** may be best expressed as "how weak we are" or "how little strength we have."

To **feel sympathy** means to understand someone "from inside," that is, "to feel with him." Often it means "to share his suffering," but the idea of suffering is not stressed here, and GeCL translates "who has no understanding for our weaknesses." The Greek word used here is related in form to the verb translated be gentle in 5.2 and is similar in meaning.

If, as has been suggested, a positive expression rather than a double negative is used in the first part of verse 15, the adversative phrase **On the contrary** should be replaced by a conjunction such as "For." The second sentence in verse 15 (TEV) simply provides the reason why Jesus Christ as High Priest is able to be fully sympathetic.

Some translators have mistakenly interpreted **who was tempted in every way that we are** as "who wanted to sin in every way that we do." It is, of course, better to translate "whom the Devil tried to make sin in every way that he tempts us."

4.16   **Let us have confidence, then, and approach God's throne, where there is grace. There we will receive mercy and find grace to help us just when we need it.**

This verse, like 4.10-11, contains some repetition which it may be better to avoid in translation. Languages have other ways than repetition by which to stress particular words and phrases. A possible translation avoiding this repetition would be "So let us go forward to God in confidence, knowing that he will freely give us all we need at the right time," or even ". . . when we need it most."

Let us have confidence is literally "with confidence"; see discussion on 3.6b. In some passages, especially of Acts, the Greek for this expression refers to confident "speaking out" in witness. Here the context shows that it refers to inner confidence. The translation of **Let us have confidence** should not suggest an unnecessary fear which people might have in approaching God. It may be necessary in some languages to translate **Let us have confidence** as "Let us not hesitate to" or "Let us be confident in."

Approach God's throne, where there is grace: most English translations have **approach** or "come forward." "Go forward" seems more natural in English, since the writer's point of view is that of human beings, not that of God.

"The throne of grace" (RSV) is one of the writer's ways of speaking indirectly about God. Indirect references to God were common among Jews and therefore among Jewish Christians. "God who is gracious" or "God who gives us such good gifts" would be non-Jewish equivalents. **Approach God's throne** may be expressed as "go before God's throne" or "go near to God's throne." But a literal rendering of this might be interpreted exclusively in the sense of "going to heaven." Furthermore, it may not be natural to speak figuratively of a **throne,** so it may be best to translate **approach God's throne** as "to approach God." If one uses "God" in place of **God's throne,** then **where there is grace** will be rendered as "who is kind" or "who shows kindness to people."

Receive mercy is difficult to distinguish from **find grace,** and there is another reference to **grace** in the first part of the verse. **Mercy** and **grace** both have the meaning of a free gift from a superior, in this case God. In Paul's writings, **grace** frequently refers to God's gift of his Son, but this is not explicit here, though 5.9 expresses the same idea without using the word for "grace." In some languages, **grace** is a word little used outside church circles. If so, the translator may need to replace it by some such word as "love" (GeCL).

We will receive mercy may be rendered as "God will be merciful to us" or "God will show us kindness." A literal rendering of **find grace** might suggest accidental discovery or coming upon as the result of searching. In fact, **find grace** is merely an equivalent of "experience kindness" or "experience love."

Accordingly, **we will receive mercy and find grace** may be restructured as "God will be kind to us and show us his love." This may be further explained as "he will help us just when we need help."

Us, following **find grace to help,** is not expressed in the Greek. The idea of asking God to help other people is not excluded.

Chapter 5

1 Every high priest is chosen from his fellow-men and appointed to serve God on their behalf, to offer sacrifices and offerings for sins. 2 Since he himself is weak in many ways, he is able to be gentle with those who are ignorant and make mistakes. 3 And because he is himself weak, he must offer sacrifices not only for the sins of the people but also for his own sins. 4 No one chooses for himself the honor of being a high priest. It is only by God's call that a man is made a high priest—just as Aaron was.

5 In the same way, Christ did not take upon himself the honor of being a high priest. Instead, God said to him,

"You are my Son;
   today I have become your
     Father."

6 He also said in another place,

"You will be a priest forever,
   in the priestly order of
     Melchizedek."ˣ

7 In his life on earth Jesus made his prayers and requests with loud cries and tears to God, who could save him from death. Because he was humble and devoted, God heard him. 8 But even though he was God's Son, he learned through his sufferings to be obedient. 9 When he was made perfect, he became the source of eternal salvation for all those who obey him, 10 and God declared him to be high priest, in the priestly order of Melchizedek.ˣ

ˣ in the priestly order of Melchizedek; *or* like Melchizedek; *or* in the line of succession to Melchizedek.

1 For every high priest chosen from among men is appointed to act on behalf of men in relation to God, to offer gifts and sacrifices for sins. 2 He can deal gently with the ignorant and wayward, since he himself is beset with weakness. 3 Because of this he is bound to offer sacrifice for his own sins as well as for those of the people. 4 And one does not take the honor upon himself, but he is called by God, just as Aaron was.

5 So also Christ did not exalt himself to be made a high priest, but was appointed by him who said to him,

"Thou art my Son,
   today I have begotten thee";

6 as he says also in another place,

"Thou art a priest for ever,
   after the order of Melchizedek."

7 In the days of his flesh, Jesusʲ offered up prayers and supplications, with loud cries and tears, to him who was able to save him from death, and he was heard for his godly fear. 8 Although he was a Son, he learned obedience through what he suffered; 9 and being made perfect he became the source of eternal salvation to all who obey him, 10 being designated by God a high priest after the order of Melchizedek.

ʲ Greek *he*

[92]

The pattern of these verses is generally clear. It follows a series of subjects to a focal point (item C below) and then reverses itself to state what that means for the subjects previously mentioned.

A. The function of a high priest is to offer sacrifices for sin (verse 1).
   B. The qualifications of a high priest are to be:
        B-1.   Gentle and understanding with people (verses 2-3, compare 4.15).
        B-2.   Appointed by God, not by himself (verse 4).
             C. Jesus has these qualifications.
        B-2'. He was appointed by God (verses 5-6).
   B-1'. He shared human sufferings (verses 7-8).
A'. So Jesus can perform the functions of a high priest (verses 9-10).

Within the argument of Hebrews as a whole, the function of this section is to move from the discussion of Jesus as Son to the discussion of Jesus as priest or High Priest. Notice how the two titles of Son and priest are used together in 3.1,6, in 4.14, again in 5.8,10, and especially in the two quotations from the Old Testament in 5.5-6.

The author of Hebrews uses the titles "priest" and "high priest" in speaking of Christ, without emphasizing the distinction between them. "Priest" renders the term used in Psalm 110.4, but by the time Hebrews was written, this could have been misunderstood to refer to someone less important than the high priest. Even when the author of Hebrews comments directly on Psalm 110.4, he sometimes uses "high priest" (5.5,10; 6.20; 7.26). In other places faithful (2.17), different (7.11,15), or great (10.21) distinguish Jesus from other priests. Therefore, wherever possible these titles should be translated by related words, not by separate terms for two ranks of priests. "High priest" means the same as great priest in 10.21.

<u>5.1</u>   **Every high priest is chosen from his fellow-men and appointed to serve God on their behalf, to offer sacrifices and offerings for sins.**

Every is singular in grammatical form but plural in meaning, and therefore **Every high priest** may need to be rendered as "All high priests." In English the terms **every** and "all" differ primarily in terms of whether the focus is upon the totality as individuals or the totality as a group, but some languages do not make this type of distinction.

Is chosen . . . and appointed implies "by God," but this is not made explicit until verse 4. However, **Every high priest is chosen from his fellow-men** may be rendered as "God chooses every high priest from among his fellow-men," if it is clearer or more natural to do so.

From his fellow-men: Leviticus 21.10 speaks of "the priest who is chief among his brethren" (RSV); compare Numbers 8.6, which speaks of Levites "from among the people of Israel" (RSV). **From his fellow-men** may be rendered in some instances as "from among those men who are like him," or "from men of his own clan," or "from men of his own tribe." Sometimes an even broader base is employed for comparison, "from men of his own nation."

To serve God on their behalf: RSV's **"in relation to God"** is literally "the (things) toward God," that is, "for the service of God." This is a general way of speaking about leading public worship, which is here linked with the task of caring for people as a pastor. If "God" is expressed as the subject of the verb "to choose," "God" should also be the subject of "to appoint," and therefore **and appointed to serve God on their behalf** would be restructured as "and God appointed every high priest to serve him on behalf of the people."

The high priest's special work was **to offer sacrifices and offerings for sins**, literally "gifts and sacrifices for sins." It is not clear whether only the **offerings** or also the **sacrifices** are **for sins**, since the phrase describes in a general way the whole system of Old Testament worship. **Offerings** may be a general term, including **sacrifices**.

To offer sacrifices and offerings for sins indicates the purpose of God in choosing and appointing every high priest. The phrase **to offer sacrifices** may need to be expressed as "to kill animals on behalf of God." However, in some contexts cereal offerings are included, so **to offer ... offerings** may be expressed as "to make gifts to God on behalf of" or "to give something to God on behalf of the people."

The phrase **for sins** can be misunderstood if translated literally, for it might suggest "in order to encourage sins" of "for the benefit of sins." The relationship of sins to the sacrifices and offerings may be best expressed in terms of cause; for example, "because of sins" or "because of the evil which people have done." **For sins** has often been translated "as payment because of sins." It is important, however, to indicate clearly that this is not a way in which people pay for the privilege of sinning. Accordingly, it is better to employ some such expression as "in order to take away sins" or "... guilt," or "in order to cause sins to be blotted out."

5.2   **Since he himself is weak in many ways, he is able to be gentle with those who are ignorant and make mistakes.**

If in verse 1 God is made the subject of the sentence, it may be important to introduce "the high priest" as the subject of verse 2; for example, "Since a high priest is himself weak in many ways."

He himself is weak is more literally "he himself is surrounded by weakness."

In choosing a term for **weak**, it is important to avoid an expression which will mean merely physical weakness. Sometimes misunderstanding may be avoided by speaking of "a person who is weak in his heart" or "someone who is not strong toward God."

The central meaning of **be gentle** is that of reacting in a moderate way to anything which might arouse anger. Like feel sympathy in 4.15, it also suggests feeling and the possibility of suffering. Unlike **to be gentle** in English, the Greek word is a rare one, not found anywhere else in the Greek Bible. **Is able to be gentle** may be expressed as "is able to feel in his heart for" or "is able to understand how others feel."

Those who are ignorant and make mistakes are probably a single group of people. However, the Greek for **make mistakes** suggests something more worthy of blame than to be **ignorant,** which means simply "not to know." GeCL translates "he has understanding for those who have done wrong unintentionally." The Old Testament background suggests that the writer means those who make mistakes because of their ignorance; see comment on <u>weaknesses</u> in 4.15. The distinction is between those sins which can be dealt with by some kind of sacrifice and those which cannot. It is important to make it clear in translation that **those who are ignorant and make mistakes** are one group of people, not two. Therefore this phrase may be rendered as "those who make mistakes because they do not know any better" or "those who do wrong because they do not know that what they are doing is wrong."

5.3   **And because he is himself weak, he must offer sacrifices not only for the sins of the people but also for his own sins.**

Because he is himself weak is perhaps a little heavy after the similar expression in verse 2, but it is clearer than RSV's **"because of this."** In the Greek, "this" certainly refers to "weakness." The rendering of **weak** in the clause **because he is himself weak** should be expressed in the same way that **weak** is translated in verse 2.

He must means "it is his duty as high priest." Brc has "he is under obligation." The background of this verse is Leviticus 16.11-14, the high priest's sacrifice for himself, and 16.15-19, his sacrifice for the people; see also Leviticus 9.7; 16.6, and the comments on Hebrews 2.17. **He must** may be expressed as "it is necessary for him" or "it is required that."

Offer is literally "bring toward" or "present." This verb is often used of presenting gifts and sacrifices to God. There is no suggestion that the sacrifice might not be accepted, though of course the Old Testament contains examples of sacrifices which were in fact refused.

In a number of languages there is no such neat contrast as **not only ... but also.** However, the same ideas may be expressed as "he must do this ... he must also do that." The last part of verse 3 may be rendered as "he must offer sacrifices to take away the sins of the people, and he must also offer sacrifices to take away his own sins."

In a number of languages a careful distinction is made between "sins" in the sense of the actual event of doing something wrong, and "sins" as guilt which results from such wrongdoing. It is the latter sense which is focal in this context.

5.4 **No one chooses for himself the honor of being a high priest. It is only by God's call that a man is made a high priest—just as Aaron was.**

The second qualification of a high priest is that he must be chosen and appointed by God. In **No one chooses,** the Greek verb often means "receive," but here the context requires "**take,**" as in RSV. FrCL, TOB have "attribute to himself." **No one** means no individual, as in 3.12-13; 4.1.

The emphasis in the first part of this verse is that no one can make himself high priest. Therefore in some languages it is important to rule out the possibility of a person making himself a high priest. This is in anticipation of the second part of the verse. Therefore **No one chooses for himself the honor of being a high priest** may be rendered as "No person can decide to give himself the honor of being a high priest." In some instances this may be expressed as direct discourse; for example, "No person can declare, 'I give myself the honor of being a high priest' " or ". . . 'I will honor myself by becoming a high priest.' "

Honor is rank, position, here almost "office." The meaning is that no one becomes a high priest simply by claiming to be one.

Call, in Greek as in English, is a common word with several meanings, including (a) to call out an order or an invitation, (b) to give someone a name, and (c) more generally, to call someone to a new way of life. Here, meaning (b) is intended. God summons someone to occupy a particular position, that of high priest. See Exodus 28.1.

By God's call that a man is made a high priest must often be restructured because of the complex relation in the phrase **by God's call** to the fact of being made a high priest. This restructuring may take the form of "a man becomes a high priest only because God has called him" or ". . . only because God has appointed him."

Just as is emphatic; BJ translates "absolutely like Aaron."

Just as Aaron was: in many languages it will be necessary to repeat "was called." It is possible to translate, like GeCL first edition, "he receives it [that is, this honor] only through God's call, just as Aaron received it." The wider context is concerned with valid appointment to the office of high priest, not so much with the call itself. **Just as Aaron was** must be modified, depending upon the manner in which the first part of the preceding clause is restructured. **Just as Aaron was** may be rendered as "this is just what happened to Aaron" or "this is the way Aaron was appointed" or "this is what happened when God appointed Aaron."

5.5 **In the same way, Christ did not take upon himself the honor of being a high priest. Instead, God said to him,**
       "You are my Son;
        today I have become your Father."

In the same way may be expressed as "This is the same thing which happened to Christ" or "This is just the same thing that happened in the case of

Christ." DuCL, GeCL use words meaning "also." Jesus has the two qualifications for being a high priest. The second qualification, mentioned in verse 4, is now applied to Christ. **Christ** is not in the Greek but is clearly implied. He has been appointed by God, not by himself.

Here we have another negative statement, **Christ did not take upon himself,** followed by a positive equivalent, **God said to him.** In some languages it may be more natural to put the positive statement first.

Christ did not take upon himself the honor of being a high priest may be expressed as "Christ did not decide to honor himself by making himself a high priest." In some languages one may only speak of honoring oneself by using a form of direct discourse; for example, "Christ never said, 'I will make myself great by becoming a high priest.' " This use of direct discourse provides a bold contrast with the second part of this verse.

Instead introduces a contrast between God and himself; FrCL "On the contrary, it is God who declared to him."

God, as often in this letter, is not named in the Greek. The first readers would have known immediately who the speaker was in the quotation **You are my Son,** but TEV and some other translations make this clear for modern readers.

The Greek word for **said** usually refers to a spoken message, but see note on the next verse. On the quotation from Psalm 2.7, see discussion on 1.5.

5.6   He also said in another place,
          "You will be a priest forever,
          in the priestly order of Melchizedek."[x]

[x] in the priestly order of Melchizedek; *or* like Melchizedek; *or* in the line of succession to Melchizedek.

Said is a different word from the one used in the last verse, but the writer often varies his choice of words for reasons of style. There is no difference in meaning.

A literal rendering of **He also said in another place** could imply that God also said something in a different geographical location. It may be useful to translate this clause as "God's words are also recorded in another part of the holy writings" or "In another place in the holy writings God also said."

You will be a priest forever is often expressed negatively as "You will never cease to be a priest." Psalm 110.4 does not refer to a "high priest" but only to a **priest,** but there is no difference in meaning.

Melchizedek's mysterious role will be discussed in detail in chapter 7. In Genesis 14.17-24 it is stated that Melchizedek was a priest, but there is no suggestion that he founded an order or succession of priests. In TEV, **priestly** is added to explain **order. In the priestly order of Melchizedek** probably means no more than "like Melchizedek" (see 7.15).[1] It may be rendered as "in the way in which Melchizedek was a priest" or "similar to the manner in which Melchizedek functioned as a priest."

[97]

The writer sometimes quotes the same text several times, making a different point each time. (See comments on 4.7 and 6.20.) This is again true of the quotation from Psalm 110.4. Here and in verse 10 the emphasis is on God, the speaker.

<u>5.7</u>   **In his life on earth Jesus made his prayers and requests with loud cries and tears to God, who could save him from death. Because he was humble and devoted, God heard him.**

Jesus also has the first qualification for being a high priest, the qualification mentioned in verses 2-3. As already stated in 2.10; 4.15, he has learned through his own suffering how to understand the suffering of others.

In his life on earth may be expressed as "While Jesus was living on earth" or "While Jesus was here in the world."

Jesus and **God** (twice) are not in the Greek, but are clearly implied.

Prayers and **requests** are similar in meaning; both imply asking God for something, whether for oneself (petition) or for someone else (intercession). The context suggests petition, especially the prayer of Jesus for himself at Gethsemane (Mark 14.32-42). In some languages it may not be possible to distinguish clearly between **prayers** and **requests,** especially since in both instances verbs may be employed rather than nouns. Therefore it may be best to translate **made his prayers and requests** as "prayed earnestly for," or as expressed idiomatically in some languages, "spoke to God with his heart open" or "spoke to God from his very insides."

Loud cries does not mean "crying" in the sense of "weeping" but "crying out, shouting." The language is similar to that of Matthew 26.37 and Luke 22.44. **With loud cries and tears to God** may be expressed as "he shouted out to God and cried" or "he spoke loudly to God and at the same time wept." It is important to relate the phrase **to God** as an aspect of the crying out or shouting rather than to the tears.

Save him, as the following words **from death** show, means "rescue him." This is a meaning of "salvation" which was noted in 1.14; see also the comment on salvation in 5.9.

Save him from death may mean either (a) prevent him from dying (as in Psa 33.19) or (b) save him, although he had already died (as in Hos 13.14). Meaning (a) fits the situation of Gethsemane better; meaning (b) would reflect belief in the resurrection, which is not emphasized in Hebrews (though see 13.20-21). Meaning (a) should probably be chosen in languages which would naturally express (a) and (b) differently, but the author may have had both ideas in mind. In keeping with the meaning of "preventing him from dying," one may render **save him from death** as "cause people not to kill him" or "to prevent people from causing his death," or even "to rescue him so that he would not have to die."

---

1 See P. Ellingworth, "Just Like Melchizedek," in <u>The Bible Translator</u>, volume 28, number 2 (April 1977), pages 236-239.

The single Greek word which RSV translates **"godly fear,"** and TEV **Because he was humble and devoted,** may mean either (a) "fear" (in the common sense of "alarm") or (b) "piety, reverence," as "fear of God" in church language. In this verse, meaning (a) would be that God listened to Jesus' prayer as a result of the fear of death which it expressed, or that Jesus' fear of death was the reason why God listened to his prayer; meaning (b) would be that God listened to Jesus because of the trustful and obedient spirit in which he prayed Not what I want, but what you want (Mark 14.36). TEV, like most translations and commentaries, follows meaning (b) with its **humble and devoted;** similarly DuCL "humble submission to God"; Phps rev "willingness to obey"; JB "he submitted so humbly"; NEB "humble submission."

The Greek word which RSV translates **"for"** may mean either "because of" or "out of." The first meaning is more likely, especially if the words which follow "for" are understood as "fear of God," not "fear of death."

God heard him: literally, "he was heard." "Hear" in biblical Greek often implies "listen and respond to." In some languages "I hear you" is a polite way of expressing disagreement; any such suggestion must be carefully avoided in translating this verse. Since the phrase **God heard him** implies far more than merely "listening," it may be clearer to render **God heard him** as "God answered him," or "God responded to him," or "God paid attention to what he said."

<u>5.8</u>   **But even though he was God's Son, he learned through his sufferings to be obedient.**

RSV's literal translation **"although he was a Son, he learned obedience . . ."** is misleading if read aloud, since it is usual for a son to learn obedience. Verse 5 makes it clear that **"Son"** here means **God's Son;** that is the translation rightly chosen by TEV. It is possible to link **even though he was God's Son** with verse 7, especially if "fear" is understood as "fear of death"; thus "God listened to him, because of the fear which he had although he was God's Son." However, TEV's interpretation is simpler and more likely to be correct.

Not all languages have the so-called "concessive clause" beginning with a conjunction such as "though" or "although." Nevertheless, the idea of concession may be expressed by an independent statement followed by some such conjunction as "nevertheless" or "despite that fact." For example, this verse could be rendered as "He was indeed God's Son, but nevertheless he learned through his suffering how to be obedient" or ". . . despite that fact he learned by suffering to be obedient." In some languages the concept of a concession is expressed only as a kind of adversative relationship; for example, "He was indeed God's Son; that is true, but he did learn to be obedient by means of his suffering."

"Learned" and "suffered" render a common play on words in Greek, where the words are similar in sound: *emathen* and *epathen*. However, this does not affect the meaning of this verse. If the play on words cannot be reproduced naturally in translation, it does not matter.

Just as <u>call</u> in verse 4 includes the ideas of speaking and summoning, so "obey" in Greek often combines the ideas of listening and responding to a summons or command. The verb translated **to be obedient** is related to the verb translated heard in verse 7, which also implies a response.

It may be necessary to make somewhat more specific the relationships between **learned, sufferings,** and **obedient;** for example, "by means of what Christ suffered he learned how to be obedient," or ". . . how to obey God," or ". . . how to always do what God told him to do."

5.9   **When he was made perfect, he became the source of eternal salvation for all those who obey him,**

Perfect translates a group of related words which are often used in Hebrews (see especially 2.10; 7.28). Between them they express various elements of meaning which usually cannot be translated by the same word or phrase. It is the translator's task to decide which element in each context is the most important. The following aspects should be considered: (a) "whole," especially "wholly faithful to God" (compare Deut 18.13 TEV; RSV's "blameless" is too negative); (b) "mature," "adult" (see Heb 5.14); (c) in the Septuagint, the ordination of a priest was often called "filling his hand," the verb for "fill" being related to **perfect.** The related Greek noun may suggest either (d) death, (e) the reaching of a goal, or both. Outside the Bible, such words are often used to express (f) reaching the goal of a spiritual journey, or being allowed to learn spiritual mysteries. Although these associations are usually less important in Hebrews, translations such as "having reached the end of his journey" fit the context well and may be appropriate in some languages. In the light of 4.15 (but did not sin), the translator should avoid any suggestion that Jesus' earlier state, before being **made perfect,** involved sin.

When he was made perfect: see comments on 2.10. Here GeCL has "after he had reached the goal"; Knox "his full achievement reached"; TOB "led to his own fulfillment." It is through suffering that Christ became mature and fully qualified as a high priest to deal with people's sins.

A literal translation of the clause **When he was made perfect** suggests imperfection in Jesus and therefore some degree of sin or guilt. It may therefore be better to avoid such a rendering. In any case, in some languages the passive construction **was made** would be difficult to render appropriately. The meaning may be expressed as "When he had accomplished his purpose," or "When he had done all that he was supposed to do," or "When he had become just what he was supposed to become."

Eternal before **salvation** suggests a contrast with rescue from physical death, which was mentioned in verse 7; however, the contrast is not emphasized. **Salvation** is a word used mainly in church circles and is therefore to be avoided in a common language translation. The corresponding verb "save" may still be part of common language. GeCL has "now he can save (rescue) for ever all who obey him."

He became the source of eternal salvation must be considerably restructured in some languages, since **source** is an expression of cause, and **salvation** is what people experience. Therefore **he became the source of eternal salvation** may be rendered as "he became the one who causes people to be saved forever" or ". . . the one who saves people forever."

Obey, here as in verse 8, involves listening and responding positively to Christ's call. As in 2.20, what Jesus does as the unique Son benefits the "many sons" who are joined to him by faith. **Those who obey him** may be rendered as "those who do what he tells them to do"; this is equivalent to "those who follow him" or "those who are loyal to his commands."

5.10   **and God declared him to be high priest, in the priestly order of Melchizedek.**[x]

     [x] in the priestly order of Melchizedek; *or* like Melchizedek; *or* in the line of succession to Melchizedek.

Declared (Syn) has a range of meaning similar to <u>call</u> (see comment on verse 4): DuCL "called him out"; GeCL "appointed"; NEB, TNT "named"; Mft, NAB, Phps rev "designated"; Knox "called"; Brc "was given . . . the title of." However, the earliest meaning of this verb is "greet," and this sense is still found in secular writings of about the same date as the New Testament. BJ translates "since he is greeted by God with the title of high priest according to the order of Melchizedek"; similarly JB "acclaimed"; TOB "proclaimed." This is a possible meaning; however, it is more likely to be an equivalent of <u>call</u>, but the author used **declared** to avoid repetition. The word does not occur elsewhere in the New Testament, and therefore the exact sense is not certain.

The meaning of the verb rendered **declared** may be expressed in some languages by direct discourse; for example, "God proclaimed, 'You are a high priest in the way in which Melchizedek was.' " For a translation of **in the priestly order of Melchizedek,** see verse 6.

The third and central part of the letter begins with 5.11 and extends to 10.39. It begins (5.11—6.20) and ends (10.19-39) with appeals to the readers. The rest of this part of the letter may be divided into three sections:
1. Christ, a high priest like Melchizedek (chapter 7).
2. The heart of the matter (chapters 8-9).
3. Christ saves for ever (10.1-18).

The author has now ended this stage of his discussion of Jesus as High Priest, and he begins his next main division with an appeal to the readers. This appeal forms a distinct section[2] on the subject of Christian maturity. In it, three possibilities are presented to the readers: (a) to remain slow of hearing (5.11; compare 6.12), content to hear simple truths repeated again and again; (b) to fall

---

[2] Some commentaries make a break after 6.8, but 6.12 appears to round off the section by returning to the point of departure in 5.11.

away from Christian faith (6.4-6); or (c) to go forward (6.1) to a full understanding of what God has promised (6.12) and now offers to men through Christ, their High Priest. The aim of this section is thus to make the readers interested in learning more about the meaning of what Christ has done.

The passage includes various words, phrases, and illustrations which were used in non-Jewish philosophical and religious teaching. The writer's main aim is to help his readers to understand Jewish traditions in the light of Christ. However, the writer knows that his readers are in touch with other ways of thinking, and he draws on these in this section. This section therefore contains no detailed analysis of Old Testament texts or of specifically Christian teaching.

TEV	**5.11-14**	RSV

Warning against Abandoning the Faith

11 There is much we have to say about this matter, but it is hard to explain to you, because you are so slow to understand. 12 There has been enough time for you to be teachers—yet you still need someone to teach you the first lessons of God's message. Instead of eating solid food, you still have to drink milk. 13 Anyone who has to drink milk is still a child, without any experience in the matter of right and wrong. 14 Solid food, on the other hand, is for adults, who through practice are able to distinguish between good and evil.

11 About this we have much to say which is hard to explain, since you have become dull of hearing. 12 For though by this time you ought to be teachers, you need some one to teach you again the first principles of God's word. You need milk, not solid food; 13 for every one who lives on milk is unskilled in the word of righteousness, for he is a child. 14 But solid food is for the mature, for those who have their faculties trained by practice to distinguish good from evil.

The section heading **Warning against Abandoning the Faith** may be expressed as an imperative; for example, "Do not give up trusting in Christ" or "Do not cease believing in Christ."

<u>5.11</u>   **There is much we have to say about this matter, but it is hard to explain to you, because you are so slow to understand.**

We probably means "I, the writer" (so Mft, Brc). There is no suggestion that the letter comes from a group of people, and ancient writers commonly used "we" as an equivalent of "I."

There is much we have to say may be expressed as "I have many words that I want to say" or "I have many thoughts that I want to write."

What is **this matter**? The Greek is literally "about this." Two translations are possible: (a) "about him," that is, Melchizedek (so NEB), or (b) "about this," that is, the subject of Melchizedek as an illustration of Christ's work (Knox "of Christ as priest"; Phps "about this high priesthood"). There is little difference in meaning. It is, however, better to make the translation specific, especially at the beginning of a section, and to avoid vague phrases such as "about this" or "about him." Most translations choose meaning (b), which may be expressed clearly as "about Christ being a high priest like Melchizedek," or more simply "about what I have just said" or ". . . have just written."

Translations should make it clear that the teaching which is to come (beginning in chapter 7) is not **hard** or difficult in itself, but hard to present in such a way that the readers will understand. As Moffatt put it in his commentary, "The fault lies with you, not with the subject." Brc translates "it is not easy for me to put it in a way that you will understand." Other possibilities for translating **it is hard to explain to you** are "it is difficult to find just the words with which I can explain this to you" or "for me to explain this to you is not at all easy."

You are so slow to understand does not mean that the readers are in a permanent state of low intelligence. They have had time to understand, but they still do not. Indeed, there is a danger that they will fall back into a state worse than the one they were in before they became Christians (6.4-6). The Greek includes both past and present: "have become and now are slow to understand." The readers have become less keen in their understanding of the Christian faith and are in danger of abandoning their faith completely.

Slow to understand here, and lazy in 6.12, are expressed by the same word in the Greek, and there seems to be a contradiction. We do not want you to become lazy (6.12) may mean (a) "we do not want you to become still lazier than you are," or (b) "we do not want you to go on being lazy" or "slow to understand." (b) is rather more likely. Knox ("listless no more") and Mft ("instead of being slack") realize the danger of translating 5.11 in such a way that it contradicts 6.12, and they therefore support (b). There seems no reason to avoid the problem, as both TEV and RSV do, by translating **slow to understand** differently in 5.11 and 6.12. The Greek word means "dull" or "hard of hearing," with the additional idea of being slack or inattentive, too mentally lazy to listen to what is said. Many translations, like TEV, replace "hear," used in a figurative sense, by the non-figurative **understand**.

Because you are so slow to understand may be rendered as "because so much time is necessary for you to understand what is meant." Sometimes **slow to understand** may be expressed better in a negative form; for example, "you do not understand at all quickly." In some instances **slow to understand** is expressed idiomatically; for example, "you listen only with your outer ears" (with the implication that the thoughts never really enter the mind) or "the words pass so slowly into your hearts."

5.12   There has been enough time for you to be teachers—yet you still need someone to teach you the first lessons of God's message. Instead of eating solid food, you still have to drink milk.

This verse develops and supports the statement that its readers have become **slow to understand** (see RSV's "**For**"). The verse contains a contrast between what the readers should be and what they are. TEV's **yet** and Brc's "but in point of fact" bring out this contrast more clearly than RSV's more literal "**though.**" Phps makes the contrast even stronger by bold restructuring: "At a time when you should be teaching others, you need teachers yourselves . . . ." TEV does not express the idea of inner obligation in RSV "**ought.**" It was a common belief that any mature person should be able to teach someone else. **Teachers** here does not mean specialized professional instructors. For this reason it may be more natural to use a verbal expression such as "by this time you should be teaching other people" (Mft, similarly GeCL).

There has been enough time may be rendered as "Already enough time has passed," but the use of a term meaning "already" and an expression of obligation may be sufficient to render **There has been enough time for you to be teachers;** for example, "Already you should have become teachers" or ". . . should have become those who could teach others."

Most modern translations and commentaries agree with the UBS Greek text, TEV, and RSV, which has **someone** rather than KJV's "which be the first principles." **Someone** suits the context better. The translation should be indefinite, since the reference is not to any individual; Phps shows this by using the plural, "teachers." 6.1-2 explains what is meant by **the first lessons of God's message** (see the comments on these verses).

You still need someone to teach you may be rendered rather impersonally as "it is still necessary for someone to teach you." In some languages this must be expressed as an obligation: "you must have someone to teach you."

The first lessons: the Greek includes some repetition for emphasis; literally, "the elements of the beginning."

God's message is literally "God's sayings." This is not the usual expression for referring to the Old Testament; it refers rather to basic elements of his revelation in general. Phps translates "the ABC of God's revelation to men"; similarly NEB. Elementary Christian teaching (see 6.1) may be included.

The first lessons of God's message may often be rendered as "what one learns first about God's message" or "what one ought to learn at the very beginning about what God has declared" or ". . . what God has said."

You still have to drink milk: RSV's second "**you need**" is literally "you have become and are people who need." Once "have become and are" has been expressed in verse 11, it need not be reemphasized here. TEV, by changing "**need**" into **have to,** makes it clear that the readers' immaturity is unusual and wrong. Brc, however, goes further than TEV's second **still** by translating "It is milk you have come to need," suggesting that the readers are even becoming less mature than they were. This fits in very well.

The connection between **the first lessons of God's message** and the final sentence of verse 12, namely, **Instead of eating solid food, you still have to drink milk,** may not be clear unless the basis for this figurative statement is made evident by introducing the fact of "being like children," as occurs in the first part of 5.13-14. It may therefore be important to transfer the reference to "being like children" into verse 12; for example, "You are like children, and instead of being able to eat solid food you still must drink milk." This provides an excellent basis for what follows in verses 13 and 14.

<u>5.13-14</u>   Anyone who has to drink milk is still a child, without any
        experience in the matter of right and wrong. 14 Solid food, on
        the other hand, is for adults, who through practice are able to
        distinguish between good and evil.

These verses expand the contrast in verse 12, but in the opposite order.
Notice, by comparison with RSV, how TEV changes the structure of verse 13. This
is in order to bring **child** closer to **drink milk.** In the Greek, "for he is a child" is
emphasized by being placed in a clause of its own at the end of the sentence.

Has to drink milk implies what RSV's "lives on milk" states explicitly, that
the readers cannot "digest" solid food, and so take nothing but milk. **Anyone who
has to drink milk** may be expressed as "Anyone who can only drink milk" or "Any
one who can consume only milk." It is important in using a term for **drink** to make
certain that this agrees with a term such as **milk.** In some languages, for example,
one "eats milk" but "drinks water."

In determining an appropriate word for **child** it is necessary to use an
expression which refers to an individual before the age of weaning. Some translations state that the **child** is still unweaned, that is, is still a baby (DuCL, SpCL,
Mft "a mere babe"; TNT "infant"; compare Knox; Brc, JB "baby"). Many languages
make an important distinction in age-grading between persons who are still unweaned and those who have been weaned, though in some societies complete
weaning may not occur until a child is two or three years of age.

It is difficult to be sure of the exact meaning of the phrase which RSV
translates "**the word of righteousness,**" and TEV **the matter of right and wrong.**
For "**word,**" CLTs generally agree with TEV in choosing a general translation,
matter; BJ has the more specific "teaching," and TOB "reasoning." Knox and TNT
(see TNT Glossary) speak of a particular "message" or "account." For "**righteousness,**" CLTs, NEB, and some other translations suggest a general, moral meaning
such as **right and wrong;** compare GeCL second edition "the language of adults."
JB, TNT, and TOB agree with RSV in using religious words like "righteousness" and
"righteous"; Knox and NAB suggest this quality more strongly by choosing terms
related to holiness.

This section does not speak in detail about special Christian teaching, so
the context favors a general meaning such as TEV's **the matter of right and
wrong.** An expanded translation or paraphrase might read as follows:

> Anyone who lives on milk is a baby who does not know by expe-
> rience what is right. But mature people, on the other hand,
> can take solid food, because they have learned by practice and
> training to be sensitive to the difference between good and
> evil.

Without any experience in the matter of right and wrong might wrongly
suggest that a small child has never done anything which is either right or wrong.
Verses 13 and 14 obviously emphasize the recognition or knowledge of what is

right or wrong. It may be appropriate to translate **without any experience in the matter of right and wrong** as "without being able to know the difference between right and wrong" or "without having learned, as yet, what the difference is between what is right and what is wrong."

Verse 14 completes the contrast; see RSV "**But**"; FrCL "On the contrary."

Solid food, on the other hand, is for adults may be expressed as "but in contrast with what happens to children, solid food is for those who are grown up" or ". . . for those who are already men and women."

TEV fourth edition, **adults, who through practice . . .** , smooths and simplifies the rather heavy translation of the first three editions: ". . . adults, who have trained and used their tastes to know the difference between good and evil," but the metaphor of athletic training is weakened. The Greek word for **practice** involves physical or mental fitness, for example, in Sirach 30.14, where it means that a person is "in good condition." The rare word which RSV translates "faculties" does not refer only to intellectual powers; in the Septuagint of Jeremiah 4.19 it includes emotional awareness.

There are certain dangers involved in a literal translation of **who through practice are able to distinguish between good and evil,** for this might be misunderstood to mean that only those who have done both good and evil would know the difference between good and evil. In other words, an individual must learn how to sin in order to know what sin is. **Through practice** might better be expressed in some languages as "by constantly using their minds," or "by repeatedly thinking in their hearts," or "by carefully and repeatedly considering in their hearts."

Distinguish means "make the right use of one's powers or faculties" (so Mft, NAB, Brc; NEB, TNT "perceptions"). Simpler words would be "senses" (DuCL, GeCL, TOB); "moral sense" (BJ); "minds" (JB). In this context there does not seem any reason to see in the passive verb translated "**trained**" (RSV) an implied reference to the activity of God.

To distinguish between good and evil may be rendered as "to tell the difference between what is good and what is evil" or "to decide in one's heart that this is good and that is bad."

Chapter 6

Throughout 5.11—6.12 the writer is trying to help his readers reach a new depth of Christian understanding and behavior. He does this by contrasting various states which are summarized in the diagram below: (A) their higher state when they first became Christians (6.1-2); (B) their present state, a lower and less favorable position, from which the writer hopes to help them progress (6.1-3); (C) the dreadful future which they can expect if they continue to go to lower positions in the Christian life (6.4-8); (D) and the position to which God will enable the readers to rise if they respond to the writer's message (6.9-12). The positions may be represented as follows:

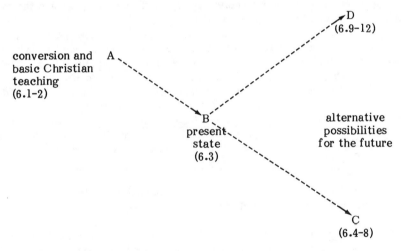

conversion and basic Christian teaching (6.1-2) — A

D (6.9-12)

B present state (6.3)

alternative possibilities for the future

C (6.4-8)

The point of **Let us go forward** is that there can be no movement from right to left, that is, from B back to A. The readers have not forgotten the basic teaching they received; they have simply lost interest in learning anything more, or in becoming better trained to distinguish good from evil.

TEV	**6.1-3**	RSV

1 Let us go forward, then, to mature teaching and leave behind us the first lessons of the Christian message. We should not lay again the foundation of turning away from useless works and believing in God; 2 of the teaching about baptisms[d] and the laying on of hands; of the resurrection of the dead and the eternal judgment. 3 Let us go forward! And this is what we will do, if God allows.

[d] baptisms; or purification ceremonies.

1 Therefore let us leave the elementary doctrine of Christ and go on to maturity, not laying again a foundation of repentance from dead works and of faith toward God, 2 with instruction[k] about ablutions, the laying on of hands, the resurrection of the dead, and eternal judgment. 3 And this we will do if God permits.[l]

[k] Other ancient manuscripts read *of instruction*
[l] Other ancient manuscripts read *let us do this if God permits*

The general pattern shown in the above diagram affects details of the translation. (a) It shows why verse 1 begins with **"therefore"** or then, not with "however." There can be no going back to the beginning of the Christian life; there must be either growth or complete collapse. This is why, despite the readers' deficiencies, the writer plans to go on (especially in chapter 7) to "solid" teaching for adults. (b) It strongly suggests that **we** in this passage is not, as in 5.11, the equivalent of "I," but includes both the writer and the readers, whom he is trying to carry forward with him. (c) It shows that **if God allows** (verse 3) does not have the narrow meaning "if I survive long enough to do it" but the wider meaning "if God allows us all to realize together what he plans for us." (d) It makes it essential to understand and to translate verses 1-3 as a whole, so that **this** in verse 3 refers, not to **lay again the foundation,** but to **go forward.** There is a real possibility of complete misunderstanding here, as RSV's ambiguous translation shows. TEV avoids this by repeating **Let us go forward** in verse 3.

6.1a   **Let us go forward, then, to mature teaching and leave behind us the first lessons of the Christian message.**

Let us go forward is not a request for permission but an appeal for action. "Moving forward" or "going forward" may not necessarily suggest progress toward any particular goal. Therefore it may be important to say "Let us go to the goal of mature teaching."

Mature teaching does not mean the teaching that is given by mature people, but the teaching which is appropriate for those who are mature, who are "adults in their faith," or "like grownups as far as believing is concerned."

Most translations and commentaries agree with TEV's **leave behind,** but the Greek may also mean "omit," "pass over" (DuCL). Knox has "We must leave on one side, then, all discussion of our first lessons in Christ, and pass on to our full growth." The difference of meaning is not great, but the translation should in any case avoid the idea that the readers are being asked to throw away the elementary teaching they had received. The writer means that he will not in this letter repeat the elementary teaching, and does not wish his readers to keep going over the same ground themselves. See verses 1b-2 and also comments on 7.11.

In order to avoid wrong connotations in the expression **leave behind**, it may be necessary to employ a negative equivalent; for example, "and not keep repeating" or "and not just stay where we are."

This verse suggests that even the milk mentioned in 5.12 consists of distinctively Christian teaching (RSV "**the elementary doctrine of Christ**"). Otherwise this verse overlaps considerably in meaning with the first lessons of God's message in 5.12. At the same time, "word," probably in contrast to 5.13, takes on the meaning of "message," that is, the Christian "Good News." **The Christian message**, literally, "the word of Christ," is a message about Christ rather than a message from Christ.[1]

The first lessons may be expressed as "what we were first taught" or "what we first learned." But if the translation "what we first learned" is combined with the **Christian message**, it may be necessary to restructure the relationship by saying "what we first learned about Christ." The meaning of **message** is, of course, combined in the expression "what we first learned."

6.1b-2   **We should not lay again the foundation of turning away from useless works and believing in God; 2 of the teaching about baptisms[d] and the laying on of hands; of the resurrection of the dead and the eternal judgment.**

[d] baptisms; *or* purification ceremonies.

In addition to the general problems discussed in the introduction to this section, these verses contain small problems of text and punctuation of the Greek, though the general sense is clear.

For the problem of punctuation, see the punctuation note in the UBS Greek text. The question is how to arrange the six items which the readers are told they **should not lay again.** These verses use two Greek words for "and," one of which may indicate a closer link than the other. If this clue is followed, the grouping would be as follows:

---

[1] The problem is that the examples of "elementary doctrines of Christ" given in 6.2 have nothing specifically Christian about them. For example, as the TEV footnote shows, the word for "baptisms" in the plural may not refer to Christian baptism, which took place once for all, but to Jewish purification ceremonies. The "elementary doctrines" are unlikely to be the teaching of Jesus during his earthly life. Perhaps "Christ" in this context has the wider meaning "Messiah," so that the "elementary teaching about the Messiah" could be partly, perhaps even entirely, Jewish teaching, which the readers would have received before they became Christian.

> turning away from dead works
> and faith in God

> baptisms and the laying on of hands and the resurrection of the dead
> and the eternal judgment.

However, it is much safer to follow the meaning of the various expressions rather than rely on a small difference in the Greek. If the meaning is followed, the grouping is clearly:

> turning away from dead works, and faith in God
> baptisms and the laying on of hands
> the resurrection of the dead and the eternal judgment.

The first pair refers to the past, the second perhaps more to worship in the present, and the third to the future.

Most translations keep the metaphor of **lay . . . the foundation,** but GeCL gives the meaning in a nonfigurative way: "So we do not want to deal once more with elementary concepts"; TNT "We have already taught you the fundamental things and we need not do it again." There are not many languages in which one can keep the figurative expression **"laying again a foundation"** (RSV), since a "foundation" normally has nothing to do with "elementary teaching" or "basic facts." It is possible to render **we should not lay again the foundation** as "we should not again talk about the first lessons," or ". . . what you must first learn," or ". . . what you first had to learn."

Turning away is a figure of speech for what is traditionally translated **"repentance,"** a complete change of mind and direction in life. However, in current English the word "repentance" is little used outside church circles, and "repentance from" something (rather than "for" past sins) is less natural than **turning away from.** The translation should, however, make it clear that the **turning away** is both inward and outward; that is, it affects both thought and action.

The foundation mentioned in verse 1b is explained as consisting of two elements, namely, **turning away from useless works** and **believing in God.** If **foundation** is translated as "first lessons" or "initial teaching," then the teaching consists of the same two elements; in other words, repentance and faith.

The phrase **turning away from** may be expressed as "no longer performing," or "no longer being involved in," or "refusing to do any longer."

"Dead works" may be (a) **useless works** (so FrCL), actions, or a way of life which does not win God's favor; or (b) "a life which leads to death" (GeCL "conduct which leads to death"; similarly TNT, DuCL, SpCL, Phps, Brc). 9.14 suggests that the "dead works" are not only useless, but that they make someone unclean, as contact with a dead body would do.

Useless works may be expressed as "what one does which does no good" or "the way in which one lives which is of no help." If, however, one adopts the meaning of "behavior which leads to death," it may be possible to speak of "the way in which one lives which results in death" or ". . . which causes one's death." This death, however, is essentially a spiritual death, and therefore it may be possible to speak of "which causes death to one's spirit."

RSV's "**faith toward God**" is awkward in English but shows that it is the opposite of turning away from "**dead works.**" GeCL has "and turning to God," implying trust in or reliance on him. **Believing in God** is the second part of the **foundation** or "first lessons." It may be necessary to render **believing in God** as "how we should believe in God" or "what trusting in God really means."

A textual problem affects the word translated **teaching.** Most manuscripts, like the UBS Greek text, have "of teaching," but two early manuscripts do not have the form corresponding to "of." This would mean that the "foundations" and the "teaching" were the same. It would probably also suggest that the "teaching" is not just about **baptisms**, but about **the laying on of hands, the resurrection of the dead,** and **the eternal judgment** as well. TEV, like RSV and most translations, agrees with the UBS Greek New Testament.

TEV's **the** before **teaching about baptisms, laying on of hands,** etc. is not in the Greek. It is added because **the** is natural in English, where a noun such as **teaching** is qualified by a phrase such as **about baptisms,** and partly in order to suggest that these subjects are already familiar to the readers. However, this is the first time that these matters have been mentioned in this passage. Except for **believing in God** (compare 4.2), this is also the first time these doctrines have been mentioned in the whole letter. Therefore there is some advantage in treating them all as "new information." This would be done by omitting **the** in English.

Teaching is probably not only about baptism (KJV "the doctrine of baptisms") but also about baptism and laying on of hands, as well as about resurrection and judgment also. Since the teaching is also a part of the foundation, it may be necessary to make this clear: "this foundation involves the teaching about . . ." or "these first lessons include teaching about . . . ."

For many readers, the plural **baptisms** is puzzling, since in the church today there is only one rite which is called baptism, and people are not usually baptized more than once. Knox's "different kinds of baptism" and TNT's "various baptisms" (see also TNT's Translational Note) show the reader that there is a problem but do not give him the information he needs to solve it. SpCL and Phps avoid the problem by translating "baptism." This, though clear, is perhaps not enough to give the meaning without a note. (See Note[1] on page 109, and compare 10.22.) The plural **baptisms** may refer simply to multiple events of people being baptized. If it is understood in this collective sense, the translation "baptism" could be used, since the phrase "teaching about baptism" would certainly imply a number of persons being baptized. However, if the plural designates various purification ceremonies (see the footnote in TEV, GeCL), it would be possible to give the meaning of "rituals for purifying people."

The laying on of hands is a traditional phrase still used by most modern translations. SpCL has the rather heavy phrase "the ceremony of laying the hands on believers," which makes it clear that **the laying on of hands** is linked with baptism, not, as elsewhere in the New Testament, with ordination or healing. If there is any danger that the phrase could be wrongly understood as meaning ordination, the translator should consider giving the correct information in a footnote or glossary note. More simply, "in baptism" could be added in the text of the translation.

A literal translation of **the laying on of hands** could be badly misinterpreted, since in some languages this is a common expression for arresting someone. It may therefore be necessary to use some such qualification as "ceremony involving laying on of hands," or even "ceremony of blessing by putting hands on someone," or ". . . by putting hands on believers."

Resurrection is literally "rising again," but the action of God is implied. FrCL has a glossary note. It may be necessary to repeat a reference to teaching when mentioning **the resurrection of the dead.** Because the teaching involves a whole series of elements, this part of verse 2 may be introduced as "also teaching about the fact that the dead will rise," or ". . . the dead will come back to life," or ". . . will live again."

The word translated **judgment** may refer either to the process of judging or to the verdict itself. In this verse it is clearly the verdict which is **eternal** in the sense of remaining valid forever. Knox has "our sentence in eternity"; "for eternity" would also be possible. In 10.27 and elsewhere in the New Testament, stress is laid on the negative aspect of judgment as condemnation, but this is not the case here or in 9.14.

The phrase **the eternal judgment** may require considerable expansion if the essential components of meaning are to be clearly indicated. It may even be necessary to specify that this is also part of **the teaching;** for example, "the teaching about how God will pass judgment on people and how his verdict will always remain" or "the teaching how God's judgment of people will always remain just that way."

6.3   **Let us go forward! And this is what we will do, if God allows.**

Let us go forward! is not in the Greek text, but it is repeated from verse 1 to make it clear what **this** is what **we will do.** NEB has "Instead, let us advance towards maturity." As already noted in the discussion of verse 1, the expression **Let us go forward** cannot always be translated literally, since it may not imply progress. It would be possible to say "Let us become mature Christians" or "Let us become more complete Christians."

This is what we will do translates a more probable Greek text than the RSV footnote "let us do this." Other ways of understanding the expression for "this we will do" are grammatically possible: (a) "I may go back and give you elementary teaching some other time, if God allows me to do so"; or (b) "God alone can allow me to introduce you into the deeper mysteries of the faith." The immediate context makes (a) unlikely, since verse 4 emphasizes the impossibility of beginning all over again. The wider context, especially chapter 7, makes (b) unlikely as well.

Literal translations such as RSV are ambiguous. **If God allows** (see 1 Cor 4.19; James 4.15) does not mean "if God lets me go on teaching you," but "if God allows us to go forward together." **We** includes author and readers. **If God allows** may be rendered as "if God permits this" or "if this is what God wants."

4 For how can those who abandon their faith be brought back to repent again? They were once in God's light; they tasted heaven's gift and received their share of the Holy Spirit; 5 they knew from experience that God's word is good, and they had felt the powers of the coming age. 6 And then they abandoned their faith! It is impossible to bring them back to repent again, because they are again crucifying the Son of God and exposing him to public shame.

4 For it is impossible to restore again to repentance those who have once been enlightened, who have tasted the heavenly gift, and have become partakers of the Holy Spirit, 5 and have tasted the goodness of the word of God and the powers of the age to come, 6 if they then commit apostasy, since they crucify the Son of God on their own account and hold him up to contempt.

These verses resemble the even stronger statement in 10.26-31. They form a single sentence in Greek, as in RSV. In dividing the sentence, TEV introduces some repetition between the first part of verses 4 and 6. So does GeCL, which numbers verses 4-6 together.

The climax comes in verse 6a, which TEV emphasizes by making it a short, separate sentence and by using an exclamation mark: **And then they abandoned their faith!** However, the tense of the Greek verb is present, "abandon." On the one hand the writer does not state absolutely that such people exist, though this is strongly implied. He states only that it is impossible to bring any such people back to repentance. On the other hand, RSV's "if" in verse 6 is perhaps too weak. Phps chooses a correct though rather heavy middle way: "When you find men who have been enlightened . . . and who then fall away, it proves impossible to make them repent as they did at first." The writer is not putting forward an abstract theory, nor is he taking on himself God's responsibility of making a final judgment on any individual. He is pointing out the danger that if the readers do not go forward (verses 1,3), they may permanently lose their faith in Christ. God's activity is implied throughout.

6.4   For how can those who abandon their faith be brought back to repent again? They were once in God's light; they tasted heaven's gift and received their share of the Holy Spirit;

It is impossible (verse 6 in TEV) begins the sentence in Greek (compare RSV). It is a strong expression which is used also in 6.18; 10.4; 11.6. The writer does not say for whom it is impossible. The implication is that it is impossible not only for man but even for God. In some languages it may be better to translate "No one can bring them back." In Greek the sentence is a statement, not a rhetorical question as in TEV. TEV introduces a question in verse 4, perhaps to avoid word-for-word repetition with verse 6.

Languages vary greatly in the extent to which they use rhetorical questions in ordinary speech or writing (see the comment on 1.5). Among European common language translations, only FrCL follows TEV in introducing a question here. In the case of languages which do not normally use rhetorical questions to express strong doubt, it may be necessary to modify the question **for how can those who abandon their faith be brought back to repent again?** and make it a negative statement; for example, "Those who abandon their faith cannot be brought back to the point of repenting again." This is a kind of summary statement which anticipates much which occurs later in verses 4-6.

Abandon their faith may be expressed as "cease believing" or "cease to trust in Christ." And **be brought back to repent** may be expressed as "cause to repent again."

They were once in God's light: "God's" is implied. As **once** emphasizes, these words refer, not to a state, but to a single event, probably baptism; FrCL "they once received God's light"; compare TNT; Brc "once people have been enlightened." The meaning is similar to after the truth has been made known to us in 10.26; see also 10.32. **Once** and once and for all are favorite words in Hebrews; see 9.7,26,27,28; 10.2,12; 12.26,27.

Though the concept of "light" is often related to moral truth, this is not so in all languages. In some languages a literal rendering of **They were once in God's light** might simply mean that they were standing in the sunlight. An equivalent might be "They once recognized God's truth" or ". . . the truth that comes from God," or "They once acknowledged the message from God as being true."

They tasted heaven's gift: the metaphor changes from light to food. Both are basic human experiences, and most translations keep the metaphors. They may be replaced if necessary by equivalent metaphors or by literal expressions; Brc "experience the heavenly gift"; similarly NEB. "Heaven" is a stylistic variant for "God." TNT has a more general expression, "They have experienced God's generosity"; DuCL, GeCL have "gifts." The writer seems to refer to a particular gift received from God at the beginning of the Christian life. Indeed, this whole passage refers to specific events, so **heaven's gift** or "God's gift" is better. This phrase is closely linked with **They were once in God's light,** and **once** may apply to both phrases: "They once received God's light and tasted his gift." The **gift,** like the **light,** is probably associated with baptism, but it is the commentator's task, not the translator's, to say what the gift is.

The Holy Spirit (compare 2.4) has a glossary note in GeCL, since it is an expression largely limited to church use. It may be necessary to translate "God's Holy Spirit" in languages where "Holy Spirit" alone would be misunderstood or not understood at all. In several parts of the New Testament, it is said that individual Christians receive different gifts from the Holy Spirit, but this is not emphasized here. The writer simply states that believers receive the Holy Spirit together, in common with one another. In much the same way, the writer said in 5.12 that young Christians "live on" milk. Mft's "participated in" or NAB's "become sharers in" therefore seems slightly better here than **received their share of** (DuCL) or "a share of" (JB, Brc, TNT). GeCL and Phps have simply "received the Holy Spirit." A literal translation of **received their share of the Holy Spirit** might wrongly suggest that the Holy Spirit is a substance which can be divided up and be distributed to believers. This implication may be avoided by translating "they together with others received the Holy Spirit."

6.5   **they knew from experience that God's word is good, and they had felt the powers of the coming age.**

TEV finds "tasted God's good word" a less natural metaphor than "tasting God's gift" in verse 4 and replaces it, as do some other translations, by the non-figurative **knew from experience that God's word is good.** "Taste" in English can have the weak meaning "eat only a small amount of," but this is not the meaning of the Greek, either here or in 2.9, where the same verb is used (see RSV). The meaning is rather that of Psalm 34.8, find out for yourself.

Word is not the same Greek term as either of those used in 5.12 and 5.13. The term used here usually means a spoken word, but may have been chosen simply for variety. The context shows that it means, not the Old Testament, but Christian teaching, which at this time would be handed on largely, though not entirely, by word of mouth. **God's word** is here "the message from God" rather than "the message about God." However, **God's word** is closely linked with **the powers of the coming age.** "Word," especially **God's word,** is commonly thought of in the Bible as active and powerful (compare 4.12). The writer may be remembering what Jesus said about the kingdom or kingly rule of God, as in Mark 1.15, or the power of the Holy Spirit just mentioned, or both.

It is rare that one can preserve the biblical figurative language of "tasting God's good word," and therefore some other expression is usually required. **They knew from experience that God's word is good** is one possibility, or more idiomatically "they felt in their hearts that God's word is good." Similarly, **God's word is good** may be rendered as "what God has said is good."

The translator should avoid any expression for **the coming age** which would suggest a time wholly in the future, for this would contradict the meaning of the past tense in "tasted" or **knew from experience.** KJV's "world to come" is misleading because the "kingdom" is a period of time, not a place.

A literal translation of **they had felt the powers of the coming age** is in danger of being radically misinterpreted or utterly obscure. Without any further qualification, **powers of the coming age** could very well be interpreted as "demonic powers" or "powers associated with evil spirits," especially if this is related directly to a verb of sensory feeling.

There is an additional difficulty involved in rendering **the coming age,** since in most languages a period of time does not "come"; it simply "happens." A literal rendering of **the coming age** or even "the age that is happening" could still be exceedingly obscure, since it would have no relationship to the rule of God. It may therefore be wise to translate **they had felt the powers of the coming age** as "they had experienced the power of the time when God is beginning to rule" or ". . . the power associated with the time when God rules."

6.6   **And then they abandoned their faith! It is impossible to bring them back to repent again, because they are again crucifying the Son of God and exposing him to public shame.**

And then they abandoned their faith is the climax of these verses (though **abandoned** is not the main verb in the Greek). **Abandoned their faith** in Christ probably suggests disloyalty or betrayal, like **exposing him to public shame.** GeCL has "turns his back to God"; FrCL "fall back into an evil life." The Greek verb is a stronger compound of the word for "fall" used in 3.17, where TEV correctly translates _fell down dead_. Though 6.6 does not refer to physical death, the loss of faith is considered just as fatal. Any suggestion of merely tripping or stumbling should therefore be avoided in translation. See also Sirach 2.7, in a similar context.

If one follows the order suggested by the TEV text, the rendering of **And then they abandoned their faith** will reflect what is employed in the first part of verse 4. The same, of course, applies to the expression **bring them back to repent again.** TEV repeats these expressions in order to make verse 6 a separate sentence.

Bring them back to repent again contains repetition for emphasis in the Greek as in the English (back . . . again); literally "again renew them towards repentance"; similarly Brc. On "repentance," see 6.1.

Most translations and some commentators agree with TEV in speaking of **again crucifying,** but the verb may also mean "to crucify up," that is, "to nail up on the cross," an emphatic form of "crucify." The second sense is chosen by Mft, JB, NAB, BJ, NEB.

Translators deal in three main ways with the phrase which RSV translates **"on their own account,"** literally "in" or "by themselves." (a) TEV and some other translations omit it. (b) Some take the meaning "in": Mft "in their own persons"; Phps "in their own souls." (c) Other translations take the meaning "by": NEB "with their own hands"; JB "willfully"; Brc "personally"; TNT "themselves." (d) The phrase may also mean "to their own harm," though this meaning is not chosen by any translation consulted. See comments on 12.3. Meaning (b) would be that the divine gifts and powers just mentioned are destroyed or killed when the one who has received them rejects Christ and loses faith in him. This involves a slight contrast between what happens "in their own persons" and the implied effect on others when Christ is "exposed to public shame." This is an argument against meaning (c), since it seems to go without saying that such a personal act would be "willful." Such apparently pointless emphasis may be the reason for choice (a), omission. Choice (b) is probably best, but (d) is possible.

The figurative meaning of **they are again crucifying the Son of God** must be marked in some languages as a simile; for example, "it is just as if they were again crucifying the Son of God" or "it is just as though they were again nailing the Son of God to a cross." If one adopts meaning (b), it is possible to say "in themselves" or "as far as they themselves are concerned." But this meaning seems presupposed in view of the figurative significance of "crucifying the Son of God." This could only have a so-called spiritual meaning with reference to the individuals themselves.

Exposing him to public shame means either (1) "holding him up as a warning to others," (2) "causing others to look down on Christ," or (3) "causing others to ridicule Christ." Here (2) or (3) fits the context better than (1). Criminals were exposed in this way by being crucified or otherwise punished in public.

7 God blesses the soil which drinks in the rain that often falls on it and which grows plants that are useful to those for whom it is cultivated. 8 But if it grows thorns and weeds, it is worth nothing; it is in danger of being cursed by God and will be destroyed by fire.

7 For land which has drunk the rain that often falls upon it, and brings forth vegetation useful to those for whose sake it is cultivated, receives a blessing from God. 8 But if it bears thorns and thistles, it is worthless and near to being cursed; its end is to be burned.

This little illustration, like Matthew 7.24-27, is divided into two contrasting parts by **But** in verse 8. Part of the contrast, items A 4 and B 2 below, is implied, as the following summary shows:

A	B
1. God blesses the soil that	1. God may curse the ground that
2. drinks in the rain, and	2. (also drinks in the rain, but)
3. grows useful plants	3. grows thorns and weeds.
4. (and prospers).	4. It will be destroyed by fire.

The reader is left to supply perhaps the most important part of the message; it may need to be made explicit in some languages. This implication is that if the readers are not to be destroyed (A 4), they must "drink in" what the writer has to tell them (B 2). The implicit parts of the message are developed in verses 9-12.

6.7   **God blesses the soil which drinks in the rain that often falls on it and which grows plants that are useful to those for whom it is cultivated.**

God blesses the soil may be rendered as "God causes good to the soil" or "God is kind to the soil." It is important to avoid a rendering of **blesses** which would suggest merely some kind of verbal formula or ritual being spoken.

The soil which drinks in the rain uses a figurative meaning of **drinks** which can only rarely be expressed in other languages. One can sometimes employ a phrase such as "the soil which absorbs the rain" or "the soil into which the rain sinks." But frequently one must use some such expression as "the soil into which the rain disappears" or "the soil which becomes moist because of the rain."

Grows plants that are useful to those for whom it is cultivated may also be translated "grows useful plants for those for whom it is cultivated," though the meaning is the same for practical purposes. (Compare no use, Luke 9.62; no good, Luke 14.35). A literal rendering of **which grows plants** might suggest the activity of a person who causes plants to grow, rather than the activity of the soil.

Therefore it may be necessary to translate **which grows plants** as "in which plants grow" or "out of which plants grow." In some instances, however, one can employ a causative expression, "the soil which causes plants to grow larger." **Plants that are useful** may sometimes be rendered as "plants which produce food" or "plants which can be eaten."

To those for whom it is cultivated may be rendered as "for those for whom someone takes care of the plants," or ". . . works the soil," or ". . . prepares the ground."

6.8   But if it grows thorns and weeds, it is worth nothing; it is in danger of being cursed by God and will be destroyed by fire.

The first half of the illustration (verse 7) recalls Genesis 1.11-12, and the second half (verse 8) echoes Genesis 3.17-18. The translator should not attempt to mark the reference by quotation marks, since only isolated words are quoted (such as **grows thorns and weeds** and **cursed**). The meaning of the sentence as a whole is rather different. In Genesis the curse makes the ground infertile; here, God curses the ground because it is infertile.

It is impossible to be scientifically certain which species of plants are referred to as **thorns and weeds** (see *Fauna and Flora of the Bible*, pages 184-186). **Weeds** are probably some kind of thistle. The point is that, far from being useful (verse 7), they interfere with desirable plants. The translator should feel free to use the names of any plants in his area which meet this condition.

If it grows thorns and weeds must be restructured in some languages as "if thorns and weeds grow in it."

It is worth nothing may be expressed as "it produces nothing," "it has no value," or even "no one wants it."

TEV and some other translations include a slight contradiction which may cause misunderstanding: the words **in danger of being cursed** are followed by the more definite **and will be destroyed by fire.** There is no contradiction in the text. It means either (a) that the land is about to be cursed and then finally burned (**will be** is implied) or (b) more probably, as GeCL puts it, that the land is "under the threat of being cursed by God and finally burned."

By God is implied.

In danger of being cursed by God may be rendered as "is near to being cursed by God" or "God is likely to curse it." The final passive expression **will be destroyed by fire** may be expressed actively as "fire will destroy it." There may, however, be a difficulty involved in suggesting that fire will destroy soil. In a sense, of course, this is a mixed figure of speech, since the text is in reality speaking about divine judgment of persons.

| TEV | **6.9-12** | RSV |

9 But even if we speak like this, dear friends, we feel sure about you. We know that you have the better blessings that belong to your salvation. 10 God is not unfair. He will not forget the work you did or the love you showed for him in the help you gave and are still giving to your fellow Christians. 11 Our great desire is that each one of you keep up his eagerness to the end, so that the things you hope for will come true. 12 We do not want you to become lazy, but to be like those who believe and are patient, and so receive what God has promised.

9 Though we speak thus, yet in your case, beloved, we feel sure of better things that belong to salvation. 10 For God is not so unjust as to overlook your work and the love which you showed for his sake in serving the saints, as you still do. 11 And we desire each one of you to show the same earnestness in realizing the full assurance of hope until the end, 12 so that you may not be sluggish, but imitators of those who through faith and patience inherit the promises.

The introduction to this Handbook, "Translating the Letter to the Hebrews," notes how smoothly the writer passes from one subject to another. It is difficult at times to decide where divisions are to be made. The writer often makes these smooth transitions with the help of what may be called "foreground" and "background" features. The translator needs to be aware of these if he is to avoid distorting the message as a whole. Hebrews 6.9-20 is a good example of this.

(a) It is generally true that verses 9-12 complete the appeal for action which began at 5.11, and that verses 13-20 begin a new section of teaching, which continues until 10.18.

(b) Within this general pattern, the writer's confidence in his readers is the main foreground feature of verses 9-12, and God's sure promise and vow are in the foreground of verses 13-20.

(c) However, verses 9-20, taken together, contain vital background features which link them with much that has already been said, and (at least by implication) with practically all that is to come. From the viewpoint of this passage, the essentials of the rest of the letter can be summed up as follows:

God made a firm promise to his people which was the foundation of the covenant generally (chapter 9) and of all its forms of worship and sacrifice (chapter 10). None of the Old Testament heroes, despite their faith, received what God promised (chapter 11); but Jesus, a High Priest of a different kind (chapter 8), like Melchizedek (chapter 7), has made it possible for us to receive it. So we must hold on to our faith in him (chapter 12) and put it into practice (chapter 13).

6.9   **But even if we speak like this, dear friends, we feel sure about you. We know that you have the better blessings that belong to your salvation.**

Until now, this section has been mainly a warning. TEV is right to mark the change of mood by putting **even if we speak like this** at the beginning of the sentence (contrast with KJV, which follows the Greek order). GeCL achieves the same result in a different way: "But for you, dear friends, we are confident, even when we speak so severely." **Even if we speak like this** may have to be rendered as "even if we write to you like this" or ". . . write to you with words like these."

On the whole, Hebrews does not seem to be a very personal letter, but these verses contain several signs that the writer cares deeply for his readers: **dear friends** here, and **great desire** and **each one of you** in verse 11. These expressions have all the greater impact because they are unusual in the Greek. Translations should reflect this by using emphatic language. Great desire is even stronger in Greek than in English.

Dear friends may be rendered as "friends whom I truly love," or even "you who are indeed my friends."

The passage makes it clear that the writer is distinguishing himself from his readers: **we** means "I" (so Mft, Syn).

We feel sure about you may be expressed as "I have confidence in you," but it is also possible to render this as a negative statement, namely, "I do not worry about you."

What are **the better blessings**, literally "better things"? The text does not say explicitly, and translations vary widely. The possibilities are as follows:

(a) "You are in a better state or situation" than that of the infertile land just mentioned; so perhaps Brc "you still possess the necessities of salvation"; TNT "You know what is good" (but "You know" is not in the text); and TOB, rather vaguely, "you are on the good side"; see also NEB.

(b) "You will take the better course," Mft, similarly FrCL; Phps "you . . . are capable of better things"; Fulfulde "you are on the good way, the way of salvation."

(c) **You have the better blessings** (compare blesses in verse 7), SpCL.

(d) "We have better confidence," Knox; Lu.

(e) "We are sure that you will be saved," GeCL.

(f) "The best is stored away for you: salvation," DuCL.

Possibilities (a) and (b) are similar, but (b) is more idiomatic, and makes a better link with "your salvation"; (c) introduces a comparison between different blessings which is not found elsewhere in the letter; (d) is not the most natural meaning of the Greek; (e) oversimplifies an admittedly difficult sentence; (f) identifies the "better things" with salvation, which leads to interpreting "better" as "best." On the whole, (b) seems the best solution; it fits in well with the general movement of the writer's thought as summarized in the diagram at the beginning of Chapter 6 of this Handbook.

If one adopts the rendering suggested by TEV, **the better blessings** may be represented by "that better way in which God has blessed you," or "the more important ways in which God has blessed you."

The final clause **that belong to your salvation** may be expressed as "this has to do with your being saved" or "this is involved in God saving you." The clause **that belong to your salvation** is in apposition with **the better blessings**. If, on the other hand, one adopts rendering (b), one may translate the second sentence of verse 9 as "we know that you will go that better way which leads to your salvation" or ". . . which involves God saving you."

6.10   **God is not unfair. He will not forget the work you did or the love you showed for him in the help you gave and are still giving to your fellow Christians.**

In place of the double negative **not unfair,** it may be best to use a positive expression; for example, "God is always just" or "God is always fair in judging."

"**Overlook**" (RSV) and **forget** are similar in meaning. **Forget** would be an example of speaking of God in terms usually used in speaking of human beings. The meaning is positive, that is to say, God will take notice or take account of the good work which the readers have done (compare Matt 25.31-46, especially verse 45). GeCL rearranges the sentence as follows: "He does not forget what you have done. You have helped other Christians and still do. In this way you show your love for him." There is no difference in meaning between TEV's **the work . . . or the love** and RSV's more literal "**your work and the love.**" **Or** is used naturally in English to link the two things which God **will not forget.**

The expression **He will not forget** also involves a type of double negative. Therefore it may be better to render the expression **he will not forget** as "he will certainly remember" or "he will always take notice of."

The work you did may be expressed as "what you did." The expression **the love you showed for him in the help you gave** may be interpreted as being synonymous with the first expression, namely, **the work you did.** Hence, **the work you did or the love you showed for him** may be rendered as "the work you did, that is to say, the love you showed for him . . . ."

For him gives the meaning of what is literally "for his name"; in biblical terms the name and the person are the same.

The love you showed for him may be expressed as "the way you showed him how you loved him" or "the way in which you showed others how you loved God."

Help is a dynamic equivalent of the literal "serve," since the Greek cannot mean that those who served were of lower status than those who were served. Nor is the writer thinking of the group of people, later called "deacons," whose special task was to give practical help (see Acts 6.1-6; 1 Tim 3.8-13).

The final part of verse 10, namely, **in the help you gave and are still giving to your fellow Christians,** may indicate the means by which the love was shown; for example, "by what you did to help and what you are still doing to help your fellow Christians."

"**Saints**" in the New Testament are not individuals of outstanding holiness, but the entire Christian community, set apart to belong to God (see comments on 3.1; also Acts 9.32; Rom 15.25-26). This is expressed by TEV's **your fellow Christians** (**your** is implied), which may be rendered as "your fellow believers" or "those who trust Christ even as you do." NEB has "his [God's] people"; GeCL "other Christians."

[121]

6.11   Our great desire is that each one of you keep up his eagerness
to the end, so that the things you hope for will come true.

Our great desire must in most languages be expressed by a verb; for example, "We desire greatly" or "We desire very much." **Our** really represents the
desire of the writer and therefore may be translated as "I desire very much."

As can be seen from RSV, this verse repeats the Greek word for "show"
from verse 10 and uses it to make a comparison. **"The same earnestness"** (eagerness, keenness) may imply (a) "be as earnest in the future as you have been in the
past" or (b) "be as earnest in your hope as you have been in your work of love."
The first alternative is simpler, since the writer has just stated that the help they
have been giving belongs to their salvation and is pleasing to God.

To the end comes at the end of the verse in Greek and is therefore emphasized. NEB does this by expansion: "until your hope is finally realized."

In a number of languages it is impossible to speak of **to the end** without
indicating what end is involved. Here, **the end** may mean either the end of the age
or the end of the readers' lives. 11.40 suggests that the writer may not have
separated the two events. In many languages it is necessary to choose either the
end of the age or the end of their lives. Sometimes it is possible to employ a
rather general phrase such as "until the time you reach your goal." This figurative
substitute may be justified in view of the obscurity of the text itself.

That each one of you keep up his eagerness to the end may be restructured
as "that each one of you continue to be eager until the end."

In 10.22, RSV's "assurance" means "confidence" (TEV has sure) and is close
in meaning to the word which TEV translates confidence in 3.6, brave in 4.16,
complete freedom in 10.19, and courage in 10.35. Here, however, the word may
mean "fullness," and **hope** may stand for "what you hope for." This would give the
meaning "show the same eagerness to the end, with a view to receiving the full
measure of what you hope for." This fits in well, both with the immediate context
(see the next verse) and with the underlying theme discussed at the beginning of
section 6.9-12.

The things you hope for may be expressed as "what you wait for patiently
and with desire" or "the good which you wait for with patience." The Greek term
for **hope** has the important components of patience, waiting for, and the expectation of something good.

6.12   We do not want you to become lazy, but to be like those who
believe and are patient, and so receive what God has promised.

On **lazy,** see 5.11, where TEV has **slow to understand.** **Lazy** fits better
here, where the context deals more with behavior than with thought, but the two
ideas are not sharply separated.

The Greek term rendered **lazy** in TEV is in bold contrast with the Greek
term rendered eagerness in verse 11. There the emphasis is upon the author's
great desire for the people to be eager, and this is expressed negatively at the

beginning of verse 12 as **We do not want you to become lazy** or "I do not want you to become lazy." The term **lazy** may be expressed as "not wanting to do anything" or "not wanting to work."

On "**faith**" or **believe**, see 4.2-3.

But to be like those who believe involves the kind of contrast that may require the repetition of a verb meaning **want**; for example, "but I do want you to be like those who believe" or ". . . trust Christ."

Patient is similar in meaning to a word which TEV in 12.1 translates determination (where JB and Brc have "perseverance"). The main idea is that of holding on to the end, but chapter 12 shows that resistance to persecution is also involved. The emphasis here of "holding on to the end" refers to the nature of what is hoped for, and therefore **patient** may be expressed as "patient (or, steady) in continuing to hope." On the other hand, **patient** may be expressed negatively as "they do not give up."

The key concept of this verse is **receive**. In Greek the word is less common than in English. Most translations use either a present tense, such as **receive**, "are now taking possession" (TNT), or a future tense, "will receive what God has promised" (GeCL, similarly Knox). If a present tense is used, the meaning must be "imitate those who are showing great faith and patience, because that is how they are receiving what God promised," but this does not seem very natural; see comments on 1.4. The meaning is probably "those who have entered and are still in possession of what God promised," or more simply, "those who have received what God promised" (Phps "came to possess the promises"). This fits in very well with the following statement on Abraham's faith and its reward, and it prepares the way for a fuller treatment of the same theme in chapter 11.

And so receive may be expressed as "and in this way they receive" or "and by doing this they receive." Or one may use a perfective tense, "and by means of this they have received."

The traditional translation, "**inherit the promises**" (RSV) may be criticized from three points of view: (a) There is no suggestion in this context of inheriting property by the will of someone who has died. (b) What is "received" is not here the promise itself, but the thing promised. (c) The text implies that God is the one who promises, and this needs to be made clear. See comments on 1.2.

What God has promised may be amplified as "what God has promised to give to them."

TEV	**6.13-20**	RSV

God's Sure Promise

13 When God made his promise to Abraham, he made a vow to do what he had promised. Since there was no one greater than himself, he used his own name when he made his vow. 14 He said, "I promise you that I will bless you

13 For when God made a promise to Abraham, since he had no one greater by whom to swear, he swore by himself, 14 saying, "Surely I will bless you and multiply you." 15 And thus Abraham,^{m} having patiently endured, obtained the

and give you many descendants."
15 Abraham was patient, and so he received what God had promised.
16 When a person makes a vow, he uses the name of someone greater than himself, and the vow settles all arguments. 17 To those who were to receive what he promised God wanted to make it very clear that he would never change his purpose; so he added his vow to the promise. 18 There are these two things, then, that cannot change and about which God cannot lie. So we who have found safety with him are greatly encouraged to hold firmly to the hope placed before us. 19 We have this hope as an anchor for our lives. It is safe and sure, and goes through the curtain of the heavenly temple into the inner sanctuary. 20 On our behalf Jesus has gone in there before us and has become a high priest forever, in the priestly order of Melchizedek.[x]

promise. 16 Men indeed swear by a greater than themselves, and in all their disputes an oath is final for confirmation. 17 So when God desired to show more convincingly to the heirs of the promise the unchangeable character of his purpose, he interposed with an oath, 18 so that through two unchangeable things, in which it is impossible that God should prove false, we who have fled for refuge might have strong encouragement to seize the hope set before us. 19 We have this as a sure and steadfast anchor of the soul, a hope that enters into the inner shrine behind the curtain, 20 where Jesus has gone as a forerunner on our behalf, having become a high priest for ever after the order of Melchizedek.

[m] Greek he

[x] in the priestly order of Melchizedek (see 5.6).

The section heading in TEV, namely, **God's Sure Promise,** may be rendered as "What God promises is certain" or ". . . will surely happen."

The statement about the danger of losing one's Christian faith in verses 4-8 is balanced by this equally strong statement about the reliability of God's promise (compare 4.1-10). The writer suggests in verse 20 what he begins to state more fully in chapter 7, that this promise has come true in Christ.

This passage illustrates the writer's method of arguing from scripture. It is similar to that of the Jewish rabbis of his period and later. As in 3.7—4.11, texts from different parts of the Old Testament are drawn into the same argument. The writer assumes that his readers know the context from which the texts are taken. For example, verses 13b-14 quote God's promise to Abraham in Genesis 22.17, but verse 13a assumes that the readers know Genesis 22.16, "By myself I have sworn" (RSV). If the readers of the translation are not likely to know this, readers' helps may be needed to give additional information.

6.13 **When God made his promise to Abraham, he made a vow to do what he had promised. Since there was no one greater than himself, he used his own name when he made his vow.**

Virtually all translations expand the text, which is literally "When God promised to Abraham." God is emphasized in the Greek by being placed at the end of the phrase.

Translators in European languages expand the text in three main ways: (a) "**made a promise**" (RSV, TNT); (b) "made the promise" (TEV first through third editions, JB, FrCL, SpCL); (c) **made his promise** (TEV fourth edition, NAB, Phps, Brc, NEB, TOB). The writer's main concern is to stress by every possible means that God's promise cannot be broken because he confirmed it by an oath. (b) and (c) therefore seem better than (a), and **his promise** is clearer and more specific than "the promise."

Made refers to a particular event in time, that is, the event recorded in Genesis 22.16-17.

In a number of languages **promise** can only be expressed as a verb, not as a noun, and therefore **when God made his promise to Abraham** may be translated as "When God promised something to Abraham" or "When God declared that he would give something to Abraham."

A vow: vows and oaths are distinct in the Bible, and neither is to be confused with cursing or general bad language. The equivalent of **vow** is often "to make a promise by calling God to witness" or "to use strong words in the presence of God." Obviously this formula cannot be used in this context, since God vows on the basis of his own name. Sometimes the most appropriate equivalent for **he made a vow to do what he had promised** is "he used strong words when he said he would do what he had promised." In some instances the only apparent equivalent is "he said that he would most certainly do what he had promised."

"**He had no one greater by whom to swear**" is the word-for-word rendering on which most translations are based, but Mft translates "since he could swear by none greater." **No one greater** may also mean "nothing greater" (GeCL), which is more inclusive, but the personal expression **no one** is more appropriate here.

Since there was no one greater than himself may be expressed as "Since no one was more powerful than himself." In some instances **greater** needs to be expressed in terms of authority, "since no one has greater authority than God himself."

The phrase **used his own name** (literally, "**by himself**," RSV) is emphasized and is the only part of the quotation on which the author comments. "**He swore by himself**" (RSV) is in fact part of the quotation, but it is not desirable to show this by double quotation marks, since the author makes these words part of his own sentence.

He used his own name when he made his vow may be almost meaningless if translated literally, since "name" may not be a substitute for someone's personality or reputation. Sometimes **he used his own name** may be rendered as "he exposed his own reputation" or "he offered himself as a witness." In some cases the process of vowing on the basis of one's own self may be rendered as "he declared that he himself would bear all the blame if he did not do what he had promised."

6.14   **He said, "I promise you that I will bless you and give you many descendants."**

The Greek is more emphatic than TEV; compare NEB "I vow that I will bless you . . . ." Ways of emphasizing statements vary from one language to another. The text uses a strong "indeed" or **"surely"** (RSV) at the beginning of the quotation, followed by an idiomatic repetition for emphasis as reflected in KJV, "blessing I will bless thee, and multiplying I will multiply thee." Such an expression is unnatural in English, as it is unnatural in Greek outside the Bible.

I promise you that I will bless you may seem rather strange in some languages if translated literally, since the declaration of blessing is itself the promise. It is in fact the certainty of the promise which is emphasized, and therefore an equivalent expression in some instances is "I will most surely bless you."

Give you many descendants may have to be rendered as a causative; for example, "cause you to have many descendants" or, more specifically, "cause you to have many children and grandchildren."

6.15   Abraham was patient, and so he received what God had promised.

This verse is linked to its context by the words **and so** (RSV "and thus"). They suggest, not merely the manner in which Abraham received the promises, but the means by which he received them. Most translations agree with TEV in taking the sentence to mean "It was because he was patient [or "endured"; see verse 12] that Abraham received what God had promised." JB, however, translates "because of that," implying the opposite: "It was because of God's promise [see verses 13-14] that Abraham was patient and saw the promise fulfilled." This is grammatically possible, but verses 12 and 15 have so much in common that it is natural to take verse 12 as a general principle which verse 15 applies to the particular case of Abraham. Abraham's patience was not just a stage in time (NAB "after patient waiting"); it played an essential part in his finally receiving what God had promised.

Abraham was patient may be expressed as "Abraham was willing to wait." It may in some cases be necessary to say "Abraham kept on trusting God for a long time."

The Greek term for **received** is a more common equivalent of the word translated receive in verse 12. As usual, the writer varies his choice of words. A strictly literal rendering of **received** may be misleading, since it might wrongly suggest that the promise was an object which God handed to Abraham. A better equivalent may be "what God had promised Abraham happened to him."

What God had promised (literally "the promise"), here as in verse 12, refers not to the act of promising but to the content of what was promised. The reference is either to Isaac's birth or to his rescue from death (Gen 22). The word translated **received** therefore refers to a single past event, unlike the same expression in 11.13,39, which refers to receiving forever what God had promised.

6.16   **When a person makes a vow, he uses the name of someone greater than himself, and the vow settles all arguments.**

Verses 16-17 illustrate a method of argument often used in Jewish writings as well as in other cultures: If "B" is greater than "A," then anything said about "A" must be even more true of "B" (compare 10.25; 12.25; Matt 6.30; Rom 5.7-9). In particular, anything good said about human beings must be even more true of God.

A person is emphatic and general; literally "people," whether men or women. As in verse 13, the Greek for **someone** may also mean "something" (Knox, JB, Seg, TOB). Some commentators think this means "God," but Matthew 23.16-22, for example, speaks of swearing by inanimate objects. The contrast is between God swearing by himself (verse 13b) and human beings swearing (verse 16). It may be helpful to make this clear by inserting some such phrase as "human beings, *on the other hand,* use the name of someone greater . . . ."

As in the case of the term **vow** in verse 13, it may not be possible to render **vow** in verse 16 with a somewhat technical formula such as "making a strong promise by calling God to witness." In the context of verse 16 it may therefore be best to translate "when a person makes a firm promise" or ". . . a strong promise," or even "when a person promises with strong words."

The expression **he uses the name of someone greater than himself** may be rendered as "he calls to witness someone greater than himself" or "he makes a promise on behalf of someone greater than himself." In this context **greater** may be a matter either of importance or of authority.

The last phrase of this verse means that, whenever people are contradicting one another, an oath acts as a guarantee and puts an end to the dispute. In this context the oath is a solemn statement such as "I swear by God that what I say is true," rather than a solemn promise to do something in the future. The statement **the vow settles all arguments** must be amplified in some languages in order to make it clear; for example, "one person calls God to witness that something is true, and in this way people no longer argue" or ". . . and because of this people no longer argue."

6.17   **To those who were to receive what he promised God wanted to make it very clear that he would never change his purpose; so he added his vow to the promise.**

The short comparison with what human beings do is over, and the writer goes on speaking about God's oath. It is natural in translation to begin a new sentence here, though verses 16-20 are a single sentence in the Greek. RSV's **"So"** loosely links verse 17 to verse 16, showing that the writer is about to develop the comparison.

What he promised is literally "the promises." The writer is moving beyond the promise made to Abraham and quoted in verse 14; he speaks now of God's

[127]

promise in general, in which the readers have an interest and a share. **What he promised** may be simply "what he had promised the people."

Those who were to receive what he promised is literally "the heirs of the promise." Although the tense of **were to receive** is not expressed in the Greek, there is no doubt that the reference is wholly to the future (contrast verse 12). It includes people of Old Testament times as well as Christians. This is confirmed by the use of we in the next verse.

Verses 17-18 are full of words which emphasize the reliability of God's promise. He wanted to make it clear, and to give proof, that his purpose could not be changed. This can only mean that God would not change his own purpose, so TEV uses an active verb and translates **he would never change his purpose.** This may be expressed as "he would never change his mind as to what he was going to do," or stated positively, "he would always do exactly what he planned to do."

The first part of verse 17 may require certain alterations in order, since those to whom God wished to make the promise clear are identified at the beginning of the sentence. In some languages this reference must occur after the verb or must be stated as a completely separate sentence. For example, one may recast the first part of verse 17 as "God wanted to make very clear to those who were to receive what he promised that he would never change his plans" or ". . . his mind." On the other hand, this rather long, involved sentence may be broken up as follows: "God wanted people to know for sure that he would not change his plans. Those whom he wanted to know this were the persons who were going to receive what he had promised."

So he added his vow to the promise may be expressed as "so he declared with the strongest possible words that he would do what he had promised" or "so he said with binding words that he would most certainly do what he had said he would do."

6.18   There are these two things, then, that cannot change and about which God cannot lie. So we who have found safety with him are greatly encouraged to hold firmly to the hope placed before us.

This verse may not be easy to understand without additional information in a footnote. The **two things** are God's promise and his oath. GeCL makes this explicit. The phrase **these two things** may be obscure if the specific reference is not made clear in translation. It would be possible to translate **There are these two things, then, that cannot change** as "What God promised and what he vowed cannot change" or ". . . cannot ever be different." A positive expression may also be employed: ". . . will most surely happen."

God cannot lie, either about his promise or about his oath, still less about both together; "He wanted to give us a double security" (GeCL). The argument is strange to many readers today, but Isaiah 45.23, for example, shows that anything spoken, especially by God, was believed to take on a life and power of its own, distinct from that of the speaker. The term translated **things** may refer to words, but the author more probably means the event of God promising something to his people.

God cannot lie may be expressed as "God is not able to say what is not true." The double negative, however, may be misleading, and a positive expression may be required: "God must surely say what is true."

We who have found safety with him: translators vary (a) in their understanding of **"we who have fled for refuge"** (RSV), and (b) in the way in which they link it with the rest of the sentence.

(a) Some translations emphasize the idea of running "away from" something: Mft "we refugees"; Knox "to us poor wanderers"; TOB "we who have left everything to seize the hope put before us." This is possible, and in other places salvation includes for this writer the idea of escape. But this idea does not seem so important in this positive passage as if it had come, for example, in 2.3 or 6.4-8. By overtranslating, Phps "we who are refugees from this dying world" shows that it is a new and somewhat unnatural idea here. Most translations therefore agree with TEV in expressing the positive aspect of running "to" God for protection: FrCL "we who have found a refuge in him"; DuCL "we who seek our refuge with him." **With him** is understood.

(b) The Greek may mean either (i) "... so that we who have taken refuge with him may have a strong encouragement to hold fast to the hope which is set before us," or (ii) "... so that we who have fled to hold fast to him may have a strong encouragement in the hope which is set before us." (i) fits in better with the general purpose of the letter, which is to encourage the readers to hold on to and develop the faith in Christ which they already have.

We who have found safety with him may be expressed as "we who have gone to him in order to be safe." In rendering **found,** it is important to avoid an expression which may suggest accidental discovery. It is possible to emphasize certain aspects of this flight to God by translating "we who have run to God in order to be safe."

Greatly encouraged: by God's vow, which gives proof of the reliability of God's promise, just as legal proof in ancient Israel required at least two witnesses to agree (see Deut 19.15; compare Matt 18.16). **We ... are greatly encouraged** may be rendered as "we are all the more sure" or "we become very certain."

Hold firmly may mean either (a) to "hold on to" something you already have, or (b) to "seize" (RSV) or reach out and grasp something you do not yet have. Translations are divided rather evenly: meaning (a), **hold firmly,** is chosen, for example, by TEV, GeCL, TNT, and perhaps by JB ("take a firm grip"). Meaning (b), **"seize,"** is chosen, for example, by RSV, FrCL, Phps ("grasp"), NEB, and BJ ("seize strongly"). The choice depends largely on whether "hope" is thought of as the act of hoping or the thing for which one hopes. In earlier verses, "to receive the promise(s)" is not simply to be given the promise itself, but to be given what was promised. This may apply to "hope" also, in which case meaning (b) would be better. This letter repeatedly insists on the need not only to resist the attacks of evil but to reach out to what the readers do not yet have. Meaning (a) would also involve some repetition with the first part of the verse. For this reason GeCL omits **who have found safety with him,** combining it with **hold firmly.** Meaning (b), slightly expanded, would give "In this way, we who have taken refuge with God have a strong encouragement to reach out and seize what he puts before us as an object of our hope."

Interpretation (a), namely **to hold firmly to the hope placed before us,** may be rendered idiomatically as "to hold close to our hearts the hope that God has placed before us." Interpretation (b) may be translated as "to take into our hearts that hope which is offered to us." In a number of instances **the hope** may need to be expressed as "that for which we wait with eager expectation."

6.19 **We have this hope as an anchor for our lives. It is safe and sure, and goes through the curtain of the heavenly temple into the inner sanctuary.**

The metaphors of **anchor** and **curtain** conflict, because **anchor** is related to the picture of a ship, while **curtain** is related to the Temple. Several translations modify at least one of these metaphors in some way. (a) The simplest way of doing this is to take **hope** rather than **anchor** as the subject of **It is safe** (RSV, GeCL, TNT). This is possible and makes no difference to the basic meaning, since **hope** is compared to an **anchor.** (b) Some English translations weaken the metaphor of the anchor by using related words like "anchoring" (Mft) or "anchorage" (Knox). (c) SpCL expands the translation so as to make the clash of metaphors less abrupt: "This hope keeps our soul firm and secure, as the anchor keeps the boat firm. This anchor which we have is firmly secured behind the curtain of the heavenly temple" (a note is added on "curtain"). (d) In principle it would be possible to replace **anchor** by a nonfigurative expression, especially in cultures where anchors are not used. Here it may be possible to use a nonfigurative expression such as "that which we hope for makes our lives secure" or ". . . causes us to live secure." It would be difficult to replace **curtain,** since this feature of Jewish worship is mentioned again in 9.3 and 10.20, and refers back to Leviticus 16.2-3,12,15.

Of these possibilities, (a) is often the best in translation, though it may not follow the grammatical structure of the original text. Grammatically, the **anchor** must be an image of **hope,** but the author is already thinking of Jesus (verse 20) as the substance or object of this hope, and this may be made explicit if it makes the translation clearer.

We have this hope must be restructured in some languages as "This is what we hope for." The statement about **hope** may then be combined with **anchor** as "This that we hope for is like an anchor for us."

On **our lives** (RSV "the soul"), see comments on "soul" in 4.12. TEV generally avoids "soul," since this word is little used outside religious language.

There is no noticeable difference in meaning between **safe** and **sure.** They are used together for emphasis, but may be combined ("absolutely secure") if this is more natural in the receptor language. Since **safe and sure** refers to **hope,** it is possible to translate **It is safe and sure** as "What we hope for makes us safe and sure" or ". . . causes us to be secure and certain."

Some translations (Mft, JB) mark "enters into the inner shrine behind the curtain" as a quotation (Lev 16.2). **"Shrine"** (RSV) or **sanctuary** is understood. To mark the phrase as a quotation does not seem necessary for such a short phrase, but a cross reference may be useful. Indeed, the **curtain** here is an example of extended meaning rather than a metaphor in the strict sense.

The equivalent for **curtain** is in many languages an expression meaning a "hanging." "Curtain" might be used only of something which is drawn across a window, while a "drape" or "hanging" may be employed across an entrance way, as in Hebrews. See also the comment on 9.3.

The heavenly temple may be rendered as "the temple in heaven," and **the inner sanctuary** may be expressed as "the holy room on the inside," or "the most holy room on the inside of the temple," or "the most holy room in the temple."

It may be meaningless in some languages to speak of "hope going through the curtain of the heavenly temple." This would make no sense, but since the object of the hope is Jesus, one may be justified in making this identification explicit. **And goes through the curtain of the heavenly temple into the inner sanctuary** may be rendered as "and the one in whom we place our hope is Jesus, who goes through the curtain of the heavenly temple into the inner sanctuary."

6.20   **On our behalf Jesus has gone in there before us and has become
a high priest forever, in the priestly order of Melchizedek.^{x}**

^{x} in the priestly order of Melchizedek *(see 5.6).*

On our behalf may be expressed as "For our benefit" or "In order to help us."

This verse brings the reader back to the subject of 5.10 and at the same time introduces chapter 7. RSV's **"forerunner"** also recalls "pioneer" in 2.10; compare RSV 12.2. **Jesus has gone in there** may be made more explicit, depending upon the relationship to the preceding verse; for example, "Jesus has gone into the inner sanctuary."

Before us is not to be understood in the sense of "in our presence" but "ahead of us."

Forever is emphasized in the Greek by a change of order in the words quoted from Psalm 110.4. However, the climax of verses 15-20, a single sentence in Greek, is reached in the word **Jesus.** Few modern translations bring this out as well as KJV "whither the forerunner is for us entered, *even* Jesus . . . ."[2]

The adverb **forever** may be emphasized as "and he will never cease to be a high priest."

The phrase **in the priestly order of Melchizedek** may be rendered as "in the way in which Melchizedek was a priest." See the comments on 5.6,10.

---

[2] Here as elsewhere KJV uses italics, not for emphasis but to mark words not expressed in the original text, though the words are clearly implied.

The ground is now fully prepared for the more advanced teaching mentioned in 6.1-3. The priesthood of Jesus is unique because it belongs to eternity and is therefore permanent and unrepeatable (7.23-28).

Chapter 7

Many commentators believe that chapters 7—9 contain the central message of Hebrews. The wider implications of its theology do not concern the translator directly. It is enough for him to be aware in advance of two related facts:

(a) By his constant references to Old Testament worship, as well as by his methods of argument, the writer shows himself to be, like Paul, "a Hebrew of the Hebrews."

(b) Nevertheless the writer states clearly what he believes to be new in what Christ has done.

These two facts mean for the translator that certain specifically Jewish or Old Testament features may need some expansion, or perhaps some explanation in marginal notes. However, this should not be done in such a way as to overshadow the distinctively Christian elements in the text.

Michel (pages 259, 269) conveniently divides this chapter into seven sections, each with its own key word:

Section	Key Word
(a) what the Bible says about Melchizedek (verses 1-3)	Melchizedek
(b) the giving of the tithe to Melchizedek (verses 4-10)	tithe
(c) the overthrow of the old priesthood (verses 11-14)	order
(d) the abolition of the Law (verses 15-19)	Law
(e) the confirmation by the oath (verses 20-22)	oath
(f) the eternity of the heavenly High Priest (verses 23-25)	forever
(g) the superiority of the heavenly High Priest (verses 26-28)	High Priest

TEV   7.1-3   RSV

The Priest Melchizedek

1 This Melchizedek was king of Salem and a priest of the Most High God. As Abraham was coming back from the battle in which he defeated the four kings, Melchizedek met him and blessed him, 2 and Abraham gave him one tenth of all he had taken. (The first meaning of Melchizedek's name is "King of Righteousness"; and because he was king of Salem, his name also

1 For this Melchizedek, king of Salem, priest of the Most High God, met Abraham returning from the slaughter of the kings and blessed him; 2 and to him Abraham apportioned a tenth part of everything. He is first, by translation of his name, king of righteousness, and then he is also king of Salem, that is, king of peace. 3 He is without father or mother or genealogy,

[133]

means "King of Peace.") 3 There is no record of Melchizedek's father or mother or of any of his ancestors; no record of his birth or of his death. He is like the Son of God; he remains a priest forever. and has neither beginning of days nor end of life, but resembling the Son of God he continues a priest for ever.

If one follows the section heading of TEV, the phrase **The Priest Melchize-dek** may be rendered as "Melchizedek was a priest" or "Melchizedek served God as a priest."

Verses 1-3 are a single complex sentence in the Greek, which RSV divides into three sentences and TEV into five. The writer's purpose is to quote his "text," that is, parts of Genesis 14.17-20, and to add a few preliminary notes on its meaning, much as a Jewish rabbi or sometimes a Christian preacher might do during a reading of scripture. Some translations show by italics the words which are quoted from Genesis. The use of italics or quotation marks is a matter of general principle to be decided for a specific translation as a whole. Common language translations avoid the use of italics in this way, since italics usually indicate emphasis. In this section the quotation is combined with the writer's own words, and so quotation marks are best avoided.

7.1   **This Melchizedek was king of Salem and a priest of the Most High God. As Abraham was coming back from the battle in which he defeated the four kings, Melchizedek met him and blessed him,**

RSV's "**For**" can have one of three functions:

(a) To link 7.1-3 with 6.20. However, this is done quite adequately by the word **This.**

(b) To make the whole of 7.1-3 a conclusion following from 6.19-20, that is, "all this is true because Melchizedek is like the Son of God." This is unlikely, and in any case can only be brought out if 7.1-3 is translated as a single sentence.

(c) JB interprets the word translated "**For**" to introduce a conclusion to be drawn from Genesis 14, and so begins "you remember that Melchizedek . . ." (with verse 4 beginning "Now think how great this man must have been . . ."); compare Knox "It was this Melchisedech." This is possible, but it is probably an over-interpretation. The Greek conjunction is common and not emphasized.

Function (a) is best, in which case "For" may be omitted, as in TEV.

The Hebrew word for **Salem** (Gen 14.18) is used also in Psalm 76. **Salem** is probably an old word for Jerusalem. However, there is no point here in using the more familiar name, since the writer of Hebrews is not interested in identifying the place but in noting that **Salem** means Peace (verse 2). It may, however, be important to identify the fact that Salem was a city rather than a country, and therefore one may translate **This Melchizedek was king of Salem** as "This person Melchizedek was king of the city of Salem."

Whatever the title **the Most High God** may have meant before it was used in biblical writings, there is no suggestion that, for the writer of Hebrews, **God** is only the highest among many gods. Such an idea should be avoided in translation. JB, NEB, TNT have "God Most High"; French translations have "the very high God"; and DuCL, GeCL "God the all-highest." In some languages it may be possible to say, for example, "God who is supreme" or "God who is very great," but for the writer it is already a traditional expression and carries no special emphasis.

A priest of the Most High God will often have to be expressed as "a priest who served the Most High God" or ". . . God who is above all." In some instances **the Most High God** may be rendered as "God over whom there is no one" or "God than whom there is no one greater."

Rather than the extended expression **from the battle in which he defeated the four kings,** it may be more appropriate to translate "from having defeated the four kings." This may be combined with the first part of the same sentence as "As Abraham was returning after having defeated the four kings."

In English the use of the phrase **the four kings** with the article **the** would suggest that these four kings are already known to the readers. This would be true for the first readers of Hebrews, but for most present-day readers it may be better to say "after having defeated four kings."

A literal rendering of **As Abraham was coming back from the battle in which he defeated the four kings** might suggest that Abraham single-handedly defeated four kings. It may therefore be necessary to say "in which he and his followers defeated four kings." And since the four kings were not alone, it may be better to say "defeated the armies of four kings" or ". . . four kings and their army." A marginal reference to Genesis 14.17-20 may be added, as in TEV.

In this context the expression **blessed him** may be rendered as "prayed to God on behalf of him." It is important to indicate that whatever Melchizedek did or said carried certain supernatural sanctions or powers. Sometimes this may be done by rendering **blessed him** as "used words which brought God's favor upon Abraham."

7.2   **and Abraham gave him one tenth of all he had taken. (The first meaning of Melchizedek's name is "King of Righteousness"; and because he was king of Salem, his name also means "King of Peace.")**

In translating this passage it is often clearer to use the names "Abraham" and "Melchizedek" rather than the pronouns "he" and "him." **And** at the beginning of this verse may be slightly emphatic; KJV, JB have "also." As the writer shows in verses 6-8, the point is that there are two ways in which Melchizedek is seen to be more important than Abraham. First, Melchizedek blesses Abraham; and second, Abraham gives Melchizedek a tithe or tenth of all he got in the battle (verse 4). The word for **gave** means "gave a share of," "shared out." In most languages there is a relatively technical term for booty, that which is taken from the enemy after the enemy has been defeated.

TEV's expansion of "everything" into **all he had taken** is based on verse 4. In some languages it may sound better to make the full statement one tenth of all he got in the battle in verse 2, and then to say simply "a tenth of everything" in verse 4. Such a small rearrangement need not involve any change of verse numbers (compare Gen 14.20 in TEV). Where it is difficult to speak of **one tenth,** it may be possible to restructure the statement as "Abraham divided all that he had taken into ten different parts and gave Melchizedek one of the parts" or "of the ten parts of all that Abraham had taken he gave one part to Melchizedek."

In the Greek, the two sentences which TEV puts in parentheses (round brackets) are a rather awkward insertion. If the Greek sentence is broken up, there is no need for parentheses, since there is no specially close connection between 2a and 3. Other common language translations do not use parentheses here. In some languages it is better to follow the verse order: 1a, 2b, 3, 1b, 2a.

TEV's **The first meaning** leads the reader to expect a second, possibly deeper, meaning of Melchizedek. In fact, what the writer does for the second meaning is to give a translation of **King of Salem.** A combination of FrCL and GeCL would give the simple meaning: "Melchizedek really means 'king of right-eousness.' He was also king of Salem, which means 'king of peace.' " **The first** indicates that the writer is beginning a systematic explanation of the Old Testament passage which he has summarized. An expanded paraphrase might read "The first thing to be said about this text [or possibly, about Melchizedek] is that his name means 'King of Righteousness.' The next point is that he is also King of Salem, which means 'King of Peace.' "

On **Righteousness** see 1.9; 5.13. **King of Righteousness** and **King of Peace** may be replaced by verbal expressions such as "king who does what is right" or "king who brings peace." The words rendered "righteousness" and "peace" in Hebrews have a wide range of meanings: for "righteousness," see 1.8 (quoting Psa 45.6); 5.13; 11.7,33; 12.11; for "peace," see 11.31; 13.20.

There is no verb in the Greek text corresponding to RSV's "**is**" before "**first**" and again before "**also king.**" TEV supplies **is** in the first place and **was** in the second. From verse 26 onward, the author is less interested in what happened in Genesis 14 than in the permanent significance of Melchizedek; therefore "**is**" in both places is perhaps better (so NEB, Phps).

7.3   **There is no record of Melchizedek's father or mother or of any of his ancestors; no record of his birth or of his death. He is like the Son of God; he remains a priest forever.**

This verse may be read as four lines of poetry, the ends of the lines corresponding to the full stops (periods) and semicolons in TEV.

Most modern translations, including TEV and other common language translations, avoid the most direct translation of the first part of this verse, which Phps gives as "He has no father or mother and no family tree. He was not born nor did he die." For ancient Jewish writers, and for the author of Hebrews, there could be deep meaning even in what the Old Testament did *not* say. The writer therefore does not hesitate to argue from silence where scripture is concerned. If the Old Testament did not give these details about Melchizedek's ancestry, birth, and death, then for the purposes of the writer's argument this is as good as a positive statement that he had no ancestors, that he was not born, and that he did not die. The purpose of TEV's apparently weaker statement, **there is no record . . .** , is to indicate the basis on which the writer claims that Melchizedek had no father or mother. It may be necessary to be more specific and translate "Scripture says nothing about Melchizedek's father or mother," especially if there is any danger of the passage being misunderstood to mean that Melchizedek was not a real human person. In any case, the context should make it clear, first, that he is a mysterious figure, and second, that he is less important than Jesus, **the Son of God.**

There is no record of may be rendered as "nothing was written in the holy books about" or "there are no written words about."

It may be important to distinguish clearly between **father or mother** and **any of his ancestors,** since all those who are prior to any particular individual are sometimes regarded as ancestors. This would then include father or mother. It is important in the choice of a word for **ancestors** to avoid what might be regarded as a contradiction.

Verse 3b, the second sentence in TEV, comes back to what is for the writer the point of the story of Melchizedek. RSV's **"but"** marks the change from negative to positive statements about Melchizedek. The equivalent in TEV is the fact of beginning a new sentence. The meaning of the sentence is the same as the quotation in 5.10 and 6.20, though different words are used (**priest** instead of high priest, and a different phrase for **forever**).

Is like (so also NEB) is literally "having been made like" (compare KJV), which may imply God's activity. This astonishing statement is neither emphasized nor explained in the text, so TEV's translation is quite adequate.[1] In Greek, as in RSV, **"resembling"** is grammatically subordinate to **remains;** but in meaning, the second phrase is as important as the first, since it defines in what way Melchizedek is **like the Son of God.** (TEV's semicolon could be a colon, pointing forward to the second half of the sentence; so DuCL, FrCL.) The relationship between the two parts of verse 3b may be indicated by saying "He is like the Son of God in that he remains a priest forever."

TEV	**7.4-10**	RSV

4 You see, then, how great he was. Abraham, our famous ancestor, gave him one tenth of all he got in the battle. 5 And those descendants of

4 See how great he is! Abraham the patriarch gave him a tithe of the spoils. 5 And those descendants of Levi who receive the priestly office have a

---

[1] The theological and literary problems of this verse are discussed in P. Ellingworth, 1983, "Like the Son of God": Form and Content in Hebrews 7,1-10 (Biblica 64, No. 2, pages 255-262).

Levi who are priests are commanded by the Law to collect one tenth from the people of Israel, that is, from their own countrymen, even though their countrymen are also descendants of Abraham. 6 Melchizedek was not descended from Levi, but he collected one tenth from Abraham and blessed him, the man who received God's promises. 7 There is no doubt that the one who blesses is greater than the one who is blessed. 8 In the case of the priests the tenth is collected by men who die; but as for Melchizedek the tenth was collected by one who lives, as the scripture says. 9 And, so to speak, when Abraham paid the tenth, Levi (whose descendants collect the tenth) also paid it. 10 For Levi had not yet been born, but was, so to speak, in the body of his ancestor Abraham when Melchizedek met him.

commandment in the law to take tithes from the people, that is, from their brethren, though these also are descended from Abraham. 6 But this man who has not their genealogy received tithes from Abraham and blessed him who had the promises. 7 It is beyond dispute that the inferior is blessed by the superior. 8 Here tithes are received by mortal men; there, by one of whom it is testified that he lives. 9 One might even say that Levi himself, who receives tithes, paid tithes through Abraham, 10 for he was still in the loins of his ancestor when Melchizedek met him.

You see, then, how great he was introduces a more detailed commentary on what Genesis 14.17-20 means for the status of Melchizedek, and therefore for the position of Christ (verses 11-28). The section is no longer a direct commentary on the Genesis text, as were verses 1-3. The transition is marked by **then**; compare NEB "consider now." Neither **then** nor "now" refers to time but to the next stage in the argument. The argument is not entirely easy for the modern reader to follow, despite what is said in 7.13. It is at least clear that Melchizedek has a higher status (a) because he received tithes from Abraham (verses 4-6a); (b) because he blessed Abraham (verses 6b-7); and (c) because he is still alive (verse 8).

7.4   **You see, then, how great he was. Abraham, our famous ancestor, gave him one tenth of all he got in the battle.**

You see is a possible literal translation of the word for "see." Most translations take it as a command, "See!" though in the case of such intellectual events, the response must be voluntary and cannot be determined by another person. Other ways of avoiding the imperative "see" are "you can see," DuCL; "notice," FrCL; Phps "look how outstanding"; "consider," TNT, NEB, BJ; "think," JB. The Greek term rendered **see** in TEV is a reference to an intellectual event and not a matter of actual vision. One may then translate the Greek verb as "You can recognize then," or "You can realize," or simply "Consider" (as imperative).

How great is an exclamation, not an expression of quantity or a question, as RSV shows: "how great!" "how important!" **Great,** as the context shows, means "important," "of high status."

The second sentence in verse 4 of TEV is the reason for recognizing the greatness of Melchizedek, and it may be useful to begin the second part with a conjunction meaning "for."

Our famous ancestor is emphasized (literally, the patriarch, TEV first through third editions). Although Abraham was himself one of the founders of Israel, the implication is that he recognized that Melchizedek was more important than himself.

The Greek term rendered **our famous ancestor** may also be translated as "the one who began our nation" or "the one who was the father of our nation."

The rare word which RSV translates **"spoils"** originally meant "first fruits," and it may imply that Abraham picked out the best of the spoil to offer to Melchizedek. NEB's "a tithe of the finest of the spoil" reflects this but is otherwise a little ambiguous; the intended meaning is "the best tenth of the spoil." Most translations take "spoils" to refer to **all he got in the battle.** **All he got in the battle** might suggest what Abraham received during the actual fighting, as though he were gathering up spoils while others fought. It may therefore be better to translate **all he got in the battle** as "all that he and his followers took from those who had been defeated."

7.5   And those descendants of Levi who are priests are commanded
     by the Law to collect one tenth from the people of Israel, that
     is, from their own countrymen, even though their countrymen
     are also descendants of Abraham.

The differences between Levites and priests are complex and partly uncertain. It is not even certain that the author of Hebrews distinguished between priests and Levites, that is, between those Levites who descended from Levi through Aaron, and those who belonged to other branches of the Levi family.

Those descendants of Levi who are priests assumes that the writer did make this distinction, but it is made nowhere else in Hebrews, not even in verse 11 where one might expect it. These words may also be translated, perhaps better, as "the descendants of Levi, that is, the priests," to contrast them with Melchizedek (verse 6), who was not a descendant of Levi at all.

Descendants is literally "sons." The essential features are (a) one or more generations after Levi, including not only "sons" but "grandsons," etc.; (b) male, thus not including female "descendants," as the English word suggests; (c) adult, thus not including "children," as in Lu.

Who are priests is more precisely "who are given the office (or function) of priests." In order to avoid some of the difficulties involved in the rendering of **those descendants of Levi who are priests**, it may be possible to employ "those men who descended from Levi and who are priests" or "those men who look to Levi as the first of their tribe and who are priests."

RSV's **"have a commandment in the Law to take tithes"** can be understood in two ways, and so can the Greek: (a) there is a law in the Torah (the Five Books of Moses) which assigns tithes to the priests; or (b) the Torah orders the priests to collect tithes. Meaning (a) is closer to the meaning of Numbers 18.21, except that in fact in this verse, all the Levites are given the right to claim tithes. Translators find it rather difficult to put this in common language; Knox "are allowed by the provisions of the law"; Phps "have the right to demand"; NAB "The law provides"; Brc "possess with it [that is, the priestly office] an injunction which legally entitles them"; TNT "are authorized to collect." Meaning (b) is chosen by NEB "are commanded by the Law"; JB "are obliged by the Law." It may be possible to say "the Law commands" or "the words of the Law say." But in many languages one cannot refer simply to "the Law," even with capitalization. It may be necessary to state more specifically "the Law given to Moses," or "the laws that God gave to Moses" or ". . . through Moses." If such an expression is used, one may translate "according to the laws given to Moses it was necessary for the descendants of Levi to collect."

The giving of "tenths" or "tithes" is a present-day custom in some cultures or groups but is unknown in others. In translations for groups to which the custom is strange, the translator should avoid any old-fashioned or specifically church-language word such as the English "tithe." In such cases the translator may need to expand the text or to explain the custom in a glossary note.

TEV's **collect one tenth from the people** could suggest the question "a tenth of what?" GeCL refers to a glossary note; DuCL translates "tenths from the income of the people"; and Phps puts "tenth" in quotation marks to identify it as a technical term. Quotation marks, however, cannot be read aloud. In speaking of "a tenth," it is sometimes necessary to say more specifically "a tenth of what the people have earned" or "a tenth of what the people have acquired." If a translation is being made for a society which makes little or no use of money, it is important not to rule out food or other goods.

The term **collect** may be rendered as "receive as offerings from." It is important to avoid an expression which would suggest "taking away by force."

Of Israel is implied. Knox's "God's people" covers too wide an area of meaning, since Christians are not necessarily included.

"Brethren" (RSV) has the wide meaning of "fellow Israelites." TEV adds **their countrymen** to make it clear that **countrymen** and not **priests** is the grammatical subject of **are.**

Descendants of Abraham is not literally "sons," as in **descendents of Levi,** but as in KJV, "they come out of the loins of Abraham" ("loins" is a common way of speaking indirectly about the male reproductive organs). This is a statement which is developed in verse 10.

Instead of the TEV word order, **from the people of Israel, that, is from their own countrymen,** it may be clearer to reverse the order, "from their own countrymen, that is, the people of Israel." The final clause of verse 5 may then be rendered as "even though their fellow countrymen are also descended from Abraham," or "even though these people of their own nation look to Abraham as their ancestor."

7.6   **Melchizedek was not descended from Levi, but he collected one tenth from Abraham and blessed him, the man who received God's promises.**

Common language translations and NEB make it clear that the Greek expression "this man" refers to Melchizedek. **From Levi** is literally "from them," that is, "from the descendants of Levi." No loss of meaning is involved in TEV. **Melchizedek was not descended from Levi** may be rendered as "Melchizedek did not count Levi as his ancestor" or "Levi was not the ancestor of Melchizedek."

As in verse 5 the verb **collected** may be rendered as "received as an offering," or in the total context of **he collected one tenth from Abraham** as "he received the tenth which Abraham gave him."

Blessed him: see comments on verse 1.

Verse 6b makes a smooth transition to the second way in which Melchizedek is seen to be more important than Old Testament priests. 6.13-15 has already identified Abraham as the one **who received God's promises** (**God's** is implied).

Received is literally "having," which Mft and Brc translate "the possessor"; Phps, JB "the holder"; and NAB translates precisely, if a little heavily, "him who had received God's promises" (similarly TNT). Here the writer probably means the act of promising rather than the content of the promises. God made a promise to Abraham (Gen 13.14-18) before Abraham met Melchizedek (Gen 14.17-20), but the promise had not yet been fulfilled.

7.7   **There is no doubt that the one who blesses is greater than the one who is blessed.**

This verse appeals to the readers' general knowledge. No one questions that a more important person blesses someone less important. **Doubt** is literally "argument," as in 6.16. This verse is itself an explanatory comment and should be easily understood, even in cultures where blessing is not much practiced, or where the inferior may bless the superior.

There is no doubt may be regarded as a double negative, since **doubt** is often rendered "not to know." Therefore **There is no doubt** may often be better rendered as "everyone knows."

In a number of languages "to bless" is always a transitive verb requiring some kind of object. Therefore **the one who blesses** must be expressed as "the one who blesses someone." In this context **blesses** might be rendered as "one who speaks well on behalf of," but it is usually necessary to indicate some supernatural sanctions involved in the speaking; for example, "speaks well to God on behalf of." (See comments on blessed in verse 1.)

In Hebrews, **greater** or better is often used in contrasts between the old and new covenants, or more generally between the situation before and after the coming of Christ (1.4; 6.9; 7.19,22; 9.23; 10.34; 11.35,40; 12.24). It is not necessary to translate the word everywhere in the same way, but it may be helpful for the translator to consider these texts together, as part of the same problem.

In this context **greater** must refer to status or rank, and this may be expressed as "is higher than," or by an expression of position such as "is out in front of," or idiomatically as, for example, "is the one to whom one must bow lower."

7.8   **In the case of the priests the tenth is collected by men who die; but as for Melchizedek the tenth was collected by one who lives, as the scripture says.**

The third point of contrast is between Melchizedek on the one hand, and Levi and his descendants on the other hand. The contrast may be only with the priests, but **In the case of the priests** is not expressed in the Greek. **In the case of the priests** may have to be rendered as "In the case of the priests descended from Levi"; otherwise "the priests" might also imply Melchizedek, since he is also called a priest.

Is collected: as in verse 5, there is no stress on the priest's initiative in "collecting."

Men who die means that the "tenth" is collected by "mortal men" (so GeCL, JB), that is to say, by "men who must die" (NEB). A strictly literal translation of **men who die** might suggest that the tithes were collected by "dying men." It may therefore be necessary to render **men who die** as "men who will ultimately die" or "men who will finally die."

The writer draws the conclusion that Melchizedek did not die from the fact that Scripture does not mention his death. NAB has "Scripture testifies that this man lives on." The Greek verb is not simply "says" but "supports by its witness"; the same word is used of Abel and Enoch in 11.4-5. **As for Melchizedek** may be rendered as "in the case of Melchizedek" or "but in speaking about what Melchizedek did."

If the passive construction **was collected by one who lives** must be rendered in an active form, it may be possible to render **but as for Melchizedek the tenth was collected by one who lives** as "but with regard to Melchizedek, he is the one who lives and is the one who collected the tenth."

7.9   **And, so to speak, when Abraham paid the tenth, Levi (whose descendants collect the tenth) also paid it.**

Verses 9 and 10 form a single sentence in the Greek. They sum up the references to Abraham, Levi, and the priests, tying them together with one another and with the text quoted in verse 1. This summing-up takes place in two stages, the first of which is not in the text but may need to be expressed in translation: (a) the priests are identified with their ancestor Levi; (b) Levi is then identified with his own ancestor Abraham. TEV's expansion for readers for whom (a) needs to be made clearer involves adding **whose descendants.** This is followed by most CLTs. **When** is not emphasized; SpCL's "at the moment when" is too strong. The text means simply that Levi paid the tithe through his ancestor Abraham.

So to speak may be rendered as "one might say" or "it is possible to say."

Abraham paid: it is important to avoid implying that Abraham was paying for something which he had received. It may be better to use some such phrase as "when Abraham gave the tenth."

Whose descendants collected the tenth may be rendered as "those who descended from Levi received the tenth which was given to them."

Levi . . . paid: see note on **Abraham paid** earlier in this verse.

In the Bible, descendants are often identified with their ancestors. In the Old Testament, "Israel" is sometimes the name of an individual, also called Jacob, but more often is the name of the people which descended from him. See also Romans 5.12-21; 1 Corinthians 15.22. How far the identification of ancestor and descendants needs to be made clear by expanded translation or marginal notes is a matter of culture rather than of language. In some cultures, including non-Christian cultures, this idea may be quite natural and therefore present fewer problems to the translator than in English.

7.10   **For Levi had not yet been born, but was, so to speak, in the body of his ancestor Abraham when Melchizedek met him.**

In verse 10, unlike verse 9, there is no **so to speak** in the Greek text. As in verse 5 the writer uses the common Hebrew expression of descendants being "**in the loins**" (RSV) of their male ancestors. To convey this idea to readers for whom it is strange, TEV (a) expands "still in Abraham's loins" to **had not yet been born, but;** (b) adds **so to speak** (TEV is not followed in this by DuCL, GeCL); and (c) replaces "loins" by **body** (compare other CLTs except GeCL, which has a word which means "seed" or "sperm").

Levi had not yet been born may be rendered as "Levi had not yet come into existence" or "Levi did not as yet exist."

The statement **but was, so to speak, in the body of his ancestor Abraham** may' be expressed as "but one might say that he was already in the body of his ancestor, who was Abraham" or ". . . in the body of Abraham, who was his ancestor."

The pronoun **him** in the clause **when Melchizedek met him** must refer to Abraham and not to Levi.

TEV	**7.11-14**	RSV

11 It was on the basis of the levitical priesthood that the Law was given to the people of Israel. Now, if the work of the levitical priests had been perfect, there would have been no need for a different kind of priest to appear, one who is in the priestly order of Melchizedek,[x] not of Aaron. 12 For

11 Now if perfection had been attainable through the Levitical priesthood (for under it the people received the law), what further need would there have been for another priest to arise after the order of Melchizedek, rather than one named after the order of Aaron? 12 For when there is a change

when the priesthood is changed, there also has to be a change in the law. 13 And our Lord, of whom these things are said, belonged to a different tribe, and no member of his tribe ever served as a priest. 14 It is well known that he was born a member of the tribe of Judah; and Moses did not mention this tribe when he spoke of priests.

in the priesthood, there is necessarily a change in the law as well. 13 For the one of whom these things are spoken belonged to another tribe, from which no one has ever served at the altar. 14 For it is evident that our Lord was descended from Judah, and in connection with that tribe Moses said nothing about priests.

x in the priestly order of Melchizedek *(see 5.6)*.

In these verses, especially in verse 13, the writer begins to turn back to the theme announced in 6.20. There is no contrast now betwen Melchizedek and Levi or between Melchizedek and Abraham. Instead, there is a positive comparison between Melchizedek and Jesus. Jesus, however, is not directly named until verse 21 (until verse 22 in the Greek), and the climax is kept for verse 25.

7.11   **It was on the basis of the levitical priesthood that the Law was given to the people of Israel. Now, if the work of the levitical priests had been perfect, there would have been no need for a different kind of priest to appear, one who is in the priestly order of Melchizedek,*x* not of Aaron.**

x in the priestly order of Melchizedek *(see 5.6)*.

On the basis of: the translator's task here, as in verse 5, is to translate what the writer of Hebrews believed to have happened, not to decide what actually did happen in Old Testament times. The text may simply mean that the Law was given "in connection with" the levitical priesthood. In fact Law and priesthood were, as TNT puts it, "closely linked" (so DuCL), and verse 12 shows that this was also the writer's view. GeCL translates "On the priesthood of Levi's descendants, the Israelite people were given clear instructions in the Law."[2] However, most translators and commentators agree with TEV in the stronger statement that the priesthood was the basis of the Law.

Of Israel is implicit.

The adjectival form **levitical** is as unusual a word in Greek as in English; SpCL has "the levite priest," which can be understood in the light of verse 5a.

The word for **priesthood** is related to the word used in verse 5. The two terms are not sharply distinguished, but the word used in verse 5 usually means the priest's ministry or function, while the word used in verses 11-12 means the priestly order as an institution.

---

[2] See Harm W. Hollander, "Hebrews 7.11 and 8.6: A suggestion for the translation of *nenomothetētai epi*," The Bible Translator 30 (1979): 244-247.

It may be difficult to use the abstract or generic vocabulary of the first part of verse 11. The first sentence may be rendered as "The priests who desended from Levi were a necessary part of the Law that was given to the people of Israel," or ". . . the Law that God gave to the people of Israel," or ". . . the laws which God commanded the people of Israel to follow" or ". . . to obey." In a number of languages one cannot use a singular form, since the so-called Law of Moses consists of a large number of regulations and rules, and in other languages this frequently requires a plural form.

Now marks a change in the argument, or at least the introduction of a new idea. The Greek term is rather emphatic (Mft translates "Further"; NAB, TNT "then"). A comparison with RSV shows that TEV puts the first part of the Greek sentence second. The effect is to emphasize it. This is helpful for the modern reader, who needs to be given this information, not like the first readers, who merely needed to be reminded of it.

The Greek word for **perfect** is related to the word for "maturity" (RSV) used in 6.1 (TEV mature teaching). It will soon become clear that the writer is concerned, not only with more advanced teaching, but with growth into a new and fully Christian life. For the moment, however, the contrast is between fulfillment in Christ and nonfulfillment in the law and priesthood of the Old Testament. The contrast is not between elementary and fully Christian faith or life. The old does not only develop into the new; the new replaces the old. The Greek word which RSV translates "**perfection**" suggests the fulfillment of a purpose. This is either the purpose for which the priesthood was set up, or more generally God's purpose for mankind. Brc translates "If that priesthood had been perfectly able to do what it was designed to do"; TNT "If then the Levitical priesthood . . . had fulfilled its purpose." The condition has not been fulfilled.

It may also be possible to translate **if the work of the levitical priests had been perfect** as "if the priests descended from Levi had done just what they should have done," or ". . . had served God as they really should have served him," or ". . . had done their work in a completely right way."

TEV and most other CLTs change the rhetorical question "**what further need would there have been?**" (RSV) into a statement. See the comment on 1.5.

There would have been no need for may also be expressed as "it would not have been necessary to have had." Sometimes the expression of necessity may be combined with the following phrase, **a different kind of priest to appear;** for example, "a different kind of priest would not have needed to appear" or "a different kind of priest would not have been necessary."

Kind of is implied, but RSV's "**another priest**" does not bring out the full meaning, since the word translated "**another**" implies "different."

One who is in the priestly order of Melchizedek is the same in Greek as in 5.10; see the comments. The most likely meaning is "just like Melchizedek." For the translator, there are two essential points in the comparison between Melchizedek and Jesus: (a) Each is unique; so words for **order** suggesting a group of people, like "Order of the Legion of Honor," are to be avoided. (b) Neither Melchizedek nor Jesus is just an isolated individual. They are linked in setting up a whole new system of priesthood and sacrifice. GeCL has "of Aaron's kind"; Mft "with the rank of Aaron." In this context the phrase **in the priestly order** refers, as elsewhere, to "a kind of priest." Therefore **one who is in the priestly order of Melchizedek** may be rendered as "one who is a priest like Melchizedek."

TEV omits RSV's **"named,"** which is simply a way of reminding the reader that the words **in the priestly order of Melchizedek** are a quotation. CLTs have a glossary note explaining who Aaron was and why he was significant.

The final phrase **not of Aaron** must be expanded in some instances as "he was not like a priest who descended from Aaron."

7.12   **For when the priesthood is changed, there also has to be a change in the law.**

Like verse 7, this is a statement of one of the principles on which the argument is based. Since the Law is based on the priesthood (verse 11), a change in the priesthood entails a change of law. There is no **the** before **law** in the Greek text. The author means that one entire legal system is replaced by another state, namely the new covenant, not that one or two of the Old Testament laws are changed. In Hebrews the main interest in the Old Testament Law is in its regulations for worship. **Has to** suggests logical necessity, not any outward pressure.

If the statement in verse 12 is to make sense, **priesthood** must be understood as "the system of priests" or "the kind of priests." Therefore **when the priesthood is changed** may be rendered as "when there is a change in the kind of priests," or "when there are no longer the same kind of priests," or "when the kind of priests is different." The manner in which one renders the clause **there also has to be a change in the law** depends on the way in which the first part of verse 12 is translated.

7.13-14   **And our Lord, of whom these things are said, belonged to a different tribe, and no member of his tribe ever served as a priest. 14 It is well known that he was born a member of the tribe of Judah; and Moses did not mention this tribe when he spoke of priests.**

These two verses contain four overlapping statements, two positive and two negative, which may be summarized as follows:

positive	negative
verse 13: Our Lord was of a different tribe.	No member of this tribe was ever a priest.
verse 14: He belonged to the tribe of Judah.	This was not a priestly tribe in the Old Testament.

The repetition is probably for emphasis. It is the writer's way of bringing home to his readers the fact that there comes a point at which they must choose between the Jewish tradition and the Christian faith. (Compare Mark 2.12-13; Gal 3.1-18.) In some languages it may be more natural and effective to avoid the repetition by shortening or rearranging the text, and this may be possible without loss of meaning.

Our Lord is not expressed in the Greek until verse 14 but is added in verse 13 for clarity. Direct use of the name "Jesus" is avoided in the text, and it should be avoided in translation until it can come in at the climax of verse 21 or 22.

Of whom these things are said probably means "said in the Old Testament" rather than "of whom we are speaking" (Brc). This makes a much better parallel to Moses in verse 14. JB even puts the verb into the past tense, "were said," to make the Old Testament reference clear, but Hebrews often uses present tenses to show the permanent value of scripture. **Of whom these things are said** may be rendered as "about whom there are words in the holy writings," or "about whom the holy writings speak," or "the holy writings contain these words about him."

Belonged to is literally "rose" (like the sun); in common language, "came from" (see Luke 1.78; Jer 23.5). **Belonged to a different tribe** may be rendered as "counted a different person as his forefather" or "did not belong to the people who looked to Levi as their forefather."

Tribe and its equivalents in some other languages are unacceptable in many parts of the world for describing ethnic groups. Where this is so, some other expression must be found which (a) describes a large kinship group within a nation, (b) has no negative "colonial" overtones, and (c) is not, like "ethnic group," a technical expression.[3] In choosing a translation for "tribe," translators should consider how they would translate the word in such Old Testament passages as Numbers 36.5-9 and Joshua 7.14-18. The expression chosen should refer to a group smaller than a people or nation, but larger than a clan or family.

No member of his tribe ever served as a priest may be expressed as "no one who belonged to the same tribe as our Lord ever served as a priest" or ". . . was ever a priest."

---

[3] The situation appears to be rather different in Africa and in some parts of Asia. In Africa, "tribe" and its equivalents in other European languages are widely rejected as implying a condescending attitude to African peoples (as do "native" and similar terms). In parts of Asia, however, members of a dominant ethnic or political group may freely refer, for example, to "hill tribes," "tribal languages," and the like. The translator needs to be sure that the expression he uses is fully acceptable to (other) native speakers, whatever their level of education; it is not enough that the term should be commonly applied to them by others. The translator should take into account, not only individual terms, but the way in which they are connected with other words; for example, the noun "a native," "the natives," usually has a derogatory meaning in modern English, but it is acceptable for someone to describe himself as "a native of Boston" or to speak of English as his "native language." At such sensitive points, careful testing of draft translations is particularly important. See Nida and Taber, The Theory and Practice of Translation, chapter 8 (pages 163-173).

It is well known, verse 14, may be expressed as "Everyone knows."

That he was born a member of the tribe of Judah may be expressed as "our Lord descended from Judah" or "our Lord belonged to the group of people who descended from Judah."

The importance which the writer gives to what Scripture does not say has already been noted in verse 3. **Moses** in verse 14 is equivalent to the Torah or Pentateuch. However, **did not mention** refers to a specific event, either the giving of the Law in general, as in 9.19, or perhaps specifically to the blessing of Levi in Deuteronomy 33.8-11.

	7.15-19	
TEV		RSV

Another Priest, like Melchizedek

15 The matter becomes even plainer; a different priest has appeared, who is like Melchizedek. 16 He was made a priest, not by human rules and regulations, but through the power of a life which has no end. 17 For the scripture says, "You will be a priest forever, in the priestly order of Melchizedek."*x* 18 The old rule, then, is set aside, because it was weak and useless. 19 For the Law of Moses could not make anything perfect. And now a better hope has been provided through which we come near to God.

x in the priestly order of Melchizedek *(see 5.6).*

15 This becomes even more evident when another priest arises in the likeness of Melchizedek, 16 who has become a priest, not according to a legal requirement concerning bodily descent but by the power of an indestructible life. 17 For it is witnessed of him,

"Thou art a priest for ever,
after the order of Melchizedek."
18 On the one hand, a former commandment is set aside because of its weakness and uselessness 19 (for the law made nothing perfect); on the other hand, a better hope is introduced, through which we draw near to God.

TEV has a new section heading, **Another Priest, like Melchizedek.** This not only serves to break up the rather long discourse of chapter 7, but it also focuses on the role of the Lord as being both a priest and also like Melchizedek. The fact that he is like Melchizedek has already been indicated in the previous section, but his role as a priest is here strongly emphasized.

Many translations begin a new section here, but not the UBS Greek New Testament. If shorter sections are required for easier reading, a break can be made at verse 13, where our Lord is first mentioned.

7.15 **The matter becomes even plainer; a different priest has appeared, who is like Melchizedek.**

In the Greek, verses 14 and 15 are linked by the use of words of similar meaning, "was descended" and "arose," and similar form, "evident" and "(even) more evident." However, the similarity of words covers a change in the argument: it is well known to everyone that Jesus was a member of the tribe of Judah (verse 14), but only Christians, and well instructed Christians at that, would be able to recognize in him a **different priest . . . like Melchizedek.**

NEB well expresses the new step in the thought: "The argument becomes still clearer, if the new priest who arises is one like Melchizedek . . . ." Unlike the if of verse 11, this condition is fulfilled: "if, as is the case." RSV tries to express this by "**when,**" implying "when we remember that another priest has arisen."

The clause **The matter becomes even plainer** may be rendered as "Now we can understand even more clearly," or "What I have been talking about now becomes clearer," or "You can now understand better what I have been talking about."

What becomes **even plainer**? Is it (a) the provisional nature of the old priesthood; (b) the change in the law; (c) both; or (d) the strength of the argument that there is really no comparison between Jesus and the levitical priests? (d) seems to fit in well with an increase of emotion which is felt from this point on. "The power of an indestructible life," for example, is emotionally stronger than "it is testified that he lives" in verse 8, RSV. Most translations agree with TEV in using some such general phrase as **The matter;** DuCL links it with the rest of the sentence: "It becomes much clearer still when we see that another priest appeared . . . ." GeCL boldly but effectively repeats material from verse 11, just as 6.3 in TEV repeats 6.1: "The levitical priesthood could not lead men to the goal. This becomes fully clear in that God has established another priest of the (same) kind (as) Melchizedek."

On **different**, see verses 11,13. **A different kind of priest,** as in verse 11, would not be too strong. NEB has "the new priest." **A different priest has appeared** may be rendered as "a different kind of priest exists."

Like Melchizedek does not translate the same expression in the Greek as does like the Son of God in verse 3, but the meaning is the same.

7.16   **He was made a priest, not by human rules and regulations, but through the power of a life which has no end.**

Priest is not in the Greek but must be repeated from verse 15. Because of the last clause of verse 16, namely, **through the power of a life which has no end,** it may be best to translate **He was made a priest** as "He became a priest." Otherwise one might wrongly assume that the passive expression would be better rendered as "God made him a priest."

There is some doubt about the exact meaning of the phrase which RSV translates "**not according to a legal requirement concerning bodily descent,**" and TEV **not by human rules and regulations.** The literal translation is "according to a law of a fleshly command." There are several aspects of the problem. (1) "Law" may also mean "principle," as in Romans 7.23, but this is not its meaning in the rest of Hebrews 7. (2) What is the relation between "law" and "command"? The most likely meaning seems to be "according to the legal force of a fleshly command"; that is, the individual command is backed by the force of the Law as a whole. (3) "Fleshly" may mean (a) generally "human," (b) "outward," "earthly," or (c) "to do with bodily descent." DuCL and other CLTs agree with TEV in choosing meaning (a), but the writer would probably not have described the Old Testament Law as "human" in this negative sense. (b) is reflected in Mft "external"; Knox "outward"; Phps "a command imposed from outside"; NEB "earth-bound"; TNT "earthly." (c) is reflected in SpCL which has simply "a law which says from which family he must come"; NAB "a commandment concerning physical descent"; Brc "any regulation based on the rule of physical descent"; compare TOB. Meaning (c) seems to fit in best with the earlier emphasis in chapter 7 on Abraham's and Levi's descendants, and on Melchizedek's lack of them.

The phrase **not by human rules and regulations** may be rendered as "he did not become a priest because of rules and regulations about being descended from a particular person" or ". . . rules and regulations about the family to which he belonged."

Finally, the expression **but through the power of a life which has no end** may be rendered as "but he did become a priest because of the power of his life which will never end" or ". . . which goes on forever."

The most probable meaning of the verse, therefore, is "He has been made a priest, not by the legal power of a rule which said from which family he must come, but by the power of a life which cannot be destroyed," or even ". . . which nothing can destroy."

7.17 **For the scripture says, "You will be a priest forever, in the priestly order of Melchizedek."ˣ**

ˣ in the priestly order of Melchizedek (see 5.6).

The key text is quoted again, this time as a whole and in the right order (unlike 6.20). RSV's literal "**it is witnessed**" means "scripture witnesses" as in verse 8, rather than "God witnesses" as in KJV, Knox, though the two ideas are closely linked. Compare 10.15, where the verb is used in the same sense (though in the active voice) of the Holy Spirit's witness in Scripture.

For the scripture says may be rendered as "For in the holy writings one may read."

You will be a priest forever, in the priestly order of Melchizedek may be expressed as "you will always be a priest of the kind that Melchizedek was" or ". . . like Melchizedek was."

7.18-19 **The old rule, then, is set aside, because it was weak and useless. 19 For the Law of Moses could not make anything perfect. And now a better hope has been provided through which we come near to God.**

These verses sum up the argument up to this point, first negatively in verses 18-19a, and then positively in verse 19b. In some languages it may be more natural to put the positive statement first. If so, the translator should change the order of the statements, since the two statements describe different sides of the same event. On the other hand, it may be more natural to speak first of the **old rule** and then of the **better hope.** Many modern translations leave the contrast implicit.

RSV's **"On the one hand . . . on the other hand"** is heavier than the Greek, but it has the same meaning. TEV's **then,** omitted by GeCL, RSV, NEB, implies that what God says in the psalm just quoted annuls the earlier commandment by instituting a different kind of priesthood. A similar argument is used in 4.7-9.

The adjective **old** should emphasize the fact that the rule in question is "the former rule" or "the rule of earlier times."

As in verse 16, the words **rule** ("command") and **Law** (**of Moses** is implied) are used in the same context. Here the two terms may have been used for the sake of variety, rather than to express any difference of meaning. The legal power of the old Law has been broken because God has set up a new kind of priesthood.

The old rule, then, is set aside may be rendered as "Therefore, the old rule has been annulled," or ". . . no longer functions," or ". . . no longer has any power."

Weak and useless translate general terms of disapproval which were chosen partly for their similar sound in Greek; there is no great difference of meaning.[4] **Useless** (Brc "ineffective") means that it did not do what it had been intended to do (see verse 11). It can therefore be called the **old,** that is, the "former, previous" commandment; it has now been made out of date (compare 8.13).

If one wishes to distinguish between **weak** and **useless,** it is possible to translate **weak** as "could not do what it was supposed to do" or "was not strong." The term **useless** may be translated as "was not good for anything" or "had no value."

The Law of Moses may be rendered, as in other contexts, as "the Law given to Moses," or "the Law which God gave through Moses," or "the laws which God caused Moses to speak to the people."

Could not make anything perfect may be rendered as "could not make anything just as it should be" or "could not make something without any defect."

A better hope must mean "a hope for something better than the old Law could give." DuCL accordingly translates "But a hope for something better has come on the scene, and this hope brings us closer to God." **Hope,** like "promise," may mean the event of promising or hoping, or that which is promised or hoped for. In this verse the context requires the second meaning. **A better hope** may sometimes be rendered as "something better for us to hope for." It may be necessary in some languages to state specifically what is being compared. It would be possible to say "what we hope for now is better than what we were able to hope for previously." Or it may be more satisfactory to use a strong positive; for example, "what we hope for now is indeed very good."

---

[4] For other examples of the use of pairs of similar expressions, see 1.1 (many times and in many ways), 6.19 (safe and sure), perhaps 11.1, and the comments on these texts.

In verse 19 the verb translated **has been provided** is not passive in Greek, but it may refer to the activity of God, meaning "God has brought in" or ". . . brought on to the scene" (Brc). GeCL's "now we have won a better hope" emphasizes human activity more strongly than does the Greek text. Instead of the passive **has been provided**, it is sometimes better to introduce God as the subject or agent. **Has been provided** may therefore be rendered as "God has caused us to have" or "God has caused us to (hope for something better)."

RSV's "**draw near to God**," still used in some more recent translations, reflects a term that originally meant coming into God's presence in Jewish Temple worship by means of a sacrifice. It may not be easy to bring this out in translation, but sacrifice is so thoroughly discussed in the following chapters that a note is probably not necessary. GeCL has "a better hope . . . which really brings us into the nearness of God," that is, "close to God." It may be extremely difficult to speak of **a better hope . . . through which we come near to God,** for hope would not normally be regarded as a means. Furthermore, hope may have to be expressed as a verb. If so, means may be expressed as a causal relation; for example, "what we now hope for, which is better, causes us to come near to God" or ". . . makes it possible for us to come near to God."

TEV	**7.20-22**	RSV

20 In addition, there is also God's vow. There was no such vow when the others were made priests. 21 But Jesus became a priest by means of a vow when God said to him,

"The Lord has made a solemn promise
and will not take it back:
'You will be a priest forever.' "
22 This difference, then, also makes Jesus the guarantee of a better covenant.

20 And it was not without an oath. 21 Those who formerly became priests took their office without an oath, but this one was addressed with an oath,

"The Lord has sworn
and will not change his mind,
'Thou art a priest for ever.' "
22 This makes Jesus the surety of a better covenant.

Before reaching the climax of the chapter and speaking directly about Jesus, the writer briefly takes up again the theme of God's oath or **vow** (see 6.13-18). God's oath is extra evidence that Melchizedek's priesthood (and therefore Christ's) is better than the Old Testament priesthood. Verses 20-22 are one sentence in Greek.

7.20   **In addition, there is also God's vow. There was no such vow when the others were made priests.**

Most CLTs, JB, and other translations like TEV, and the UBS Greek New Testament, end the verse after **were made priests;** KJV, Mft, RSV, NEB end it after **vow.** This Handbook follows TEV and the UBS Greek New Testament.

The writer does not often begin sentences with "**And**" (RSV), so TEV is right to emphasize it here by **In addition.** In rendering **In addition,** it is frequently necessary to indicate clearly what is added to what. One may say "In addition to the better hope," or "We have this better hope, but there is also God's vow," or ". . . what God vowed."

TEV makes it explicit that the **vow** was God's. It also changes the double negative "**not without**" (RSV) to a simpler positive form, **there is.**

There was no such vow: as in verses 3,14, the author argues on the basis of what Scripture does not say.

For the translation of **vow**, see the comment on 6.13. The word for **vow** used twice in this verse refers strictly to the act of taking a vow rather than to the vow itself, but the difference in meaning is slight: "God did not take a vow when the others were made priests."

7.21   **But Jesus became a priest by means of a vow when God said to him,**
        "The Lord has made a solemn promise
           and will not take it back:
        'You will be a priest forever.' "

By means of: it may be difficult to introduce **means** when a verb or an event such as taking a vow is involved. Therefore **Jesus became a priest by means of a vow** may need to be expressed as "God made a vow when Jesus became a priest" or "when Jesus became a priest God vowed." **Vow** may sometimes be rendered as "made a strong promise."

God said: the Greek has "he said," but TEV avoids confusion by using the noun **God** instead of the pronoun "he."

There is a serious problem involved in the reference to **The Lord,** since in this context **The Lord** refers to God. It may be necessary to begin the quotation as "I, the Lord God, have made a solemn promise."

Not take it back may need to be expressed as "will not change my mind" or "will not decide to do something different."

In the quotation from the first part of Psalm 110.4, the first line is emphasized and Melchizedek is not mentioned. Modern editions of the Greek text omit the words which KJV translates "after the order of Melchisedec."

The second line of the quotation partly repeats the meaning of the first. This is common in Hebrew poetry but may not be necessary in translation. In languages where "and" suggests that new information is to follow, it may be better to omit **and** here and to translate as follows:

    "The Lord has made a vow,
        he will not change his mind . . . ."

You will be a priest forever may be expressed negatively as "You will never cease to be a priest" or "There will never be a time when you will not be a priest."

[153]

7.22 This difference, then, also makes Jesus the guarantee of a better covenant.

Difference is not in the Greek, but it is added (as in DuCL and GeCL) to bring out the full meaning of the text. It is not God's oath-taking itself which establishes a **better covenant**; it is because the new covenant included an oath that it is **better** than the old.

With a phrase such as **This difference**, it is often necessary to specify the basis for the difference, since this may not be clear from the context. One may, for example, translate **This difference** as "This difference concerning an oath" or "The fact that in the case of Jesus, God made a solemn promise."

As was noted on 2.9 and 6.20, the name **Jesus** by itself usually carries great emphasis in this letter, and this is so again here.

The Greek for **guarantee** is not used elsewhere in the New Testament, but it is common in other parts of the Greek Bible; see especially Sirach 29.14-19. Its meaning is clear. The term describes someone called a "guarantor" (NEB and TNT) or "**surety**" (Mft, RSV) who was responsible for seeing that the terms of a contract were carried out. He also promised to pay the penalty if the contract was broken. The word is similar in meaning to "mediator" (8.6; 9.15; 12.24). Some translations make it explicit that Jesus guarantees "to us" that the contract will be maintained; FrCL "Therefore Jesus is . . . the one who guarantees us a better covenant"; JB "our guarantee." In translating **guarantee** as "one who guaranteed a covenant," it may be possible to translate "Jesus is the one who causes a better covenant to be fulfilled." It may also be possible to say "Jesus is the one who makes possible this better covenant."

If it is necessary to indicate the basis for the comparison, **a better covenant** may be contrasted with "the previous covenant" or "the covenant made through Moses."

It is an astonishing sign of the care with which this letter was written that the key word **covenant** has not been used before but has been kept in reserve until this point. The way was prepared in earlier chapters by a series of comparisons between Jesus on the one hand and angels, Moses, and high priests on the other. Then came statements earlier in this chapter about the new priesthood which involved a new Law. These statements mean that the whole basis of Israel's special relationship with God has been changed. Israel had been the "people of the covenant," but now the old covenant has been replaced by a new one. Until now the writer was not ready to suggest this, and even now he only mentions it in passing. The full discussion will come in chapter 9.

The translation of **covenant** is a test of one's ability to follow dynamic equivalence translation principles, especially at the level of common language. For detailed discussion, see Appendix B, "The Translation of 'Covenant.' "

The translator may be able to find a word or phrase used to describe an agreement which (as in many African societies) has a religious aspect, and which at least has nothing in it which conflicts with the essential features of the biblical covenant. If such an expression is available it should be used. The biblical context will allow this expression to make its meaning fuller and clearer where this is necessary.

If such an expression is not available, the translator should consider using a secular word for "agreement" or "treaty." It will then be possible to show that the biblical covenant is based on God's initiative, and the translation can use such phrases as "the agreement which God proposed" or "the arrangement which God made."

Where neither of these things is possible, the translator will probably have to use a traditional term, where one exists, or some otherwise inadequate expression, and then explain it in a glossary note. It is important in the choice of a word for **covenant** to avoid any expression which will suggest a kind of "compromise" or "deal" by which both sides work out an arrangement by which they realize some kind of reciprocal benefit. There are, of course, mutual obligations in a covenant, but in the Bible, covenants are made by God, not reached by bargaining.

The FrCL glossary note, and parts of the GeCL glossary note, may be adapted to give the amount and type of information that the intended readers need and can use. The glossary notes are as follows:

FrCL: treaty or agreement which God made, on his own initiative, with Abraham (Gen 17.1-8), then, later, with the people of Israel (Deut 29.10-15), and finally with all who believe in Christ.

GeCL: ... The covenant between God and his people is not a contract between equal partners. The initiative is always with God, who offers his covenant to an individual or to the people of Israel, and who makes promises to the partner in the covenant, but also lays obligations upon him (Gen 9.8-17; 15.18; 17.1,4,10; Exo 19—24).

The Old Testament prophets, who experience Israel's breaking of the covenant with God by the worship of idols and by social injustice, speak of a future "new covenant." This expectation, according to the New Testament, is fulfilled in Jesus Christ. He became by his death on the cross the founder of the new covenant, which exists between God and the new covenant people from all nations, the Christian people.

	7.23-25	
TEV		RSV

TEV	RSV
23 There is another difference: there were many of those other priests, because they died and could not continue their work. 24 But Jesus lives on forever, and his work as priest does not pass on to someone else. 25 And so he is able, now and always, to save those who come to God through him, because he lives forever to plead with God for them.	23 The former priests were many in number, because they were prevented by death from continuing in office; 24 but he holds his priesthood permanently, because he continues for ever. 25 Consequently he is able for all time to save those who draw near to God through him, since he always lives to make intercession for them.

7.23   There is another difference: there were many of those
other priests, because they died and could not continue their
work.

The words **There is another difference** and **other** are implied in the Greek of
verse 23; this passage clearly marks a contrast between Jesus and the priests just
mentioned.   Other translations show this contrast in different ways: "Under the
old covenant" NAB; "Under the levitical system" Brc. Mft, Brc, and others translate "became priests," but the event of being ordained priest is not stressed here
as it is in verse 20. **There were many of those other priests** gives the meaning.

The main idea, well expressed in both TEV and RSV, is that Old Testament
priests died and therefore could not remain in office, but that Jesus lives on
forever (verse 24) and therefore remains permanently in office.   This idea is
further complicated by the thought that it is more effective to have a single
priest than a large number of priests.

There is another difference may require some indication of the basis for the
difference, or of the context in which there is a difference.   Therefore **There is**
another difference may be expressed as "There is another difference between the
old covenant and the new covenant" or ". . . between the old covenant and this
better covenant."

There is a problem involved in the rendering of **those other priests**, since they
have not been specifically identified. It may therefore be important to speak of
"those priests of previous times" or "those priests of the earlier covenant."

Because they died does not follow logically from **there were many of those**
other priests. Basically, the meaning is "there had to be many of those earlier
priests, for each of them died and thus could not continue his work." What is
important is not the fact that there were many priests but the necessity of having
a long series of such priests.

Continue their work is a strong form of the Greek word for "remain," which
here means "remain in office."

Could not continue their work may be expressed as "were not able to continue
to serve God as priests" or "were not able to keep on being priests."

7.24   But Jesus lives on forever, and his work as priest does not pass
on to someone else.

Jesus is literally "he," as in RSV. This word is slightly emphasized and corresponds to the you of Psalm 110. 4, quoted in verse 21.

RSV's **"because"** is expressed in the text; TEV leaves it to be understood in
verse 24, since it has already been expressed in verse 23, where the Greek is
similar.

On **his work as priest**, literally "priesthood," see 7.5,11.

Does not pass on to someone else is expressed by one word in the Greek. This
word is not used elsewhere in the New Testament and has not been found in any
secular writing in this sense.   But many commentators and translations, for

example Barclay and TNT, accept this meaning because it fits the context well. However, the usual meaning of the word outside the Bible is "permanent," "unchangeable," "inviolable," and this is probably what the word means here. This meaning is chosen by many other translations, including GeCL and NEB.

The rendering of **does not pass on to someone else** is a negative manner of expressing permanence and unchangeableness. It is possible to render **his work as priest does not pass on to someone else** as "no one else will take on his work as priest" or "no one else will become a priest as he is."

7.25   **And so he is able, now and always, to save those who come to God through him, because he lives forever to plead with God for them.**

And so marks the conclusion of the whole argument; FrCL "that is why."
On **save**, see 5.7.

Translations are divided on the meaning of **he is able, now and always, to save**. It is almost certain that the phrase **now and always** goes with **save** and not with **is able**; NAB's "he is always able" is too weak. These words may mean either (a) "**for all time**" (RSV, TNT), **now and always** (FrCL); or (b) "completely" (KJV, Phps, JB; "utterly certain" JB; "absolutely" NEB, BJ). "Definitively" (GeCL, TOB) combines both meanings, with a slight emphasis on (a). (a) fits the immediate context well, emphasizing the fact that Christ lives on forever (verse 24; compare 25b). (b) fits the wider context somewhat better. The idea is that the old priesthood failed, not because it could save people for only a short time (though see 9.28), but because it could not do so completely. That is, it could not completely fulfill the purpose for which it had been set up (verses 11,18-19).

Now and always may be rendered as "now and always in the future." Since **able** only qualifies the capacity to **save**, the temporal expression is thus related to the entire act of salvation. Therefore the first part of verse 25 may be rendered as "And so now and always he can save those." If, on the other hand, the Greek term translated **now and always** in TEV is to be rendered as "completely" or "fully," the first part of verse 25 may be rendered "And therefore he can completely save . . . ." There may, however, be an implied contradiction in talking about "to save completely," since "to save" suggests a complete act and not something which occurs partially. It may therefore be better to relate "completely" or "absolutely" to the capacity to save. One may thus render the first part of verse 25 as "And so he is completely able to save."

Come translates the same Greek word translated approach in 4.16. Like "draw near" in verse 19 (RSV), it is often associated with sacrifice. This idea is developed in verse 28.

The expression of means or causative agent in the phrase **through him** may require some restructuring. For example, **those who come to God through him** may be expressed as "those for whom he makes possible their coming to God" or "those who come to God because of what he has caused to happen."

Plead in this context means to speak to someone on behalf of someone else. In English **plead** can have associations with the law courts, but "**make intercession**"

(RSV) and "intercede" are associated almost entirely with public prayer and are thus too narrow in meaning and are not common language. "Appeal to God for them" or, at a higher level of language, "intervene with God on their behalf" are other possibilities. **To** before **plead** means "in order to," "with a view to." The purpose of Christ's life in heaven is to speak with God in favor of men and on their behalf.

In translating the term **plead**, it is important to avoid any implication that God is himself hostile to men and that he requires some kind of unusual pleading on the part of Christ in order to remove his ill will toward humanity.

With God is implied.

For them means "on their behalf," "in their favor," not in this context "instead of them."

| | TEV | 7.26-28 | RSV |

26 Jesus, then, is the High Priest that meets our needs. He is holy; he has no fault or sin in him; he has been set apart from sinners and raised above the heavens. 27 He is not like other high priests; he does not need to offer sacrifices every day for his own sins first and then for the sins of the people. He offered one sacrifice, once and for all, when he offered himself. 28 The Law of Moses appoints men who are imperfect to be high priests; but God's promise made with the vow, which came later than the Law, appoints the Son, who has been made perfect forever.

26 For it was fitting that we should have such a high priest, holy, blameless, unstained, separated from sinners, exalted above the heavens. 27 He has no need, like those high priests, to offer sacrifices daily, first for his own sins and then for those of the people; he did this once for all when he offered up himself. 28 Indeed, the law appoints men in their weakness as high priests, but the word of the oath, which came later than the law, appoints a Son who has been made perfect for ever.

In this passage there is both a summary and a confession of faith, or hymn in praise of Christ. The writer includes two themes which have been mentioned already in passing and which will be developed later; first, the contrast between the one Jesus and the many priests (see verse 23), and second, the sacrifice of Jesus. This sacrifice is not only something which Jesus offered, but also something which he was in his own person. The words used to describe him in the translation of verse 26 should if possible be suitable to describe a sacrifice. These verses thus develop the thought of verses 23-24, in which the writer contrasted the Old Testament priests with Jesus by saying that the Old Testament priests died and so had to be replaced, but Jesus continues forever.

7.26   **Jesus, then, is the High Priest that meets our needs. He is holy; he has no fault or sin in him; he has been set apart from sinners and raised above the heavens.**

For **High Priest,** see comments on 2.17.

Most translations adopt a translation similar to **the High Priest that** (or "who") **meets our needs.** This phrase develops the meaning of It was only right (2.10). Expressions suggesting that Christ "meets our claims" or "our demands" should be avoided. NEB gives the meaning in literary language: "Such a high priest does indeed fit our condition." "Indeed" corresponds to "and" in the Greek text, which TEV and RSV omit. The idea is, we not only have in Jesus the kind of high priest described in verses 24-25; we also need him.

That meets our needs may be expressed as "that does for us all that is necessary" or "that helps us in every way possible."

Holy is not the common Greek word used elsewhere (for example, in 3.1) which means "set apart to belong to God." Here the meaning is "pleasing to God," like an unblemished sacrifice; elsewhere it can mean "pious, saintly." The meaning "pleasing to God" is reinforced by the two negative adjectives which follow: "innocent" (**has no fault;** literally "unstained"), which is used in the Greek translation of Jeremiah 11.19 to describe a sacrificial lamb; and "unstained" (**has no . . . sin**), which is used in 2 Maccabees 14.36 to describe the Temple; NEB "undefiled."

He is holy may be rendered as "He is the one with whom God is pleased." But in some languages it may be better to use an expression such as "He is good in God's eyes" or "God looks on him as good."

He has no fault or sin in him may be expressed as "he has done nothing wrong nor has he any guilt." It may be wrong to render the expression **sin in him** as literally "**unstained**" (RSV), since this might suggest only some physical imperfection or accidental blemish.

Set apart from sinners and raised above the heavens: TEV is right to link these expressions closely together, since they represent negative and positive aspects of the same event. On earth, Jesus shared human life to the full (2.18), but now in heaven he is no longer in daily contact with sinners. **He has been set apart from sinners** may be expressed in the active as "God has set him apart from sinners" or ". . . from those on earth who sin."

Above the heavens is what the text says (see 2 Cor 12.2), but some translations modify this in order to avoid stressing details of the writer's picture of the universe which may be strange to a modern reader; GeCL "raised up into heaven"; DuCL "someone who lives untouchable by sin and close to God." A literal rendering of **raised above the heavens** might be understood to mean that Christ was himself exalted above God. If so, some such translation as "God raised him up into heaven" is more satisfactory.

7.27   He is not like other high priests; he does not need to offer sacrifices every day for his own sins first and then for the sins of the people. He offered one sacrifice, once and for all, when he offered himself.

Other is implied, as in verse 23. The background of this verse is the order of worship on the Day of Atonement; see Leviticus 9.7; 16.6,15 (where "Aaron" means the high priest); also Hebrews 5.3. This, however, was an annual, not a daily event. If **other** is added in translation (as in TEV), it may be necessary to choose between the meanings "different in kind" and "different as individuals." In this context the meaning "different in kind" is appropriate.

This verse includes a double contrast which should be kept in translation: (a) **every day . . . once and for all;** (b) **offer sacrifices . . . offered himself.**

He does not need to offer sacrifices may be expressed as "it is not necessary for him to offer sacrifices" or ". . . to sacrifice." In some languages **sacrifices** may be rendered as "to kill gifts for God" or "to kill animals as gifts to God."

In rendering **for his own sins,** it is essential to avoid a wording which would suggest "for the benefit of his sins" in the sense of "to enhance his sins." It is also important to avoid a rendering of **for** which will suggest "to pay for," as though sacrifices were made in order to pay for sins and thus to enjoy them.

TEV's second sentence in the Greek is literally "for this he did once-for-all, having offered himself." "For" introduces the reason for the statement in the first part of the verse. "This," in the light of 4.15, cannot mean "offered sacrifice both for his own sins and those of the people." It means "offered sacrifice for the people." This is the basis of TEV's rearrangement.

Offered (9.28; 13.15; James 2.21; 1 Peter 1.5) is often used of "offering up" or "carrying up" a sacrifice to an altar. The meaning here is that of offering a sacrifice "up" to God, but this is not emphasized and TEV leaves it implicit. This theme will be developed in chapter 9.

Once and for all and "once" (compare 6.4) in the Greek are key words in the letter: "once and for all" 9.12; 10.10; "once" 9.7,26-28; 10.2; 12.26,27. **Once and for all** is an English idiom which means the same as "once," but it is more emphatic, like the Greek word which it translates. It means "one time for all times," not "for all people."

When he offered himself may be rendered as "when he gave himself to God" or "when he gave himself to God as a sacrifice."

7.28   The Law of Moses appoints men who are imperfect to be high priests; but God's promise made with the vow, which came later than the Law, appoints the Son, who has been made perfect forever.

The Law of Moses: of Moses is implied, as in verse 19. The original readers knew which Law was meant, but most present-day readers need to be told.

In some languages the verb **appoints** requires the use of direct discourse; for example, "the Law of Moses declares, 'You men who are imperfect are to become high priests.' " However, it may be impossible to speak of "the Law of Moses appointing men," since only a person may appoint someone else. **The Law of Moses appoints men . . . to be high priests** may be rendered as "according to the Law of Moses men become high priests." In this type of context **who are imperfect** may involve a concession; for example, "according to the Law of Moses, men, even though they are imperfect, are appointed to be high priests."

Imperfect is literally "weakness" (4.15; 5.2). The words "weak" and "weakness" cover a wide range of meaning including sickness, moral weakness, and ritual imperfection. A sick animal could not be offered as a sacrifice, and a human being suffering from certain types of illness was not allowed to take part in sacrifice. See 4.15 and 5.2. **Imperfect** in this context may be rendered in some languages as "who are unable to do what they should."

God's promise made with the vow is literally "God's oath-taking," as in verses 20-21; compare 6.16,17.

There may be a problem in speaking of "God's promise . . . appointing the Son" since, as in the case of the Law of Moses, a "promise" cannot do any appointing. It is, however, possible to say "God appoints his Son by means of a vow" or ". . . by means of a strong promise."

Which came later than the Law: some cultures assume that what is older is more worthy of respect than what is more recent. Where this is so, it may be necessary to make explicit that God's vow not only **came later,** but superseded what had gone before; compare 4.6-8; 7.18; 8.7. It was an accepted principle among the rabbis that "a new act of God supersedes the old" (see Jer 6.16 and Luke 5.39). It may be necessary to restructure the clause **which came later than the Law,** since two events are involved, both of which include God as an agent. Therefore **which came later than the Law** may be expanded as "God made his solemn promise at a time later than he gave the Law through Moses" or ". . . caused Moses to announce the laws."

Appoints is not the same Greek word as that which was translated chose in 3.2, but the meaning is similar. See comments on 3.2.

The Son: literally "a son"; so "one who has the title and status of son," as in 1.2 (see the comments). In many languages a "son" must be possessed, so it is impossible to speak of "the Son"; one must say "his Son."

Made perfect, as in verse 11, for example, implies more than being without sin. "Who has reached his full achievement" (Knox) is part of the meaning. Two other ideas are also involved: (a) "fulfillment of a purpose," and (b) "fulfillment not only for Christ himself but for others." If (as perhaps in English) **perfect** is understood too narrowly in moral terms, it may be slightly expanded in translation as "one who, as Son, has done forever all that God intended him to do." One may also render **has been made perfect** as "has become the one who is able to do everything that he should."

Chapter 8

Jesus Our High Priest

1 The whole point of what we are saying is that we have such a High Priest, who sits at the right of the throne of the Divine Majesty in heaven. 2 He serves as high priest in the Most Holy Place, that is, in the real tent which was put up by the Lord, not by man.

3 Every high priest is appointed to present offerings and animal sacrifices to God, and so our High Priest must also have something to offer. 4 If he were on earth, he would not be a priest at all, since there are priests who offer the gifts required by the Jewish Law. 5 The work they do as priests is really only a copy and a shadow of what is in heaven. It is the same as it was with Moses. When he was about to build the Covenant Tent, God told him, "Be sure to make everything according to the pattern you were shown on the mountain." 6 But now, Jesus has been given priestly work which is superior to theirs, just as the covenant which he arranged between God and his people is a better one, because it is based on promises of better things.

7 If there had been nothing wrong with the first covenant, there would have been no need for a second one.

1 Now the point in what we are saying is this: we have such a high priest, one who is seated at the right hand of the throne of the Majesty in heaven, 2 a minister in the sanctuary and the true tent[n] which is set up not by man but by the Lord. 3 For every high priest is appointed to offer gifts and sacrifices; hence it is necessary for this priest also to have something to offer. 4 Now if he were on earth, he would not be a priest at all, since there are priests who offer gifts according to the law. 5 They serve a copy and shadow of the heavenly sanctuary; for when Moses was about to erect the tent,[n] he was instructed by God, saying, "See that you make everything according to the pattern which was shown you on the mountain." 6 But as it is, Christ[o] has obtained a ministry which is as much more excellent than the old as the covenant he mediates is better, since it is enacted on better promises. 7 For if that first covenant had been faultless, there would have been no occasion for a second.

[n] Or tabernacle
[o] Greek he

This section forms another stage in the "teaching for mature people" which stretches without any major break from 7.1 to 10.18. It is full of contrasts between features of the old and new covenants. Some of these contrasts are contained in a single phrase or sentence; others only appear from the wider context. They may be listed as follows:

verse	feature	contrasted with	
		feature	reference
1	our high priest	other high priests	7.28; 9.7 etc.
2	in heaven	on earth	8.4
2	real tent	copy	
			8.5
5	pattern	shadow	
2	the Lord (God)	man	8.2
6	better covenant	first covenant	8.7
13	new covenant	old covenant	8.13

These contrasts, which continue into chapter 9, should be carefully distinguished from the points of similarity, mentioned in verse 3, on which the comparisons are based; for example, **Every high priest.**

This new stage in the teaching is marked by a change of Old Testament texts, from Genesis 14.17-20 and Psalm 110.4 to Exodus 25.40 and Jeremiah 31.31-34.

The TEV section heading for chapter 8, **Jesus Our High Priest,** may be rendered as "Jesus is a high priest for us," or "Jesus serves God as our High Priest," or "Jesus helps us as High Priest."

8.1   **The whole point of what we are saying is that we have such a High Priest, who sits at the right of the throne of the Divine Majesty in heaven.**

The whole point: NAB and NEB "the main point"; RSV and Brc "**the point**"; FrCL "the most important point." Some translations introduce a metaphor: DuCL "the kernel"; Knox, following Coverdale, "the very pith." This main point covers verses 1-2. Strictly speaking it is not a summary, as Phps' "to sum up" suggests. Verse 2, especially the word real, introduces new ideas.

It is not certain whether **the whole point** is what the writer has just been saying (Brc, Mft, Phps, JB) or what he is about to say (GeCL "I come now to the decisive point"; similarly Knox). In fact it is both, and some commentators bring this out by using a general phrase such as "to crown the argument." The writer intends to distinguish such "details" as the furniture of the sanctuary (9.2-5) from the central message of 7.1—10.18. TEV and other CLTs are therefore right to keep the present tense of the original with **what we are saying.**

The whole point of what we are saying may be rendered as "The real meaning of what I am saying," or "What I am saying really means that," or "The real purpose of what I am saying is that."

The language of this verse recalls 1.3. **Such a High Priest** implies "as Jesus," referring back to 7.26-28, which describes Jesus as High Priest; Phps "an ideal High Priest such as has been described above"; compare JB. It is possible to omit **such:** GeCL "we have a high priest"; DuCL "we have someone as high priest who . . . ."

The "place" of the new High Priest is described in impressive picture language, to emphasize the contrast with the old covenant.

The **right** side is the place of honor. Where readers may have difficulty in understanding the significance of **right,** it may be good to translate the final clause of this verse as "who sits at a place of honor beside God in heaven."

The Divine Majesty is a reverent way of speaking of God. **Divine** is implied. However, it may be impossible in translation to talk about **the Divine Majesty.** This is a title of God, so it may be better to say "God" or "God, who is wonderful." **Who sits at the right of the throne of the Divine Majesty in heaven** may be rendered as "who sits at the right of God's throne in heaven."

Heaven is literally "the heavens" (KJV), as in 4.14 and 7.26. There is probably no special significance in the use of the phrase here, and the singular **heaven** is clearer for most modern readers.

8.2 He serves as high priest in the Most Holy Place, that is, in the real tent which was put up by the Lord, not by man.

The writer of Hebrews seems to draw his information about the earthly sanctuary from the Old Testament, not from personal knowledge of worship in Jerusalem in his own lifetime. He is interested in the simple mobile tent or sanctuary which the Israelites used at the time of their escape from Egypt. It is therefore good in translation to use words which suggest a temporary construction rather than a permanent building such as a temple. From this point of view, "put up" (verse 5, TEV first through third editions), is better than TEV fourth edition, build.

As high priest is repeated from verse 1. The Greek word for **serves** strongly suggests the work of a priest. **He serves as high priest** may be rendered as "He serves God as high priest," or it may be better to say "He is a high priest."

The words translated **the Most Holy Place** probably refer to the Old Testament sanctuary as a whole, not only to its inner room. Other CLTs therefore translate simply "sanctuary," and this is better.

There may be some complications in rendering **the Most Holy Place,** especially if **Holy** is generally translated as "dedicated to God." How can a place be more dedicated to God than some other place or thing? It may be possible to use "that place which is especially dedicated to God" or "that very special place which is dedicated to God."

RSV's **"sanctuary"** and **"true tent"** are the same place, as TEV's **that is** shows; GeCL translates them both as "holy place."

Real introduces a new contrast, common in Greek thought, between (a) the heavenly pattern (verse 5) of the **real** temple, and (b) the earthly temple, which is only a copy or shadow (verse 5) of the heavenly one. The writer may be influenced by the view of the philosopher Plato and his followers, that the visible world was a reflection of a real but invisible world. The context shows that here **real** is the opposite of "material." Compare John 15.1. **The real tent** may be rendered as "that which is truly the tent." "That which is the perfect tent" may be a satisfactory equivalent.

The real tent which was put up by the Lord refers to Numbers 24.6, which has the plural "tents." The author of Hebrews adds **real;** the reason for this will become clear in verse 5. In some languages it may be more natural to put the negative statement first: "not by human beings but by the Lord." In Hebrews it is not certain whether **the Lord** is God, as for example in 7.21, or Jesus, as in 2.3 and 7.13-14. In Numbers 24.6 it is clearly God, and neither here nor in Hebrews 9.11 does the author think of Jesus himself as the maker of the heavenly tent. In translation it may be essential to show that **the Lord** refers to God. It may therefore be clearer to translate **the real tent which was put up by the Lord** as "the real tent which the Lord God put up."

The Greek word translated **man** is a quite general term for "human beings."

8.3 **Every high priest is appointed to present offerings and animal sacrifices to God, and so our High Priest must also have something to offer.**

The writer has finished outlining his "main point" (verse 1), and he now prepares to develop certain aspects of it in greater detail. This is what RSV's **"for"** implies; most CLTs omit it (DuCL has "now"). Before contrasting Jesus with other high priests, the writer briefly states what they have in common. This verse is very similar to 5.1.

The verb for "appoint" is the same as that used in 7.28 and means "appoint to an office." The passive **is appointed** is used because the writer is not now emphasizing that the Old Testament high priests were appointed by God. However, the translator may have to make God the explicit subject of the active verb if his own language does not make much use of passives.

The phrase which TEV fourth edition translates sacrifices and offerings in 5.1 and, more precisely, **offerings and animal sacrifices** here in 8.3 is exactly the same in the Greek. **Animal sacrifices** in the Greek is a single word, which is sometimes used of sacrifices generally. The whole phrase **offerings and animal sacrifices** refers to all kinds of gifts made to God in Old Testment worship. "Animal" is omitted by DuCL, FrCL, SpCL, probably correctly, since this verse includes reference to Jesus, who did not offer any animal sacrifice. **To present offerings and animal sacrifices** may be rendered as "to make gifts and sacrifices." It would, however, be wrong to suggest that these offerings and sacrifices were at the high priest's own expense. His function was to make such gifts and sacrifices on behalf of the people.

The second half of the verse moves from high priests in general to **our High Priest** (literally "this man" KJV), referring to Jesus in particular. It is not until

9.12 that the writer specifies what **our High Priest** has to offer, namely, his own blood.

Must also have something to offer may need to be expanded in some languages to indicate the person to whom the offering is made; for example, "must have something to give to God."

8.4 If he were on earth, he would not be a priest at all, since there are priests who offer the gifts required by the Jewish Law.

The contrast between the heavenly and earthly priesthood is complete. As already stated in 7.14, Jesus is not qualified to be a member of the earthly, Old Testament priesthood. The emphatic negative **not . . . at all** (similarly DuCL, JB, Phps, Brc, TNT) is the probable meaning. Another possible meaning is "not even" (FrCL, NEB, TOB), which implies "not a high priest, and not even a priest." The first meaning is more likely, since the writer seldom contrasts "priest" and "high priest."

In some languages it is difficult, if not impossible, to imply a condition contrary to fact, such as **If he were on earth, he would not be a priest at all.** The closest equivalent may be a contrast between the earthly and the heavenly conditions: "He is a priest in heaven, but if he is on earth he is not a priest." Or it may combine causal relations and the matter of location: "Because he is in heaven he is a priest, but on earth he is not a priest."

The verb **required** may be expressed as a type of necessity. For example, **the gifts required by the Jewish Law** may be rendered as "the gifts which the priests must offer because of the laws which the Jews must follow."

Jewish is implied; compare Law of Moses in 7.19,28.[1] **The Jewish Law** may be rendered as "the laws which the Jews follow" or "the laws which the Jews must obey."

8.5 The work they do as priests is really only a copy and a shadow of what is in heaven. It is the same as it was with Moses. When he was about to build the Covenant Tent, God told him, "Be sure to make everything according to the pattern you were shown on the mountain."

The first part of this verse is grammatically a subordinate part of the long sentence in Greek which includes verses 4-6. In meaning, however, it is a separate statement, and it should therefore be translated as such.

The work they do as priests may be rendered as "What these priests do." **Only** is implied.

---

[1] Strictly speaking, "Jewish" should not be used for the period before the end of the Babylonian exile (586 B.C.), and the phrase "the Jewish Law" is not found in the New Testament (Rom 2.17 is not a real exception).

Copy and **shadow** are two figurative ways of saying that earthly forms of worship are similar to, but less "real" than, the heavenly ones. The Greek word for **copy** was used in 4.11 to describe a bad human example of disobedience, as they did. In 10.1, where the context is similar, TEV translates the Greek word for shadow as faint outline. GeCL has "only a shadow-picture, only an imperfect reproduction." TEV's **a copy and a shadow** could be misunderstood as suggesting that two different things are spoken of; in fact, the same thing is described in two ways. "A copy or shadow" would be clearer.

Is really only a copy and a shadow of what is in heaven may be rendered as "is really only similar but not the same as what is in heaven," or ". . . as what takes place in heaven," or ". . . what happens in heaven," since what is being compared here is a series of events and not one particular thing. In order to indicate clearly that the ritual on earth is only an imperfect reproduction of what takes place in heaven, it may be necessary to say "is not really the same but is similar to," or "looks like but is not identical with," or "appears to be similar but is not really the same."

What is **the same as it was with Moses**? TNT thinks that these words refer to acts of worship: "They are performing a service . . . just as Moses . . . was instructed to do." This does not fit the context of the verse quoted, that is, Exodus 25.40, which deals with the construction of the tent rather than its use. It seems likely that the writer is not making a detailed comparison, but simply preparing to introduce its key word, **pattern,** by means of the quotation. This is well brought out by Phps: "Moses, you will remember . . . was cautioned by God . . . ." One might translate "It is the same as happened with Moses," "This is what happened when God spoke to Moses," or simply "It was the same with Moses."

God's name is avoided throughout this verse; literally, "Moses was instructed," "he said," "it was shown to you." Passives may be turned into active verbs in languages which speak more freely of God: "As God instructed (or, told) Moses . . . ," "like the pattern I showed you." See also the comments on the next verse.

Build does not translate the same word as put up in verse 2. Here the Greek uses a more common verb meaning "complete, fulfill," and sometimes "construct." Rather than use **build** in reference to **the Covenant Tent**, it may be more appropriate to use "make." Some languages have a specific term for putting up tents, for example, "to stretch," or even "to weave."

The Covenant Tent is literally "the tent." The context makes it clear that this is the earthly tabernacle set up by Moses, not the heavenly tabernacle mentioned in verse 2. TEV adds **Covenant** because modern readers may not know which tent is referred to in verse 5, and may even confuse it with the tent or tabernacle mentioned in verse 2. TEV's example is followed by GeCL and the Italian common language translation (ItCL), and this solution should be adopted wherever possible (see also the next paragraph). In some languages it may be necessary to use some equivalent of "a (covenant) tent."

Hebrews adds **everything** to the quotation. The author may be thinking of Exodus 25 as a whole, or of verse 9 of that chapter, where the same Greek word is used.

The words for **copy** and **pattern** belong closely together, because the "heavenly sanctuary" became a **pattern** for Moses when he was told to copy it. Unfortunately, in other contexts such as Romans 5.14, the word translated pattern may itself mean copy, but this need not confuse the translation of this passage. It is unnecessarily complicated to suppose that what God showed Moses in heaven was itself a copy of some still higher reality, so that the "earthly sanctuary" was only a "copy of a copy."

Some languages may lack a term for **pattern** which could be applied to a tent. In such cases, **according to the pattern you were shown on the mountain** may be rendered as "according to the way in which you saw it on the mountain" or even "according to what you saw on the mountain."

You were shown refers in the Greek to a completed action occurring entirely in the past. (The Septuagint uses a verb suggesting an uncompleted or recent action.)

8.6 But now, Jesus has been given priestly work which is superior to theirs, just as the covenant which he arranged between God and his people is a better one, because it is based on promises of better things.

This verse continues the contrast with verse 4. **But now** suggests a contrast of present time with past time, as well as a contrast in the kind of **priestly work.** As RSV's note shows, **Jesus** or "Christ" is implied. **Has been given,** more literally "has received," means "God has given him," as a permanent possession.

The statement **Jesus has been given priestly work** may require some restructuring; for example, "God has appointed Jesus to serve as a priest" or "God has assigned Jesus to work as a priest."

The old and new orders are contrasted at three points: the new order includes (a) **superior . . . priestly work,** (b) **a better . . . covenant,** and (c) **promises of better things** (literally, "better promises"; compare "hope of something better" in 7.19; see comment). The relation between these three contrasts is as follows: contrast (a) is as great as contrast (b). Contrast (c) is literally "which is enacted on better promises." (Compare 7.11.) The basic idea is "God has given Jesus a higher priestly function (or, office) as mediator of a better covenant which is based on promises of better things."

Work which is superior to theirs may be rendered as "work which is higher than theirs." But **superior** must usually be understood as "more important." Therefore **work which is superior to theirs** may be rendered as "what Jesus does is far more important than what they do" or ". . . what other high priests do."

The "mediator" is usually an arbitrator or go-between who deals impartially with both parties who have made a contract. TEV brings out the meaning clearly. The idea of a conflict between the parties is not emphasized. "Mediator" here carries some of the same meaning as guarantee in 7.22 (see comment).

In this context it may be better to translate **arranged** as "made possible," because the Greek does not state in detail what the role of Jesus was. It would be wrong to suggest that Jesus served as a kind of go-between to work out a compromise between God and his people.

The tense of the verbs, as of the verb for <u>told</u> in verse 5, emphasizes the fact that the new covenant is permanent and remains valid.

It may be necessary to indicate what is being contrasted in the phrase **a better one.** This can be done by expanding the central part of verse 6 to read "just as the covenant which Jesus made possible between God and his people is better than the one arranged by Moses" or ". . . the one God made through Moses."

It may be difficult to render satisfactorily the final clause of verse 6, namely, **because it is based on promises of better things. It is based** suggests the establishment of the covenant, and **promises** may need to be expressed as a verb. If so, the final clause must be restructured and made more explicit, "because God established this agreement by promising that people would have better things," or ". . . would enjoy greater benefits," or ". . . would be benefited much more."

8.7   **If there had been nothing wrong with the first covenant, there would have been no need for a second one.**

This verse partly repeats 7.11b. There it is the priesthood which is in focus, not the covenant, but 8.6 has just shown how closely priesthood, covenant, and promises are linked.

If there had been nothing wrong . . . : the first covenant was shown to be defective because it could not do what it was set up to do (7.11), that is, deal effectively with sin. RSV's **"faultless"** does not mean that a covenant could itself have some moral defect. TEV makes it clear that the defect is one of function, that is to say, the covenant did not work.

If there had been nothing wrong with the first covenant may be expressed as "If the first covenant had been able to do everything it should have done" or "If there had been nothing which the first covenant could not do."

There may, however, be serious problems in rendering verse 7, because of the condition which is contrary to fact. Therefore the structure may require some modification; for example, "There was something wrong with the first covenant, and therefore a second one was necessary" or "Because the first covenant was not able to do all that it should, it was necessary to have a second covenant."

There would have been no need for a second one gives the meaning of a Greek idiom, literally "look for," which should not be translated literally; Phps rev "no need to look for a second" and TNT "God would not have been seeking a place for a second" (similarly Brc) try unsuccessfully to do so.

A second one: not until verse 13 does the author call the first covenant <u>old</u>, implying "out of date." But since in this verse the contrast between **first** and **second** is one of temporal sequence, it may be necessary to speak of "former" and "latter."

	TEV	**8.8-13**	RSV

8 But God finds fault with his people when he says,

> "The days are coming, says the Lord,
> when I will draw up a new covenant with the people of Israel and with the people of Judah.

9 It will not be like the covenant that I made with their ancestors
> on the day I took them by the hand and led them out of Egypt.
> They were not faithful to the covenant I made with them,
> and so I paid no attention to them.

10 Now, this is the covenant that I will make with the people of Israel
> in the days to come, says the Lord:
> I will put my laws in their minds and write them on their hearts.
> I will be their God,
> and they will be my people.

11 None of them will have to teach his fellow citizen or tell his fellow countryman,
> 'Know the Lord.'
> For they will all know me,
> from the least to the greatest.

12 I will forgive their sins and will no longer remember their wrongs."

13 By speaking of a new covenant, God has made the first one old; and anything that becomes old and worn out will soon disappear.

8 For he finds fault with them when he says:

> "The days will come, says the Lord,
> when I will establish a new covenant with the house of Israel
> and with the house of Judah;

9 not like the covenant that I made with their fathers
> on the day when I took them by the hand
> to lead them out of the land of Egypt;
> for they did not continue in my covenant,
> and so I paid no heed to them, says the Lord.

10 This is the covenant that I will make with the house of Israel
> after those days, says the Lord:
> I will put my laws into their minds,
> and write them on their hearts,
> and I will be their God,
> and they shall be my people.

11 And they shall not teach every one his fellow
> or every one his brother, saying,
> 'Know the Lord,'
> for all shall know me,
> from the least of them to the greatest.

12 For I will be merciful toward their iniquities,
> and I will remember their sins no more."

13 In speaking of a new covenant he treats the first as obsolete. And what is becoming obsolete and growing old is ready to vanish away.

Verses 8b-12 consist of the longest quotation in the New Testament. Its text does not correspond exactly with the Hebrew of Jeremiah 31.31-34, because as usual the writer is quoting on the basis of the Septuagint, with some additional minor changes. The translator should not attempt to harmonize the text of Hebrews with the Hebrew text of Jeremiah. See the introduction to 1.4-14.

The writer draws two conclusions from the quotation: (a) the first covenant has now been made out-of-date (verse 13); (b) the new covenant is concerned with the forgiveness of sins (verse 12). This will be repeatedly emphasized in chapter 9. Part of this quotation is repeated in 10.16,17, where point (b) is emphasized.

8.8 **But God finds fault with his people when he says,**
  "The days are coming, says the Lord,
    when I will draw up a new covenant with the people
    of Israel and with the people of Judah.

Neither the Greek text nor the meaning of the words which introduce the quotation is quite certain.

There is fairly equal manuscript evidence for two texts: (1) "he says, having found fault with them," and (2) "he says to them, having found fault." The difference in meaning is slight. In any case, "them" is "the people of the first covenant just mentioned." The finding of fault is ultimately directed to the people, though in the Greek, as in TEV and RSV, the people are addressed in the third person throughout. **God finds fault with his people** may be expressed as "God blames his people." If necessary, this may be expressed in some languages as direct discourse; for example, "God says to his people, 'You have done wrong.' "

The expression rendered **finds fault with** seems strange in introducing a quotation which is mainly a promise rather than a condemnation. However, **finds fault with** or "blames" is certainly the meaning. The same rare Greek verb is found in 2 Maccabees 2.7 (reprimanded).

He says . . . says the Lord: the repetition of **says** is in the text: the first **says** introduces the quotation, and the second **says** is part of the quotation. Some CLTs avoid the repetition in various ways; for example, DuCL "but God criticizes his people with these words: 'The days are coming,' says the Lord . . . ." There may be some complication or misunderstanding involved if the quotation is introduced as coming from **God,** and then within the quotation the expression **says the Lord** occurs. This might suggest that God is quoting the Lord or possibly, in this context, quoting Jesus. It may therefore be necessary in some languages to omit the expression **says the Lord** and in this way avoid the impression that there are two persons involved in this declaration.

The days are coming cannot always be expressed literally since "days" do not "come." The closest equivalent may be "it will happen that . . ." or ". . . in the future." GeCL has "the time is near."

Draw up a new covenant: draw up is not a technical term in Greek but a common word meaning "conclude, complete, establish." On the meaning and translation of **covenant,** see Appendix B and comments on 7.22. **I will draw up a new covenant** may be expressed as "I will make a new agreement." The Greek for **new** suggests not only "fresh" but "different."

People (see note on 7.14) is literally "house," as in verse 10a. "With the people(s) of Israel and Judah" could be clearer, since only one new covenant is to be made.

[171]

In the phrases **the people of Israel** and **the people of Judah,** the preposition **of** marks a relation of apposition; in other words, the one group of people are Israel and the other group of people are Judah. Therefore **a new covenant with the people of Israel and with the people of Judah** may need to be expressed as "a new covenant with the people who are Israel and with the people who are Judah," or simply ". . . with Israel and Judah."

The argument of verses 9-10 needs to be made clear in translation. The new covenant will not be like the old for two reasons: on the one hand, because the old covenant has been broken; and on the other hand, because the new covenant will be written on people's hearts and therefore cannot be broken.

8.9   **It will not be like the covenant that I made with their ancestors**
 on the day I took them by the hand and led them out of Egypt.
They were not faithful to the covenant I made with them, and so I paid no attention to them.

It will not be like the covenant . . . : as verse 10 shows (I will be their God, and they will be my people, see Lev 26.12), the new covenant has something in common with the old (see comment on 7.22). The difference is that the new covenant will be based on inward obedience to a different kind of law (7.12). Verse 10 will make this clear. Hebrews uses the ordinary Greek word for **made,** which is different from the more technical term used in the Septuagint. TEV preserves this distinction by using draw up in verse 8.

It may be necessary to repeat "The new covenant" rather than employ a pronoun such as **It.** Therefore the first part of verse 9 may be rendered as "The new covenant will not be like the covenant that I made with their ancestors."

I took them by the hand is an idiom meaning "to guide carefully" or "to lead with care." Therefore **I took them by the hand** may be rendered as "I carefully guided them."

In rendering **led them out** it is essential to use an expression which is applicable to people and not merely to animals.

"The land of" before Egypt is omitted in TEV, DuCL, and GeCL, though it is in the Greek. The readers of the translation are expected to know that Egypt is the name of a country.

They were not faithful brings out the meaning of "did not continue in." They did not keep the promise to be "God's people." **They were not faithful to the covenant** may be rendered as "They did not continue to do what the covenant said they should do" or ". . . what they should do in accordance with the agreement."

Paid no attention to means "disregarded" or even "rejected." **I paid no attention to them** may be rendered negatively as "I let them go their own way," or one may employ some such expression as "I abandoned them" or "I went off and left them."

8.10   Now, this is the covenant that I will make with the people
          of Israel
       in the days to come, says the Lord:
    I will put my laws in their minds
       and write them on their hearts.
    I will be their God,
       and they will be my people.

The adverb **Now** functions in this context as a transitional, similar to "Therefore."

This is the covenant must be expressed in some languages as "this is the kind of covenant," since it is the nature of the covenant and not the fact of the covenant which is in focus.

As in other contexts, **in the days to come** may be expressed as "in the future."

As in verse 8 there may be complications with the phrase **says the Lord,** which may make it seem that two persons are involved. It is often possible to render **says the Lord** as "I, the Lord God, am speaking." In this way "the Lord" is made identical in reference with "God."

Laws: not "law," as in Jeremiah 31.33.

Minds . . . hearts: the most likely Greek text is "mind" in the singular, followed by **hearts** in the plural (so KJV; similarly NEB). The change is not significant, and translators are right to use either the singular or the plural in both places, whichever is more natural in their own language.

Minds and **hearts** are similar in meaning. Another Greek word of similar meaning is translated "conscience"; the writer uses it three times (RSV 9.9,14; 10.2) in his commentary on this passage of Jeremiah (see also 10.22). TEV translates this term heart in 9.9 and 10.22; conscience in 9.14; and feel guilty in 10.2. (See the comments on these verses, especially 9.9.) In biblical language the "heart" is the seat of the understanding, not of the emotions.

The figurative expressions **I will put my laws in their minds and write them on their hearts** may require some adjustment; for example, "I will cause them to think about my laws, and they will keep them in their hearts" or ". . . their hearts will truly know them."

The last part of this verse is literally "I will be to them a God, and they shall be to me a people" (Phps). This does not suggest "one God among others" or even "one people among others." It points to the conviction that God had freely chosen Israel as his people and had not always been linked to Israel, for example, by God's being the ancestor of the tribe.

Since in some languages one cannot, as it were, possess God, it is not possible to say **I will be their God.** However, it is normally possible to say "I will be the God whom they will worship" or "They will worship me as God."

They will be my people may likewise require some modification, since "to possess people" may be equivalent to having people as slaves. Accordingly **they will be my people** may be rendered as "they will be the people whom I will care for" or ". . . who will look to me for help."

[173]

8.11   **None of them will have to teach his fellow citizen
or tell his fellow countryman,
'Know the Lord.'
For they will all know me,
from the least to the greatest.**

Fellow citizen is the text preferred by the UBS Greek New Testament and most modern translations, rather than "neighbour," followed by JB (but not BJ), TNT. **Fellow citizen** may be translated in some languages as "one who belongs to the same nation."

RSV's "**fellow**" and "**brother**" are expressed by parallel terms in Hebrew poetry, and these are similar in meaning. SpCL combines the two phrases: "No one will have to teach anyone, neither his companion nor his brother, so that they know the Lord . . . ." In this type of context **fellow countryman** may be rendered as "person of the same clan." The term rendered **fellow citizen** is often more inclusive than the term rendered **fellow countryman,** but in a poetic passage such as this the difference is not emphasized.

It may seem strange to command people to "know" someone; GeCL has "learn to know," "get to know the Lord." For **they will all know me,** GeCL has "everyone will know who I am." However, "to know someone," for Hebrew thought, involved experience and a personal relationship. Because of the awkwardness in commanding someone to "know" an individual, it may be better to place this type of statement in an indirect form with some kind of auxiliary or affix indicating obligation or necessity; for example, "No one of them will have to teach anyone of the same nation or of the same clan that he should know the Lord" or ". . . come to know the Lord." In some instances it may be better to translate **Know the Lord** as "Acknowledge the Lord as God."

For they will all know me may be expressed as "For they will all acknowledge that I am their God" or "They will all recognize me as God."

The phrase **from the least to the greatest** involves status in society and may be rendered as "from the least important to the most important" or possibly "from the little people to the big people." Sometimes this is expressed idiomatically in terms of the kinds of houses that people have; for example, "from those who live in the smallest houses to those who live in the largest houses."

8.12   **I will forgive their sins
and will no longer remember their wrongs."**

KJV's "and iniquities" is the correct text in Hebrews 10.17, but not in this verse nor in Jeremiah 31.34 (Septuagint Jer 38.34). The two halves of this verse are similar in meaning. They form the climax of the whole passage, both in Jeremiah and in Hebrews. The writer of Hebrews shows this in 10.16-18. As in similar contexts **I will forgive their sins** must be expressed as "I will forgive their guilt."

Remember (see 2.6) is the literal translation, and it is kept by most modern versions with only slight variations (GeCL "I will never think of their guilt again";

JB "never call their sins to mind"). However, to "remember" in the Old Testament involved taking action; see Genesis 9.15,16, about God "remembering" his covenant, and 1 Kings 17.18, about Elijah "remembering" the sins of the widow. The meaning is virtually "I will take no action against them because of their sins."

A strictly literal translation of **will no longer remember** might suggest merely a failure of memory on the part of God. But God's negative action is purposeful, and so **will no longer remember** may be rendered as "I purposely will not think about any longer."

Wrongs means wrong things done by God's people, not to them.

8.13   By speaking of a new covenant, God has made the first one old; and anything that becomes old and worn out will soon disappear.

The writer emphasizes once again that the new covenant is not merely better than the old but takes the place of the old. See the introduction to chapter 7. The meaning is not simply that talk of a "new" covenant makes the earlier covenant "old" by comparison, but that God himself, **by speaking of a new covenant,** has declared and therefore **made the first one old.** The tense of the Greek verb refers to a past event whose effect continues into the present.

The expression of means by a phrase such as **By speaking of a new covenant** may be difficult to render adequately in some languages. Sometimes such a phrase may be combined with what follows by the addition of an expression such as "in this way" or "thus"; for example, "God spoke about a new covenant and in this way he made the first one old" or ". . . thus he caused the first one to become old."

Some languages have different words for "old," one for referring to old people and another for referring to old cloth or similar objects. This latter meaning is more suited to this context.

Worn out means essentially the same as **old;** NEB "old and ageing." Both expressions may, if necessary, be translated by a single word.

The verb for **disappear** is sometimes used of laws which are abolished or which fall into disuse. The phrase **will soon disappear** may be expressed as "will soon no longer exist" or "in a short time will not exist."

Chapter 9

Earthly and Heavenly Worship

1 The first covenant had rules for worship and a man-made place for worship as well. 2 A tent was put up, the outer one, which was called the Holy Place. In it were the lampstand and the table with the bread offered to God. 3 Behind the second curtain was the tent called the Most Holy Place. 4 In it were the gold altar for the burning of incense and the Covenant Box all covered with gold and containing the gold jar with the manna in it, Aaron's stick that had sprouted leaves, and the two stone tablets with the commandments written on them. 5 Above the Box were the winged creatures representing God's presence, with their wings spread over the place where sins were forgiven. But now is not the time to explain everything in detail.

1 Now even the first covenant had regulations for worship and an earthly sanctuary. 2 For a tent[p] was prepared, the outer one, in which were the lampstand and the table and the bread of the Presence;[q] it is called the Holy Place. 3 Behind the second cutain stood a tent[p] called the Holy of Holies, 4 having the golden altar of incense and the ark of the covenant covered on all sides with gold, which contained a golden urn holding the manna, and Aaron's rod that budded, and the tables of the covenant; 5 above it were the cherubim of glory overshadowing the mercy seat. Of these things we cannot now speak in detail.

[p] Or *tabernacle*
[q] Greek *the presentation of the loaves*

Verses 1-22 and the following section (9.23—10.18) tie together the themes of sacrifice (7.1—8.3) and forgiveness (8.4-13).

This section heading may be rendered "The worship of God on earth and in heaven" or "The way God is worshiped on earth and in heaven."

<u>9.1</u>   **The first covenant had rules for worship and a man-made place for worship as well.**

RSV's "**Now**" (NEB "indeed"), omitted by TEV, shows that the writer is taking up the argument again at the point at which he left it before the quotation from Jeremiah. The phrase which RSV translates "**Now**" may also begin a comparison or contrast which is later completed by the word translated <u>But</u> in verse 11.

The first covenant: covenant is implied. "The first tent" is grammatically possible but is not the meaning chosen by any of the translations consulted. Most manuscripts include a word meaning "**even**" or "also," which is included in RSV, JB, BJ, Lu, and some other translations. The UBS Greek text prints it in square brackets. If this is part of the original text, it is a way of stating what the two covenants had in common, before going on to contrast them (compare 3.2 and 8.3, RSV). GeCL misleadingly translates the word for "even" as "but." In fact, the contrast begins with **man-made** (see below).

In English it seems perfectly natural to speak of "a covenant having rules," but this involves a particularly complex relationship, and in many languages a covenant cannot possess anything, much less rules. The meaning of **The first covenant had rules for worship** may be expressed by translating "In order to act in accordance with the first covenant, there were certain rules for ways in which people should worship God," or "In order to keep the first covenant, people had to worship God according to certain rules," or ". . . according to certain ways that were necessary." Or perhaps "The first covenant was given with rules . . . ."

Worship, as the context shows, means not "the spiritual content of worship" (that is, "adoration"), but "liturgical forms."

Man-made, like on earth in 8.4, means "belonging to this world," not to heaven (8.5). TEV is followed by GeCL; DuCL has "on earth"; like RSV, FrCL has "**earthly.**" This correctly suggests not only the location but the nature of the place for worship, like SpCL "of this world" and NEB "material." **Man-made** or "**earthly**" is emphasized in the text in order to show that the writer is moving away from what the two covenants have in common to what makes them different. This is brought out by Brc "it had a sanctuary, although a this-worldly one." The **place** rather than the "maker" of the sanctuary is what matters here. There is a good note in the TEV Word List on "Tent of the LORD's presence."

And . . . as well indicates that the rules for worship were closely related to the place for worship. The Greek is literally "the," not "a" **place for worship.** This is because the writer could assume that his readers knew about it. However, modern readers may not, so **a** is correct.

Place for worship or "sanctuary," literally "holy place," is the entire place of worship. It is also called a **tent** in 8.2. It is not the same expression in the Greek as the one designating the Holy Place in verse 2 (literally, "holy places"), which is the outer part of the sanctuary. The position is, however, complicated by the fact that the same word for tent is used to describe the whole building (8.2), the Holy Place (9.2), and the Holy of Holies or Most Holy Place (9.3). GeCL solves the problem by beginning verse 2 "Two tents had been put up." JB is more precise: "There was a tent which comprised two compartments." The writer was not interested in the details of any particular sanctuary, but the details which he does give may be fitted together within a general picture of a large room divided into two parts by a curtain:

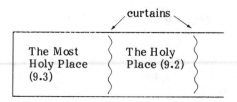

"sanctuary," <u>place for worship,</u> <u>tent,</u>
"tabernacle" (8.2; 9.1).

In some languages it may be strange to speak of **a man-made place,** since a term for **place** may only suggest a location rather than a construction. Because the reference in this context is to the sanctuary, it may be necessary to translate **a man-made place** as "a tent which was made by people."

Instead of adding **as well** to the end of verse 1, it may be necessary to relate more closely the phrases **a man-made place for worship** and **rules for worship.** The resulting translation may be "rules for how to worship God and also a tent for worship which had been made by people."

9.2 **A tent was put up, the outer one, which was called the Holy Place. In it were the lampstand and the table with the bread offered to God.**

Notice how verses 2-5 balance one another, as seen in the literal translation of RSV:

Contents of outer tent, verse 2a	Contents of inner tent, verses 4-5
name of outer tent, verse 2b	name of inner tent, verse 3b

Second Curtain,
verse 3a

This balance, called chiasmus, is common in biblical language. If it sounds strange in the receptor language, the translator should feel free to change the order.

RSV's "**For**" does not imply that verse 2 gives a reason for the statement in verse 1, but that verse 2 will develop the content of verse 1. Therefore the word can often be omitted in translation.

Put up may mean "built," "equipped," or both; RSV and NEB "**prepared.**" TEV translates the same word <u>arranged</u> in verse 6, where it refers to the contents of the sanctuary rather than the building itself. There is little difference between the translations "The place of worship was equipped with the lampstand . . ." or "the place of worship was built, and in it were put the lampstand . . . ."

As already mentioned, it may be necessary to render **was put up** in rather different ways, depending upon the receptor language; for example, "was stretched," or "was hung on posts," or "was tied down."

Outer is literally "first," the first which anyone enters. The appositional and explanatory phrase **the outer one** must be more specifically marked in some languages; for example, "a tent was put up, I mean the outer one" or ". . . the first one"; or "a tent was put up, that is, the first one to be entered" or ". . . the first one that anyone could enter."

TEV logically brings together RSV's **"outer one"** and **"the Holy Place,"** since they identify the room being described.

There may be complications in speaking of the first part of the sanctuary as being **the Holy Place,** since as in some languages "place" only indicates a location and not an enclosure. Therefore **the Holy Place** must be rendered in some languages "the Holy Room."

The lampstand . . . : the shows that the first readers will know about these objects, not that they have been mentioned before. An indefinite article, or its equivalent, may be more natural for readers to whom these things are not familiar. However, modern European translations keep "the." The use of the definite article **the** shows that **lampstand** and **table with the bread offered to God** were unique objects. As such, the phrases **the lampstand** and **the table with the bread offered to God** become practically equivalent to proper names. The equivalent of these phrases in some languages is a phrase such as "a special lampstand" and "a particular table with the bread offered to God."

The **lampstand** is described in Exodus 25.31-39 and Leviticus 24.1-4. **The bread offered to God** (Lev 24.5-9; compare Mark 2.26) was kept on the **table** (Exo 25.23-30; 37.10-16), so TEV translates **the table with the bread offered to God** rather than literally "the table and the bread." As Leviticus 24.5-9 shows, **bread** is plural, that is, "loaves," and it may be necessary to render **bread** as "loaves of bread." They were shaped like large pancakes (probably 24-30 centimeters, 9-12 inches, across, and a centimeter or two, or less than an inch, thick).

Bread offered to God may be expressed as "the bread which the priests had offered to God," or ". . . had set aside for God," or ". . . had given to God."

9.3 Behind the second curtain was the tent called the Most Holy Place.

The second curtain: there is no reference to a "first curtain" in Greek, only to a "first tent" in verse 2, and to a "second curtain" and "a tent called Holy of Holies" in verse 3. TEV attempts to distinguish the two tents by referring to the "first tent" as **the outer one,** but this leaves the confusion of mentioning a **second curtain** without a first curtain having been mentioned. Late Jewish writers mention a first curtain in front of the Holy Place. Phps avoids this difficulty by omitting "second." Most modern English translations prefer **curtain** to the traditional "veil," which now suggests an article of clothing. Since no mention has been made of a first curtain, it may be best to translate **Behind the second curtain** as "Behind a curtain" or "Behind a drape."

[179]

A literal rendering of **the tent called the Most Holy Place** may wrongly imply two different tents rather than a single sanctuary consisting of two parts. In order to avoid such complications, it may be better to translate the phrase as "the part of the tent called the Most Holy Room," since, again, a literal rendering of **Place** might not suggest an enclosed area.

The traditional expression rendered **"Holy of Holies"** (RSV) is a Hebrew idiom meaning **the Most** (FrCL "Very") **Holy Place.** GeCL refers to a glossary note on "Temple." In order to indicate clearly the significance of **the Most Holy Place,** it may be possible to speak of "that room which belongs to God more than any other place" or "that room which has been dedicated to God more than any other room."

9.4　　**In it were the gold altar for the burning of incense and the Covenant Box all covered with gold and containing the gold jar with the manna in it, Aaron's stick that had sprouted leaves, and the two stone tablets with the commandments written on them.**

The Greek word here translated **altar for the burning of incense** usually means a censer or incense-holder. But here it must refer to the wooden box, overlaid with gold, on which incense was burned twice a day (see Exo 30.1-10). This altar was in fact kept in the outer part of the sanctuary (see Exo 30.6), but it would be wrong to change the statement in Hebrews to agree with the statement in Exodus 30. A literal rendering of **the gold altar** might suggest that the altar was made entirely of gold, but in reality it was merely covered with gold. It may therefore be appropriate to translate **the gold altar** as "the altar which was covered with gold."

In some languages **incense** is referred to as "sweet-smelling resin," and in a few cases it is "sweet-smelling medicine." Where there is no specific term or phrase for **incense,** it may be described as "a sweet-smelling substance" or even "a sweet-smelling powder."

Covenant Box: TEV and other CLTs rightly use **Box** in place of the traditional "ark," which is no longer part of common language, except for Noah's ark, which was quite different. This **Box** is described in Exodus 25.10-16. It was called the **Covenant Box** because it contained various objects, all mentioned in this verse, which were closely linked with the making of the covenant between God and Israel. According to 1 Kings 8.9, "the box" contained nothing but the two stone tablets, but the writer of Hebrews seems to have ignored this text. The Greek of Hebrews 9.3-4 cannot mean that the **Most Holy Place** contained **the gold jar,** etc.

In selecting an appropriate term for **Box,** it is important to choose an expression such as "Chest," which will refer to a container used in preserving or storing important objects.

There may, however, be some difficulty in relating **Covenant** to **Box.** One may use a phrase such as "Box which symbolizes the Covenant," or "Box which

[180]

points to the Covenant," or "Box which tells about God's agreement," or "Box which shows God's agreement." TEV fourth edition **and containing** replaces the clearer TEV third edition "The box contained."

On the **jar,** see Exodus 16.33. **The gold jar** which contained the manna was of a size to hold approximately two liters. The expression **gold jar** can be translated "jar made of gold." In some languages there are a number of different terms for jar, depending on its shape, its size, the material of which it is made, and whether or not it has a top. It is impossible to determine precisely the shape of the jar involved, and therefore, if possible, one should select a term having a general meaning.

On **Aaron's stick,** see Numbers 17.8-10. **Aaron's stick** may be rendered as "Aaron's walking stick" or "the stick which Aaron used when he walked." The clause **that had sprouted leaves** may be rendered in some languages as "from which leaves had come out" or "on which leaves had grown."

On the **stone tablets,** see Exodus 25.16 and Deuteronomy 10.3-5. The phrase which RSV literally translates "**the tables of the covenant**" is found in the Septuagint of 1 Kings 8.9, and a similar phrase is found in Deuteronomy 9.9,11. Several translations expand this phrase to make it clearer for the modern reader; DuCL "the stone tablets with the law of the covenant." **Two** is not in the Greek text; but see Exodus 32.15 and Deuteronomy 10.1. In modern English, "table" usually means a piece of furniture, so TEV uses the diminutive **tablets.** The Old Testament passages referred to show that they must have been small enough to carry, but large enough for the commandments to be cut into the stone. **The two stone tablets** may be expressed as "the two tablets which were made out of stone" or "the two slabs of stone."

With the commandments written on them may be rendered as "with God's commandments written on them" or "with words about what God had commanded." It is important in rendering **the commandments** to use the same type of expression which is used in the Old Testament.

9.5   **Above the Box were the winged creatures representing God's presence, with their wings spread over the place where sins were forgiven. But now is not the time to explain everything in detail.**

There is no doubt that RSV's "**above it**" means **Above the Box. The winged creatures** (TEV third edition "glorious creatures") are the "cherubs" or "cherubim" who were signs of God's glory or presence. RSV's "**cherubim of glory**" is the literal translation of a Hebrew idiom. GeCL keeps the word "cherubs," with a glossary note explaining that the "cherubim" are "winged creatures in the shape of animals and men, who were represented as watchers over the Ark of the Covenant."

Winged creatures: there are particularly difficult problems involved in rendering in English the term "cherubim" (TEV **winged creatures**), which is a Greek borrowing from Hebrew. For most English-speaking people the term "cherubim" is completely meaningless, and in order to indicate clearly that it is plural, one

[181]

would be compelled to use the expression "cherubims." However, this is not a recognized form. The proper plural form, "cherubs," usually refers to beautiful and innocent people, especially children. "The winged animals" does not do justice to the composite nature of these ancient symbols. Their one distinguishing characteristic was the fact of having wings. But to refer to the objects themselves, it seems necessary to use some such expression as "creatures" or perhaps "beings." Yet these objects were actually representations made of hammered gold. It may be appropriate to speak of "winged images" or "winged figures."

The phrase **representing God's presence** may be even more difficult to translate than the phrase **the winged creatures**. In some languages, **representing God's presence** may be rendered as "standing for God's presence," "pointing to God's presence," "showing that God was present," or "symbolizing God's being there."

These objects are described in Exodus 25.17-22, together with **the place where sins were forgiven** (RSV "mercy seat"). The "mercy seat" or "cover" (RSV note on Exo 25.17) was a covering for the ark or **Covenant Box**. This "cover" was splashed with blood once a year on the Day of Atonement, as a sign that Israel's sins were forgiven. The same word is used with an extended meaning in Romans 3.25 to describe Jesus as "the means by which men's sins are forgiven."

With their wings spread over the place where sins were forgiven may have to be rendered as a separate sentence; for example, "Their wings were spread over the place where sins were forgiven" or "Their wings cast a shadow over the place where sins were forgiven."

The passive expression **where sins were forgiven** may need to be made active in translation, "where God forgave sins."

Everything, literally "of which" (plural), refers back to verses 1-5a as a whole, or perhaps to the **rules for worship** mentioned in verse 1, but certainly not to the cherubim alone.

Now is not the time to explain everything in detail seems to be a reference to time, but in reality it is a reference to the location in this letter, though it can be interpreted as "the period of time in which the author was writing this letter." It may be better to translate the last sentence of verse 5 as "but this is not the place to explain everything with many words," in which the phrase "with many words" may be the equivalent of **in detail**.

TEV	**9.6-10**	RSV

6 This is how those things have been arranged. The priests go into the outer tent every day to perform their duties, 7 but only the High Priest goes into the inner tent, and he does so only once a year. He takes with him blood which he offers to God on behalf of himself and for the sins which the people have committed without

6 These preparations having thus been made, the priests go continually into the outer tent,ᵖ performing their ritual duties; 7 but into the second only the high priest goes, and he but once a year, and not without taking blood which he offers for himself and for the errors of the people. 8 By this the Holy Spirit indicates that the way into the

knowing they were sinning. 8 The Holy Spirit clearly teaches from all these arrangements that the way into the Most Holy Place has not yet been opened as long as the outer tent still stands. 9 This is a symbol which points to the present time. It means that the offerings and animal sacrifices presented to God cannot make the worshiper's heart perfect, 10 since they have to do only with food, drink, and various purification ceremonies. These are all outward rules, which apply only until the time when God will establish the new order.

sanctuary is not yet opened as long as the outer tent[p] is still standing 9 (which is symbolic for the present age). According to this arrangement, gifts and sacrifices are offered which cannot perfect the conscience of the worshiper, 10 but deal only with food and drink and various ablutions, regulations for the body imposed until the time of reformation.

[p] Or *tabernacle*

<u>9.6</u>   **This is how those things have been arranged. The priests go into the outer tent every day to perform their duties,**

This verse marks a minor step in the argument, expressed by KJV's "Now," and in other translations by beginning a new paragraph. Verses 2-5 have described the sanctuary; verses 6-7 will describe what happened there.

The first few words are literally "these things having thus been prepared." Before translating **This is how those things have been arranged,** it is essential to determine whether the sentence in question refers back to the preceding paragraph (and thus involves the location of various objects) or whether this sentence refers to what follows, namely, the various rituals to be performed. If, as is more probable, the first sentence of verse 6 refers specifically to the arrangement of objects, it may be combined with the preceding paragraph as a concluding statement; for example, "This, then, is how the various things in the sanctuary have been arranged" or ". . . were arranged." If another possible interpretation of the Greek is used, and the first part of verse 6 is combined with what follows, it may be rendered as "In view of how the objects in the sanctuary are arranged, the following is what happened." The Greek word for **arranged** is the same used in verse 2 (TEV <u>put up</u>). Here as in other places the author passes smoothly from one aspect of the subject to another—in this case, from the description of what the tent contained to an account of what went on in it. **This** and **those things** probably refer back to verses 1-5. Knox emphasizes this by linking 6a with 5: "We have no time to treat of these more particularly, but this was the general fashion of it." GeCL links this phrase with what follows, but somewhat undertranslates it: "so the whole holy place consists of two parts. Each day the priests go into the first tent . . . ." The translation will vary slightly according to whether the **"preparations"** (RSV) are thought of as being (a) for a particular service, for example, lighting the candles, preparing the bread, or (b) the more permanent furnishings of the sanctuary. (b) fits the context better; this is brought out by Phps' "Under this arrangement" and JB's "Under these provisions."

9.6

On **tent,** see 8.2 and 9.1-2. Brc translates "first tent" here and "second tent" in verse 7 as "the outer part" and "the inner part of the tabernacle." It is often better to speak of **the outer tent** as "the first part of the tent" or "the first room of the tent."

Every day is more precisely "**continually**" (RSV). The priests, in fact, went twice a day into the outer part of the sanctuary; see Numbers 18.2-6.

To perform their duties may be rendered as "to do what they must do" or "to do what their work as priests requires them to do." On **duties,** see comments on "worship," verse 1.

9.7   but only the High Priest goes into the inner tent, and he does
       so only once a year. He takes with him blood which he offers
       to God on behalf of himself and for the sins which the people
       have committed without knowing they were sinning.

In this context it must be made clear in translation that there is only one **High Priest** at any time. **The High Priest** may be expressed as "the priest who is above all other priests" or "the priest who commands all the other priests." In some languages this can be simply expressed as "the most important priest."

Once a year: only is understood. This phrase refers to the Day of Atonement, on which offerings were made in order to obtain God's forgiveness for all but the most serious sins. The liturgy is described in Leviticus 16, especially verses 2,14,15,29,34; see also Exodus 30.10.

He takes with him blood simplifies a double negative which is literally "not without blood." The original is a little stronger, equivalent to "he must take blood with him." The blood is that of the sacrifice made in the outer part of the sanctuary for the high priest's own sins and those of the people. It may be necessary in some languages to specify the source of such blood; for example, "He takes with him the blood from a sacrificed animal" or ". . . blood from an animal which has been sacrificed." Otherwise the implication might be that this blood was his own blood.

For **on behalf of,** see 7.25,27 and comments.

Without knowing they were sinning: FrCL "through ignorance"; GeCL "without ill-will," perhaps "without intending to sin." The text is a single word which can mean "oversight" in the sense of "something left undone by mistake"; see Genesis 43.12; Sirach 23.2; 51.19.

Without knowing they were sinning may be expressed as "when they did not know that what they were doing was sin" or "when they did not realize that they were sinning."

9.8   The Holy Spirit clearly teaches from all these arrangements
       that the way into the Most Holy Place has not yet been opened
       as long as the outer tent still stands.

GeCL and Phps start a new paragraph here. The writer has now finished his description of the forms of Old Testament worship and moves on to a Christian interpretation of its inner meaning.

On **The Holy Spirit,** see comment on 2.4.

The verb which TEV translates **clearly teaches** (Brc "makes it clear") has a general meaning here: "shows" FrCL; **"indicates"** RSV; "signifies" NEB; "means" Mft; "meant us to see" Knox.

From all these arrangements is simply "this" in the Greek text. The text seems rather to refer to the restrictions on entry into the **Most Holy Place,** that is, to verse 7 rather than to the whole of verses 1-7. If so, "by this rule" would be a clearer translation.

The meaning of the second half of the verse, from **that the way into the Most Holy Place,** is not at all clear. It must be understood in the light of verses 11-12. A rather literal translation would be "By this the Holy Spirit shows that the way of [that is, to or into] the holy (places) has not yet been revealed, as long as the first tent still has (its) standing [or existence]." The difficulties may be summed up as follows, using the wording of the literal translation:

I. Does "the holy (places)" mean
   (a)   the earthly sanctuary, as in 8.2; 9.2, or
   (b)   the heavenly sanctuary, as in 9.12?
   Knox's translation "the true sanctuary" chooses (b); other translations leave the question open.

II. Does "the holy (places)" mean
   (a)   the whole sanctuary, as in 8.2,
   (b)   only the outer part, as in 9.2, or
   (c)   only the inner part?
   Most translations either choose (c), like TEV, or leave the question open; Knox appears to prefer (a).

III. Does "the first tent" mean
   (a)   the outer part of the earthly sanctuary, as in 9.2,6, or
   (b)   the earthly sanctuary as a whole, contrasted with the greater and more perfect tent of verse 11?
   (a) is chosen by TEV, JB, and TNT; (b) is chosen by NEB "earlier tent," Knox and probably Phps. If (a) is chosen, "first" will mean "first in place"; if (b) is chosen, "first" will mean "first in time."

IV. Does "has (its) standing" mean
   (a)   continue to exist, or remain in use, or
   (b)   maintain its status?
   Among translations consulted, only Knox chooses (b).

This list shows the need for translations to show clearly which of the various possibilities they have chosen. In case of doubt, an equally clear alternative may be given in a note. In making their choice, translators cannot rely only on the way in which the writer varies from verse to verse. In any case, the expression "has (its) standing" is not used anywhere else in the New Testament. The translator must also take into account the wider context.

The most probable translation of verse 8 would be "The Holy Spirit shows us by this means that the way into the real tent had not yet been opened as long as the old tent still remained in use."

The Most Holy Place: since "the real tent" (the suggested probable translation of this phrase) is a reference to the Holy Place in heaven, it may be good to make this explicit. Accordingly, one may translate "the Holy Spirit shows us in this way that the entrance into the Holy Room of the heavenly sanctuary had not been opened as long as the tent of the old sanctuary was still in use" or ". . . was still being used." It would also be possible to speak of "the sanctuary of the old covenant." Though these expressions do not reflect precisely the wording of the Greek text, the reference is clear.

In languages in which the passive of **has not yet been opened** would be unnatural, it may be necessary to use an expression of state, namely, "was not yet open."

Verses 9-10 involve a slight change in point of view. In this chapter the main contrast is generally between the old covenant and the new. The "new covenant" has been set up by Christ, as the writer will state in verses 11-15. It is effective now (verses 24,26; compare verse 11). Yet the results of what he has done remain at least partly in the future; they are something to hope for (7.19 and 10.23). In verse 8 the old temple and all that it stands for are in the past. Yet in verses 9-10 the present time, in which the old sacrifices still have some value as a symbol or illustration, is contrasted with **the time when God will establish the new order** (verse 10). God and the new order are implied, as RSV shows.

The problem for translators is to decide whether or not the writer thinks of the **new order** as already established. In order to decide this, it is first necessary to discover in what sense the writer thinks of Old Testament forms of worship as still having any value. The key to the problem is given in the middle part of verses 9-10 and is reflected in Knox's translation, "that allegory still holds good at the present day." The "symbolic" value of the Old Testament sacrifices is negative, not positive. What the Old Testament says about worship under the "old covenant" is proof that something more effective was needed.[1]

Translators solve this problem in one of two ways, corresponding broadly to the translations **will establish** and "established," verse 10. The second translation makes a smoother transition in the immediate context and is rather more likely. See also comments on verse 11. Another possibility is for the **new order** to be understood as future for those who shared in Old Testament worship, but present for the writer and his readers. So GeCL "these rules only had meaning until God set up the new order"; similarly Phps and JB.

---

[1] GeCL understands the new order or "time of reformation" as future for those who shared in Old Testament worship, but present for the writer and his readers: "These rules only had meaning until God set up the new order." Similarly Phps, "only intended to be valid until the time when Christ should establish the truth."

9.9 **This is a symbol which points to the present time. It means that the offerings and animal sacrifices presented to God cannot make the worshiper's heart perfect,**

What **is a symbol**? Translations which take the "first tent" in verse 8 to be the outer tent of the earthly sanctuary will take **This** to be the outer tent too; Phps "For in this outer tent we see a picture of the present time." Translations which take "the first tent" to mean "the former tent" or "sanctuary" will understand **This** in verse 9 in a more general sense. Grammatically **This** is the tent, but all these arrangements connected with worship are included too.

In view of the fact that so much is potentially included in the symbolism of the sanctuary, it may be legitimate to translate the first sentence of verse 9 as "All of this is a symbol which points to the present time," or "All this shows us something about the present time," or "All of this is a picture about what is important now."

In place of **It means** it may be legitimate to repeat the subject of the first sentence; for example, "All this means" or "All this shows."

Offerings and animal sacrifices: animal is implied since the reference is only to Old Testament worship, not as in 8.3. **Animal sacrifices** are contrasted with the sacrifice of Christ, to be mentioned in verses 11-14. The **animal sacrifices** were also **offerings**; one might translate "animal sacrifices and other offerings."

Cannot make may be expressed as "cannot cause to be" or "cannot cause to become."

Worshiper is "one who shares in the public worship" mentioned in verse 1.

Heart in Greek is literally "conscience," as in verse 14; 10.2,22; 13.18; compare Wisdom 17.10. **Heart** and **make ... perfect** are key words for describing the purpose of sacrifice, and thus of what Christ has done. See comments on 2.10 and 5.9.

The word usually translated "conscience" in the New Testament sometimes has the general meaning "consciousness," especially consciousness of having done right or wrong. The function of the conscience is to cause inward pain when one has done wrong. However, sin often makes the conscience function badly, so that someone may not be conscious of the wrong he has done (a possibility suggested in 1 Cor 4.4), or he may suffer the pain of conscience over matters which should not trouble a Christian at all, because Christ has set him free (see 1 Cor 10.25-29). In Hebrews, except in 13.18, the situation is as follows: those who do not have faith in Christ suffer the pain of conscience because of the wrong they have done. The Old Testament sacrifices can do nothing to put this right. Christ's sacrifice of himself on the cross makes believers clean from their sins, and thus their consciences cease to give them pain. The thought of this verse is developed in 9.14, and more fully in 8.10-11. In all these passages, the "conscience," like the heart, is an aspect of a human being's whole nature, and of his relationship to God.

In some languages the focal element of the feelings, will, and personality may not be the heart or even the conscience, but the liver, or the abdomen, or even the throat.

In speaking about the perfection of the heart or the conscience, one may talk about the way in which something "ought to be." Therefore, **cannot make the worshiper's heart perfect** may be rendered as "cannot cause the worshiper's heart to be as it ought to be" or ". . . as good as it ought to be."

9.10   **since they have to do only with food, drink, and various purification ceremonies. These are all outward rules, which apply only until the time when God will establish the new order.**

The pronoun **they** must refer clearly to the offerings and animal sacrifices. It may be important to repeat at least some aspects of the previous statement, for example, "the things offered to God," to make the meaning clear.

Food and **drink** are plural in the text: "things to eat and drink," referring to Old Testament regulations about what might or might not be eaten and drunk. **Food, drink** may be rendered as "what one should eat and what one should drink" or "what God allows people to eat and drink."

Various purification ceremonies is literally "baptisms"; see comment on 6.2. **Various purification ceremonies** may be rendered as "various ways in which people could purify themselves," or ". . . could become pure," or ". . . could get rid of what made them unclean."

Most translations are based on the same text as the UBS Greek New Testament, in which **outward rules** includes **all** the **rules to do with food, drink, and various purification ceremonies.** Phps and Zür follow a less likely text which makes the **outward rules** another item in the list: "various washings and rules for bodily conduct." The word for **rules** is the one used in verse 1. Some translations put **outward rules** first and give the examples later; for example, JB "they are rules about the outward life, connected with foods and drinks and washing at various times." The "rules about the outward life" are contrasted with the heart or "conscience" (verse 9).

The expression **outward rules** may be almost meaningless if translated literally. It may be possible to speak about "rules about how one performs rituals," but it may be clearer to translate **outward rules** as "rules which have nothing to do with one's heart" or "rules which have nothing to do with the person inside of each of us."

Establish the new order (RSV **"reformation"**) translates a Greek word related to an adjective meaning "straight," "upright." In order to give the full meaning of "putting things straight," TEV fourth edition (like GeCL, TNT) uses the phrase **the new order.** JB's "until it should be time to reform them," that is, "the rules about worship," is too narrow. Brc's "only until the time when by the action of God religion is totally reformed and reconstructed" gives the meaning precisely but is rather long. The text refers to the fulfillment of the Jewish hope for a new world, not a mere improvement of this world.

TEV fourth edition avoids words like "reform" and "reformation" perhaps because in current English they are increasingly used to refer to some superficial improvement in the existing situation. **Establish the new order** may be expressed in some languages as "make everything new," or "cause everything to be new and different," or "cause a new way of living to come into existence."

TEV   **9.11-14**   RSV

11 But Christ has already come as the High Priest of the good things that are already here.[e] The tent in which he serves is greater and more perfect; it is not a man-made tent, that is, it is not a part of this created world. 12 When Christ went through the tent and entered once and for all into the Most Holy Place, he did not take the blood of goats and bulls to offer as a sacrifice; rather, he took his own blood and obtained eternal salvation for us. 13 The blood of goats and bulls and the ashes of a burnt calf are sprinkled on the people who are ritually unclean, and this purifies them by taking away their ritual impurity. 14 Since this is true, how much more is accomplished by the blood of Christ! Through the eternal Spirit he offered himself as a perfect sacrifice to God. His blood will purify our consciences from useless rituals, so that we may serve the living God.

[e] already here; *some manuscripts have* coming.

11 But when Christ appeared as a high priest of the good things that have come,[r] then through the greater and more perfect tent[p] (not made with hands, that is, not of this creation) 12 he entered once for all into the Holy Place, taking[s] not the blood of goats and calves but his own blood, thus securing an eternal redemption. 13 For if the sprinkling of defiled persons with the blood of goats and bulls and with the ashes of a heifer sanctifies for the purification of the flesh, 14 how much more shall the blood of Christ, who through the eternal Spirit offered himself without blemish to God, purify your[t] conscience from dead works to serve the living God.

[p] Or *tabernacle*
[r] Other manuscripts read *good things to come*
[s] Greek *through*
[t] Other manuscripts read *our*

This paragraph consists of two long sentences in the Greek. The first sentence describes the event, the second its significance. Together they sum up several aspects of the contrast between Old Testament sacrifices and the sacrifice of Christ. These are:

(a) the earthly tent contrasted with the heavenly tent;
(b) the animal sacrifice contrasted with Christ's sacrifice of himself;
(c) the once-for-all, eternal sacrifice contrasted by implication with the many sacrifices of 7.27;
(d) "purification of the flesh" contrasted with "purification of the conscience";
(e) dead works contrasted with the living God.

These contrasts are complicated in verses 13-14 by a **how much more** type of comparison, common in Hebrews (2.1-3; 3.3; 8.6; and 10.28-29) and found also in other books of the New Testament (for example, Luke 11.13; Rom 11.12,24).

[189]

As comparison with RSV shows, TEV divides the sentence at the end of verse 11, and puts into verse 12 the words **When Christ went through the tent,** which in the Greek belong to verse 11. **The tent in which he serves is** is not expressed in the Greek text but is added to make a separate sentence as in GeCL quoted below.

GeCL's extensive restructuring of this passage is worth quoting in full:

> 11 Meanwhile Christ came. He is the High Priest who really brings reconciliation. He went through the tent which is greater and more perfect, that was not built by man, and is not part of this world. 12 Once for all he entered the Most Holy Place. Nor did he have to t ke with him the blood of goats and calves; rather he entered with his own blood. So he has freed us for all time from our guilt. 13 People who are impure in the sense of the religious rules are sprinkled with the blood of goats and bulls and the ashes of a cow, and so outwardly cleansed from their stain. 14 But through the blood of Christ, much more is accomplished. Filled with God's Spirit, Christ offered himself to God as a perfect sacrifice. His blood cleanses us inwardly from our guilt, so that we must no longer do what leads to death, and we can serve God, the giver of life.

9.11　　**But Christ has already come as the High Priest of the good things that are already here.**[e] **The tent in which he serves is greater and more perfect; it is not a man-made tent, that is, it is not a part of this created world.**

[e] already here; *some manuscripts have* coming.

Since verse 8, the writer's main interest has no longer been in the two compartments of the "sanctuary." What matters in verses 11-12 is the comparison between (a) the high priest going through the <u>curtain</u> into the <u>Most Holy Place</u> on the Day of Atonement, and (b) Christ, by his <u>sacrifice</u> of himself, passing into heaven to take up the highest and holiest "place" beside God.

But probably completes the contrast prepared in verse 2 (see comments). There may, however, be difficulty in introducing a conjunction such as **But** at the beginning of verse 11, since the clause which it introduces is not in direct conflict or opposition to the immediately preceding clause. It introduces a contrast with the entire paragraph which precedes. It may therefore be necessary to use a somewhat expanded expression such as "In contrast with all of this" or "On the other hand."

Christ has already come: already is implicit. The phrase probably refers neither to his coming to earth nor to his arrival in heaven after his ascension, but to his "appearing" or "being shown" as High Priest (compare verse 26). If, however, one wishes to avoid indicating precisely the point to which Christ has come, it may be possible to translate **Christ has already come as the High Priest** as "Christ has already become the High Priest."

Manuscript evidence is rather evenly balanced between "**the good things that have come**" (RSV text and UBS Greek New Testament text, TEV text, JB note, NEB text, TOB note) and "good things to come" (KJV, RSV note, Mft, JB text, TEV note, NEB note, Brc, TOB text). "Good things to come" fits in too easily with the context and with 10.1, so the more difficult reading, "good things that have come," is rather more likely to be the original text.

It may be difficult to relate **the High Priest** to the expression **the good things that are already here**. It may be possible to translate **High Priest of the good things that are already here** as "the High Priest who provides the good things that are already here" or "the High Priest who has caused to happen the good things that are already here." It is important when rendering **the good things** to avoid an expression referring only to material things. The reference is to the good experiences which people have, and therefore **the good things that are already here** may be expressed as "the good experiences that we already have" or "the good which we have already experienced."

The tent in which he serves is literally "through the greater . . . tent." **In which he serves** is implied. In Greek as in English, this may mean either "from one end to the other of the tent" or "by means of the tent." The first meaning, referring to space, seems more natural here.[2] A suggested translation would therefore be "But Christ has come as a priest of the good things that are already here. He has passed through the tent (or, "a tent," since it is not clearly identified in this context) which was not made by men; indeed it is not a part of this created world."

When one translates **The tent in which he serves**, it may be necessary to indicate the person who is served. It would, however, be wrong to suggest that Christ simply "serves God," for this would mean that Christ had become merely a servant to help God with the daily things which he might require. Therefore **the tent in which he serves** can perhaps best be expressed as "the tent in which he works on our behalf" or ". . . where he serves for our sake."

Comparatives such as **greater and more perfect** may require explicit indication of the item with which something is compared. Therefore it may be

---

[2] It is not clear whether the writer thinks of the heavenly sanctuary, like the one on earth, as having two compartments, a Holy Place and a Most Holy Place (see comments on 9.8, question 2). The use of "through," here and in 4.14, suggests two divisions in the heavenly sanctuary also. Alternatively, by a slight change in imagery, the earth in which Jesus lived and died may be compared with the outer part of a sanctuary, of which heaven is the Most Holy Place, and Jesus' death the curtain between them (compare Mark 15.38). In any case, since verse 8 the writer's main interest has no longer been in the two compartments of the sanctuary. What matters now is the comparison between (a) the high priest going through the curtain into the Most Holy Place on the Day of Atonement, and (b) Christ, by his sacrifice of himself, passing into heaven to take up the highest and holiest "place" beside God.

necessary to say "is greater and more perfect than the one on earth." **Greater** must be understood in the sense of "more important" rather than simply "larger." **And more perfect** may be expressed as "more as it should be."

Most translations, like TEV and RSV, understand **not a man-made tent** to mean the same as **not a part of this created world.** The second statement is wider than the first, hence the word "indeed" in the translation suggested above. It does not seem necessary to link the two statements by "because," as in GeCL, quoted in the introduction to this section.

Not a man-made tent may be expressed as "no people made such a tent" or "no person made the tent." **It is not a part of this created world** may be expressed as "it is not something which exists here in the world and which has been created."

There is no break in the Greek between verses 11 and 12; literally ". . . through the greater and more perfect tent not made with hands, that is, not of this creation, 12 neither by the blood of goats and bulls . . . ."

9.12   When Christ went through the tent and entered once and for all
into the Most Holy Place, he did not take the blood of goats
and bulls to offer as a sacrifice; rather, he took his own blood
and obtained eternal salvation for us.

When Christ went through the tent: comparison with RSV shows that TEV has restructured the sentence to make the meaning clearer. In the Greek, the words translated **when Christ went through** are part of verse 11. TEV then repeats **the tent** because a new sentence has been started in verse 12. The tent in question is the sanctuary in heaven, and it may be important to make this clear.

On **once and for all,** see comment on 7.27.

The Most Holy Place, as in verse 8, is "the holy (places)," but in this verse TEV's translation fits the context better. There is no difference in meaning between "holy" in its singular and its plural form.

The Greek says, literally, "not *through* the blood of goats and bulls, but *through* his own blood, he entered . . ." (see RSV note). "Through" means in this context "by means of (his own blood)"; it does not express passing "through" something, as it does in verse 11. It means that the blood was the means by which he was allowed to enter into the Most Holy Place. TEV and RSV state that he **took his own blood,** but only TEV shows that the blood was the means by which he entered when it adds **to offer as a sacrifice** to make this explicit.

It may be necessary to indicate the manner in which Christ **did not take the blood of goats and bulls** into the Most Holy Place, for example, by using a phrase such as "took in a bowl" or "carried in a small vessel."

The phrase **to offer as a sacrifice** may present certain difficulties, since the animals from which the blood had been obtained had already been sacrificed. Therefore, **to offer as a sacrifice** may perhaps be best expressed as "to offer as a gift to God." The meaning of **sacrifice** would then be implicit.

It may be important to emphasize the contrast expressed by **rather.** One may say "he didn't do that but . . ." or "instead of doing that . . . ."

If **he took his own blood** is translated literally, it might appear that he was carrying into the Most Holy Place a bowl of his own blood. It may therefore be important to render **he took his own blood** as "he gave his own life." A footnote may then introduce the literal rendering of the Greek expression in order to indicate the parallel with the preceding statement.

In both Old and New Testaments, "blood" often has the wider meaning of "life," especially "life violently destroyed," therefore involving "death" (as in 12.4). This is part of the meaning here. The principle "the life is in the blood" (Gen 9.4 and Lev 17.14) runs right through this letter. However, verse 13, with its reference to "sprinkling," requires the literal translation blood. A note may be necessary, as in TNT, to show the wider meaning, though in many cultures blood, life, and death are closely linked.

And obtained eternal salvation for us, more literally, "securing eternal redemption." It is a short, emphatic phrase at the end of the Greek sentence. It may be better translated as a separate sentence and somewhat expanded, as in the GeCL paragraph quoted above. The verb refers to an action at a given point in time, not over a period. **Eternal** means not only "not needing to be repeated," as in 7.27, but also "not limited to this creation" (verse 11b). DuCL has "permanent." This sacrifice is thus different in kind from the Old Testament's way of dealing with sin, which never fulfilled its purpose. The word for **salvation** meant originally "setting free from slavery," sometimes with the idea of paying a sum of money, but often, as in Luke 1.68 and 2.38, with the wider meaning of "liberation." Brc and TNT have "eternal deliverance." It will sometimes be better to use a verb phrase such as GeCL's "set free for all time from our guilt."

Obtained eternal salvation for us must often be expressed as a causative; for example, "caused us to be set free from our guilt forever" or "caused us to be delivered for all time to come."

9.13 The blood of goats and bulls and the ashes of a burnt calf are sprinkled on the people who are ritually unclean, and this purifies them by taking away their ritual impurity.

A literal translation of **The blood of goats and bulls and the ashes of a burnt calf** might suggest that all of these substances were mixed together and then sprinkled on the people. In reality, the reference is to quite different events. In addition, the passive expression **are sprinkled** must be changed into an active form in some languages, and this would mean that "the priests" would need to be introduced as the agents. Therefore the first part of verse 13 might be rendered as "The priests sprinkled on the people who are ritually unclean the blood of goats, and the blood of bulls, and the ashes of a calf which has been completely burned."

Bulls probably refers to the "young (male) bullock" (Lev 16.3) which Aaron had to offer as a sin offering for himself and his family. The writer does not clearly distinguish this from the **burnt calf** of verse 13, which is the "red heifer" (female) described in Numbers 19.1-10 (RSV). In both cases only one animal was sacrificed at a time. A comparison between 9.12 "goats and calves" NEB; 9.13

goats and bulls; 9.19 "calves" NEB (some manuscripts "calves and goats"); 10.4 **bulls and goats,** shows that the author is not concerned either with particular animals or with consistency in this respect. Here as elsewhere, the translator of Hebrews must not distort its meaning in order to conform more closely to the Old Testament text.

Sprinkled in the Greek refers grammatically only to **ashes,** which were mixed with water, but the meaning must include **the blood of goats and bulls** also. "Sprinkling," in Greek as in English, is more often associated with liquids like blood than with a powder such as ash. The writer may be remembering that according to Numbers 19.9 the ashes were mixed with water. In any case, translators should use the most suitable expression in their language for scattering a powder. It may be necessary to use two different verbs and translate "The blood of goats and bulls is sprinkled, and the ashes of the burnt calf are scattered . . . ." It may even be necessary to expand the text to include "mixed with water."

On a first reading, TEV seems very different from the literal translation of RSV, but TEV simply brings out more clearly the fact that the text is speaking of **ritual impurity,** not moral impurity. TEV fourth edition makes this even clearer by replacing TEV third edition "make them clean" with **this purifies them** (similarly in verses 10,14,22,23; 10.2). In other words, the "sprinkling" served to put people back into a state in which they could once again legally take part in temple worship. This has nothing to do with inward consciousness of moral sin, so there is no contradiction with 10.4.

The pronominal reference of **this** in the statement **this purifies them** might suggest that only one action is involved in the preceding statement. It may therefore be necessary to use some kind of plural reference; for example, "these actions" or "these ceremonies."

The term **purifies** indicates the removal of what may be called "negative taboo," that is to say, anything which defiles. In some languages **purifies** is expressed as "takes away that which defiles." Accordingly, **this purifies them by taking away their ritual impurity** may be expressed as "these actions take away from the people all that causes them to be defiled" or ". . . causes them to be unclean." In this context, however, a term meaning "unclean" must refer to ritual uncleanness and not to physical dirt.

9.14   **Since this is true, how much more is accomplished by the blood of Christ! Through the eternal Spirit he offered himself as a perfect sacrifice to God. His blood will purify our consciences from useless rituals, so that we may serve the living God.**

RSV makes clear the grammatical connection between verses 13 and 14, but most CLTs divide them into two sentences. DuCL links 14a with 13: "If the blood of goats and bulls, and sprinkling with the ash of a young cow, can make impure people holy, so that they are pure according to the law, 14 how much more then the blood of Christ!"

Since this is true may be expressed as "Since this is what does take place" or "Since people are purified in this way."

On **how much more**, see 2.1-3; 3.3; 8.6.

Is accomplished is not in the text, but it is essential to bring out the meaning and to avoid the misleading suggestions that Christ's sacrifice is merely a better way of making people ritually clean, or that Christ's sacrifice cleanses the conscience more effectively than animal sacrifices made people ritually clean. The first suggestion would contradict verse 14b, and the second, though doubtless true in itself, is not what this text means. There is no contrast between the present tense of **is accomplished** and the future **will purify**. **Is accomplished**, as already noted, is not expressed in the Greek text, but **will purify** is implicitly present in meaning: "if the argument is correct, this consequence follows" or ". . . will follow."

The blood of Christ: though grammatically **blood** is a noun, the rest of the verse shows that it means the event of Christ's dying as a sacrifice.

Rather than an exclamation such as **how much more is accomplished by the blood of Christ!** some languages require an emphatic statement; for example, "the blood of Christ accomplishes so much more" or ". . . is even more powerful."

If a literal reference to **the blood of Christ** can be retained, this is useful, since it continues the analogy between the Old Testament sacrifices and the death of Christ. But in some instances it may be important to render **by the blood of Christ** as "by the death of Christ," and therefore **how much more is accomplished by the blood of Christ!** may be expressed as "how much more Christ accomplished when he died as a sacrifice" or ". . . when he shed his own blood." However, in rendering "shed his own blood" it is important to avoid any implication of suicide.

Through the eternal Spirit may be expressed as "By means of the Spirit that lives forever." This is usually understood as a reference to God's eternal Spirit, and it may be necessary to make this clear by translating "By means of God's Spirit which always exists."

Sacrifice is implied, both by the word for **offered** (see 5.1) and by the word for **perfect**, which recalls Numbers 19.2; compare 1 Peter 1.19. In Numbers perfect means that "the animal has no defect which would disqualify it for use as a sacrifice." However, in Psalms 15.2 and 18.24 the same term is used of human worshipers.

He offered himself as a perfect sacrifice to God may involve some readjustment in some languages; for example, "he gave himself to God as a perfect sacrifice." But the phrase **as a perfect sacrifice** must be understood in a figurative sense, since he really died on a cross. Therefore in translation it may be necessary to render this clause as "when he died he was just like a sacrifice and, as such, he was just what he should be."

Translations and commentaries are divided about the meaning of **Through the eternal Spirit.** Some give an alternative translation in a note, and some leave the meaning unclear when the verse is read aloud (BJ "an eternal Spirit").

(a) CLTs, RSV, JB, TNT spell **Spirit** with a capital "S," suggesting either "the Holy Spirit" (Knox) or "the divine nature of Christ."

(b) Mft "in the spirit of the eternal," Phps, NAB "in the eternal spirit," TOB, Brc, NEB "a spiritual and eternal sacrifice" spell it with a small "s," either suggesting "the unique but human spirit of Christ," or leaving the meaning unclear.

In favor of (b) it may be said (i) that "eternal spirit" does not have "the" in the text (but this argument is not decisive); (ii) that the writer speaks several times of the Holy Spirit, and there seems no reason why he should not have done so here if that was what he meant; and (iii) that "eternal spirit" may mean the same as the power of a life which has no end in 7.16.

It is therefore possible, as an alternative to TEV and RSV, to translate with NEB "a spiritual and eternal sacrifice" or "an eternal and spiritual sacrifice." This solution should not, however, be adopted if there is any danger of the reader thinking that Christ's sacrifice itself, rather than its effects, took place eternally. This would conflict with clear statements that his sacrifice took place "once for all" (for example, see verse 26).

On **consciences**, see comment on **heart** in verse 9. The UBS Greek New Testament, CLTs, and most other translations except Mft read **our** rather than "your" **consciences**. The manuscript evidence is rather evenly divided, but **our** fits better in a part of the letter which consists of teaching rather than calls to action.

On **useless rituals** or "**dead works**," see comment on 6.1, and then GeCL quoted in the general comment on 9.11-14. There is a rather complex problem in rendering **His blood will purify our consciences from useless rituals**. The implication is that the **useless rituals** (or literally "**dead works**") actually make the conscience unclean or impure, or even cause death. But what makes the person impure is not the ritual as such but its uselessness, in that it does not take away sin or guilt. **His blood** is a reference to Christ's sacrificial death. It may therefore be possible to translate **His blood will purify our consciences from useless rituals** as "By his sacrificial death Christ will purify us from what remains as the result of the rituals which accomplish nothing."

Serve here renders the word used for liturgical worship in verse 9, **worshiper**.

GeCL's "God, the giver of life" is at least part of the meaning of **the living God**, and it has a fresher impact than the traditional phrase.

So that we may serve the living God may be rendered as "in order that we may serve the God who lives" or ". . . the God who gives life." But "to serve God" must be expressed in some languages as "to do what God wants us to do."

TEV	**9.15-22**	RSV

15 For this reason Christ is the one who arranges a new covenant, so that those who have been called by God may receive the eternal blessings that God has promised. This can be done because there has been a death which sets

15 Therefore he is the mediator of a new covenant, so that those who are called may receive the promised eternal inheritance, since a death has occurred which redeems them from the transgressions under the first

people free from the wrongs they did while the first covenant was in effect.

16 In the case of a will it is necessary to prove that the person who made it has died, 17 for a will means nothing while the person who made it is alive; it goes into effect only after his death. 18 That is why even the first covenant [f] went into effect only with the use of blood. 19 First, Moses proclaimed to the people all the commandments as set forth in the Law. Then he took the blood of bulls and goats, mixed it with water, and sprinkled it on the book of the Law and all the people, using a sprig of hyssop and some red wool. 20 He said, "This is the blood which seals the covenant that God has commanded you to obey." 21 In the same way Moses also sprinkled the blood on the Covenant Tent and over all the things used in worship. 22 Indeed, according to the Law almost everything is purified by blood, and sins are forgiven only if blood is poured out.

[f] COVENANT: *In Greek the same word means "will" and "covenant."*

covenant. [u] 16 For where a will [u] is involved, the death of the one who made it must be established. 17 For a will [u] takes effect only at death, since it is not in force as long as the one who made it is alive. 18 Hence even the first covenant was not ratified without blood. 19 For when every commandment of the law had been declared by Moses to all the people, he took the blood of claves and goats, with water and scarlet wool and hyssop, and sprinkled both the book itself and all the people, 20 saying, "This is the blood of the covenant which God commanded you." 21 And in the same way he sprinkled with the blood both the tent [p] and all the vessels used in worship. 22 Indeed, under the law almost everything is purified with blood, and without the shedding of blood there is no forgiveness of sins.

[p] or *tabernacle*
[u] The Greek word here used means both *covenant* and *will*

The blood of Christ in verse 14 implied "the death of Christ," and the writer now turns briefly to discuss death in general, in its relation to the legal execution of a will. Verses 16-17 are incidental to the main argument, which is related to Mosaic rather than secular law. The key word, rendered **covenant** in verse 18, is probably used in the sense of a will. (TEV fourth edition and RSV explain this in a note.) Mft tries to combine the two meanings in verse 18 with "the first covenant of God's will." GeCL, more successfully, adds at the beginning of verse 16 "with the covenant which God sets up, it is like a will."

9.15   For this reason Christ is the one who arranges a new covenant, so that those who have been called by God may receive the eternal blessings that God has promised. This can be done because there has been a death which sets people free from the wrongs they did while the first covenant was in effect.

For this reason probably points forward: "The reason why Christ arranges a new covenant is so that those who have been called . . . may receive the eternal blessings . . . ." TEV seems to suggest that **For this reason** may sum up the thought of the previous verses, but **Christ is the one** is not emphasized in the

Greek. If **For this reason** refers backward, it may have the weakened meaning "so, in this way" (as in GeCL, which begins a new section here). **Christ** is understood.

If **For this reason** points forward, then the first part of verse 15 may be rendered as "The purpose of Christ's arranging a new covenant is so that those who have been called by God may receive the eternal blessings." If, on the other hand, **For this reason** points back to the previous paragraph, one may translate "Because of what Christ has done, Christ is the one who arranges a new covenant so that those who have been called by God may receive the eternal blessings."

On **the one who arranges a new covenant,** see 8.6. **One who arranges a new covenant** may be expressed as "one who causes a new covenant to exist."

Those who have been called by God may be expressed as "those whom God has called." It is important, however, to avoid an expression for **called** which would mean "to shout at" or "to call to." In some languages the most appropriate equivalent is "those whom God has invited to become his own" or ". . . to become his people."

The eternal blessings that God has promised literally, "the promise of the eternal inheritance," as in 11.8; compare 9.11. "The promise" is clearly God's promise, and TEV rightly makes this explicit. **Blessings** is a rather general word in English; the Greek refers more specifically to what God promised to give his people and has now given them in Christ. In Old Testament times he gave his people the Promised Land; now, in Christ, he has given them forgiveness of sins.

May receive the eternal blessings may require some restructuring, since **blessings** involves an event of blessing and **may receive** can be regarded as a kind of substitute passive. Accordingly, **may receive the eternal blessings that God has promised** may be rendered as "may be forever blessed by God in the way that he promised."

This can be done is added in order to divide the sentence. **This can be done** may be expressed as "This can happen" or "This happens."

A death this phrase is quite general. It is used to prepare the way for the discussion of **will** in verses 16-17. TEV shows this more clearly than "his death" in JB and TOB. **Sets people free** renders a noun meaning "liberation," which is related to the word translated salvation in verse 12 (see the comment). It may be essential in some languages to specify whose death is meant by the term translated **a death.** One might attempt some such rendering as "someone has died and this sets people free." But this would probably refer to almost anyone's death. The second part of verse 15 may rather be rendered as "this can happen because Christ died, and this causes people to be set free from the wrongs . . ." or ". . . from the sins that they committed."

On **wrongs,** see comments on 2.2 and 8.12.

While the first covenant was in effect suggests "sins which were connected with the first covenant," that is, the sins which hurt the conscience and therefore prevent people from really "drawing near" to God in worship. The first covenant could not deal with these (compare 10.4). **While the first covenant was in effect** may be rendered as "while the first covenant still existed" or "while there still was the first covenant."

9.16 In the case of a will it is necessary to prove that the person who made it has died,

TEV is so clear as to need little further comment. TEV third edition was even simpler in style: "it has to be proved that the man who made it has died." "Man" is generally avoided in TEV fourth edition in places where both men and women are meant.

In a number of languages there is no term for **will** in the sense of a document which specifies who is to receive various parts of a dead person's property or estate. It may therefore be necessary to use some descriptive phrase; for example, "a paper which tells who will get a dead person's property" or ". . . who will receive the things that a dead person has left."

It is necessary to prove may be expressed as "one must show" or "it is necessary to know."

The person who made it must be expressed in some languages as "the person who wrote it," or "the person who caused it to be written," or "the person who said it."

9.17 for a will means nothing while the person who made it is alive; it goes into effect only after his death.

TEV reverses the two halves of this verse, putting the negative statement first. This is natural in English, but in some languages it may be better to keep the order of the Greek and RSV.

A literal translation of **a will means nothing** may be misleading. What is important in some languages is a statement to the effect that "a will has no power while the person who made it is alive" or "a will doesn't cause anything to be given to anybody while the person who wrote the will is still alive."

The adjective translated **goes into effect** is used by the writer in various senses. In this legal context it means "valid."[3] It may be better to omit **only**, which is not expressed in the Greek. This strengthens the positive statement and prepares for verse 18.

His death: his is understood; NEB "a testament is operative only after a death."

It goes into effect only after his death may be expressed as "it causes a person's possessions to be distributed only after that person has died."

---

[3] Elsewhere it means "to be relied upon." It is used in 2.2 of the "word spoken by angels," in 6.19 of the "secure anchor," and in 3.14 (and some manuscripts of 3.6) of holding on "firmly" to the confidence which is one aspect of Christian faith. The related verb means "confirm, prove to be true" (2.3), or "make strong" (13.9). A related noun is used in 6.16, in a similar context to 9.17, of an oath "confirming" what someone says.

9.18 **That is why even the first covenant^f went into effect only with the use of blood.**

f COVENANT: *In Greek the same word means "will" and "covenant."*

The writer now turns back from the illustration of a will to the main subject, which is the **covenant**. **That is why** is a possible translation of the Greek, but this verse does not in fact draw a logical conclusion from verses 11-17. The link between verses 16-17 and 18 is the play on different senses of the word for will or **covenant**. This play on words is made possible by the fact that **blood** or "death" was involved in both. JB has "the earlier covenant needed something to be killed in order to take effect." A comparison or analogy, not a proof, is involved. Therefore some more general translation, such as "So," "In this way" (GeCL and TOB), **"Hence"** (RSV, Mft, NAB), or "Thus," may be more appropriate than **That is why** or "It was for this very reason" (Bre).

The Greek word used for **went into effect** is not a legal term. It is most often used in the Bible in speaking of the dedication or inauguration of the Temple; in 10.20 it means "to open a path." Here and in verse 19 the writer is concerned with the ceremonies which took place when the first covenant came into effect. The Greek is different for reasons of style, but the meaning is close to the term translated goes into effect in verse 17, with the added suggestion of a ceremony. GeCL has simply "So the first covenant became valid only through blood."

The concept of **went into effect** or "was inaugurated" is sometimes expressed idiomatically; for example, "was cut," or "was made to stand," or "was tied," or "bound the persons."

As in verse 7, TEV simplifies the double negative, meaning "not without blood," into **only with the use of blood,** which is more usual in common language. **With the use of blood** may be expressed as "by means of blood" or "by means of death."

9.19 **First, Moses proclaimed to the people all the commandments as set forth in the Law. Then he took the blood of bulls and goats, mixed it with water, and sprinkled it on the book of the Law and all the people, using a sprig of hyssop and some red wool.**

First may be expressed as "The first thing Moses did."
Proclaimed: a word suggesting speaking, such as "told," **"declared"** (RSV), or "recited" (NEB), is better than a word suggesting reading, as in DuCL, Knox.[4]

---

[4] There is nothing to suggest that the author sees any importance in the exact order in which the ceremonies were performed. However, the probable order of events implied in Exodus 24 is: (a) the Law is told to the people; (b) the Law is written down (verse 4); (c) oxen are sacrificed (verse 5); (d) half the blood

The people is strictly "all the people," "the whole people," in the first half of the verse as well as the second. TEV omits "**all**" (RSV) to avoid repetition. The writer combines references to Exodus 24.3,6-8; Leviticus 14.4; and Numbers 19.6. Throughout this passage the Greek word for "all" is repeated three times in verse 19 and once each in verses 21 and 22.

All the commandments as set forth in the Law may be expressed as "all that God had commanded, as written down in the laws," as in a number of languages it is impossible to use a singular form, "the Law," since "Law" cannot be used as a collective term for a series of commandments or rules.

Bulls and goats: there is a minor textual problem. Many good manuscripts add "and goats" after **bulls.** These words are included in square brackets in the third edition of the UBS Greek New Testament, and are included in the fourth edition of TEV, but not in FrCL, NEB, TNT. It is more likely that the author wrote the words translated "and goats," but that copyists omitted these words because goats are not mentioned in Exodus 24.5.

Though in English it is easy to speak of **the blood of bulls and goats,** in some languages it is necessary to use a plural, since the substances are different; for example, "the bloods of bulls and goats" or "the blood of bulls and the blood of goats." It may also be necessary in rendering **took** to indicate the way in which the blood was taken or carried. If a plural is used in referring to **the blood,** it is usually necessary to make the appropriate modifications in the pronominal references of **it.**

The book of the Law may have to be expressed as "the book which contained the laws." It may even be preferable to use "the scroll" rather than "the book."

It may be necessary to distinguish the different senses in which **the book** and **the people** are sprinkled with **blood** and **water, hyssop** and **red wool.** The situation is complicated by the fact that "hyssop" is not known in many areas, and no one can be sure exactly which plant is meant here or in Numbers 19.6 (see *Fauna and Flora of the Bible,* pages 129-130). Small branches of the "hyssop" plant were probably tied together with "scarlet wool," dipped into the mixture of "blood" and "water," and used as a "sprinkler." FrCL's glossary note reads: "Small plant whose branches were used to scatter blood in certain ceremonies of Jewish worship." A different plant may be mentioned in John 19.29. TEV fourth edition makes the meaning clear: **and** before **some red wool** implies "tied with." For **red,** earlier editions of TEV had "scarlet," and DuCL has "deep red."

The final phrase expressing means, namely, **using a sprig of hyssop and some red wool,** may be best expressed as a separate sentence; for example, "He did this by means of a sprig of hyssop and some red wool." The relation between the small sprig or branch of hyssop and the red wool may be expressed as "He used a small twig of hyssop to which some red wool had been tied" or ". . . tied with some red wool."

---

is thrown on the altar (verse 6); (e) the Book of the Covenant is read out (verse 7); (f) half the blood is thrown on the people (verse 8).

9.20   He said, "This is the blood which seals the covenant that God
has commanded you to obey."

He said: literally ". . . saying." TEV divides the Greek sentence, which runs
without a break from verse 18 to verse 21. "As he did this, he said" would be
possible. The quotation is from Exodus 24.8, with some changes, probably influenced by the story of the Last Supper (Mark 14.24).

The reference of **This** may need to be more explicit; for example, "What I
am sprinkling."

Which seals is implied and brings out the meaning of "blood of the covenant." The verb **seals** is a dead or dying metaphor in English, since the practice of
fastening documents with a seal has become rare. It would be possible to bring
out the meaning in a nonfigurative way, for example, by translating "this is the
blood which confirms the covenant to which God has ordered you to be faithful."

It is unusual to speak of one party to an agreement commanding the other
to obey it. But the biblical covenant was unique; see the comment on 7.22. This
idea is seriously weakened by GeCL's "through this blood is sealed the covenant
which God has concluded with you."

In some languages "to seal a covenant" or "to confirm a covenant" may be
expressed as "to make a covenant strong." But the concept is often expressed
somewhat more idiomatically; for example, "it ties you to the covenant" or "it
makes you one with the covenant."

To obey is implied in **commanded.**

The clause **that God has commanded you to obey** may have to be expressed
as direct discourse; for example, "God has commanded, 'You must obey the covenant' " or " '. . . obey what the covenant says you must do.' "

9.21   In the same way Moses also sprinkled the blood on the Covenant Tent and over all the things used in worship.

In the same way: that is, in the way described in verse 19b; other CLTs
have simply "also."

In this verse, **the Covenant Tent** is the sanctuary as a whole.[5]

All the things used in worship (see 1 Chr 9.28) includes objects such as
those mentioned in verses 4-5.

9.22   Indeed, according to the Law almost everything is purified by
blood, and sins are forgiven only if blood is poured out.

---

[5] Leviticus 8.15 speaks of pouring blood on the altar, which in fact stood in
the outer part of the sanctuary, but which the writer puts in the Most Holy Place
(see comment on 9.4).

This verse forms a summary and also introduces the next stage in the argument. Verse 22 is to be understood in the light of **according to the Law.** TEV's frequent addition of Moses (7.28) is not necessary here, since Moses has just been mentioned. The meaning is not "no one may forgive anyone else unless blood is poured out," but "the Law does not provide for sin to be dealt with in any other way than by a sacrifice which involves pouring out blood."

According to the Law may be expressed as "the Law says that," or "as it is written in the Law," or ". . . the laws."

A literal rendering of **everything is purified by blood** might wrongly suggest that everything is made clean by blood. In reality, of course, blood stains. Therefore it may be best to speak of "everything is made pure by the shedding of blood," for it is death which causes purification, not the mere substance of blood itself. This is emphasized in TEV by the second clause, **sins are forgiven only if blood is poured out.**

From this point, the middle of verse 22, the forgiveness of sin becomes the central theme. In verse 22a it is not clear whether the writer is still thinking of ritual purification, or whether he is already thinking of forgiveness of sin. Verse 22a may thus mean either (a) "almost all sins are dealt with by means of blood," or (b) "almost all objects to do with worship are made ritually pure by blood." The writer sometimes uses the word for "cleanse" with human beings as the object (see 9.23; 10.2), but in this verse the word rendered **everything** is most naturally understood to include the objects just mentioned. The BJ note quotes Leviticus 5.11 as an illustration of **almost,** that is, something which is an exception to the rule because it is not cleansed by blood. **Almost** is surprisingly emphasized in the Greek. On might translate "it is almost true" or "one could almost say that according to the law everything is purified by blood . . . ."

Sins are forgiven translates the last word in the Greek sentence; it is therefore emphatic. NEB's "forgiveness," implying "of sins," is quite sufficient. Some modern translations, Mft, Knox, Phps, JB, keep the rather literary expression "remission" for **sins are forgiven,** to show that it is not a mere statement of the type "I forgive you," but a process which effectively deals with sin. The meaning is similar to that of verse 26, where the word for **sin** is expressed.

The passive expression **sins are forgiven** may need to be expressed in an active form as "God forgives sins."

The word for "pouring out blood" seems to have been invented by the writer, but the meaning is clear from such texts as 1 Kings 18.28, where a similar phrase occurs. It does not refer only to shedding blood when an animal or human being is killed, but to collecting blood in basins and then pouring it out.

TEV	**9.23-28**	RSV

Christ's Sacrifice Takes Away Sins

23 Those things, which are copies of the heavenly originals, had to be purified in that way. But the heavenly

23 Thus it was necessary for the copies of the heavenly things to be purified with these rites, but the

things themselves require much better sacrifices. 24 For Christ did not go into a man-made Holy Place, which was a copy of the real one. He went into heaven itself, where he now appears on our behalf in the presence of God. 25 The Jewish High Priest goes into the Most Holy Place every year with the blood of an animal. But Christ did not go in to offer himself many times, 26 for then he would have had to suffer many times ever since the creation of the world. Instead, now when all ages of time are nearing the end, he has appeared once and for all, to remove sin through the sacrifice of himself. 27 Everyone must die once, and after that be judged by God. 28 In the same manner Christ also was offered in sacrifice once to take away the sins of many. He will appear a second time, not to deal with sin, but to save those who are waiting for him.

heavenly things themselves with better sacrifices than these. 24 For Christ has entered, not into a sanctuary made with hands, a copy of the true one, but into heaven itself, now to appear in the presence of God on our behalf. 25 Nor was it to offer himself repeatedly, as the high priest enters the Holy Place yearly with blood not his own; 26 for then he would have had to suffer repeatedly since the foundation of the world. But as it is, he has appeared once for all at the end of the age to put away sin by the sacrifice of himself. 27 And just as it is appointed for men to die once, and after that comes judgment, 28 so Christ, having been offered once to bear the sins of many, will appear a second time, not to deal with sin but to save those who are eagerly waiting for him.

These verses form a gradual transition to chapter 10. There is little or no difference in meaning between **to offer himself** in verse 25 and **through the sacrifice of himself** in verse 26; between **to take away . . . sins** in verse 28 and **sins are forgiven** in verse 22; between **appeared** in verse 26 and (apart from the tense) **will appear** in verse 28, although in each case the Greek is different. As usual, the writer repeats the same ideas in fresh words. Verses 23-24 contain many echoes of 8.1-6: copies, heavenly 8.5, better 8.6, sacrifices 8.3; copy is related to pattern in 8.5, real 8.2, now 8.6.

The TEV section heading, **Christ's Sacrifice Takes Away Sins**, was introduced in order to break up this rather long and involved chapter. It may be rendered as "Christ gives himself as a sacrifice and in this way takes away sins" or "By dying Christ takes away sins."

9.23   **Those things, which are copies of the heavenly originals, had to be purified in that way. But the heavenly things themselves require much better sacrifices.**

Those things probably sums up the objects mentioned in verse 19. In order to show clearly what **those things** are, it may be necessary to employ an expression such as "Those things just mentioned" or "What has just been spoken about." It is essential that **Those things** be explicit and specific, so that the clause **which are copies of the heavenly originals** may be understood as nonrestrictive. In fact in some languages a nonrestrictive clause can only be introduced as a kind of parenthetical expression; for example, "they are copies of the heavenly originals" or "they are just like the ones in heaven which were copied."

The term for **had to** is in an emphatic position at the beginning of the Greek sentence. As usual the expression refers to a legal requirement (see also 7.12,27; 9.16). Other links with the previous verses are (a) RSV's **"Thus"** or "Therefore"; this is a summary of the requirements mentioned in earlier verses; and (b) **Those things,** pointing backward to the same items. TEV's **Those things, which are copies** makes this link clearer than RSV, though TEV omits "thus." RSV's **"rites"** is not in the text, and TEV's more general **in that way** may be better (so FrCL and GeCL; DuCL has "through sacrifices"; SpCL "these sacrifices").

Had to be purified may need to be expressed as "it was necessary to purify them." **In that way** may be expressed as "in the way just mentioned."

The writer suggests in passing that **the heavenly things,** like the **copies,** needed to be purified. He is now increasingly stressing the uniqueness of Christ's sacrifice, and therefore the contrast (**better**) between the old order and the new. The plural **sacrifices** means "a better kind of sacrifice." The verses which follow will emphasize that under the new covenant, there is in fact only one sacrifice.

But the heavenly things themselves require much better sacrifices may be expressed as "But it is necessary for much better sacrifices to be made for the things in heaven" or ". . . for the sake of the things in heaven."

9.24   **For Christ did not go into a man-made Holy Place, which was a copy of the real one. He went into heaven itself, where he now appears on our behalf in the presence of God.**

Verses 24 and 25 make two parallel negative statements which contrast the sacrifice of Christ with Old Testament sacrifices. A corresponding positive statement occurs in verse 26 with Instead.

Caution must be employed in rendering **For,** since the initial clause of this verse is not a specific reason for the immediately preceding clause in verse 23. In fact, in some languages it may be better to omit a conjunction expressing cause, since to suggest an immediate relationship may be too explicit.

On **Holy Place** here and Most Holy Place in verse 25, see comments on 8.2. The context (especially every year in verse 25) suggests that the writer is comparing the earthly sanctuary, or possibly its inner part, with the immediate presence of God in heaven.

As in other contexts it may be necessary to render **Holy Place** as "Holy Room," and **man-made** may be expressed as "made by people."

The Greek word for **copy** is literally "antitype," the converse of pattern or "type" in 8.5. As in 8.2 and 9.11, the writer insists that the **real** sanctuary is not **man-made.** **Copy** is a different Greek word from copies in verse 23, but the meaning is the same.

The nonrestrictive clause **which was a copy of the real one** may have to be expressed as a separate sentence or as a parenthetical expression; for example, "it was just like the real one" or "it was similar to the real one."

Went into refers to a single event, but its consequences are **now** (compare 2.8 and 8.6) and **on our behalf** (as in 6.20; compare 7.25).

Now appears on our behalf is similar in meaning to lives forever to plead with God for them in 7.25 (GeCL actually uses the same verb). In English, "plead" and "appear" are both used to describe an advocate's efforts for his client in a court of law. This is not so in the Greek. Translations in other languages use different but equivalent expressions for **appears on our behalf:** DuCL "has now appeared before God to take care of our cause," and FrCL "he presents himself now for us before God."

In some languages a literal rendering of **appears** would be misleading, because it might suggest suddenly coming onto the scene. A more satisfactory rendering of **where he now appears on our behalf in the presence of God** may be expressed as "where he now is in God's presence for our sakes" or ". . . in order to help us."

The presence of God is literally "the face of God" (as in Exo 33.20,23). For a Jewish Christian, this would be a strong expression of Christ's nearness to God.

9.25   **The Jewish High Priest goes into the Most Holy Place every
        year with the blood of an animal. But Christ did not go in to
        offer himself many times,**

The phrase **The Jewish High Priest** must be rendered in such a way as to indicate not merely the national origin of the high priest but the fact that he serves as a high priest for the Jews.

The phrase rendered "**the Holy Place**" (RSV) is the same in the Greek as in verse 2, but the context shows that **the Most Holy Place** is meant.

Blood of an animal is literally "blood which is not his own," but phrases suggesting the "blood of some other human being" (like "someone else's blood") should be avoided. **With** before **the blood** means "by," "by means of." The Old Testament Law forbade anyone to enter the Most Holy Place without an offering of blood. Though it is true that **with the blood of an animal** specifies a necessary accompaniment, it could be misleading to translate **with the blood of an animal** as "by means of the blood of an animal," since this would suggest that the blood of an animal was some kind of instrument by which the high priest entered. In order to show the obligatory nature of the blood of an animal, it may be possible to translate the first sentence of verse 25 as "when the Jewish High Priest went into the Most Holy Place every year, he had to carry with him the blood of an animal" or ". . . take with him some of the blood of an animal." It may also be necessary to specify the particular manner in which the blood was taken, namely, in some kind of bowl or jar.

Christ did not go in must be understood in a figurative sense. As far as the earthly sanctuary was concerned, Christ never went into the Most Holy Place, but as far as the heavenly sanctuary was concerned Christ did enter, that is, in terms of the analogy drawn by the writer of Hebrews. If one assumes that the reference is to the earthly sanctuary, it is possible to translate the second part of verse 25 as "but Christ did not, as it were, go into the Most Holy Place to offer himself many times." But this would be out of keeping with the argument of this letter. The reference must be to the heavenly entrance into which Jesus did enter. The negation, therefore, is to be placed with the offering; for example, "Christ went in but it was not to offer himself many times."

9.26   **for then he would have had to suffer many times ever since the creation of the world. Instead, now when all ages of time are nearing the end, he has appeared once and for all, to remove sin through the sacrifice of himself.**

The main contrast is between the many Old Testament sacrifices and the one sacrifice of Christ. There is also a contrast of time, as in 1.1-2, between **the creation of the world** and **when all ages of time are nearing the end.** The exact meaning of **when all ages . . . are nearing the end** is not clear, either in the Greek or in TEV. It is literally "at . . ." or "near the end of the ages." This expression is not used anywhere else in the New Testament, though Matthew (13.39,40,49; 24.3; 28.20) uses the same word for "end" with "age" in the singular. "The end of the ages" may be a poetic equivalent of this, but with the same meaning. The related verb often has the meaning "fulfill" or "accomplish"; so DuCL's "at the high point of history" is possible, as are Knox's "at the moment when history reached its fulfillment" and Brc's "at the consummation of history." However, the writer and his contemporaries believed that they were living near the end of time (see 10.25); hence the contrast with **the creation of the world.**

The expression **for then he would have had to suffer** implies a condition contrary to fact; for example, "for if he had done that, he would have had to suffer" or "for if he had done that, it would have been necessary for him to suffer." Sometimes this kind of condition contrary to fact may be expressed as "for if he did that (and he didn't) then it would be necessary for him to suffer."

Ever since the creation of the world may be expressed as "ever since the world was first created" or "ever since the time God created the world."

The main contrast marked by **Instead** (RSV "But") is between the annual sacrifices of the Old Testament Day of Atonement (verse 7) and the one sacrifice of Christ (6.4; compare once and for all in 7.27). **Instead** also marks a secondary contrast, repeated from verses 7.8 but not emphasized here, with the high priests' offering of blood of an animal in verse 25.

Some commentators think that **now** in verse 26 is used simply to reinforce the contrast and does not refer to time at all. This view is followed by RSV ("**as it is**"), Mft, Knox, NEB, Brc, TOB; all CLTs, Phps, JB, NAB, TNT have **now.** The contrast is probably between the present and Old Testament times.[6]

---

[6] In favor of the translation "as it is," one can say (a) that the same expression is used in 8.6, where TEV translates it as as it is (see also RSV, 11.16 and 2.8); (b) the writer has used now in verse 24, and tends to give words different meanings when he repeats them; (c) now is slightly awkward with the past tense he

It may be almost impossible to translate literally **when all ages of time are nearing the end.** In the first place, it may be impossible to speak of ages "nearing" something. Furthermore, it may be necessary to specify what is involved in **the end.** An equivalent of **now when all ages of time are nearing the end** may be "now when we are near the end of all the ages" or "now when we are living in the last days of all the ages." The expression **all ages** may be rendered as "all periods of time" or "all long successions of days" or "all long series of years."

Suffer: a few manuscripts have "die," which is a correct interpretation of **suffer** in this context (compare 2.9).

He has appeared once and for all may be rendered as "he has come just once" or "he has come once and will not do so again."

To remove sin may be expressed as "to cause people to have no guilt" or "to cause sins to be forgiven."

On **sacrifice,** see 5.1 and 7.27. **Through the sacrifice of himself** may be expressed as means; for example, "by sacrificing himself," or "by giving himself over to die," or "by causing (or, allowing) himself to be killed like a sacrifice."

9.27-28   **Everyone must die once, and after that be judged by God. 28 In the same manner Christ also was offered in sacrifice once to take away the sins of many. He will appear a second time, not to deal with sin, but to save those who are waiting for him.**

These verses are partly an aside; the main theme is taken up again in 10.1. However, they are also related to the main subject by the repetition of **offered in sacrifice once** and by the mention of "salvation."

Must renders a different word from that used in 2.1. It refers to something "in store," either literally, as in Luke 19.20, or figuratively, as in Colossians 1.5; 2 Timothy 4.8. FrCl "is destined to die"; NEB "it is the lot of men to die."

Everyone must die once may be expressed as "All people die once." This is, of course, a reference to physical death.

After that be judged by God: by God is implied. These words are not an aside, as TOB suggests; they reinforce the general statement **Everyone must die once** by adding a specifically Christian statement. TEV shows this by ending the sentence at the end of the verse. The clause **after that be judged by God** may be rendered as "and after that happens, God judges them."

The rendering of **In the same manner** may cause complications, because such a phrase could refer to the immediately preceding statement about being

has appeared. However, none of these arguments is conclusive. (a) The same expression is used in 12.26 with a clear reference to time (TEV, RSV now); (b) the writer uses once in the same sense in verses 26,27, and 28 (the Greek is the same); and (c) the writer does not contrast the time at which he writes with the time of Christ's death; the contrast is rather between the present and Old Testament times.

judged by God. The phrase **In the same manner** must refer to the entire process of sacrificial offering.

If the writer of Hebrews has Isaiah 53 in mind, as the phrase translated **take away the sins of many** suggests, it is possible to understand **Christ** as a title, "the Messiah," not as a proper name. See the TEV Word List.

One might assume that the passive expression **was offered** could be shifted into an active form with God as the agent. However, this would introduce a concept which is not in accordance with New Testament expression, for it would then appear that God offered Christ as a sacrifice. This would suggest the wrong idea of God's offering Christ to someone else as a sacrifice. It is often best to change the passive **was offered** into a reflexive form, "Christ offered himself as a sacrifice."

TEV is right to emphasize **once,** which is repeated in verse 28a as the point of the comparison between verses 27 and 28a. It adds this emphasis by making the verb rendered **was offered** a main verb, and by then turning 28b, which contains a new thought, into a separate sentence.

The term translated **many,** as in Isaiah 53.12; Mark 10.45; Hebrews 2.10, does not mean "many but not all," but "many, not just one or a few." It renders a Hebrew idiom, used here to mark a contrast between the one sacrifice of Christ and the large number of people who benefit from it.

He will appear a second time may also be rendered as "He will come again."

Not to deal with sin: literally "without" or "apart from sin." DuCL's "freedom from the burden of sin" is not the likely meaning here. This part of the verse qualifies the first part. An expanded translation would be "He will, it is true, appear a second time, but this will not be to deal all over again with sin, for he has done that once for all. It will be for the final rescue of those who are waiting for him." **Deal with sin** and **save** are positive and negative aspects of the same event. **Save** here probably includes not only rescue from death, but giving all God has promised.

It may be more natural in some languages to introduce the positive before the negative part of the contrast, namely, "he will come again to save those who are waiting for him. He will not come the second time to deal with sin" or ". . . When he comes the second time, it will not be in order to deal with sin." In place of the rather generalized expression **to deal with sin,** it may be possible to translate "to cause the forgiveness of sins."

The last part of the sentence could also mean "those who are waiting for him to save them" (so TOB), but almost all translations and most commentaries take the same meaning as TEV. In translating **who are waiting for him,** it is important to suggest positive expectations rather than passive endurance. Accordingly, **who are waiting for him** may be rendered in some languages as "who are expecting his coming."

Chapter 10

1 The Jewish Law is not a full and faithful model of the real things; it is only a faint outline of the good things to come. The same sacrifices are offered forever, year after year. How can the Law, then, by means of these sacrifices make perfect the people who come to God? 2 If the people worshiping God had really been purified from their sins, they would not feel guilty of sin any more, and all sacrifices would stop. 3 As it is, however, the sacrifices serve year after year to remind people of their sins. 4 For the blood of bulls and goats can never take away sins.

5 For this reason, when Christ was about to come into the world, he said to God:

"You do not want sacrifices and offerings,
but you have prepared a body for me.

6   You are not pleased with animals burned whole on the altar
or with sacrifices to take away sins.

7   Then I said, 'Here I am to do your will, O God,
just as it is written of me in the book of the Law.' "

8 First he said, "You neither want nor are you pleased with sacrifices and offerings or with animals burned on the altar and the sacrifices to take away sins." He said this even though all these sacrifices are offered according to the Law. 9 Then he said, "Here I am,

1 For since the law has but a shadow of the good things to come instead of the true form of these realities, it can never, by the same sacrifices which are continually offered year after year, make perfect those who draw near. 2 Otherwise, would they not have ceased to be offered? If the worshipers had once been cleansed, they would no longer have any consciousness of sin. 3 But in these sacrifices there is a reminder of sin year after year. 4 For it is impossible that the blood of bulls and goats should take away sins.

5 Consequently, when Christ[v] came into the world, he said,

"Sacrifices and offerings thou hast not desired,
but a body hast thou prepared for me;

6   in burnt offerings and sin offerings thou hast taken no pleasure.

7   Then I said, 'Lo, I have come to do thy will, O God,'
as it is written of me in the roll of the book.' "

8 When he said above, "Thou hast neither desired nor taken pleasure in sacrifices and offerings and burnt offerings and sin offerings" (these are offered according to the law), 9 then he added, "Lo, I have come to do thy will." He abolishes the first in order to establish the second. 10 And by that will we have been sanctified through the offering of the body of Jesus Christ once for all.

O God, to do your will." So God does
away with all the old sacrifices and
puts the sacrifice of Christ in their
place.   10 Because Jesus Christ did
what God wanted him to do, we are all
purified from sin by the offering that
he made of his own body once and for
all.

ᵛ Greek *he*

Verses 1-10 have been called the writer's "final verdict" on Old Testament worship. They continue the thought of 9.26 and develop it in two ways. First, by means of the quotation in verses 5b-7 of Psalm 40.6-8, they show the readers that the Old Testament itself states that animal sacrifices are not enough; secondly, they emphasize that Christ's sacrifice is not only unique and final, but that it is also a personal act of obedience.

10.1　　　　　The Jewish Law is not a full and faithful model of the real things; it is only a faint outline of the good things to come. The same sacrifices are offered forever, year after year. How can the Law, then, by means of these sacrifices make perfect the people who come to God?

Jewish is implied, as in verse 11. This term is not historically correct, since Israelites were not called "Jews" until after the exile, while the first five books of the Bible are set in an earlier period. However, the writer is not concerned with the distinction between the various periods of Old Testament history. Nor are most modern readers concerned, for whom "Jews" are a recognizable group, whereas "Israelites" or "Hebrews" are not. **Jewish** is therefore widely used in CLTs. See comment on 8.4.

The phrase **The Jewish Law** may be rendered as "The Law given to the Jews" or "The Law for the Jews." Note, however, that in many languages it may be necessary to employ a plural form, namely, "The laws given to the Jews."

As a comparison with RSV shows, TEV reverses the original order of **not a full and faithful model** and **only a faint outline**. This change makes the verse easier to understand, by putting the more important negative statement first. The translator should consider whether or not this is natural and effective in his own language.

In contrasting the **full and faithful model** and the **faint outline,** the writer returns to the contrast expressed in partly different words in 8.5 between the <u>pattern</u> and the <u>shadow</u> (also Col 2.17). For **model,** KJV uses "image," which is appropriate in Mark 12.16 and Colossians 1.15, but is misleading here; the writer does not mean "the image of an original" but the original itself, the reality itself, of which the Old Testament worship is only a "shadow."

Not a full and faithful model has a textual problem. For the Greek, "not the true form," one early manuscript has "and the true form," and others have different readings. Both old and modern translations choose the same text as TEV and RSV.

[212]

The expression for **the real things** is as general in meaning in the Greek as its equivalent is in English; all the stylistic emphasis falls on "true form."

The phrase **the real things** can be almost completely obscure, especially in a literal translation in which the equivalent of **things** may indicate merely objects. It would appear that **the real things** must in some way be related to the good things to come, but in view of what has been said about what is real in the previous two chapters, **the real things** may relate to "that which exists in heaven."

Is not a full and faithful model of the real things may be expressed as "does not look just like the real things."

The **good things** were **to come**, from the point of view of the Law, but have now already come, from the point of view of the writer (see 9.11). For this reason GeCL's "a weak indication of what God wanted to do for men in the future" is preferable to Mft's "a mere shadow of the bliss that is to be" or Brc's "no more than a shadow of the good things which are to come." Phps has "a dim outline of the benefits Christ would bring," and NEB "the good things which were to come." These renderings are similar to that of GeCL.

It may be difficult to translate the phrase **a faint outline of the good things to come.** In some languages the equivalent may be "words which are difficult to understand about the things that are to come," or "only some few words about the things that are to come," or "only a picture which is difficult to see clearly, which shows those good things that are to come," or ". . . those good things in the future."

On **sacrifices,** see comments on 5.1; 7.27.

The passive **are offered** is like the English impersonal pronoun "they," since it does not specify who does the offering; it means quite generally "people offered." The writer is now less concerned with the High Priest than with the sacrifice. **The same sacrifices are offered** may be expressed in some languages as "The same sacrifices happen" or ". . . occur."

The writer is more interested in Old Testament texts on worship than with what was happening in the Jerusalem Temple in his own lifetime. The writer is unlikely to have meant that sacrifices would go on being offered **forever** in the Temple (see 8.13; 9.8), but rather "repeatedly" or "indefinitely" (see TOB; similarly GeCL).[1] The NEB text solves this problem by taking the Greek for **forever** ("continually") with **make perfect,** thereby translating "can never bring the worshippers to perfection for all time." However, this translation, and the NEB footnote "bring to perfection the worshippers who come continually," go against the natural flow of the Greek sentence.

It may be possible to indicate in an effective and idiomatic way the meaning of **forever, year after year** as "day after day, year after year, always." Instead of **are offered forever** one may use a negative expression, for example, "never cease," and then add "day after day and year after year."

---

[1] This is true whether or not the Jerusalem Temple was still in use when Hebrews was written. On this matter scholars disagree.

RSV's **"never"** is strongly emphasized. TEV brings this out by turning the negative statement **"it can never . . . make perfect"** into a rhetorical question, **How can the Law . . . make perfect . . . ?** Translators must decide how far it is natural to follow this example in their own languages.

Instead of RSV's **"it** (that is, the Law) **can never,"** many good manuscripts have "they can never," referring to "sacrifices" or to those who offer them, leaving "the Law" without futher explanation. Translations and commentators generally choose the text followed by RSV, but one or two mention the alternative in a note.

On **make perfect,** see comments on 2.10.

On **come to God** or **"draw near,"** see comments on 4.16.

It may be difficult to speak of "the Law making something perfect," for in many languages the Law is not regarded as being an agent. However, one can often say "How can the people who come to God become perfect by following the laws which tell about these sacrifices?" or ". . . the laws which indicate how sacrifices are to be performed?"

10.2   **If the people worshiping God had really been purified from their sins, they would not feel guilty of sin any more, and all sacrifices would stop.**

This sentence may be understood either as a rhetorical question, as in RSV and the UBS Greek New Testament, or as a statement, as in TEV. Even if the Greek text is punctuated as a question, here again the translator must decide whether rhetorical questions are natural and easily understood in the receptor language.

TEV arranges the three parts of the verse in their most natural order for English, although this is not necessarily the most natural order for other languages: (a) **purified,** (b) **not feel guilty,** (c) **sacrifices would stop.** The translator should not follow TEV or any other translation mechanically. He should instead consider the relation between the following statements:

(a) The worshipers have once been purified.

(b) People are no longer conscious of sin.

(c) Sacrifices stop.

Part (b), and less directly part (c), are consequences of part (a). When the translator has found a provisional translation for these three statements, he should then take account of the fact that all this is an unreal condition, that is, something which would have happened if things were different, but which in fact did not.

Really translates the writer's characteristic expression "once." It contrasts with year after year in verses 1 and 3 and could therefore be kept in translation.

The noun phrase **the people worshiping God** may be restructured as a noun expression followed by a relative clause, for example, "the people who worship God."

It may be difficult to speak of "being purified from sins," and therefore it may be more appropriate to speak of "becoming rid of one's sins" or "having one's sins removed." Sometimes the expression may be more effective in a negative form; for example, "had become no longer defiled by their sins."

Feel guilty translates the Greek word which was translated heart in 9.9 and consciences in 9.14. As here, it usually implies "consciousness of sin," that is, "a bad conscience." **They would not feel guilty of sin any more** may be expressed as "they would no longer feel guilty because of the sins they had done." However, the concept of "being guilty of sins" is often expressed in idiomatic ways; for example, "their hearts would no longer feel heavy because of their sins," or "their sins would no longer be following them," or "their minds would no longer be killing themselves because of their sins."

All sacrifices would stop may be rendered as "there would be no more sacrifices," or "people would no longer offer sacrifices," or ". . . cause sacrifices to be made," or ". . . cause animals to be sacrificed."

10.3   **As it is, however, the sacrifices serve year after year to remind people of their sins.**

As it is translates a strong Greek word for "But" (RSV). TNT has "In fact the opposite happens." **As it is, however** may be rendered as "But it happens that" or "Nevertheless, the truth is that."

RSV's "**in these sacrifices**" more probably means "by means of these sacrifices." This means the same as TEV, **the sacrifices serve . . . to,** but TEV restructures the sentence.

"**In**" (RSV) or "by these sacrifices" is literally "in them." This phrase includes the confession of sin which went with the sacrifice.

Year after year is repeated for emphasis from verse 1. RSV's "**reminder**," which TEV turns into a verb (**remind**), is better than the traditional "remembrance" of KJV and Knox. For sacrifice as a reminder of sin, compare Numbers 5.15. A "**reminder**," here as in Luke 22.19 and 1 Corinthians 11.24, is something said and done to make someone remember a past event.

Serve . . . to remind people of their sins may be rendered as "cause people to continually think about their sins" or "cause people never to forget about their sins."

10.4   **For the blood of bulls and goats can never take away sins.**

It may be impossible to translate literally **the blood of bulls and goats.** Two kinds of blood are involved, so it may be necessary to talk about "the bloods of bulls and of goats" or "the blood of bulls and the blood of goats."

Never translates the emphatic "it is impossible"; it is not an expression of time. For the writer's typical phrase "it is impossible" (RSV), see 6.4,18; 11.6.

Take away in Greek is a compound verb used with **sins** or "sin" in both the Old and the New Testaments; see Romans 11.27, which refers back to Isaiah 27.9. John 1.29 in Greek uses the simple form of the same verb (without the equivalent of **away**). An expression for **take away,** in the Greek as in English, is here a dead metaphor. It does not make the reader ask "where are the sins taken?" but means essentially the same as "forgive" (9.22) or deal with (9.28).

Can never take away sins may be rendered as "cannot at all cause guilt to disappear" or "can never cause sin to be forgiven." Expressions for forgiveness often involve idiomatic expressions; for example, to forgive guilt may be "to take guilt back" or "to throw guilt away."

10.5   **For this reason, when Christ was about to come into the world, he said to God:**
"You do not want sacrifices and offerings,
but you have prepared a body for me.

For this reason (or "That is why") points back to verse 4. This makes a contrast with what, for the writer, is the main point of Psalm 40.6-8. The underlying argument, made clear in verses 9b-10, is as follows: animal sacrifices cannot deal with sin, because the animals have no choice about whether or not they will be sacrificed. Christ, on the other hand, offered himself, by his own choice, in response to his Father's will.

The first part of this verse assumes three things: first, that Christ existed before he became man (see 1.2-3); second, that parts of the Old Testament can be understood as having been spoken by Christ (see 2.12-13); and third, that Psalm 40.6-8 refers to the time of Christ's beginning his life as a human being (see 1.6 and comments).

Christ is implied (see RSV footnote). Most modern translations supply the name **Christ; Christ** was used in 9.24,28. One or two even use "Jesus," but this is less satisfactory, since Hebrews keeps this name for use with special emphasis (2.9; 3.1; 6.20; 10.19; 12.2).

Most commentators take the term rendered **the world** to mean "the earth." A different Greek word is used in 1.6. The psalm quotation would then refer to the incarnation, probably in contrast to 1.6, rather than to Christ's entry into the heavenly world when he was enthroned at the right hand of God.

The clause **when Christ was about to come into the world** may be expressed as "when there was not much time before Christ was to come into the world," or "when Christ was soon to come into the world," or "when Christ was almost coming into the world."

To God is added, to explain **You** in the next line. **He said** is literally "he says," and **when Christ was about to come** is literally "coming." The writer uses the present tense, because this passage of the Old Testament is still available to him as he writes, and is still valid. Some translations put both the original "he says" and "coming" into the past tense, since it was in the past that Christ came into the world: GeCL "therefore Christ said, when he came into the world, to God . . ."; Brc "this is why Christ, as he was coming into the world, said to God . . . ."

The tenses in the quotation, verses 5b-7, need careful examination. RSV's verbs refer to completely past events. "I have come" (verse 7, RSV) suggests a past event, the consequences of which continue into the present. TEV's Here I am (verse 7) emphasizes this present aspect to the exclusion of the past. The time at which Christ "said" the words in verse 7 is fixed by verse 5, that is, "when Christ came into the world." Hebrews emphasizes the difference between the past system of sacrifices and the later event of Christ's coming (then, verse 7, repeated in verse 9). In English "you did not want" (verse 5) and "you took no pleasure" (verse 6) are appropriate tenses to show that this was God's attitude in the past toward the sacrificial system.

Sacrifices and offerings are singular in the Greek of this verse, which means "You do not want any sacrifice or offering." For the writer of Hebrews, the meaning is the same, as he shows by using the plural again in verse 8. **You do not want sacrifices and offerings** often requires expansion in translation, since **sacrifices and offerings** imply certain events in which people participate. Therefore "You do not want people to offer sacrifices and to give you gifts" or "You do not desire people to sacrifice animals and to make offerings to you."

A body: the Septuagint of Psalm 40 differs from the Hebrew, which has "ears"; the RSV footnote translates "ears thou hast dug for me" in Psalm 40.6. There is no doubt that TEV and RSV give the meaning of the way the Psalm is quoted in Hebrews. A strictly literal translation of **you have prepared a body for me** might suggest that the body was a kind of supernatural strait jacket into which Christ's personality would temporarily fit. It may be clearer to employ some such translation as "you have given me a body" or "you have caused me to have a body."

10.6 **You are not pleased with animals burned whole on the altar or with sacrifices to take away sins.**

You are not pleased is expressed by a past tense in the Greek, meaning "you took no pleasure in." Most translations keep the past tense, but FrCL, GeCL, and Mft use the present. What in the English sentence is the complement of the verb **pleased** must be made the causative subject in some languages; for example, "When animals are completely burned on the altar or when sacrifices to take away sins are performed, these do not cause you to be pleased" or ". . . these do not make you happy."

Animals burned whole on the altar or with sacrifices to take away sins translates only four Greek words, but the expansion is necessary to give the full meaning. The Hebrew Old Testament has the singular for "burnt offering," which is followed by some manuscripts of the Septuagint and of Hebrews. The plural is used in Psalm 51.16. There is no difference in meaning here. The expression rendered "**sin offerings**" (RSV) is literally "for sin," but "sacrifice(s)" or something similar must be added to make the meaning clear.

10.7   Then I said, 'Here I am
              to do your will, O God,
              just as it is written of me in the book of the Law.' "

Then I said is unavoidably awkward after he said in verse 5, since the writer is fitting an Old Testament quotation into a new setting. (In Psalm 40, verse 6 is part of the psalmist's meditation, and it is quoted in Hebrews 10 as verses 5b-6; and verses 7-8a, which are quoted in Hebrews 10.7, describe the next event.) Not only is this expression **Then I said** somewhat awkward at the beginning of verse 7, but it is completely misleading, for many readers will interpret the **I** as being the writer of the letter. It may therefore be necessary in some languages to translate **Then I said** as "Then Christ said," with adjustment of quotation marks as necessary.

Here I am is better than RSV's "**I have come**," since the only movement implied is probably in the opposite direction, away from God to earth.

A vocative expression such as **O God** normally occurs at the beginning of a direct quotation addressed to a particular person. The quotation may be rendered as "O God, I am here to do your will" or ". . . what you want me to do." However, it may be impossible to insert a direct vocative into direct discourse, and therefore it may be necessary to relate **God** to the statement "then Christ said." The beginning of verse 7 may thus have "then Christ said to God, I am here to do your will."

The third line of this verse in TEV appears as the second line in the Greek. It is an aside, that is, a parenthetical remark. **It is written** renders an expression often used in introducing quotations from scripture. This introduction is not used anywhere else in Hebrews, but it is very common in the rest of the New Testament; see, for example, Mark 1.2; Acts 7.42; Romans 1.17. It suggests "it has been written, and the writing remains valid." **Just as it is written of me** may be expressed as "in the same way that the words speak about me" or "just as what is written is about me."

Of the Law is not part of the text of Hebrews, nor is it part of the Hebrew text of Psalm 40.8. The writer may be thinking of a heavenly book in which people thought that God wrote down everything people did (see Psa 139.16; Heb 12.23). GeCL suggests that the reference is to the Old Testament as a whole, "as it is foretold in the Holy Scriptures." However, in the light of constant references to the "Law" of Moses, for example, in 7.5 and 10.8, **book of the Law** is adopted by FrCL and TNT. Other translations simplify the Greek "roll of the book" to "scroll" (NEB) or "book" (SpCL and NAB). **The book of the Law** may be expressed in some languages as "the book which contains the laws" or "the book containing the laws given through Moses." In this way the reference is specifically to the Torah, in other words, the first five books of the Old Testament.

10.8-9a   First he said, "You neither want nor are you pleased with sac-
              rifices and offerings or with animals burned on the altar and
              the sacrifices to take away sins." He said this even though all

> **these sacrifices are offered according to the Law. 9 Then he said, "Here I am, O God, to do your will."**

By making a few verbal changes in the quotation from Psalm 40, Hebrews has emphasized the contrast between the end of the old order and the basis of the new. The quotation is now repeated in a rather different form, but with no major change of meaning. **First** or "**above**" (RSV) may mean "earlier in what I am writing," or more probably, "earlier in the quotation," in contrast with Then, verse 9.

In view of the way in which the direct quotations are introduced in verses 5 and 7, it may be good in verse 8 to render **First he said** as "First Christ said." It may be necessary to introduce God as the person to whom the statement is made, since only in this way is the referent of the pronoun **You** made clear.

The rendering of the direct quotation in verse 8 depends largely on the way in which similar expressions are rendered in verses 5 and 6.

He said this even though all these sacrifices are offered according to the Law is an aside, or parenthetic expression, as RSV shows by using parentheses. Nowhere else does Hebrews speak so positively about the Law of Moses, and the meaning here may be only "these sacrifices belong to the old order, governed by the Law." Since the Greek participle, literally "saying," is translated **he said**, it would be possible to put **are offered** into the past tense also. A better solution is GeCL's "although all these sacrifices are prescribed (or, laid down) in the Law"; or Brc's "and these are the offerings which the law prescribes" (similarly TNT).

Some languages do not use a concessive clause introduced by a conjunction such as **though** or **even though**. However, it is always possible to express a concession by introducing a conjunction such as "nevertheless"; for example, "all these sacrifices were made as the Law said they should be made, but nevertheless he said this."

As in verse 7 it may be necessary to alter the position of **O God** or to incorporate it as an indirect object of the verb **said**; for example, "Then he said to God, I am here to do your will."

10.9b-10 **So God does away with all the old sacrifices and puts the sacrifice of Christ in their place. 10 Because Jesus Christ did what God wanted him to do, we are all purified from sin by the offering that he made of his own body once and for all.**

Translations are usually longer than the texts they translate. This passage is so compressed in the Greek that translations may need to be much longer if they are to bring out the full meaning.

The translator also has to choose between different ways of making explicit what is implicit in the text. The main problems may be listed as follows, using RSV as a basis. The first two questions must be studied together: (a) Who "**abolishes the first in order to establish the second**"? And (b) what is "**that will**"? There are two possibilities:

[219]

(a) "he abolishes . . ."   (i) God abolishes: (ii) Christ abolishes:
                                 TEV, FrCL   RSV, GeCL,
                                                        Phps, JB (?),
                                                        Brc (?).

(b) "that will"   (i) God's will (in   (ii) Christ's act of
                        general): DuCL,   obedient sacrifice:
                        Knox (?), NEB   TEV, FrCL,
                                                GeCL,TNT.

Many translations irresponsibly leave the reader to choose; those translations are not mentioned in this summary. If necessary, an alternative translation may be added in a footnote.

(a) There are two arguments in favor of choice (i), TEV **God does away . . .**: first, if "Christ" is the grammatical subject, the conclusion "the body of Jesus Christ" is a little awkward. Second, it is usually God rather than Christ who is said to establish or change the Law, priesthood, and forms of worship. On the other hand, in favor of choice (ii) is the fact that "Christ" has been the subject of all the main verbs since verse 5. Most translations therefore imply or state that "Christ" is the subject here also.

(b) **"That will"** is literally "by which will," referring back to "thy will" in verse 9. "Thy will" there means "God's will." The question arises whether the "**will**" that people should be **purified from sin** is (i) God's will or (ii) the specific act by which Christ offered himself in sacrifice, in response to **what God wanted him to do.** Choice (ii) fits in more clearly with the context, and choice (i) could have been more naturally expressed in Greek in other ways.

On this basis other questions are more easily settled. (c) **Does away with** means "abolishes" a "law," rather than having the general meaning "destroys." (d) "The first" means **the old** animal **sacrifices** mentioned in verses 5-6, and "the second" is Christ's willing obedience to God (verse 7), expressed in the sacrifice of his death. (e) In **we are all purified** or "made holy," **we** includes all Christians. The Greek for been purified in verse 2 is different from the word used here, and so is the Greek for made perfect in verse 1, but the meaning is very similar. Alternatively **purified** may mean "set apart to belong to God in a special way." TNT combines the two: "we are cleansed and set apart for his service." Brc emphasizes that for the writer, the purpose of holiness is to make possible a real meeting with God in worship: "we have been made fit to enter God's presence." GeCL (see below) emphasizes the inner purpose of worship as the removal of guilt, as in verses 17-18.

Even though the Greek text of 9b says only "he does away with the first in order to establish the second," it is important to make clear what are the first and the second, and this is precisely what TEV has attempted to do. But **does away with** should not be understood in the sense of "destroying" or "throwing away." A more satisfactory rendering may be "declares that all the old sacrifices no longer have any power," or "causes all the old sacrifices to no longer have power" or ". . . no longer be able to accomplish anything." The rendering of **puts the**

sacrifice of Christ in their place must be translated in such a way as to complement the first part of 9b. If the first part of 9b is translated "God takes away the power of all the old sacrifices," one may translate the second part of 9b as "and he causes the sacrifice of Christ to have power."

As in other contexts **we are all purified from sin** may be best expressed negatively: "we no longer have sin" or ". . . have guilt."

The offering . . . of his own body[2] is the same as the sacrifice of himself in 9.26; compare 9.12. No contrast is implied between **body**, the key word of verse 5, and "soul" or "spirit." **Offering**, as in verse 8, is used in the sense of a "sacrifice." The expression of means in the phrase **by the offering that he made** may be rendered in some languages as cause; for example, "because of the offering he made" or "because of the way he offered."

In order to avoid the implication that **his own body** was something external to Christ himself, it may be best to translate **by the offering that he made of his own body** as "by the way in which he offered himself."

Once and for all, in the Greek as in TEV, comes at the end of the sentence, and is thus even more emphatic than usual. The tense of the verb indicates a past action, the effects of which continue into the present. GeCL and some commentators understand the sentence to mean "we have been purified once for all," but GeCL first edition's very clear translation is more probable: "Once for all he offered himself."

GeCL sums up many of the choices recommended above: "In this way Christ puts an end to the old sacrifices and puts his own (sacrifice) in their place. Thus he did what God wanted of him. Once for all, he offered himself (emphasized). By this, we have been freed from all guilt."

	TEV	**10.11-18**	RSV

11 Every Jewish priest performs his services every day and offers the same sacrifices many times; but these sacrifices can never take away sins. 12 Christ, however, offered one sacrifice for sins, an offering that is effective forever, and then he sat down at the right side of God. 13 There he now waits until God puts his enemies as a footstool under his feet. 14 With one sacrifice, then, he has made perfect forever those who are purified from sin.
15 And the Holy Spirit also gives us his witness. First he says,

11 And every priest stands daily at his service, offering repeatedly the same sacrifices, which can never take away sins. 12 But when Christ[w] had offered for all time a single sacrifice for sins, he sat down at the right hand of God, 13 then to wait until his enemies should be made a stool for his feet. 14 For by a single offering he has perfected for all time those who are sanctified. 15 And the Holy Spirit also bears witness to us; for after saying,
16 "This is the covenant that I will
make with them
after those days, says the Lord:

[2] One manuscript has "blood," as in verse 29, but this is most unlikely to be correct here.

16 "This is the covenant that I will
make with them
in the days to come, says the
Lord:
I will put my laws in their hearts
and write them on their minds."
17 And then he says, "I will not remember their sins and evil deeds any
longer." 18 So when these have been
forgiven, an offering to take away sins
is no longer needed.

I will put my laws on their
hearts,
and write them on their minds,"
17 then he adds,
"I will remember their sins and
their misdeeds no more."
18 Where there is forgiveness of these,
there is no longer any offering for sin.

w Greek *this one*

The main purpose of verses 11-18 is (a) to show that what Christ did as priest and as sacrifice was entirely successful; and (b) to emphasize once more that the purpose of what he did was to deal with sin. Point (a) links this passage with the beginning of the letter (1.3, like 10.12,13, refers to Psalm 110.4); and point (b) recalls 8.10-12 (which refers to Jer 31.33-34; compare 9.22).

In this as in other contexts, **once and for all** may be rendered as "once and never again."

Note the chiastic structure of verses 11-12, with items occurring in A-B-B'-A' order:

A	Every priest stands	(Christ) sat down	A'
B	daily	for all time	B'

Translators must decide whether this structure is used in their own languages.

10.11 Every Jewish priest performs his services every day and offers the same sacrifices many times; but these sacrifices can never take away sins.

Some manuscripts have "High Priest," but "priest" was more likely to be changed by copyists into "High Priest" (5.1 and 8.3) than the opposite. For this and other reasons the UBS Greek text has "priest."

Jewish is implied; see comments on 8.4 and 10.1. This verse adds little to previous statements. **Every Jewish priest** may be rendered as "every priest who is a Jew." But this misses the point that in this context **Jewish** refers more to the religious system than to an individual as such. Therefore **Every Jewish priest** may be better rendered in some languages as "every priest of the Jewish religion" or "every priest who performs . . . on behalf of the Jews."

Performs his services every day may be rendered as "does his work as priest every day." See 7.27.

Many times: see comments on 6.7 and 9.25.

Take away translates a different verb from those used in verses 4 and 8, but the meaning is practically the same. In translation it may be necessary to use some such phrase as "the same type of sacrifices," to make it clear that the identical animals are not offered **many times.**

10.12   **Christ, however, offered one sacrifice for sins, an offering that is effective forever, and then he sat down at the right side of God.**

However marks a strong contrast between verses 11 and 12a; GeCL "Christ, on the other hand . . . ."

Christ is implied; literally "this man"; TNT "this priest."

Christ . . . offered one sacrifice for sins could be misunderstood to imply that on one occasion Christ functioned as a priest in the temple and offered a sacrifice for sin or, as a layman, brought a sacrifice to the temple to be offered for sin. It may therefore be necessary to translate "but Christ offered himself as a sacrifice for sin."

Effective is implied.

Forever may be linked either (a) with **offered,** as in TEV, RSV, NEB, and TNT, or (b) with **sat down,** as in DuCL, GeCL, and TOB. The following factors should be considered in choosing between these two constructions.

(1) Offered and forever certainly go together in verse 1. However, in that verse forever means "repeatedly," not "continuously," as in verse 12.

(2) **Sat down** is part of the reference to Psalm 110.1, but **forever** is not. However, verse 13 suggests that the writer may be trying to meet a possible difficulty caused by adding **forever** to the quotation. (Compare his addition in verse 8 of neither want nor to the quotation from Psalm 40.6.)

(3) In the other three places where the writer uses this Greek phrase translated **forever,** it is connected with what precedes; but the author's style is too flexible for this to prove that the same is true here.

(4) To connect **forever** with **offered** involves giving **forever** an unusual meaning, not "offered forever a single sacrifice," but "offered a single sacrifice which is valid forever." The balance of evidence therefore seems slightly on the side of (b) "sat down forever," but (a) **offered . . . forever** may be included in a footnote.

Interpretation (a), **an offering that is effective forever,** may be rendered as "this offering always takes away sins," or "this offering is always able to take away sins" or ". . . to cause the forgiveness of sins." Interpretation (b), combining **forever** with **he sat down,** might imply that the writer is making this statement from a position at the end of time. It may therefore be necessary to render **forever** as "permanently" or "he sat down on the right side of God to stay."

10.13   **There he now waits until God puts his enemies as a footstool under his feet.**

Now in this context is an expression of time, meaning "from this (or, from that) time on," "henceforth" (NEB, BJ, TNT).

As in other contexts, the rendering of **waits** should be such as to suggest patient expectation rather than mere inaction.

Until God puts is literally "until they put," but "they" is impersonal, meaning "until his enemies are put," and probably implies here the activity of God.

In place of **God puts his enemies as a footstool under his feet** it may be necessary to change the order; for example, "God puts his enemies under his feet as though they were a footstool." However, this figure of speech may seem quite ridiculous in some languages, and it may therefore be necessary to introduce the meaning of the idiom in the text, and the literal rendering may be placed in a marginal note, if necessary.

10.14   With one sacrifice, then, he has made perfect forever those
who are purified from sin.

Here, as in verse 12, **With one sacrifice** may be translated as "By means of once having sacrificed himself" or "When once he offered himself as a sacrifice."

"Making perfect" and "making pure" are difficult to distinguish. "Making people pure" means that God sets them apart to belong to him, or to be dedicated to him. "Making people perfect" involves dealing completely with sin and so cleansing the conscience from guilt. GeCL translates simply, "So he has with a single sacrifice brought to the goal those who are made pure by him"; similarly TNT.

As in other contexts, **made perfect** may be rendered as "made to be as they should be" or "made to be without guilt."

Those who are purified from sin in 2.11 the same Greek phrase is translated **those who are made pure.** In some contexts it may be rendered as "those whom God has made to belong to himself" or "those who are dedicated to God."

10.15-17   And the Holy Spirit also gives us his witness. First he
says,
16   "This is the covenant that I will make with them
in the days to come, says the Lord:
I will put my laws in their hearts
and write them on their minds."
17 And then he says, "I will not remember their sins and evil
deeds any longer."

Throughout these verses, it is important to make clear in translation to whom the verbs of speaking refer. These verbs are:
(a) **gives us his witness,** literally "witnesses," verse 15;
(b) **he says,** literally "to have said," verse 15;
(c) **says the Lord,** verse 16.
With these should be considered:

(d) **and then he says,** verse 17, though there is no verb in the Greek, which is literally "and."

Verbs (a) and (c) present no problems. (a) The person who "witnesses" is **the Holy Spirit.** (c) The one who **says** is **the Lord,** which here almost certainly means God, not Christ. The tense of verb (b), **says,** and also the context, suggest that the subject is probably the Holy Spirit, but the translation "it says," meaning "scripture says," is also possible. It is unlikely that the author made a sharp distinction between the two, and it is simpler in translation to keep **the Holy Spirit** as the subject of (b) as well as (a).

Verb (d) is practically meaningless if translated literally, since the sentence has no main verb to follow verb (b), **"after saying"** (RSV). Even some of the scribes copying manuscripts of Hebrews added in verse 17 expressions such as RSV's **"then he adds."** This is not what the writer of Hebrews wrote, but it is almost certainly the way in which he intended the last line of the quotation to be understood. TEV and RSV are therefore right not to include verb (d), "and" or its equivalent, as part of the quotation, even though this word occurs at this point in the Greek translation of Jeremiah. If some such expanded translation as **then he says** or **"then he adds"** is chosen, the implied subject of the verb must be the same as the subject of verb (b), **says,** probably the Holy Spirit. It may be necessary to make this explicit.

On **the Holy Spirit,** see comments on 2.4; he is mentioned as the author of an Old Testament quotation in 3.7. Hebrews 7.8,17; 10.15; 11.2,4 also speak of what God "witnesses" or "testifies" in scripture. **Us** includes the writer and his readers. **The Holy Spirit also gives us his witness** may be rendered as "the Holy Spirit also speaks to us about this."

This is the covenant: the covenant has been discussed in 9.1-22, and it is grammatically possible for **this** to refer back to this passage. But it is much more probable that **this** looks forward to the particular kind of covenant which is mentioned in the second part of verse 16, "a covenant which is put into the hearts and written on the minds of the people."

In the days to come may be rendered as "in the future" or "later."

As in 8.8, the repetition **he says . . . says the Lord** may be misunderstood, for one might think that there are two persons speaking, one the Holy Spirit and the other the Lord. It may be more satisfactory to introduce the direct quotation in the following way: "first the Holy Spirit says that the following is what the Lord has said, 'This is the covenant that I will make . . . .' "

For a discussion of some of the problems involved in rendering **I will put my laws in their hearts and write them on their minds,** see the discussion under 8.10.

The quotation is from Jeremiah 31.33-34, which was first quoted in 8.10,12.

As in 2.13 (Isa 8.17,18), the writer emphasizes the point by dividing a quotation into two parts. The effect is to underline the second part of the quotation: "Not only does the new covenant involve a law written on people's hearts; it also brings the forgiveness of sin." The author of Hebrews quotes Jeremiah more freely than in 8.10-12: (a) **with them** in verse 16a summarizes with the people of Israel in 8.10; (b) **hearts** and **minds** in verse 16b are mentioned in the opposite order from 8.10; (c) and **evil deeds** in verse 17 is added to Jeremiah 31.34.

For a discussion of some of the problems involved in rendering **I will not remember their sins and evil deeds any longer,** see the suggestions made under 8.12.

As in 8.10-12, there are many differences of detail between the text quoted here and the text of Jeremiah in the Hebrew and even in the Greek Septuagint. The translator's task is to translate the Greek text of Hebrews. He should not be influenced by the Old Testament wording.

10.18   **So when these have been forgiven, an offering to take away sins is no longer needed.**

This verse, like verses 9b-10, is concentrated and leaves certain details implicit. **Forgiven** translates the same word used in 9.22. **These** are clearly their sins and evil deeds just mentioned. **When** is a logical expression, literally "where"; there is no special reference to the place or time of forgiveness. The meaning is "in a situation in which sins have been forgiven, no sacrifice is needed any longer to take them away." **No longer,** however, refers to time; therefore CLTs, JB (but not BJ), and Brc translate **when.**

The verse contains no verb in Greek: literally "but where forgiveness of these, no longer offering for sins." Different translations supply different verbs in the second phrase: (a) **"there is,"** RSV, NEB, NAB; compare Mft, "an offering for sin exists no longer"; (b) "no more offering for sin takes place" Lu; similarly TOB; (c) **an offering to take away sins is no longer needed,** CLTs, Brc, TNT; (d) "there is no longer any room for a sin-offering," Knox; JB "there can be no more sin offerings"; (e) Phps expands the whole sentence: "Where God grants remission of sin there can be no question of making further atonement." In choosing between these possibilities, it should be remembered that this statement comes in a very emphatic position, at the end of the longest section of teaching in the whole letter. This is perhaps an argument for preferring a stronger statement of type (d) or (e), rather than the less emphatic translation (c). On **offering to take away sins,** see comments on verse 6.

In some languages the conclusion in verse 18 may be effectively rendered as "therefore, when God has forgiven people's sins, it is no longer necessary for priests to make offerings which are supposed to take away sins" or ". . . cause the forgiveness of sins."

TEV   **10.19-25**   RSV

Let Us Come Near to God

19 We have, then, my brothers, complete freedom to go into the Most Holy Place by means of the death of Jesus. 20 He opened for us a new way, a living way, through the curtain—that

19 Therefore, brethren, since we have confidence to enter the sanctuary by the blood of Jesus, 20 by the new and living way which he opened for us through the curtain, that is, through his

is, through his own body. 21 We have a great priest in charge of the house of God. 22 So let us come near to God with a sincere heart and a sure faith, with hearts that have been purified from a guilty conscience and with bodies washed with clean water. 23 Let us hold on firmly to the hope we profess, because we can trust God to keep his promise. 24 Let us be concerned for one another, to help one another to show love and to do good. 25 Let us not give up the habit of meeting together, as some are doing. Instead, let us encourage one another all the more, since you see that the Day of the Lord is coming nearer.

flesh, 21 and since we have a great priest over the house of God, 22 let us draw near with a true heart in full assurance of faith, with our hearts sprinkled clean from an evil conscience and our bodies washed with pure water. 23 Let us hold fast the confession of our hope without wavering, for he who promised is faithful; 24 and let us consider how to stir up one another to love and good works, 25 not neglecting to meet together, as is the habit of some, but encouraging one another, and all the more as you see the Day drawing near.

At the beginning of this new section, verses 19-39, the writer reaches perhaps the most important turning point in his letter. From now on he is mainly concerned to encourage his readers to apply in their own lives the results of what Christ has done.

However, even here there is no sharp break; teaching and appeals for action, theology and preaching, are related to one another, and both are grounded in the Old Testament. There is some connection between this section and earlier passages, and some of the same words and ideas recur.

This section is divided in the UBS Greek New Testament, TEV, and RSV into three paragraphs, all of which have links with earlier chapters: (a) verses 19-25 recall the appeal of 4.14-16; (b) verses 26-31 recall the warning of 6.4-8; and (c) verses 32-39 recall the more positive and hopeful statement of 6.9-12. In each case the thought of earlier passages is more fully developed in the light of all the teaching given in 6.13—10.18.

In translating the section heading, **Let Us Come Near to God**, it is important to avoid in the rendering of **Let Us** any implication of request for permission. This is simply an exhortation and may need to be expressed as "We should therefore come near to God."

10.19   **We have, then, my brothers, complete freedom to go into the Most Holy Place by means of the death of Jesus.**

The writer begins to apply his teaching in a long sentence which in Greek continues without a break until verse 25. It will usually be necessary to divide this in translation, especially in a common language translation. In the Greek text the three main verbs are "draw near" (verse 22), "hold fast" (verse 23), and "consider" (verse 24). If the sentence is divided, it is necessary to find other means of making the translation as solemn and impressive as the original. This can be done by using some words which are near the upper limits of common language, and by paying particular attention to the style and form of the translation, and to points of special emphasis.

The second word in the Greek is a strong word for "therefore" (under-emphasized by TEV's **then**; FrCL has "thus"). This Greek word is usually used in Hebrews to mark (a) the beginning of a new section, as in 4.14; 9.1,23; (b) a transition from a statement to an appeal ("let us . . ." do something), as in 4.1,11,16; 10.35; 13.15; or (c) a conclusion drawn from an Old Testament quotation, as in 2.14; 4.6. In this verse "therefore" is both (a) and (b). The transition is also marked by **my brothers** (that is, "fellow Christians," as in 3.1,12; 13.22). **Brothers** does not exclude "sisters"; but neither does it suggest any blood relationship, and it is important in many languages to avoid an expression which would mean literally **my brothers.** In many languages an expression for "fellow Christians" is either "relatives" or "those of the same clan," since the fellowship among Christians suggests the establishment of a new kind of family relationship based upon God being the father of all those who believe.

Complete freedom renders a single word in the Greek. Here, as in 3.6 and 4.16, it means confidence in approaching God, rather than as in 10.35, courage in facing opponents. In Ephesians 3.12 TEV translates boldness. The underlying idea is that of having been given the right or permission to enter God's presence. **Complete freedom to go into** may even mean "the right to use the way into," that is, the path which Christ has opened up by his death. **Go into the Most Holy Place** recalls 9.7 and also 4.16; all Christians can now approach God as freely and closely as the high priests did under the old covenant. **Most** is implied, as in 9.25.

In rendering **we have . . . complete freedom to go into the Most Holy Place,** it may be important to indicate the symbolic or figurative nature of the expression, or to indicate by a note that this does not refer literally to the right of Christians to go into the Most Holy Place in the Temple. The author is speaking of access to God in a spiritual sense. Some translators have wanted to translate **into the Most Holy Place** as "into the Most Holy Place in heaven." But this can be misinterpreted as meaning that "believers have complete freedom to go to heaven when they die." The figurative meaning may be made clear by translating as "we have complete freedom to go, as it were, into the Most Holy Place," or ". . . into the Most Holy Room," or . . . into the Most Holy part of the sanctuary."

It is important not to translate either "blood" here, or body in verse 20, as if they were separate objects, distinct from Christ's whole offering of himself in death. For this reason TEV, in this verse as in 13.20 (sacrificial death), replaces the literal translation "blood" by **death.** However, this is not done in chapter 9 or in 10.4,29, where blood has its literal meaning, which is necessary to the argument. Sometimes a verb may be used, that is, where "blood" refers to an event. TEV does this in 12.4: you have not yet had to resist to the point of being killed. TNT chooses this solution in 10.19, "Jesus has died for us"; compare GeCL "because Jesus has sacrificed his blood."

By means of the death of Jesus means the same as through his own body in verse 20 (see comments below), though the Greek is different. **By means of the death of Jesus** may have to be expressed as a separate clause or sentence; for example, "this is possible because Christ died."

Jesus by itself is emphatic as usual; see comments on 2.9.

<u>10.20</u>   **He opened for us a new way, a living way, through the curtain
—that is, through his own body.**

The translation presents several related problems which affect the verse as
a whole.

(a) The second **through** is implied. As in 9.11-12 (see comments there on
through), there is probably a transition from the meaning of movement **through
(the curtain)** to the instrumental meaning "by means of" (**his own body**). The two
phrases will almost certainly need to be translated differently, if this difference
of meaning is to be made clear.

(b) If the second **through** does not mean "by means of," it must continue the
metaphor of movement **through the curtain.** Two constructions are possible:

(i) ". . . that is, (through the curtain of) his flesh," GeCL.

(ii) "that is, (the way of) his flesh."

(ii) is grammatically more difficult than (i).

The TEV rendering **through the curtain—that is, through his own body** is
both obscure and somewhat misleading, since it tends to equate **the curtain** with
his own body. It is symbolically strange to equate the body which was offered as a
sacrifice, with the curtain which divided the outer sanctuary from the inner
sanctuary. Though it is true that in English **through** has two different meanings,
the first involving movement and the second involving means, this is certainly not
clear to the average reader. Therefore, **through the curtain—that is, through his
own body** may be better expressed as "passing through the curtain, that means, he
did this by offering himself as a sacrifice."

(c) Is the **curtain** thought of as a "barrier" (compare 9.8; also Mark 15.38) or
as a "means of access" (equivalent to **way**)? The translation of "by means of the
curtain" is possible, but less likely than the literal **through the curtain,** which
would make the **curtain** a "barrier" through which Christ had passed.

The Greek word for **opened** is the word which was translated <u>went into</u>
<u>effect</u> in 9.18, where there was a suggestion of "inaugurating" the covenant by
some ceremony. Here the object of **opened** is **way,** not "covenant," and the idea of
ceremony is not important. **New** implies "which did not exist before Jesus opened
it" (see 6.20, where Jesus enters before us).

The term **way** may be both obscure and misleading unless some goal is
specified. **He opened for us a new way** does not refer directly to a new "way of
life." The implication is rather that Christ opened for the believer a new kind of
access to God. Therefore **He opened for us a new way** may be rendered as "He
opened for us a new way to God."

A living way may be unnatural in some languages; how can a **way** be
"alive"? The meaning may be "we can enter the Most Holy Place with perfect
freedom by means of Jesus, who sacrificed himself in death but is now alive." In
other words, the **living way** is Jesus, more particularly Jesus reigning (verses
12-13) and "appearing on our behalf in the presence of God" (9.24). This meaning

[229]

of **a living way** may be expressed as "Jesus is that way and he is alive." Alternatively, **living** may be understood as "a way which leads to life"; GeCL has "a new way to life," just as in 9.14 GeCL translated "the living God" as "God, the giver of life"; compare verse 31 and comments.

His own body: TOB's "his humanity" is misleading; it was not till long after New Testament times that the theology of Christ's human and divine natures was developed in any systematic way. **Body** does not refer to his human nature but, like "blood" in verse 19 (RSV), to Christ's whole offering of himself in death.

10.21   **We have a great priest in charge of the house of God.**

The expression for **great priest** is used for the sake of variety, instead of "High Priest" (see Septuagint, Lev 21.10; Num 35.28). However, there is no need to use a different expression in translation, since the meaning is the same.

In charge of the house of God translates the same phrase as in 3.6, with the same meaning. There may be complications in rendering **in charge of the house of God,** since the expression "the house of God" is frequently used as a name for the Temple in Jerusalem. Because the reference here is certainly to the heavenly temple or sanctuary, it may be best to indicate that fact, either in the text by some such expression as "the house of God in heaven," or by a marginal note saying that this is a reference to a heavenly sanctuary rather than to the Temple in Jerusalem.

10.22   **So let us come near to God with a sincere heart and a sure faith, with hearts that have been purified from a guilty conscience and with bodies washed with clean water.**

So shows that verses 22-25 logically depend on the statements in verses 19-21. In summary: "We have a way into God's presence, and a High Priest; therefore **let us come near** . . . hold on . . . be concerned" (verses 22-24). Throughout this passage the author includes himself and his readers in the words "we" and "us."

On **come near**, see 4.16, where TEV has approach. **Come near** does not imply that the writer is nearer to God, even figuratively, than are his readers. **To God** is implied. These words did not need to be expressed in the Greek, because **come near** renders a well-known expression related to worship, but it needs to be made clear in translation.

Since the expression **come near to God** is figurative in meaning, it may be necessary to mark it as such; for example, "Therefore, let us, as it were, come near to God." However, a verb meaning "come" may not be appropriate, since the movement is from the place where people are to a different point close to God. Accordingly, it may be necessary to translate "let us go near to God."

A sincere heart gives the meaning of "a true heart"; JB translates a similar expression in Isaiah 38.3, "with sincerity of heart"; NEB "loyal." It is the opposite of the attitude described in James 1.8 as "unstable" (RSV; compare James 1.6). **Heart,** as usual, stands for the whole person, especially what is central to the personality; it has no special reference to emotion. See comment on 3.8.

A sure faith is similar in meaning to **a sincere heart.** GeCL avoids the word for **faith,** since it is not often used outside church language, and instead translates "firm trust" ("in God" is understood, as in TEV). TNT uses a verb, "sincerely and fully believing in him," where "believe in" must mean "trust" rather than "believe that he exists."

The phrase **with a sincere heart and a sure faith** expresses what is called "attendant circumstances." That is, this phrase describes the situation which should exist when people approach God. The meaning of the phrase **with a sincere heart and a sure faith** may be expressed as "when we approach God, we must be sincere and trust him" or ". . . our hearts must be pure, and we should have no doubts."

The rest of the verse recalls Ezekiel 36.25-26, though it is not a direct quotation. This is not a poetic passage, but the writer of Hebrews produces something very similar to a couplet of Hebrew verse, in which the two lines have a similar meaning:

"hearts . . . made clean from a guilty conscience,
and bodies washed with pure water."

Some commentators link the second line with verse 23, but this suggestion is not followed by translators.

Hearts and **bodies** are not contrasted any more than are "blood" and body in verses 19-20.

On **purified** or "sprinkled," see comments on 9.13. On **conscience,** see comments on 9.9. It may be difficult to so k of "hearts being purified from a guilty conscience." Since in this context "hearts" refers to individuals and not to some part of the personality, it may be possible to translate **with hearts that have been purified from a guilty conscience** as "being purified from a sense of guilt" or "with our sense of guilt having been taken away."

Bodies washed with clean water may suggest a comparison of Christian baptism with the washing done by Old Testament priests (see 6.2 and 9.10). Knox's "hallowed water" is not a natural meaning of the Greek or even of the Vulgate. The tense of the words for **purified** and **washed** emphasizes the permanent effect of these events.

Since **bodies** also refers to the persons as such, the expression **and with bodies washed with clean water** may be expressed as "and we, as it were, washed with clean water." In this way one may avoid the suggestion of merely taking a bath. With the expression "as it were," the figurative meaning of the final phrase is clearly marked. However, if the reference is to Christian baptism, **water** will not be figurative, and **clean** may imply "cleansing." In this case it may be possible to translate "our whole selves washed and made clean by a special bath."

10.23   **Let us hold on firmly to the hope we profess, because we can trust God to keep his promise.**

After faith in the previous verse come hope and love respectively, here and in verse 24. These three nouns are linked in various parts of the New Testament, especially 1 Corinthians 13.7,13. If possible they should be dealt with in the same way in translation, to mark the relation between them. For example, if one is translated by a verb, all three should be. The text of KJV, which has "faith" instead of hope, is not to be followed. Both TEV and RSV in different ways lose a little of the meaning by restructuring. The word translated firmly is not an adverb but an adjective modifying hope; and here as in some other passages, hope probably means the objects of hope, not a feeling with which we look to the future. The text therefore probably means "Let us hold on to our confession of (faith in) the unshakable things we hope for." In Hebrews, as in the Old Testament, "faith" and "hope" are very close in meaning.

Let us hold on firmly to the hope may be expressed as "Let us continue to hope firmly" or ". . . strongly." Sometimes this may even be expressed more effectively in a negative form; for example, "Let us not cease to hope for a moment." If, however, the emphasis is to be placed upon "what is hoped for," one may translate "Let us have complete confidence in what we hope for."

Profess is a noun in the Greek, "profession (of hope)," and therefore does not have a tense. Most translations, like TEV, use a verb in the present tense; Brc "the hope which we tell the world we possess." TNT uses a past tense, linking the "profession of hope" with the time of baptism, "the hope which we have professed." This is possible, since verse 22 refers to baptism. However, the following verses speak of Christian living in the present. A wider meaning, including both past and present action, is more likely. TEV brings out the meaning of the second part of the verse, which RSV translates literally. The focus, however, is on God, not on believers: "God, who gave the promises (6.13-19), is to be relied on."

It may be useful to render we profess as a distinct clause, or even a separate sentence related to hope; for example, "this is the hope we have spoken about to others" or "this is the hope which we have said we have confidence in."

Because we can trust God to keep his promise may be rendered as "because we know that God always does what he has promised to do" or ". . . will do what he has promised to do."

10.24   Let us be concerned for one another, to help one another to show love and to do good.

The two parts of this verse are more closely linked than TEV suggests. Be concerned with renders the word translated Think of in 3.1. The verse as a whole means "Let us think how to stimulate one another to show love and do good." Show is implied; love is linked with human action both here and in 6.10. Translations should avoid any word for love which implies a mere emotion.

In place of Let us be concerned it may be clearer to translate "We should be concerned."

The word translated help . . . to show is unusual and strong, suggesting in this context a demonstration of affection.

Love may include love both for fellow Christians and for others. However, verse 25 suggests that the writer is thinking primarily of love within the Christian fellowship. "Brotherly love" in 13.1 is specifically love for fellow Christians. Unfortunately, an expression such as **to show love** might suggest merely outward demonstration of affection. Therefore a more satisfactory rendering of **to show love** may be "to show kindness to one another."

Since **concerned** in the first part of this verse is directly linked to the second part, one may translate the whole verse as "We should be concerned to help one another, to show love for one another, and to do good to one another." **To do good** may be best expressed as "to help one another," provided this phrase was not already used in the first part of this verse.

<u>10.25</u>   **Let us not give up the habit of meeting together, as some are doing. Instead, let us encourage one another all the more, since you see that the Day of the Lord is coming nearer.**

This verse prepares for the warning in verses 26-31. General commentaries discuss what this verse may tell us about the circumstances in which the readers lived. This, however, does not directly concern the translator, and the meaning of the text itself is generally plain.

GeCL reverses the order of the first sentence so as to make the meaning clearer: "Some have formed the habit of staying away from meetings of the Christian community. That is not good; instead, you must rather encourage one another." As in GeCL, it may be better to render the clause **as some are doing** at the beginning of verse 25. **As some are doing** may be more effectively expressed in a negative manner; for example, "some people are not attending the meetings of the congregation." Such a statement may then be followed by a positive exhortation, "but we must go on meeting together."

Encourage: it may be necessary to anticipate the question "Encourage them to do what?" In this case, "give one another courage," "strengthen one another," "cause one another to have courage," or "cause one another to have strong faith" are possible translations. The word may mean "encourage by words," "exhort," as perhaps in 3.13, where RSV has "exhort" and TEV help. JB (not BJ) makes the meaning very specific: "encourage each other to go," implying "to meetings of the community." This is possible since verses 26-31 could be understood as an encouragement not to abandon the Christian community and its faith, because judgment is near (verses 27,30). However, there does not seem sufficient evidence to abandon the wider meaning **encourage** (by word and deed).

The attributive phrase **all the more** may be expressed as "more and more" or "even more than we have done."

Day of the Lord: "Day" is emphasized in Greek as the last word in this long sentence. **Of the Lord** is implied, as it often is in the Old Testament expression meaning "in that day . . . ," for example, Isaiah 2.11 and Jeremiah 39.17 (RSV; see also 1 Cor 3.13). GeCL is still more explicit: "the day on which the Lord comes," understanding "the Lord" as "Jesus," which is probably correct. In some languages it will have to be made explicit whether "Lord" is a reference to "Lord Jesus" or "Lord God." "The day" without some addition is meaningless to most modern readers. Some translations write with a capital letter, "Day," but this does not help when the verse is read aloud. JB and some other translations add a note. Knox, Brc, Syn have "great day"; Phps "final day." In general, the expression **the Day of the Lord** refers to a time of judgment, and this fits the context of verses 26-31. Therefore **the Day of the Lord** may be translated as "the Day when the Lord will judge."

It is often impossible to speak of "a Day coming near," for in most languages days do not move. It is often possible, however, to say "the Day of the Lord is soon," or "the Day of the Lord will soon happen," or "we are very near to the Day of the Lord."

TEV   **10.26-31**   RSV

26 For there is no longer any sacrifice that will take away sins if we purposely go on sinning after the truth has been made known to us. 27 Instead, all that is left is to wait in fear for the coming Judgment and the fierce fire which will destroy those who oppose God! 28 Anyone who disobeys the Law of Moses is put to death without any mercy when judged guilty from the evidence of two or more witnesses. 29 What, then, of the person who despises the Son of God? who treats as a cheap thing the blood of God's covenant which purified him from sin? who insults the Spirit of grace? Just think how much worse is the punishment he will deserve! 30 For we know who said, "I will take revenge, I will repay"; and who also said, "The Lord will judge his people." 31 It is a terrifying thing to fall into the hands of the living God!

26 For if we sin deliberately after receiving the knowledge of the truth, there no longer remains a sacrifice for sins, 27 but a fearful prospect of judgment, and a fury of fire which will consume the adversaries. 28 A man who has violated the law of Moses dies without mercy at the testimony of two or three witnesses. 29 How much worse punishment do you think will be deserved by the man who has spurned the Son of God, and profaned the blood of the covenant by which he was sanctified, and outraged the Spirit of grace? 30 For we know him who said, "Vengeance is mine, I will repay." And again, "The Lord will judge his people." 31 It is a fearful thing to fall into the hands of the living God.

The words all the more in verse 25 are explained and developed in this paragraph, verses 26-31. Its center, verses 28-29, is a "how much more" comparison of the type found, for example, in 2.1-4 and 9.14. This paragraph is similar to 6.4-6 but is more concerned with the coming judgment. The theological difficulties of these verses are perhaps greater than the translation problems they contain, except in verse 28.

10.26   **For there is no longer any sacrifice that will take away sins if we purposely go on sinning after the truth has been made known to us.**

There is no longer any sacrifice, that is, "for us." The writer does not mean that there was once such a sacrifice, but that it exists no longer. This possible misunderstanding occurs because TEV reverses the two halves of the sentence. One solution would be to translate "If deliberately (emphasized) we go on sinning after we have come to know the truth, there is no other sacrifice left which can deal with our sin." Verse 27 would then begin as a new sentence, "As it is, however . . . ."

"Sin-offerings" are the sacrifices to take away sins mentioned in 10.6.

In place of the English construction with an anticipatory particle such as **there,** one may use a somewhat shorter initial clause such as "no sacrifice can any longer take away our sins" or ". . . cause our sins to be forgiven."

The key word of this passage is **purposely,** which is the first word in the Greek sentence; Knox "wilfully"; Brc, TNT "deliberately." On the distinction between deliberate and accidental breaking of the Law, see Numbers 15.25-31. The "sinning" is not only deliberate but repeated or continued, as **go on sinning** shows; similarly NEB "if we persist in sin." **If we purposely go on sinning** may be rendered as "if we decide we want to go on sinning," or "if we make our plans so that we can go on sinning" or ". . . continue to sin."

After the truth has been made known to us: TEV is right to emphasize that "the receiving of the truth" is an event, probably associated with baptism; compare 6.4-5 and 10.22. The **truth** indicates Christian teaching, not "truth" in any general philosophical sense. Phps' "after we have known and accepted the truth" seems on first reading rather more than the text says, but "accepted" may be implied by the fact that knowledge in the Bible includes experience. GeCL has "after we have got to know the truth."

The passive expression **has been made known** in the clause **after the truth has been made known to us** may seem rather weak in some languages, since it might suggest merely "after the truth has been told to us." A more satisfactory expression may be "after we have known what the truth really is" or even "after we have known what the truth of the Good News is."

10.27 **Instead, all that is left is to wait in fear for the coming Judgment and the fierce fire which will destroy those who oppose God**

This verse recalls Isaiah 26.11 in the Septuagint. A literal translation of **all that is left** may be confusing, since it might suggest that something has been "left" in the sense of being abandoned. The meaning is simply "the only thing we can do" or "there is nothing else for us to do but . . . ."

To wait in fear for the coming Judgment repeats in more detail the reference to the "Day" in verse 25. The Greek contains an element of indefiniteness which KJV translates "a certain fearful looking for of judgment." The judgment is certain, but exactly what it will involve is not. The Greek for "fearful" means "causing fear" or "(rightly) to be feared." See also 10.31 and 12.21.

To wait: The noun which RSV translates "**prospect**," and NEB more literally "expectation," is related in form and meaning to the verb translated <u>waits</u> in 10.13 and <u>waiting</u> in 11.10.

The phrase **to wait in fear** may need to be expressed by two verbs; for example, "to wait and to fear" or "while we are waiting, to fear."

For the coming Judgment may be expressed as "God's judging will soon happen" or "the time when God will judge is near."

The fierce fire may be expressed as "the hot fire" or "the very hot fire," but it may be better to speak of the fire in terms of its extent; for example, "the very great fire" or "the exceedingly large fire."

Destroy is literally "eat"; TNT "devour," but clearly in an extended meaning, making **fire** assume the figure of a wild beast.

Those who oppose God may be rendered as "those who are enemies of God" or "those who fight against God." However, the writer avoids the common Greek word for "enemies," except in quotations from the Old Testament; a somewhat milder word such as "**adversaries**" (RSV) may be appropriate in translation. In **those who oppose God**, in the Greek <u>God</u> is implied as in Isaiah 26.11, to which the writer may be referring; Hebrews 10.29 suggests that opposition to Christ may also be included.

10.28   **Anyone who disobeys the Law of Moses is put to death without any mercy when judged guilty from the evidence of two or more witnesses.**

This and the following verses look at the Old Testament, to compare it with the new order. Penalties for breaking the Law of Moses were severe (Deut 17.2-17); the quotation comes from Deuteronomy 17.6; compare Deuteronomy 19.15; 28.15-68.

This apparently simple verse presents a surprising number of translation problems.

The verb translated **disobeys** has a range of meanings from "declare invalid," as in 7.18, to "reject." The word for **disobeys** is a strong word, used not of incidental sins, but of breaking the whole covenant (Ezek 22.26), for example, by idolatry (Deut 17.2-7), false prophecy (Deut 18.20), or blasphemy (Lev 24.13-16). In order to emphasize the willful disobedience involved in **disobeys,** it may be well to translate the first part of verse 28 as "Anyone who refuses to obey the laws given through Moses" or "If a person refuses to obey the Law of Moses."

The main verb, meaning **is put to death** or "dies," is in the present tense. It is uncertain whether, even before the destruction of Jerusalem in A.D. 70, Jewish courts had the legal right to inflict the death penalty. People were sometimes lynched, as in Acts 7.57-60, but that is a different matter. The writer is generally more interested in the earlier history of Israel than in current events. Here he is concerned with what the Law demanded, not with how it was applied in his own time. In any case, the verb for **is put to death** is part of a free quotation. It may therefore be better to translate **is put to death** as "was put to death." In some instances, however, it may be necessary to change the passive **is put to death** into an active form, and therefore to introduce "the authorities" or "the officials"; for example, "the authorities put him to death" or "the officials executed him."

The phrase **without any mercy** may be expressed in some languages as an entirely separate clause; for example, "they did not at all show mercy" or "they did not think twice when they put him to death."

The **witnesses** should not be emphasized in this verse, but will come into focus in 12.1.

When judged guilty from the evidence of two or more witnesses may best be expressed as a conditional clause; for example, "if two or more witnesses gave evidence against the person and as a result he was judged guilty."

It may be necessary in some languages to specify what was involved in being witnesses; for example, "if two or more persons saw what the man did and told about it, and if then the man was judged to be guilty."

10.29   **What, then, of the person who despises the Son of God? who treats as a cheap thing the blood of God's covenant which purified him from sin? who insults the Spirit of grace? Just think how much worse is the punishment he will deserve!**

This second half of the "how much more" comparison identifies three aspects of the same sin, not three separate sins. This sin is a deliberate turning away from faith in Christ (verse 26).

There are four possible ways to punctuate, the first two of which are essentially the same. (a) TEV makes three separate questions which are not linked by "and." (b) The UBS Greek New Testament, like RSV and several other translations, punctuates this sentence as a single question, "How much more . . . ?" (c) Other editions and translations take it as a statement: TNT "Think how much severer punishment a man will deserve . . ."; or (d) an exclamation, as in TEV. The choice between these possibilities depends on what is most natural in the receptor language. It makes little difference to the meaning, since the question, in any case, is rhetorical.

Despises is a nonfigurative translation of a vivid metaphor meaning "tramples underfoot." In the Old Testament the phrase for "trample underfoot" is used literally, of cities, buildings (Isa 26.5), or even people (Dan 8.10); it is used also in the weakened metaphorical sense of "show great contempt for" (Micah 7.10; Mal 4.3; Psa 56.1-2). TEV, probably correctly, understands "trample underfoot" to have a metaphorical sense here (compare Phps "poured scorn on," GeCL similarly). If the metaphor is common in the receptor language and has the same meaning as in Greek, it should be kept, as in many translations. Otherwise, the translator should consider using a different but equivalent metaphor, or a nonfigurative expression. The translator must decide how natural the metaphor sounds in his own language, and whether it will be understood as a metaphor. In some languages the equivalent figurative expression for "trample underfoot" is "to throw away," or "to cast aside," or "to consider as rubbish."

The Son of God: the thought recalls 6.6, but the wording of this verse is different.

The three rhetorical questions in verse 29 are incomplete in themselves. Even the first question, **What, then, of the person who despises the Son of God?** contains no main verb, and in some languages it is essential to fill out the question, "What then is likely to happen to the person who despises the Son of God?" It may then be possible to introduce the following two question fragments as essentially appositional to the first question; for example, "to the person who treats as a cheap thing . . . ?" "to the person who insults the Spirit of grace?"

The second aspect of the "unforgivable sin" depends on the biblical distinction between what was "holy" or fit for use in worship, and what was "common" and therefore not to be used in worship, or even generally by the people of Israel, who were themselves a "holy" people. See comments on 3.1, and compare Acts 10.14. In some parts of the world, this distinction is not recognized. For this reason TEV translates the expression for "thinks common" as **treats as a cheap thing.** Translations in other (especially non-Western) languages may be able to express more directly the distinction between what is ritually holy and what is common, even in a common language translation. It is necessary to avoid in translation any word for "holy" which implies belonging to an evil or destructive supernatural power. If one follows the meaning **who treats as a cheap thing,** one may employ an expression such as "who considers as worthless" or "who thinks of something as being of no value."

The **covenant** is, of course, the new covenant. The **blood** is Christ's sacrifice of himself. **God's** is implied. See comments on **covenant** in 7.22. The relationship between **the blood** and **God's covenant** may need to be made more explicit; for example, "the blood which was involved in establishing God's covenant." However, in languages in which **blood** cannot be used as a symbol for death, it may be possible to render **the blood of God's covenant** as "the sacrificial death of Christ which established God's covenant."

The clause **which purified him from sin** is a reference to **the blood,** and it may be necessary to express this as a separate clause; for example, "the blood is what purified him from sin" or "Christ's sacrificial death caused him to be free from guilt."

Insults may be expressed as "to speak against" or "to say bad words against." Most languages have a number of words for verbal insulting.

GeCL makes explicit the probable meaning of **the Spirit of grace:** "the Spirit from whom he received grace," or more literally "to whom he is indebted for grace." On (Holy) **Spirit,** see comments on "wind" and "spirit" in 1.7; on **grace,** see comments on 2.9. **The Spirit of grace** may be rendered as "the Spirit that shows us loving kindness."

In view of the fact that **punishment** is so often expressed as a verb, the final statement of verse 29 may be rendered as "Just think how much more that person will deserve to be punished," or "Just consider how much more that person deserves to have God punish him" or ". . . cause him to suffer."

10.30   **For we know who said, "I will take revenge, I will repay"; and who also said, "The Lord will judge his people."**

We, that is, the writer and his first readers, **know** that God was the speaker in Deuteronomy 32.35-36 (compare Psa 135.14 and Rom 12.19). However, some present-day receptors may not know this, or at least may be puzzled for a moment. To make the meaning plain for modern readers, SpCL translates "We know that the Lord (God) has said . . . ."

In other places where the writer divides a quotation taken from the Old Testament, the result is to emphasize the last part of the quotation. This may be the case here. If so, the implied meaning will be "God will take revenge, not only on his adversaries in other nations (see verse 27), but also, indeed especially, on his own people." This would fit the context well, since the rest of the chapter is concerned with the Christian community.[3]

If this explanation is correct, translators will need to find some way of emphasizing the second part of the quotation, perhaps by expanding the words which introduce it (literally, **"And again"** [RSV], as for example in the Greek of 1.5). The translation of the introductions to the quotations in 5.5,6 may serve as a model; there the meaning is "God calls Christ not only his Son, but also a priest . . . ."

The introductions to both parts of the quotation in 10.30 may need expansion for other reasons also. **We know who said** may be rendered "we know who it was who said," "we know that it was the Lord who said" or ". . . that it was God who said." The word for **know** suggests knowledge of facts, not in this context knowledge of people. Similarly, **and who also said** may be translated "we also know who it was who said."

The meaning of the first quotation may need expansion; for example, "I will pay you back for the wrong you have done," or if there is any danger of "pay back" being misunderstood as referring to compensation or reward, "I will certainly make you suffer for the evil you have done."

In its Old Testament context, the second quotation means "The Lord will prove his people right," but **The Lord will judge his people** is certainly how the writer of Hebrews understands the Old Testament text. In some languages this must be adjusted to "I will judge my people," since God is the assumed speaker.

10.31   **It is a terrifying thing to fall into the hands of the living God**

Terrifying renders the same Greek word which was translated to wait in fear in verse 27. It does not mean in general terms "something very bad," but specifically "a thing to be feared."

---

[3] It is likely that the existing Hebrew text of Deuteronomy 32.35, and followed in Hebrews and Romans 12.19, is an abbreviation of the original "in the day of judgment," preserved in the Septuagint and other witnesses.

To fall into the hands of simply means "to come under the power of," or "to be subjected to," or "to be controlled by."

The living God, in English and some other languages, is a rather conventional biblical phrase which is best avoided in a modern translation. GeCL first edition had "God is alive; to fall into his hands is fearful!" (also in 9.14). Compare 3.12; 12.22.

It may be necessary to restructure the items in this verse; for example, "To have the living God get control of a person is something to be greatly feared." The suggestion of some degree of hostile control may be expressed as "If the living God grabs hold of a person . . ." or "If the living God catches a person . . . ."

TEV   **10.32-39**   RSV

TEV	RSV

32 Remember how it was with you in the past. In those days, after God's light had shone on you, you suffered many things, yet were not defeated by the struggle. 33 You were at times publicly insulted and mistreated, and at other times you were ready to join those who were being treated in this way. 34 You shared the sufferings of prisoners, and when all your belongings were seized, you endured your loss gladly, because you knew that you still possessed something much better, which would last forever. 35 Do not lose your courage, then, because it brings with it a great reward. 36 You need to be patient, in order to do the will of God and receive what he promises. 37 For, as the scripture says,
 	
"Just a little while longer,
  and he who is coming will
    come;
  he will not delay.
38 My righteous people, however,
    will believe and live;
  but if any of them turns back,
  I will not be pleased with him."
39 We are not people who turn back and are lost. Instead, we have faith and are saved.
	32 But recall the former days when, after you were enlightened, you endured a hard struggle with sufferings, 33 sometimes being publicly exposed to abuse and affliction, and sometimes being partners with those so treated. 34 For you had compassion on the prisoners, and you joyfully accepted the plundering of your property, since you knew that you yourselves had a better possession and an abiding one. 35 Therefore do not throw away your confidence, which has a great reward. 36 For you have need of endurance, so that you may do the will of God and receive what is promised.
	37 "For yet a little while,
	    and the coming one shall come
	      and shall not tarry;
	38 but my righteous one shall live by
	     faith,
	   and if he shrinks back,
	   my soul has no pleasure in him."
	39 But we are not of those who shrink back and are destroyed, but of those who have faith and keep their souls.

This section, verses 32-39, is related to other parts of the letter in two main ways. First, it contains a positive message which contrasts with the stern warning of verses 26-31. Second, it prepares the way for chapters 11 and for 12.1-4 by the forward-looking message of verses 35b-38, and by the reference to struggle and public exposure in verses 32-33, which are related to the idea of running a race in 12.1 (see comments on these verses).

The structure of this section is generally clear and simple. Verses 32-34 look back to the time immediately following the readers' conversion to Christianity. Verse 35 forms a bridge between past (**Do not lose**) and future (**a great reward**). Verses 36-38 reemphasize the Christian hope, with the help of quotations from the Old Testament. Verse 39 is a summing up which also introduces the key word of the next chapter, **faith.**

10.32   Remember how it was with you in the past. In those days, after God's light had shone on you, you suffered many things, yet were not defeated by the struggle.

RSV's "But" marks the contrast between warning (verses 26-31) and encouragement. The imperative **Remember** suggests that the readers are being asked to make some effort to recall earlier times. Many translations have "**recall**" (RSV) or some equivalent; Brc "Cast your minds back." "**Former**" (RSV) simply means "earlier than the present," hence **in the past**. The closest equivalent of **Remember** in this type of context may be simply "think about." But **how it was with you** may be "what happened to you." **In the past** may be expressed as "before" or "before now."

In those days is added in TEV to link the two sentences; it is literally "in which," implying "days." A literal rendering of **In those days** may be too specific; "Then" or "At that time" may be better.

After God's light had shone on you translates a single word for "having been enlightened." The passive indicates the action of God, and "**enlightened**" (RSV) refers here, as in 6.4, to a single act, probably becoming a Christian and being baptized. The writer certainly does not mean that the readers were "enlightened" in the past but are now in "darkness." The meaning in nonfigurative terms is "when you first became Christians," "when you first came to understand the Good News," or "when you first believed the Good News."

The meaning of the last part of the verse is very compressed. TEV uses eleven English words to translate four Greek ones; literally "you-endured much struggle of-sufferings." The picture is that of an athlete engaged in some kind of hard competition, perhaps a race (compare 12.1), or possibly a wrestling match. Who the other competitors are is not stated; the main idea is that of struggle and hardship. This struggle is made necessary by what the readers **suffered**. Yet despite their suffering, the readers had not given up the struggle or abandoned their faith. **You suffered many things** may be translated "you suffered much."

Not defeated expresses negatively what the Greek, followed by RSV, states positively by "endured." The meaning is not simply that the readers suffered without complaint, but as TEV makes clear, that they still survived as Christians when the sufferings had done their worst. 12.4 states that martyrdom had not been involved, so **suffered** here does not mean "died," as it does for example in 2.18.

[241]

Yet were not defeated by the struggle may be expressed as "but the struggle did not defeat you," or "but even though you struggled, you did not give up" or ". . . you continued strong."

10.33   **You were at times publicly insulted and mistreated, and at other times you were ready to join those who were being treated in this way.**

The two halves of this verse are clearly distinguished by the words trans-lated **at times . . . at other times.** These are not strictly expressions of time, but express two different aspects of the new converts' behavior. On the one hand, sufferings (being **publicly insulted and mistreated**) were imposed upon them; on the other hand, they willingly shared other peoples' sufferings. GeCL distinguishes, not two **times,** but two "groups" among the readers: "Some were publicly insulted and mistreated, and the others joined with them." This makes good sense, since the writer is speaking of a single "time," when the readers first became Christians.

At times may be rendered as "on some occasions" or "there were occasions when."

The metaphor of athletic competition is continued in this verse. The word for **publicly insulted** contains the Greek word for "theater," suggesting a public entertainment, though not yet the idea of Christians being killed by lions in an arena (see 12.4).

The adverb **publicly** may often be rendered by a clause, "while people looked on" or "in the presence of many people who were there."

Insulted translates a noun which TEV translates scorn in 11.26, and shame in 13.13. It is closely linked with **mistreated;** the same events, or at least the same group of events, were both insults and ill-treatment. In place of the passive **You were . . . insulted and mistreated,** it is possible to use an active form, "people spoke bad words against you and caused you to suffer."

At other times may be rendered as "on other occasions" or "on other days."

As RSV shows, **ready to** is not in the Greek. It is added to make it clear that the readers had shared one another's sufferings willingly. It is important to avoid the suggestion that the readers were merely "ready" but did not actually "join." Therefore **you were ready to join those who were being treated in this way** may be rendered as "you willingly joined those who were being insulted and mis-treated" or ". . . whom people spoke against and caused to suffer."

10.34   **You shared the sufferings of prisoners, and when all your be-longings were seized, you endured your loss gladly, because you knew that you still possessed something much better, which would last forever.**

The text of this verse is uncertain at three points.

(a) Modern translations have **prisoners,** but some manuscripts have "bonds," or as in KJV "my bonds." It is easy to understand that this would be popular when Paul was thought to be the writer of this letter, but **prisoners** is more likely to be correct.

(b) **You still possessed:** some manuscripts, followed by KJV, have "in yourselves" instead of "**yourselves**" (RSV). Early editions of TEV, but not other CLTs, followed manuscripts which have "for yourselves." The fourth edition of TEV adopts the reading of the UBS Greek New Testament, "yourselves," to give the translation **you still possessed.** "**Yourselves**" is not emphasized here.

(c) Some manuscripts, followed by the first but not the revised edition of Phps, add "in Heaven" at the end of the verse.

"**For**" (RSV) at the beginning of this verse shows that it expands and supports the last statement in verse 33. **Shared the sufferings of** renders the verb which in 4.15 was translated feel sympathy for. See comment on that verse.

In rendering **You shared the suffering of prisoners,** it is important to indicate that the readers actually suffered themselves. Unfortunately, in some languages the verb meaning **shared** suggests distributing or handing out something, and therefore by implication causing others to suffer. It is possible to translate **You shared the suffering of prisoners** as "You suffered along with prisoners" or "You joined with prisoners in their sufferings."

Prisoners is literally, as in RSV, "**the prisoners.**" Since no prisoners have been mentioned before, the writer is probably referring to prisoners whom he and his first readers knew well. The context suggests that they were Christians. Modern readers do not know these people, so TEV omits "the." If **prisoners** sounds too general (as if the readers visited everyone in the public prisons), some such expression as "those who had been put in prison" may be used.

All before **your belongings** is implied. It is not clear whether the readers' **belongings** were **seized** by the authorities, as Mft's "confiscation" suggests, or by a mob, as in JB "being stripped of your belongings." If the first alternative is chosen, it may be useful to translate **when all your belongings were seized** as "when the authorities seized all that you owned" or "when the officials took away from you what was yours." The word for **seized** implies violence or force, whether or not backed by legal authority.

The word here translated **endured** is not as strong as the word which RSV translates "endured" in verse 32. Here the meaning is "**accepted**" (RSV), and this idea is developed in the second part of the verse. In rendering **you endured your loss gladly,** it is important to avoid the impression that the people were happy to have lost their belongings. The implication is that the persons in question put up with the loss and continued to be joyful.

There is an obscurity in the clause **because you knew that you still possessed something much better.** This could be misinterpreted to mean that the persons in question had been able to hide their better possessions and thus avoid the seizure of them. It is possible to interpret these better possessions as treasures laid up in heaven, but the reference is to the "promises of God" which have been mentioned in preceding passages and will be mentioned again in verse 36. It may therefore be possible to translate the latter part of verse 34 as "because you knew that you still possessed the things which God promised, which are much better and which last forever."

Forever is implied. The phrase **which would last forever** is literally "remaining," that is, after the upheaval of the final judgment (see 12.27 and 13.14).

10.35   Do not lose your courage, then, because it brings with it a great reward.

Lose is literally "**throw away**" (RSV), not simply "mislay," but "discard as something worthless." **Do not lose your courage** may be rendered as "Do not give up" or "Do not cease to have confidence when you face opposition." In 4.16; 10.19, the same Greek term is used to mean "confidence in approaching God."

Then, literally "**Therefore**" (RSV), draws a conclusion from what has just been said: "You have shown yourselves to be good Christians so far; so do not give up now." The equivalent of **then** in the sense of "Therefore" is usually clearer if it is placed at the beginning of the verse.

On **reward**, see comments on 2.2 and 11.26. The **reward** is closely related to God's promise, discussed in detail in 6.12-20, and which will be mentioned in the next verse, and again in 11.9,13,17,33,39.

Brings with it is literally "has," not "will have"; the reward is so close in the future, as the following verses emphasize, that it is almost present. The pronoun **it** (which occurs twice) relates to **courage**, but it may be impossible to speak of "courage bringing something." Therefore it may be necessary to modify the second clause of this verse as "because if you continue to have courage, you will receive a great reward."

10.36   You need to be patient, in order to do the will of God and receive what he promises.

You need strongly suggests that the readers do not at present have the necessary endurance to carry them through to the end, so the meaning is "you lack," "you still need." See 5.12. The meaning of **need**, in the sense of lack as well as obligation, may be expressed by a modal form equivalent to "must"; for example, "You must be patient," implying both the necessity of being patient in the future, as well as the implied lack of it in the present.

To be patient translates a noun related to the verb for "endure" used in verse 32 (see RSV). Verse 34 uses a different Greek word for endured. "Waiting" is suggested in the verses which follow. This is not a passive attitude of mind, but an active refusal to let go of one's faith.

TEV does not make any explicit link between **be patient, do the will of God,** and **receive what he promises.** The most likely connection is that "patience" or "endurance" is a necessary condition for "doing the will of God," and "doing the will of God" must come before "receiving what he promises." Brc brings this out well with "What you need is the power to see things through. If you have that, you will obey the will of God, and so receive what he has promised." **What he promises** is literally "the promise," but **God** has just been mentioned and is thus clearly implied. Similarly, **the will of God** implies an event and may be translated "what God wants (you to do)." On **the will of God**, see comments on 10.10. The purpose clause in this verse may be rendered in some languages as "in order to do what God wants you to do and in this way obtain what he promises to give you." This indicates the relation between the various elements in the purpose clause.

10.37-38 **For, as the scripture says,**
> **"Just a little while longer,**
> > **and he who is coming will come;**
> > **he will not delay.**
> **38** **My righteous people, however, will believe and live;**
> > **but if any of them turns back,**
> > **I will not be pleased with him."**

As the scripture says is implied. Some such phrase is necessary, even when this passage is read aloud, to show that it includes a quotation from the Old Testament. The first line of the quotation in TEV comes from Isaiah 26.20, and the rest from Habakkuk 2.3-4, part of which is also quoted in Romans 1.17 and Galatians 3.11. As usual, the writer quotes rather freely from the Septuagint. Often one cannot translate **as the scripture says** literally, since scriptures do not "speak." One can, however, employ an expression such as "as one may read in the Scriptures" or "according to the words of the holy writings."

Just a little while longer may be expressed as "In a very short time" or "Not long from now," or even "Soon."

The key words, for Hebrews as for Paul, are **righteous** (see 11.4,7,33; 12.11,23, where this or related Greek words are used) and "faith" (TEV **believe**).[4] The writer of Hebrews emphasizes the future aspect of the text by quoting Habakkuk 2.3, as well as verse 4.

He who is coming will come: the writer emphasizes this by adding a definite article: "the one who is coming." It may seem odd and repetitious to say "the one who is coming will come." It may be better, therefore, to render this clause as "the one who is coming will arrive."

He will not delay may be rendered as "he will not be long in coming."

---

[4] The meaning of the text as quoted here must be confused neither with the meaning of the Hebrew and Greek texts of Habakkuk, nor with the meaning which Paul gives to the text. Habakkuk's message was that in the time of crisis which was coming, anyone who was "righteous," that is, who did God's will as expressed in the Law, would survive. For Paul the meaning is very different: those who have the kind of "righteousness," or "being right with God," which comes from relying on God through faith in Christ, not from obeying the letter of the Law, will experience what life really is.

The translation of verse 38a is complicated by a textual problem. TEV, RSV, and most translations follow the UBS Greek text. Other manuscripts have "the righteous by faith," sometimes with "in me" added. These texts are influenced by the text of the Septuagint, and possibly by Paul, and are not likely to be correct.

My righteous people is literally "My righteous (one)," grammatically singular, as in most translations except TEV and DuCL. However, **any of them** later in the sentence shows that the meaning is "anyone who has a right relationship with me," and TEV brings this out. The writer of Hebrews emphasizes at various points his concern for each one of his readers, but always addresses them as a group; he does not mention individuals by name. TEV means "my righteous nation." However, the transition from **my righteous people** (singular) to **any of them** (plural) and then back to the singular **him** may be awkward in some languages. If so, it may be best to use plural expressions throughout, since the author is certainly referring to more than one righteous individual.

The emphasis of the expression **My righteous people** is that these are people who do God's will. In a sense, therefore, **My righteous people** implies "My people who do what I want them to do."

However is literally "but" (RSV), and **but** in the next line is literally "and," as in RSV. The word translated **however** is less emphatic than "however" in English. The word translated "**and**" in RSV may in some contexts indicate a contrast, like the English **but**. It is necessary to see where contrasts are indicated or suggested in this passage. The general direction of the argument suggests that there is no contrast between Christ's coming, and God's people believing and living; but that there is a contrast between believing and living on the one hand, and turning back on the other hand. So GeCL translates "The person who trusts me and remains true to me can stand before me and will live. But the person who loses his courage, I will have nothing to do with him" (similarly DuCL, ItCL).

It is sometimes necessary to have some complement to a verb such as **will believe**. The tendency for some translators is to expand **will believe** to "will believe the Good News." But the correct interpretation of **will believe** involves trusting in God, and therefore **will believe** may be rendered as "will trust me."

Since **and live** indicates the result of trusting, it may be possible to render **and live** as "and so live."

The TNT note indicates that "faith" is stressed. This is not obvious from the form of the Greek sentence, but it is clear from the wider context (verse 39 and chapter 11). TNT accordingly translates "It is by faith that my righteous one shall live."

For the writer of Hebrews, though not in Habakkuk, the last part of this verse is spoken by God. As a comparison with RSV shows, **any of them** is implied. In English **any** may be either singular or plural, and the last part of this verse may very well be rendered as "if any turn back, I will not be pleased with them." Certainly the implication is for more than one person being likely to turn back. The Greek verb for **turns** is singular, but refers to any one of a group of people, so a plural verb is often clearer in translation.

The metaphor of **turns back** may be related to thinking of the Christian life as "the Way" (see Acts 9.2); or it may mean "draws back" in fear, "shrinks back" (NEB), with a meaning similar to the term for "looking back" in Luke 9.62. The meaning "draw back from involvement in the world" has been suggested but does not seem to fit in with the message of the letter as a whole.

In some languages the idea of "turning back" would not be a natural figure of speech to describe giving up one's faith. "To turn back" may simply be equivalent to "turning around." Therefore **if any of them turns back** may be rendered as "if any refuse to follow me further," or "if any give up trusting in me," or "if any no longer trust me."

TEV is right to understand "my soul" as equivalent to **I**, but the Greek for **I will not be pleased with him** is the climax of the quotation. The language is similar to that of Luke 2.14b (peace on earth to those with whom he is pleased!). The thought of God being "pleased" with people is closely linked with the idea of his "choosing" them for particular tasks; see 10.6,8.

10.39 **We are not people who turn back and are lost. Instead, we have faith and are saved.**

This verse applies verse 38 to the readers' situation. TEV omits "**But**" (see RSV) to avoid repetition of the but in verse 38.

There is an alternation of positive and negative statements. Verse 38, line 1 (in TEV and RSV) is positive, and lines 2-3 of that verse are negative. Verse 39 includes a negative statement, but is generally positive and brings this part of the letter to a strong conclusion.

We is emphatic; BJ and other French translations have "as for us . . ."; SpCL means "we are not among those who turn back." The Greek is literally "we are not of falling back . . . , but of faith." This means "we do not belong to the group (or kind) of people who fall back . . . , but to the group (or kind) of people who go on believing . . . ." More concisely, one might translate "We are not the kind of people . . . ."

The rendering of **who turn back** in verse 39 will depend upon how the similar expression is translated in verse 38.

And are lost is the result of **turn back**. Accordingly, one may translate **and are lost** as "and so are lost." In some languages, however, the expression "to be lost" has nothing to do with a person's spiritual state, and therefore it may be better to translate **and are lost** as "and so perish" or "and so suffer destruction."

The second half of the verse, from **Instead,** is similar to the first in form, though opposite in meaning. "**But**" (see RSV) is emphasized in the Greek; "on the contrary." TEV omits "**souls**" (RSV) for two reasons: first, because the English word is not much used outside church circles; and secondly, because it could be misunderstood as a distinct part of the personality. **Saved** does not translate the Greek word most commonly used; it means rather "keep," implying "keep safe from attack." Neither TEV nor RSV makes any explicit connection between **turn back** and **are lost,** and between **have faith** and **are saved.** "As a result" is implied in both parts of the verse.

[247]

In order to show the proper relation between **we have faith** and **are saved,** it is possible to translate "we trust God and so are saved," or ". . . and so he saves us," or ". . . and so he rescues us."

Chapter 11

Faith

1 To have faith is to be sure of the things we hope for, to be certain of the things we cannot see. 2 It was by their faith that people of ancient times won God's approval.

3 It is by faith that we understand that the universe was created by God's word, so that what can be seen was made out of what cannot be seen.

4 It was faith that made Abel offer to God a better sacrifice than Cain's. Through his faith he won God's approval as a righteous man, because God himself approved of his gifts. By means of his faith Abel still speaks, even though he is dead.

5 It was faith that kept Enoch from dying. Instead, he was taken up to God, and nobody could find him, because God had taken him up. The scripture says that before Enoch was taken up, he had pleased God. 6 No one can please God without faith, for whoever comes to God must have faith that God exists and rewards those who seek him.

7 It was faith that made Noah hear God's warnings about things in the future that he could not see. He obeyed God and built a boat in which he and his family were saved. As a result, the world was condemned, and Noah received from God the righteousness that comes by faith.

8 It was faith that made Abraham obey when God called him to go out to a country which God had promised to give him. He left his own country

1 Now faith is the assurance of things hoped for, the conviction of things not seen. 2 For by it the men of old received divine approval. 3 By faith we understand that the world was created by the word of God, so that what is seen was made out of things which do not appear.

4 By faith Abel offered to God a more acceptable sacrifice than Cain, through which he received approval as righteous, God bearing witness by accepting his gifts; he died, but through his faith he is still speaking. 5 By faith Enoch was taken up so that he should not see death; and he was not found, because God had taken him. Now before he was taken he was attested as having pleased God. 6 And without faith it is impossible to please him. For whoever would draw near to God must believe that he exists and that he rewards those who seek him. 7 By faith Noah, being warned by God concerning events as yet unseen, took heed and constructed an ark for the saving of his household; by this he condemned the world and became an heir of the righteousness which comes by faith.

8 By faith Abraham obeyed when he was called to go out to a place which he was to receive as an inheritance; and he went out, not knowing where he was to go. 9 By faith he sojourned in the land of promise, as in a foreign land, living in tents with Isaac and Jacob, heirs with him of the same promise. 10 For

without knowing where he was going. 9 By faith he lived as a foreigner in the country that God had promised him. He lived in tents, as did Isaac and Jacob, who received the same promise from God. 10 For Abraham was waiting for the city which God has designed and built, the city with permanent foundations.

11 It was faith that made Abraham able to become a father, even though he was too old and Sarah herself could not have children. He^g trusted God to keep his promise. 12 Though Abraham was practically dead, from this one man came as many descendants as there are stars in the sky, as many as the numberless grains of sand on the seashore.

he looked forward to the city which has foundations, whose builder and maker is God. 11 By faith Sarah herself received power to conceive, even when she was past the age, since she considered him faithful who had promised. 12 Therefore from one man, and him as good as dead, were born descendants as many as the stars of heaven and as the innumerable grains of sand by the seashore.

^{g} It was faith . . . children. He; *some manuscripts have* It was faith that made Sarah herself able to conceive, even though she was too old to have children. She.

This chapter is the best-known part of Hebrews and generally the easiest to understand. It is also to some extent different from anything else in the letter. It has something in common with Stephen's summary of Old Testament history in Acts 7.2-53. However, since Hebrews is addressed to Christians and not to non-Christian Jews, the theme of Israel's disobedience is not emphasized. The comments on the last section showed how the subject of patient endurance, discussed in 10.32-39, is taken up again in chapter 12. Nevertheless chapter 11 also has links with the rest of the letter. It may be compared with the passages on Moses in 3.1-6 and Melchizedek in 7.1-19, which strengthen the argument by evidence drawn from the Old Testament. In those passages, however, the Old Testament was quoted in order to show that Jesus is unique and supreme. In this chapter, as 12.1-4 will show, the purpose is rather to encourage the readers to hold on to their faith in him. Similar lists are found in Wisdom of Solomon 10 and Sirach 44—50.

The chapter may be divided into a general statement about faith (verses 1-2), two series of examples (verses 3-12 and 17-38), a general comment (verses 13-16), and a short conclusion (verses 39-40) which also introduces the application in chapter 12. In this Handbook, additional divisions are made for convenience at verses 23 and 32.

Instead of the TEV section heading **Faith**, it may be more appropriate to use a clause; for example, "How people trusted God" or "How people in ancient times trusted God."

11.1   To have faith is to be sure of the things we hope for, to be certain of the things we cannot see.

RSV's **"Now"** has nothing to do with time; it indicates a new step in the argument. On the key word **faith**, see comments on 4.2. GeCL, alone among the CLTs, usually avoids the noun for **faith**, because the translators did not feel that it belonged to common language. **Faith** may also suggest a body of teaching rather than a relationship with God; this would be quite unsuitable for a chapter full of examples of faith expressed in action. **To have faith** or "to trust God" shows that "faith" is an event, not an object. For example, GeCL begins the verses which are to follow with "because we trust God" (verse 3), "because Abel trusted God" (verse 4), "because Moses' parents trusted God" (verse 23), "because the Israelites trusted God" (verses 29-30). In several places the subject of the verb "trusted" is implicit. However, nowhere in this chapter is there any doubt that God is the one who is "trusted." See Appendix C: "The Translation of 'Faith.' "

To be sure: the Greek word which RSV translates **"assurance"** has been understood in three ways:

(a) From early times, some translators and commentators have thought it had the meaning "substance" or "underlying reality" which it has in 1.3 (God's own being). This interpretation is chosen by KJV "substance"; Knox and NEB text "gives substance to our hopes."

(b) Most translations understand the word as **"assurance"** or **"conviction"**: RSV and NEB footnote "assurance"; Phps "full confidence"; NAB "confident assurance"; or verbal expressions like **to be sure**; Mft "we are confident."

(c) Some French translations have "guarantee," perhaps because "the word was often used in legal documents of the time for the title-deeds of a piece of property" (TNT note); Seg, BJ; TOB "faith is a way of already possessing what one hopes for"; JB "Only faith can guarantee the blessings that we hope for."

A suggested translation would be "Those who trust God are sure that he will give them what they hope for; they are certain that things they do not yet see are real." Like TEV and RSV, this translation generally follows (b). "God" and "that he will give them" are implied. There is no "and" before "certain," since the meaning of the second half of the sentence largely overlaps with that of the first, expressing the same thought in terms of space rather than time. "And" before "certain" would suggest that the writer intends to make a new statement in the second half of the verse.

The word which RSV translates **"conviction"** (**to be certain**) is not used anywhere else in the New Testament. It probably refers to objective "proof" rather than to subjective "conviction," but the writer may have intended both these aspects. In any case, "proof" in chapter 11 as a whole is not logical demonstration but evidence used for convincing people of the truth.

The word translated **things** is even more general in meaning in Greek, since it can cover both events and objects; "certain of what we cannot see."

It is not always possible to employ an infinitive phrase such as **To have faith** as the subject of a sentence in which the predicate, **to be sure of the things we hope for,** equals the subject. In many languages there is no way in which one can employ such verbal expressions as subject and predicate of an equational sentence, that is, one which states that the predicate equals the subject. In reality, **To have faith** indicates a condition, and therefore the closest equivalent of the TEV construction would be a conditional clause; for example, "If we have faith." Such a condition can be easily combined with the rest of verse 1: "If we have faith, we can be sure of what we hope for, and we can be completely certain of what we cannot see." In place of "If we have faith" one may employ "If we trust God."

If one wishes to emphasize the certainty suggested in the second part of this verse, it is possible to translate "we can be absolutely certain," or express negatively "there is no reason at all for us to doubt."

11.2   It was by their faith that people of ancient times won God's approval.

RSV's "**For**" underlines the fact that faith is not simply a subjective feeling of certainty but, as in 6.12, has an active role in salvation. The Greek shows that RSV's "**by it**" means **by . . . faith.**

People of ancient times means essentially the same as our ancestors in 1.1, not KJV's "the elders," which suggests ordination. The rest of the chapter, especially verses 3-12, shows that "**men**" (RSV) of this period are mainly in the writer's mind, but "women" are not excluded; see comments on verse 11, and compare verses 31,35. GeCL specifies "exemplary people of earlier times," and this is certainly implied.

Won God's approval is literally "were witnessed (to)," but verse 4 makes it clear that God is the one giving a favorable judgment. The meaning may more precisely be "God speaking in scripture."

In the Greek, **faith** is related to **God's approval** by an expression of means, but it may have to be expressed as a cause; for example, "Because people of ancient times trusted God, they won his approval."

It may be difficult to translate **won God's approval** literally. This can, however, be made a causative expression, "caused God to approve of them" or "did what caused God to approve of them." The causative is not, however, essential for the meaning; for example, "Because people of ancient times trusted God, he approved of them" or ". . . he showed that he was happy with them."

11.3   It is by faith that we understand that the universe was created by God's word, so that what can be seen was made out of what cannot be seen.

This verse is the first example of the general statement in verse 1. It is, however, of a different kind from all the other examples, and for this reason CLTs, following the UBS Greek New Testament, make it a separate paragraph.

As in verse 2, the expression **It is by faith** may be restructured as cause; for example, "Because we have faith, we understand . . ." or "Because we trust God, we understand . . . ."

Understand is not emphasized, but the use of this word shows that in Hebrews "faith" is not opposed to "understanding"; the two belong together.

This verse contains two examples of the need to choose clearly between alternative meanings of a word. The Greek word for **created** sometimes means "repaired," and the word for **the universe** sometimes means "the ages," but these choices would obviously be wrong here.

The Greek term for **word**, as in 1.3, usually means a spoken rather than a written word, and this is so here; see Genesis 1.3 and Psalm 33.6,9. However, there is no sharp distinction between the two Greek terms for **word** which are used in Hebrews: (a) in 1.3; 6.5; and here; and (b) in 4.12 and 13.7.

The statement **we understand that the universe was created by God's word** may be restructured; for example, "we understand that God used his word to create the universe" or ". . . the heavens and earth." It is also possible to render **the universe was created by God's word** as "God spoke and in this way created the universe."

So that probably means "with the result that," not "in order that"; it is an expression of result rather than purpose.

TEV uses **seen** twice to translate two different Greek words, used for the sake of variety but having the same meaning.

Was made implies "and still exists," like the English "came into being," but there is no emphasis, as there is in 1.3, on the idea of God's "maintaining" or "upholding" the universe by his "word."

TEV and RSV agree in taking the Greek word for **"not"** with **"appear"** (**cannot be seen**), to give the paraphrase "To say that the world came into being by God's word is to say that the visible world was made out of something which cannot be seen." It is grammatically possible, but less likely, to link "not" with the whole clause, to give the meaning "it was not out of the world of visible things that the visible world came into being."

The most probable text means **what can be seen** (singular), though the Greek for **what cannot be seen** is plural (so RSV). The change is probably made only for the sake of variety, but TEV and GeCL use parallel expressions (both singular) to make the contrast clearer. The final statement of result, namely, **so that what can be seen was made out of what cannot be seen,** may be rendered as "as a result God made what can be seen by using what cannot be seen." But the passive expression in **can be seen** and **cannot be seen** may require some modification; for example, "God used what no one can see in order to make what we do see."

11.4   It was faith that made Abel offer to God a better sacrifice than Cain's. Through his faith he won God's approval as a righteous man, because God himself approved of his gifts. By means of his faith Abel still speaks, even though he is dead.

The Greek text is uncertain at two points: (a) some manuscripts omit **to God** after **offer;** (b) for RSV's **"God bearing witness,"** some manuscripts have "he (Abel) having borne witness" or other variants. RSV, CLTs, and most translations follow the UBS Greek text.

As elsewhere in Chapter 11, the expression **It was faith that . . .** may be expressed as "Because he had faith." In verse 4 the rendering would be "Because Abel had faith" or "Because Abel trusted God."

Better translates a word which usually means "more" or "greater." However, the context shows that the quality, not the size, of the offering is in the writer's mind.

It may be better to translate **a better sacrifice** as "a more appropriate sacrifice," or "a more fitting sacrifice," or "he sacrificed to God in a more fitting way." The entire comparative expression may then be rendered as "Abel sacrificed to God in a more fitting way than Cain sacrificed to God."

Through his faith: literally, **"through which,"** as in RSV. This could mean "through his sacrifice," which is how KJV, RSV, and probably Phps understand it. Many translations are ambiguous; for example, JB "for that"; NAB "Because of this." Many translations agree with TEV's **Through his faith.** This translation is strongly supported by the immediate context and also by the word righteous . . . by faith in 10.38. The expression of means in **Through his faith** may also be reproduced in some languages as cause; for example, "Because Abel trusted God, God approved of him."

He won God's approval is literally "he was witnessed"; here as in verse 2, "witnessed" refers to God speaking, probably through scripture.

Since God's approval implies a declaration, this may need to be expressed as direct discourse; for example, "God declared, 'You are a righteous man' " or ". . . 'You are a man who does what I want you to do.' "

Righteous translates a word which is rare in Hebrews, though common elsewhere in the New Testament; see 10.38 and 12.23, where TEV fourth edition has good people. **Righteous** (not the same as "self-righteous") is disappearing from common English, as is the corresponding word in German; so GeCL has "Because he relied on God, he was able to stand before him." DuCL keeps "righteous" but restructures the sentence to show that God's approval is closely related to God's declaring Abel "righteous": "Because of his faith, God declared him righteous." It is possible to translate "God declared that he was pleased with him" or ". . . approved of him."

This **approval,** as the rest of the verse shows, was shown by God accepting his **gifts.** The repetition of **approval . . . approved** can be avoided if this is more natural; for example, "God showed that he was pleased with him by accepting his gifts."

God's approval of Abel's gifts may be expressed by direct discourse; for example, "God said, 'Your gifts are the right kind of gifts' " or ". . . 'What you have given is right' " or " '. . . appropriate.' "

The last part of the verse probably means that because the story of Abel's faith is permanently recorded in the Old Testament, his example still speaks to us (see Brc). The writer is probably referring to the fact that Genesis 4.10 uses a present tense, <u>Your brother's blood is crying out to me from the ground</u>, suggesting that the consequences of Cain's crime continue. Nevertheless, the underlying meaning is probably that Abel **still speaks** because of the faith which enabled him to become the first true worshiper recorded in scripture (see 12.24). Genesis 4.10 uses a present tense, rendered <u>is crying out</u>, to which the writer of Hebrews gives a deeper meaning.

Abel is made explicit in the last sentence, since both Cain and God have been mentioned more recently than Abel. KJV's literal "he being dead yet speaketh" brings out a contrast expressed by TEV's **even though** and by RSV's "but," though less strongly.

A strictly literal translation of **By means of his faith Abel still speaks, even though he is dead** could lead to serious misunderstanding. What spoke to people in New Testament times was the action of Abel as recorded in the Scriptures. This may be communicated as "Because Abel trusted God, what he did still speaks to us even though Abel himself is dead," or ". . . what he did means something to us . . . ." However, in many languages, actions don't speak. Perhaps "what he did continues to have a message for us," or retaining the expression of the Greek, "because Abel trusted in God, we can say that even though he is dead, he still speaks today, because what he did continues to have a message for us."

11.5   It was faith that kept Enoch from dying. Instead, he was
‾‾‾   taken up to God, and nobody could find him, because God had
       taken him up. The scripture says that before Enoch was taken
       up, he had pleased God.

This verse cites the two halves of Genesis 5.24, but in reverse order, to emphasize the fact that Enoch **pleased God.**

Kept Enoch from dying: RSV's **"see death"** is a literal translation of a Hebrew idiom meaning "experience death" (compare Phps) or simply "die." The first sentence of this verse, namely, **It was faith that kept Enoch from dying**, may be rendered as "Because Enoch trusted God, he did not die."

This verse contains some repetition: the writer first states <u>he was taken up to God</u>, and then cites the verse from Genesis on which this statement is based. It is difficult to make this clear in translation without producing a heavy sentence. "Instead, he was taken up to God; 'nobody could find him, because God had taken him up' " gives the meaning, but quotation marks cannot be read aloud. GeCL is similar, but without quotation marks, and with a full stop instead of the semicolon.

Taken up to God is unusual in English; DuCL has "taken him away," and FrCL adds "(to be) with him," that is, with God. GeCL says explicitly "was taken to God." The statement **he was taken up to God** might be assumed to mean "the angels took Enoch up to God," but this is contradicted by the later clause **because God had taken him up.** It may be necessary to combine the two clauses referring to Enoch's being taken up, translating the second sentence of verse 5 as "Instead, God took him up to heaven, and therefore no one could find him."

[255]

And before **nobody** should be omitted in most languages, since it misleadingly prepares the reader for new information. The function of **and** in the text is simply to introduce the quotation.

Nobody could find him uses an active verb in place of RSV's literal passive, "**he was not found**," which is less clear in English. The Hebrew for **nobody could find him** is literally "and he was not."

The scripture says is the translation generally adopted in modern versions. The literal translation is "it has been witnessed." This renders a Greek verb used in 7.8,17 and 10.15 of the direct "witness" of scripture, and in 11.2,4 of the "witness" or "approval" of God (probably also in scripture). The tense of the Greek verb here suggests the meaning **The scripture says**; TOB "before his taking up . . . he had received the witness that 'he had been pleasing to God.' "

As in other instances, the statement **The scripture says** may have to be modified; "As one may read in the Scriptures" or "As it is written in the Scriptures."

The clause **before Enoch was taken up** may be made active by rendering it as "before God took Enoch up to heaven."

The meaning of the Greek for **pleased God** is very close to the expression rendered God's approval in verse 4. The writer as usual follows the Septuagint; the Hebrew text has literally "Enoch walked with God." **He had pleased God** may be rendered as "he had caused God to be pleased with him," or "he had caused God to be happy because of what he, Enoch, had done," or "he had pleased God's heart."

11.6   **No one can please God without faith, for whoever comes to God must have faith that God exists and rewards those who seek him.**

This verse, especially the second part, explains and applies verse 5. Genesis 5.24 does not mention Enoch's "faith," so the writer has to show that it is implied. The phrase **without faith** may be restructured as "unless he has faith" or "if he does not have faith."

Comes to God implies "worship," as in 4.16 and 7.25. Usually, CLTs use more verbs and less nouns than the Greek, but here TEV replaces "**believe**" (RSV) by **have faith**. The meaning is unchanged, and in Greek, "believe" and "faith" are expressed by related words.

The indefinite relative clause **whoever comes to God** may be transformed into a conditional clause, "if anyone comes to God." This may be rendered as "if anyone seeks to worship God" or ". . . wants to worship God."

Must indicates a way of doing things which God has set up, not an arbitrary command.

The two phrases translated **God exists** (literally, "is") and **rewards those who seek him** are closely linked. The stress falls on **rewards**, not on **God exists**, a fact which Jewish, though not Greek, readers would take for granted. RSV's repetition of "**that he**" misleadingly gives equal stress to both statements.

God exists may be expressed in some languages simply as "God lives."

Seek him, like **comes to God,** implies "in worship."

And rewards those who seek him is often expressed as "and is good to those who seek him" or ". . . come to him." It would be wrong to render **seek him** by expressions which would suggest "going out to find" or "looking around in order to discover."

<u>11.7</u>　　　　**It was faith that made Noah hear God's warnings about things in the future that he could not see. He obeyed God and built a boat in which he and his family were saved. As a result, the world was condemned, and Noah received from God the righteousness that comes by faith.**

See Genesis 6.13,14. The main evidence of Noah's **faith** is the building of the **boat.** Neither the Greek here, nor Genesis 6.13-14, states that **faith . . . made Noah hear God's warnings,** but TEV makes this explicit in dividing the sentence. The verb translated **hear . . . warnings** means "given authoritative information about" (compare 8.5). The context, with its reference to the future, requires the meaning "warn."

A literal translation of **made Noah hear God's warnings** may miss the point. It may be more satisfactory to translate "made Noah pay attention to God's warnings" or "made Noah pay attention to what God said, when God warned him about things in the future."

Things in the future that he could not see, literally "things not yet seen," develops the thought of verse 1b. This phrase may be rendered as "what was going to happen, which he could not, as yet, see" or ". . . could not, as yet, know about," in languages which do not use **see** in speaking about future events.

GeCL and TEV fourth edition replace the traditional "ark" by "ship" or **boat,** which makes the meaning clear.

He obeyed God and built a boat is clearer than Mft's "reverently constructed an ark." The point is that Noah showed his reverence for God in a practical way, by doing what God told him; **obeyed** is implied. The relation between obedience and building a boat may be expressed as "he obeyed God by building a boat," or "he built a boat because he was obedient to God," or "he did what God told him to, and built a boat."

Saved in this context has its literal meaning of "escaped"; see comments on 1.14.

As a result (TEV third edition "In this way") is literally "By means of this," referring either to the **boat** or more probably to faith; GeCL "because he relied on God."

The world was condemned, as expressed in the Greek and in most translations (including TEV third edition), is "he (Noah) condemned the world," not by words, but by what he did. The thought is similar to verse 38a. The context gives **world** an evil sense here, though not in 10.5. GeCL brings out the contrast in another way: "Because he relied on God, he cut himself off from people who rejected God." The idea is similar to that expressed in 10.39 (see comments).

Since the condemnation of the world resulted from Noah's behavior, not specifically what he said, it is possible to translate **the world was condemned** by "what Noah did showed that the world was wrong" or ". . . showed that the people of the world were evil."

On **received from God**, literally "became heir," see comments on 1.2 and 6.17. The writer is not thinking of "inheriting" property from someone who has died.

The righteousness that comes by faith: as in verse 4, there is some overlap between being "righteous" and being "approved by God"; **righteousness** is understood as a right relationship with God, based on "faith" and "obedience." **Righteousness,** like "righteous," is disappearing from common language English. FrCL restructures to give "He . . . obtained, by means of faith, that God consider him righteous."

The final statement in verse 7, namely, **Noah received from God the righteousness that comes by faith,** is more complex than it seems. In the first place, Noah's receiving **righteousness** is a result of God's declaration or consideration of him as righteous, and this may involve direct discourse. The final statement, **that comes by faith,** shows the manner in which Noah's trusting God caused him to be declared righteous. Accordingly, it may be necessary to restructure the final statement of this verse; for example, "God declared that Noah was righteous because Noah trusted God" or "Because Noah trusted God, this caused God to declare, 'Noah does what is right.' "

11.8   **It was faith that made Abraham obey when God called him to go out to a country which God had promised to give him. He left his own country without knowing where he was going.**

See Genesis 12.1-2. From this point until verse 20, the writer is mainly concerned with Abraham, but this theme is interrupted in verses 13-16 by a more general statement, and perhaps in verse 11 by a reference to Sarah (see comments). It is impractical, as well as a distortion of the author's careful method of writing, to rearrange the verses in order to bring everything on Abraham together.

Made Abraham obey: a different word for **obey** from that used in verse 7 is used here, but there is no difference in meaning. It may be necessary to state who obeys whom; for example, "because Abraham trusted God, Abraham obeyed him."

When God called him makes explicit what is implied in the passive "when he was called." **God called him** means "when God told him to leave Haran for an unknown destination," not "when God gave him the name Abraham" (see Gen 17.5), as in some manuscripts.

It may be impossible to employ a literal rendering of **to go out to,** since this would suggest leaving an enclosure such as a room or house. An equivalent may be "to go away to," or "to leave in order to go to," or simply "to go to."

A country is quite general in meaning; literally "a place" (KJV). **Which God had promised to give him** makes God explicit and shows that **"inheritance"** (RSV), as in the previous verse, has its more general meaning of "a gift," in this case from God. In some languages it may be necessary or more natural to state from where Abraham **went out.**

He left his own country is literally "he went out," as in the first part of the verse.

It may be necessary to reverse the order of **He left his own country** and **without knowing where he was going;** for example, "Even though he did not know where he was going, he left his own country" or "He did not know where he was going, but he left his own country."

11.9   **By faith he lived as a foreigner in the country that God had promised him. He lived in tents, as did Isaac and Jacob, who received the same promise from God.**

See Genesis 23.4; 26.3; 35.12; compare Genesis 35.27.

Lived . . . in the country; lived in tents: as in other places, the writer uses two different words for "live in," for the sake of variety. The first means "to stay for a time," "to make a temporary home." The second usually means "to take up permanent residence," but **in tents** makes this difficult. However, the writer may be being deliberately ironical, as "settle down in tents" could be in English.

As a foreigner is literally "as in a foreign land." At first sight it seems to make no difference whether one says that Abraham was foreign to the country or the country foreign to Abraham, but there is a change of focus. TEV fourth edition, **as a foreigner,** replaces TEV third edition, heavier but less ambiguous, **as though he were a foreigner.** The point is that the country was only in a manner of speaking "foreign," since God had promised to give it to Abraham's descendants.

By faith he lived as a foreigner may be rendered as "Because he trusted God, he lived as a foreigner would live," or ". . . as a person who had no rights in that place," or ". . . as a person who was a stranger in that land." The clause **that God had promised to him** may be expanded; for example, "that God had promised to give to him" or "that God had promised, I will give it to you."

A literal rendering of **He lived in tents** may cause problems. In the first place, the use of the singular pronoun **he,** without mention of anyone else, might suggest that Abraham lived alone. Secondly, to say that **he lived in tents** might appear as though he alone lived in several tents. It may therefore be necessary to translate **He lived in tents** either as "He lived in a tent" or "He and those with him lived in tents."

As did Isaac and Jacob weakens TEV third edition with Isaac and Jacob, which is difficult to reconcile with the chronology of Genesis (see especially Gen 26.1). The Greek, however, cannot mean anything but "with." FrCL, GeCL, and ItCL have "with"; DuCL, the Portuguese common language version (PoCL), NEB, the New International Version (NIV), and TNT have "as," under the influence of Genesis. "With Isaac and Jacob" may be translated "in company with Isaac and Jacob" or "in the same place as Isaac and Jacob."

On **promise,** see comments on 4.1 and 6.12. The last part of the verse probably means "Isaac and Jacob, who were also to receive what God had promised," not "Isaac and Jacob, to whom the same promise had been made." Both are grammatically possible because no tense is expressed in the Greek. The first explanation fits in better, both with the writer's usual use of the word for **promise** and also with the next verse.

11.10 For Abraham was waiting for the city which God has designed and built, the city with permanent foundations.

The Greek text has **the** before both **city** and **foundations** (**permanent** is implied). To this extent RSV and TEV are formally more accurate than KJV "a city" (in verse 16 the Greek has no article). However, this verse makes a transition from the idea of a country (verse 9) to that of a **city.**

A literal rendering of **For Abraham was waiting for the city** may be both obscure and misleading. It is easy enough to speak of "waiting for the arrival of a person," but "to wait for a city" may be meaningless, unless one is waiting for "the existence of such a city," or even better, "the coming into existence of such a city." The most appropriate equivalent may be "For Abraham was looking forward to living in the city which God had designed and built."

TEV, unlike other CLTs, reverses the order of **with permanent foundations** and **which God has designed and built.** The latter clause **which God has designed and built,** like its equivalent in Greek, makes a stronger climax in English. **Designed** and **built** correspond to Greek nouns for "designer" and "builder." These nouns are never used elsewhere in the New Testament in speaking of God, though "builder" is used in pagan writings in speaking of less important gods. The meaning here does not contradict the idea of God as creator, but in fact presupposes it; see verse 3. **Designed and built** may be rendered as "planned and constructed" or "of which God was the architect and builder."

The phrase **the city with permanent foundations** may involve problems in translation, since foundations normally belong to buildings, not to cities themselves. What is important about the **foundations** is the aspect of permanence, so that this is a reference to "the eternal city" or "the city which will always exist."

11.11 It was faith that made Abraham able to become a father, even though he was too old and Sarah herself could not have children. He^g trusted God to keep his promise.

^{g} It was faith . . . children. He; *some manuscripts have* It was faith that made Sarah herself able to conceive, even though she was too old to have children. She.

See Genesis 17.19; 18.11-14; 21.2. The textual difficulties of this verse are discussed in Metzger's *A Textual Commentary on the Greek New Testament* (pages 672-673); he refers to articles in which these problems are discussed in more detail. There is also a translational difficulty which involves the question of whether Abraham (TEV) or Sarah (RSV) is the subject of the sentence.

The text of the UBS Greek New Testament ("D" rating) may be translated rather literally as follows, with implied words in parentheses: "By faith, even though Sarah was barren, (Abraham) received power to beget (children), even though (he was) too old." This basic text is followed by TEV, FrCL, GeCL, and Brc, and is probably the best available, though it is by no means certain. The same text, slightly modified by marks which would not usually be part of the oldest manuscripts, could mean "By faith (Abraham) also, together with barren Sarah, received power to beget (children), even though (they were) too old." If this text is chosen, "barren" may be omitted (as in DuCL), following many manuscripts, but it is included in the text of the UBS Greek New Testament. These choices, like TEV, make Abraham the subject of the sentence.

If Sarah is the subject of the sentence, the possiblities are: (a) "By faith, even though Sarah was barren, she received power to conceive (children) even though (she was) too old." This text is followed by Knox and TNT text. (b) "By faith, even Sarah received power to conceive (children), even though (she was) too old." This text is followed by KJV, RSV, NEB, and many other translations. The main difficulty in taking Sarah as the subject is that "received power to beget" is a more natural meaning of the Greek than "received power to conceive." In other words, the verb usually has a man as its subject. It is true that the reference to being "too old" applies more naturally to Sarah than to Abraham. In Genesis 18.12,13, Sarah's age is emphasized, but both are mentioned, and Abraham's age is certainly mentioned in Genesis 18.12 as well as 21.2. On the whole it seems more likely that the subject is Abraham, and this fits in better with the passage as a whole.

It was faith that made Abraham able to become a father may be rendered as "Because Abraham trusted God, he was able to have a son," or ". . . was able to have a son born to him," or ". . . was able to cause his wife to bear him a son."

It may be better to render **even though he was too old** as "even though he was very old indeed." If one renders the statement **he was too old**, it may be necessary to indicate a complement; for example, "too old to have a son" or "too old for a person to have a son born to him."

Early in the verse there is a word which KJV translates "also," but TEV and RSV omit, though it is implied in TEV's **even**. KJV's "also" is most unlikely to be correct. In the Greek, "even Sarah herself" is emphasized.

TEV and other translations restructure the text so as to bring the two "even though" clauses together ("even though barren" and "even though too old"), producing a smoothly flowing sentence.

Some translations omit **could not have children** ("barren"), perhaps for stylistic reasons, because of partial repetition with **too old**. However, the two expressions do not mean the same, and in fact Sarah was barren before she was old.

The last sentence in TEV is much simpler than the rest of the verse. **He trusted** does not refer directly to Abraham's attitude of faith, but means "He considered God faithful" or ". . . to be trusted." **God** is implied, as RSV shows. **He trusted God to keep his promise** may be rendered as "He was sure God would do what he had promised" or "He was certain that God could be trusted and therefore would do what he had promised."

Though Abraham was practically dead, from this one man came as many descendants as there are stars in the sky, as many as the numberless grains of sand on the seashore.

This verse quotes Genesis 22.17, a passage referred to in various parts of the Old Testament and also in Romans 4.19.

Though is an idiomatic equivalent for RSV's **"and him."** Most of the rest of the verse, except **as many,** comes directly from Genesis 22.17. For languages which do not possess a concessive clause introduced by a conjunction meaning "though" or "even though," one may express the meaning as "Abraham was practically dead but nevertheless he . . . ." It may, however, be important to indicate that the expression **was practically dead** is figurative; for example, "was, as it were, almost dead."

The word **came** is not strictly a translation of the UBS Greek text, which means "there were born"; this text is followed by other CLTs and RSV. The expression **from this one man came as many descendants** may be expressed as "this man had as many descendants," or "this one man produced as great a lineage," or "the people who descended from this one man were as many as."

The comparison of the descendants of Abraham with the number of **stars in the sky** or the **grains of sand on the seashore** is a kind of literary hyperbole or exaggeration, and these comparisons are to be understood as such. The statement **as many as the numberless grains of sand on the seashore** may be expressed as "his descendants are as many as the grains of sands on the seashore which cannot be counted" or ". . . which no one can count."

TEV   **11.13-16**   RSV

TEV	RSV
13 It was in faith that all these persons died. They did not receive the things God had promised, but from a long way off they saw them and welcomed them, and admitted openly that they were foreigners and refugees on earth. 14 Those who say such things make it clear that they are looking for a country of their own. 15 They did not keep thinking about the country they had left; if they had, they would have had the chance to return. 16 Instead, it was a better country they longed for, the heavenly country. And so God is not ashamed for them to call him their God, because he has prepared a city for them.	13 These all died in faith, not having received what was promised, but having seen it and greeted it from afar, and having acknowledged that they were strangers and exiles on the earth. 14 For people who speak thus make it clear that they are seeking a homeland. 15 If they had been thinking of that land from which they had gone out, they would have had opportunity to return. 16 But as it is, they desire a better country, that is, a heavenly one. Therefore God is not ashamed to be called their God, for he has prepared for them a city.

11.13   **It was in faith that all these persons died. They did not receive the things God had promised, but from a long way off they saw them and welcomed them, and admitted openly that they were foreigners and refugees on earth.**

In faith renders a different wording from "By faith" in the RSV of verses 8,11, and earlier. It would be a mistake to translate **It was in faith** in the same way as similar expressions in verses 3,4,5,7, and 8. Verse 13 does not involve a causal relation, and one would not want to say "Because they trusted God, all these persons died." A more satisfactory rendering would be "All of these persons trusted God until the time they died" or "All these persons who trusted God died." **All these persons** means the people mentioned by name earlier in this chapter, not the **numberless . . . descendants.** GeCL specifies "Abraham, Isaac and Jacob."

In meaning, though not in grammar, **They did not receive** is more closely linked with **in faith** than with **died.** There is a double contrast between (a) **in faith,** (b) **not having received,** and (c) **they saw** and **welcomed;** both (a) and (c) are contrasted with (b). In order to indicate the relationship between the trust in God and the people not having received **the things** that **God had promised,** it is possible to render the first part of the verse as "All these people who trusted God died without having received the things that God promised."

TEV's **they did not receive the things God had promised** (similarly RSV) is clearer than KJV's "not having received the promises," since Abraham and the others did receive a promise but not its fulfillment. The meaning is similar to receive what God has promised in 6.12, though the Greek is different. In the same way, what the patriarchs saw **from a long way off** was not the promises themselves, which are in any case invisible, but what God had promised. The picture language is drawn from the story of Moses looking at the promised land **from a long way off** (see Deut 34.1-4). "From a long way off," in the Greek as in TEV, refers to distance in space, not time, and really refers to such texts as Deuteronomy 32.49,52 and 34.4. The idea of "greeting" inanimate objects is strange (see RSV). The writer means that the patriarchs looked forward with joy and confidence to receiving what God had promised; Phps "hailed them as true"; GeCL "rejoiced about it."

From a long way off they saw them may have to be modified so as to emphasize the temporal aspect and to indicate that **saw** is used in a figurative sense; for example, "long before what God promised took place, they, as it were, saw it" or ". . . saw what would happen." The expression **and welcomed them** may be rendered as "and were very happy."

Admitted openly translates a word which can be used to speak of "confession," either of faith or of sin. Here **admitted openly** suggests something of which people might be expected to be ashamed. As Genesis 23.4 and 47.9 show, people living outside their own country were often despised. **Admitted openly** may be rendered as "freely told people" or "did not hesitate to say to people."

The Greek word for **foreigners** is harsher than the word used in the Septuagint translation of Genesis 23.4, which means "strangers." **Refugees** is a little stronger than the Greek, which does not suggest people who have escaped from trouble in their own country, but simply "resident aliens"; see comment on verse 38.

11.14-16 **Those who say such things make it clear that they are looking for a country of their own. 15 They did not keep thinking about the country they had left; if they had, they would have had the chance to return. 16 Instead, it was a better country they longed for, the heavenly country. And so God is not ashamed for them to call him their God, because he has prepared a city for them.**

The writer's thought is generally clear, but the translator needs to look at the passage as a whole if he is to avoid difficulties later. The writer's main interest is not in the "promised land" of Exodus or Joshua, but in the city with permanent foundations in heaven (verse 10). For this reason he gives more space to the patriarchs and Moses than to those who lived after the exodus, and the patriarchs themselves are mentioned as heroes of faith rather than those who established the nation of Israel. So in verses 14-16 the movement is from the patriarchs' starting point (Ur of the Chaldees, Gen 12.1 and 11.8), through a period of wandering, to the heavenly promised land. When the writer says in verse 33 that those who came after the exodus received what God had promised, he means that they were given the land of Israel, the earthly promised land, or in a more general sense, God's help in various struggles and difficulties.

The rendering of **Those who say such things** may need to be somewhat more specific: "Those who admit they are foreigners and refugees" or "Those who say they do not belong to that country."

Make it clear that may be rendered as "say so clearly that" or "are really saying that."

A country of their own: the writer describes the heavenly promised land as "a homeland" (RSV). This usually means the country in which a person is born, but this idea must be avoided here. **"Seeking a homeland"** (RSV) is awkward, since it may suggest "looking for a place in which to be born." TEV's **a country of their own** (also Brc) gives the meaning well; other translations specify "their true homeland" (Phps; similarly JB). **Looking for** suggests, not something that has been lost, but something still to be obtained. Translations of **they are looking for a country of their own** must avoid any implication of "looking around for." One may express the meaning as "they are expecting to possess a country that will belong to them."

Verses 15-16 form a contrast, as TEV's **Instead** shows. **Keep thinking about the country they had left** implies "When they called themselves foreigners and aliens, they did not mean that they had left their homeland in Chaldaea, but that they had not yet reached the country of their own which God had promised to give them in heaven." This involves taking "foreigners and aliens" as the key phrase of verses 14-16, and emphasizing by repetition or in some other way that verses 14-16 belong together. Phps is a model in this respect:

> They freely admitted that they lived on this earth as exiles and
> foreigners. Men who say that mean, of course, that their eyes
> are fixed upon their true homeland. If they had meant the
> particular country they had left behind, they had ample
> opportunity to return. No, the fact is that they longed for a
> better country altogether, nothing less than a heavenly one.

This seems to make stronger sense of the passage as a whole than DuCL
(similarly GeCL), which translates verse 15 "If they had been homesick for the
country they had left, they could easily have gone back"; but this translation is
also possible.

Chance or **"opportunity"** (KJV, RSV, NEB) fits the context better than
"time" (Mft and TOB). It is not always necessary to specify "a chance" or "an
opportunity," since the meaning of **they would have had the chance to return** may
very well be expressed as "they could have returned" or "there was nothing to stop
them from returning."

Instead, "but as it is," or "but in fact" (JB; not "now" KJV) marks the contrast with verse 15 (as in 8.6). **Longed for** is a less common and stronger equivalent of the expression rendered **keep thinking about** in verse 15.

It may be necessary to expand the adversative adverb **Instead;** for example,
"Instead of longing for the country they had left, it was a better country they
were longing for."

The appositional phrase **the heavenly country** may be made more explicit as
"that is to say, it was the country in heaven." It is important to avoid a rendering
of **the heavenly country** which would suggest a country on earth which is merely
like heaven.

Call him their God may refer to "calling on God" in worship, but if so, this
is not emphasized here. The last part of verse 16 serves only to summarize
verses 13-15 and link them with verse 10.

The meaning of **because** is not very clear. The second half of the verse
may be partly paraphrased: "God shows that he is not ashamed of them, by preparing a city for them." But this is not the whole meaning. The writer does not
use the word for "covenant," which was so important in chapters 8—9. However,
he has in mind the sentence which expressed the essential content of the covenants with Abraham (Gen 17—18) and Moses (Exo 29.45), and of the new covenant
of which Jeremiah (31.33; Heb 8.10) and Ezekiel (11.20) had spoken: "I will be their
God, and they shall be my people." In English the conjunction **because** wrongly
suggests that the preparation of a city is directly related to people calling God
their God. A more indirect causal relation may be expressed by the conjunction
"for." The basic idea of the last sentence of this section is that one may know
that God is not ashamed to be called their God, since he has shown that fact by
preparing a city for them. The two halves of the sentence belong so closely
together that it would be possible to translate it "God is not ashamed to acknowledge them as his people, and so he has prepared a city for them," or even "... and
this is shown by the fact that he has prepared a city for them to live in."

17 It was faith that made Abraham offer his son Isaac as a sacrifice when God put Abraham to the test. Abraham was the one to whom God had made the promise, yet he was ready to offer his only son as a sacrifice. 18 God had said to him, "It is through Isaac that you will have the descendants I promised." 19 Abraham reckoned that God was able to raise Isaac from death—and, so to speak, Abraham did receive Isaac back from death.

20 It was faith that made Isaac promise blessings for the future to Jacob and Esau.

21 It was faith that made Jacob bless each of the sons of Joseph just before he died. He leaned on the top of his walking stick and worshiped God.

22 It was faith that made Joseph, when he was about to die, speak of the departure of the Israelites from Egypt, and leave instructions about what should be done with his body.

17 By faith Abraham, when he was tested, offered up Isaac, and he who had received the promises was ready to offer up his only son, 18 of whom it was said, "Through Isaac shall your descendants be named." 19 He considered that God was able to raise men even from the dead; hence, figuratively speaking, he did receive him back. 20 By faith Isaac invoked future blessings on Jacob and Esau. 21 By faith Jacob, when dying, blessed each of the sons of Joseph, bowing in worship over the head of his staff. 22 By faith Joseph, at the end of his life, made mention of the exodus of the Israelites and gave directions concerning his burial.[x]

[x] Greek *bones*

11.17-18   **It was faith that made Abraham offer his son Isaac as a sacrifice when God put Abraham to the test. Abraham was the one to whom God had made the promise, yet he was ready to offer his only son as a sacrifice. 18 God had said to him, "It is through Isaac that you will have the descendants I promised."**

As a sacrifice (twice) is implicit; the word for **offer** is often used of making "sacrifices" to God, as in 5.1. **God** is implied by the Greek passive verbs for "was tested" and (in verse 18) "it was said." **His son** is also implied.

The first sentence of verse 17 may be rendered as "Because Abraham trusted God, he offered his son as a sacrifice to God when God put him to the test," or ". . . when God tested Abraham," or ". . . when God wanted to see what Abraham would do." However, in rendering **It was faith that made Abraham offer his son Isaac as a sacrifice**, it is important to avoid the implication that this actually took place. Therefore one may translate "Because Abraham trusted God, he was prepared to offer his son Isaac as a sacrifice" or ". . . was about to offer his son Isaac as a sacrifice."

There is some repetition between **made Abraham offer** and **he was ready to offer**. The same event (Gen 22.1-10) is seen from two points of view: first, as a whole, as the next event in the series of examples of faith; and second, with a special focus on the moment when Abraham's hand was stretched out to kill Isaac, but God told him not to do so.

[266]

There is room for great variety in restructuring these verses. It may be possible to combine them; for example:

> It was faith that made Abraham offer his son Isaac as a sacrifice, when God put him (Abraham) to the test. God had promised him, "It is through Isaac that you will have descendants," yet he was ready to offer his only son as a sacrifice.

"God had promised him" is literally "having received the promises," but the only example of a "promise" given here is the quotation from Genesis 21.12. "Received" here suggests more than a passive attitude; rather it means a willingness to take what God offered (see verse 13).

Another possible restructuring is that of GeCL: "Because Abraham trusted God, he offered him his son Isaac as a sacrifice when he was put by God to the test. He was ready to offer his only son, although God had promised him . . . ." It is important to make it clear whether Abraham, Isaac, or God is the subject or object of each verb.

The reference to **descendants** introduces a new idea into this chapter, though a country of their own in verse 14 implies that future generations will live there. Although in Genesis 21.12 through Isaac is emphasized, Isaac has already been mentioned here in verse 17, so the main emphasis in the quotation is now on **descendants.**

11.19 **Abraham reckoned that God was able to raise Isaac from death**
   —and, so to speak, Abraham did receive Isaac back from death.

In the Greek this verse is part of the same sentence as verses 17-18. Most modern translations begin a new sentence, since it is at this point that the writer passes from a summary of the story of Isaac to a comment on it.

Reckoned suggests a process of thought or reasoning; Brc "he had reasoned it out"; TOB "even a dead man, he said to himself, God is able to resurrect him."

God was able to raise Isaac from death may be expressed as "God was able to cause Isaac to live again" or ". . . to come back to life."

So to speak is literally "in a parable," but the word for "parable" in biblical Greek has a much wider meaning than its English equivalent, since it can include proverbs and various other types of figurative language (see symbol in 9.9). The point here is that Isaac was practically dead, like Abraham for different reasons in verse 12. ItCL brings out the meaning more fully than TEV: "God restored the son to him (that is, gave his son back to him), and this fact has the value of a symbol."

The phrase **so to speak** marks the final statement of verse 19 as being a simile. In some languages this may be introduced, "as though to say," or "as though it were," or "as it might seem."

11.20 **It was faith that made Isaac promise blessings for the future to Jacob and Esau.**

At the beginning of the Greek verse, after "By faith," there is a word meaning "also" or "and," which is omitted by some manuscripts and most translations, including TEV, GeCL, RSV, NEB. It is not directly related to Isaac as the next example of faith. It may mean "also, like previous examples," or "also, for the future," or it may link the whole verse with what precedes.

All the examples of faith are related in some way to future events which are now coming true, as verse 40 will suggest. However, he now says explicitly that the blessing by Isaac of his children is "about the future."

The future includes both future time and what will happen in it. This is clear from Genesis 27.28,29,39,40, especially since Jacob and Esau were thought of not merely as individuals but as the ancestors of Israel and Edom respectively. The translator should avoid the idea that Isaac would only bless his children "in the future." It is important to show that the blessing is not only about the future, but helps to bring the future about. GeCL does this in two sentences: "Because Isaac trusted God, he blessed Jacob and Esau. He relied on (the fact) that the words of blessing would some time be fulfilled."

Promise blessings for the future: the Greek, "to bless about the future," is difficult for two reasons: (a) a "blessing," like a "promise," is a present act whose results lie in the future; (b) the role of "blessing" may vary in different cultures. The solution of the second problem will vary from one area to another. In cultures in which blessing plays an important part, translation of this phrase may raise no problems. In western European cultures, where blessing is unusual, especially of one human being by another (7.1-2), translation will be difficult. For example, Phps' "his words dealt with what should happen in the future," and Mft's "blessed Jacob and Esau in connection with the future," give correct information, but the blessings are mere statements, whereas in Hebrew thought a "blessing," "curse," "promise," "vow," "prophecy," or almost any solemn statement was a power which helped to bring about the things of which it spoke. The words may be restructured: "say that God would do good to Jacob and Esau in the future."

This verse may also be expressed as "Because Isaac trusted God, he blessed Jacob and Esau by speaking about the blessings which would come to them in the future." However, the real problem is often that of finding a satisfactory term for "blessing." In some instances one can use a phrase such as "to speak well on behalf of." But in the biblical context there are certain supernatural sanctions which are associated with blessings. Sometimes this may be expressed by saying "to speak good and powerful words on behalf of." In some languages the only equivalent is "to speak well about, with God listening." The phrase "with God listening" provides the kind of supernatural sanction which makes the promises of good things more secure.

11.21 **It was faith that made Jacob bless each of the sons of Joseph just before he died. He leaned on the top of his walking stick and worshiped God.**

This verse adds little to the last one, except an essential link in the series of generations. The verse as a whole refers to Genesis 48.15-16, but the quotation in the second half comes from the Greek translation of Genesis 47.31. This is different from the Hebrew, which has the word for bed instead of for **walking stick.** A **walking stick** is a stick or cane which a person may use as a support or help while walking.

In rendering **He leaned on the top of his walking stick,** it is important to avoid a statement which will seem ridiculous. One can, for example, "lean against a building" or "lean on a table," but in some languages it would be impossible to say "to lean on a walking stick." It may, however, be possible to say "he steadied himself by means of his walking stick."

God is implied. There is no basis for the suggestion that the walking stick in this verse had anything to do with "worship." The sentence may be restructured: "he worshiped God as he leaned on his walking stick."

11.22   **It was faith that made Joseph, when he was about to die, speak of the departure of the Israelites from Egypt, and leave instructions about what should be done with his body.**

See Genesis 50.24-25. The author uses a different word for **die** from verse 21 (literally "end," see RSV), but only for reasons of style.

Departure, like "exodus" in English, had the special meaning of the "great trek" or "long march" of Israel out of Egypt. **From Egypt** is added to make this clear.

The Israelites is literally "the sons of Israel," a very common expression indicating the whole people.

It may be awkward to introduce the temporal clause **when he was about to die** in the statement concerning Joseph speaking about the departure of the Israelites from Egypt. Accordingly, the first part of this verse may be rendered as "Because Joseph trusted God, he spoke about how the Israelites would leave Egypt; he said this when he was about to die."

And leave instructions about what should be done with his body may be rendered as "and he told people what they should do with his body."

The point about Joseph's **body** was that he ordered it to be carried out of Egypt when the Israelites left. The reference to the **body** may be puzzling to some readers unless it is explained by a note, or at least a reference to Genesis 50.25. **Body,** as RSV's footnote states, is literally "bones," meaning "remains."

TEV	11.23-31	RSV

23 It was faith that made the parents of Moses hide him for three months after he was born. They saw that he was a beautiful child, and they

23 By faith Moses, when he was born, was hid for three months by his parents, because they saw that the child was beautiful; and they were not

were not afraid to disobey the king's order.

24 It was faith that made Moses, when he had grown up, refuse to be called the son of the king's daughter. 25 He preferred to suffer with God's people rather than to enjoy sin for a little while. 26 He reckoned that to suffer scorn for the Messiah was worth far more than all the treasures of Egypt, for he kept his eyes on the future reward.

27 It was faith that made Moses leave Egypt without being afraid of the king's anger. As though he saw the invisible God, he refused to turn back. 28 It was faith that made him establish the Passover and order the blood to be sprinkled on the doors, so that the Angel of Death would not kill the first-born sons of the Israelites.

29 It was faith that made the Israelites able to cross the Red Sea as if on dry land; when the Egyptians tried to do it, the water swallowed them up.

30 It was faith that made the walls of Jericho fall down after the Israelites had marched around them for seven days. 31 It was faith that kept the prostitute Rahab from being killed with those who disobeyed God, for she gave the Israelite spies a friendly welcome.

afraid of the king's edict. 24 By faith Moses, when he was grown up, refused to be called the son of Pharaoh's daughter, 25 choosing rather to share ill-treatment with the people of God than to enjoy the fleeting pleasures of sin. 26 He considered abuse suffered for the Christ greater wealth than the treasures of Egypt, for he looked to the reward. 27 By faith he left Egypt, not being afraid of the anger of the king; for he endured as seeing him who is invisible. 28 By faith he kept the Passover and sprinkled the blood, so that the Destroyer of the first-born might not touch them.

29 By faith the people crossed the Red Sea as if on dry land; but the Egyptians, when they attempted to do the same, were drowned. 30 By faith the walls of Jericho fell down after they had been encircled for seven days. 31 By faith Rahab the harlot did not perish with those who were disobedient, because she had given friendly welcome to the spies.

11.23 It was faith that made the parents of Moses hide him for three months after he was born. They saw that he was a beautiful child, and they were not afraid to disobey the king's order.

See Exodus 2.2-3. The way in which Moses' parents showed their faith is stated in the second part of the verse, beginning with RSV's **"because."** This may be made even clearer by translating "It was faith which gave Moses' parents courage to disobey the king's order, and hide him for three months after he was born, because he was a beautiful child." It is in any case important to show that this verse is about the faith of Moses' parents, not of Moses himself.

If quotation marks are used for indicating a passage from the Old Testament, they should be put around the words **saw that he was a beautiful child** (the subject of the verb "saw" in Exo 2.2 is Moses' mother). The text probably means more than "he was such a beautiful baby that it was a shame for him to be killed." Physical beauty or height was sometimes thought of as a sign of God's special favor; see 1 Samuel 9.2; 16.12; Luke 1.80; 2.40; Acts 7.20.

They saw that he was a beautiful child may be related to the preceding sentence by translating "they did this because they saw that he was a beautiful child" or ". . . a beautiful baby."

To disobey is implied. **Order** suggests a solemn official edict; the language of Exodus 1.17 is less formal.

Verses 24-26 form a single sentence in the Greek, similar in general structure to verses 17-19. First, in verse 24 the writer refers to an Old Testament story, in this case, Exodus 2.10-12. Then he adds his explanation. This is in the form of a double comparison, first with Moses' own times (verse 25), and then with the future (verse 26), that is, to the times in which the writer is living. Most modern translations begin new sentences in each verse, though verses 25-26 are more closely linked with one another than with verse 24.

11.24   **It was faith that made Moses, when he had grown up, refuse to be called the son of the king's daughter.**

See Exodus 2.11,12. **Be called** implies really having the position and privileges of Pharaoh's grandson; Syn has "renounced the title of." **The king's** is literally "of Pharaoh." "Pharaoh" is the title of kings of Egypt, not a proper name. There are various ways of dealing with this unfamiliar title, depending on the intended readers and whether the translation of Hebrews is to be published as a separate book or in a complete Bible. Normally the title "Pharaoh" should be translated the same way in both the Old and the New Testaments. Possibilities include (a) using the title "Pharaoh," but anticipating that it will be understood in the light of the king in verse 27; (b) adding a glossary note, as for example in TEV and GeCL; (c) translating as "the king of Egypt" as in GeCL and SpCL. Choice (a) is possible for readers who know the Bible well, but (b) is better for others, and (c) may be necessary in translations of Hebrews which are published separately.

Moses . . . refused to be called the son of the king's daughter may be rendered as "Moses refused to have people treat him as the son of the king's daughter," or as in some languages, "the adopted son of the king's daughter," or ". . . as the person whom the king's daughter had adopted" or ". . . had adopted as her son."

The temporal clause **when he had grown up** must sometimes be made a separate sentence; for example, "He did this when he had grown up" or "This is what he did after he had become a man."

11.25-26   **He preferred to suffer with God's people rather than to enjoy sin for a little while. 26 He reckoned that to suffer scorn for the Messiah was worth far more than all the treasures of Egypt, for he kept his eyes on the future reward.**

There is a close parallel between these two verses, especially in a rather literal translation such as RSV:

Verse 25	Verse 26
choosing rather	he considered . . . greater wealth
to share	suffered
ill-treatment	abuse
with the people of God	for the Christ
than to enjoy the fleeting pleasures of sin	than the treasures of Egypt
	for he looked to the reward

He preferred may be rendered as "He thought it was better" or "He decided that it was better."

As in RSV, different expressions for **suffer** are used in Greek in verses 25 and 26 for the sake of variety. In verse 25 the writer uses an unusual compound verb, meaning "be badly treated with."

Enjoy sin for a little while: in 4 Maccabees 5.8 and 8.6, a pagan emperor invites faithful Jews to "enjoy" the rewards of giving up their faith; the meaning is similar here, though "**pleasures**" is implicit (see KJV, RSV, NEB).

GeCL brings out clearly the relation between "enjoyment" and "sin" in 25b: "He preferred to suffer with God's people, rather than to live well for a short time, and so burden himself with guilt." The verb translated **suffer with** is related to that translated suffering in 13.3, and mistreated in 11.37. These verbs are not used anywhere else in the New Testament. The writer of Hebrews uses the more common Greek word for suffer only in speaking of the death of Christ (2.9,10,18; 5.8; 9.26). Translators must decide whether it is natural to keep this distinction in their own language. In Greek as in English, the verb for mistreated, unlike that for **suffer**, clearly expresses the evil nature of those who cause the suffering.

To suffer with God's people may be expressed as "to suffer in a way in which God's people were suffering." **To suffer** may be translated "to experience pain" or "to be pained."

Verse 26, **scorn for the Messiah,** is literally "the shame (or, insult) of the Christ" (compare 13.13). This expression raises two questions:

(a) Who is "the Christ" in this context? In Psalm 89.51 "the Christ" (RSV "anointed") is probably God's servant or chosen king. In translating Hebrews the usual equivalent for "Messiah" or "God's chosen one" should be used: **Messiah** or "God's Anointed" (NEB), or "God's promised king," rather than "**the Christ**" (RSV) or "Christ," as in GeCL and most older translations. The idea of Moses suffering insults directly for the sake of Jesus is unnecessarily difficult.

(b) What is the meaning of the word "of" in the Greek expression for "the shame of the Christ"? In other words, what is the relation between Moses' "sufferings" and "the Christ"? It is part of the translator's responsibility to make this clear, and the literal translation "the reproach of Christ" (Phps), even with quotation marks, does not convey any clear meaning. Translators follow two main lines: (i) suffering for **the Messiah**, TEV; GeCL "the contempt which one takes on oneself for Christ"; SpCL "for the cause of Christ"; TNT "for God's Anointed One"; or (ii) suffering like God's anointed: Brc "the insults and injury, which God's Anointed One must suffer"; JB "the insults offered to the Anointed"; NEB "the stigma that rests on God's Anointed"; NAB "the reproach borne by God's Anointed." "Suffering as (being) God's Anointed" is impossible; Moses anointed Aaron and his sons (Exo 28.41) but was not himself anointed. The insults which Moses "suffered" had a meaning related to Jesus, and also indirectly to the "suffering" of the people of God (verse 25a). To some extent (ii) includes (i) and is to be preferred.

It may be difficult to say that suffering is worth more than all the treasures of Egypt, since **to suffer scorn for the Messiah** could be interpreted as a type of condition. It may therefore be possible to render the first part of verse 26 as "He reasoned that if he suffered the scorn of the people for the sake of God's Anointed One, that was far more valuable than possessing all the treasures of Egypt."

He kept his eyes on prepares the way for 12.2, though the Greek is different.

Instead of the figurative expression **kept his eyes on,** it may be better to use a nonfigurative expression; for example, "for he kept thinking about the reward which would come in the future" or ". . . the reward which would be given to him in the future," or "he kept hoping for the reward."

On **reward,** see comments on 2.2 and 10.35.

11.27   **It was faith that made Moses leave Egypt without being afraid of the king's anger. As though he saw the invisible God, he refused to turn back.**

This verse is similar to verse 23 and may be treated similarly in translation: "Because Moses trusted God, he did not fear the king's anger, but left Egypt." **The king** is "Pharaoh"; see comment on verse 24.

Commentators discuss whether this verse refers to (a) Moses' running away from Egypt after killing an Egyptian (see Exo 2.11-15), or (b) the exodus of Israel as a whole from Egypt (see Exo 12.51). This problem affects the translation of the second part of the verse, especially **he refused to turn back.** The difficulty with (a) is that Exodus 2.14 says that Moses was afraid, and verse 15 states that Pharaoh tried to kill him. The difficulty with (b) is that the Israelites, as distinct from Moses himself, are not mentioned in this passage until verses 28-29. Mft's solution is to take verse 27 as referring to Exodus 2, but as modifying or explaining Exodus 2.14: "It was by faith that he left Egypt—not from any fear of the king's wrath."

It was Moses' faith which not only made him leave Egypt but made it possible for him to be unafraid of the king's anger. This may be expressed as "Because Moses trusted God, he left Egypt; he was not afraid of the king who was angry" or ". . . he was not afraid even though the king was angry." This use of two statements side by side may be natural in languages which do not employ a preposition combined with a participial phrase, such as **without** combined with **being afraid of the king's anger.**

The invisible God: God, once more, is implied. Mft contrasts the visible, angry king of Egypt and the invisible king in heaven, and translates "the King Invisible." This does not seem necessary, and one would expect such a contrast to be stated explicitly. **As though** correctly implies that Moses did not in fact see God. **The invisible God** may be rendered as "the God whom no one can see."

The clause which TEV translates **he refused to turn back** has been understood in various ways:

(a) TEV fits in better with a reference to the exodus proper, rather than to Moses' flight after killing the Egyptian. Exodus 16.3 and other passages refer to difficulties which could have led the Israelites to **turn back** and return to Egypt.

(b) Many modern translations give a more general meaning, such as "He held inflexibly to his chosen course" (Brc), leaving it open whether the "course" was a literal journey or a plan of action. DuCL "he carried through, persevered"; FrCL "he remained firm"; Seg, Syn, TOB "he held firm"; JB and TNT "he held to his purpose."

(c) A few translations reemphasize Moses' fearlessness at this point: GeCL "that gave him courage"; Mft "he never flinched."

(d) Older German translations (Lu and Zür) link Moses' endurance directly with seeing the invisible: "he held on to the one whom he did not see, as if he saw him."

(e) There is some evidence that the verb can mean "fix one's eyes upon," and although this meaning is not adopted by translations consulted, it would fit in well with verse 26, **he kept his eyes on the future reward**, and with 12.2.

On the whole, interpretation (b) seems the most probable, but since we do not know to which incident the verse refers, it is impossible to be certain.

The relation between **As though he saw the invisible God** and **he refused to turn back** may seem complicated, for the first clause did not happen, while the second clause did happen; yet the first clause expresses cause, while the second expresses result. This may be expressed as "It was as though Moses saw the invisible God and so refused to turn back," or ". . . he refused to change his course," or ". . . he continued straight ahead." In some languages the two clauses are inverted in order, but the difference between what did happen and what did not happen must be maintained. For example, "Moses refused to turn back, as though he saw the invisible God."

11.28   **It was faith that made him establish the Passover and order the blood to be sprinkled on the doors, so that the Angel of Death would not kill the first-born sons of the Israelites.**

See Exodus 12.12-42, especially verses 21-30. It is implied that Moses showed his trust in God, and therefore his belief in Israel's future, by obeying

God's instructions. Here, as usual, faith is forward-looking and is expressed in active obedience to God.

The clause **so that the Angel of Death would not kill the first-born sons of the Israelites** is related only to **order the blood to be sprinkled on the doors**, not to **establish the Passover.**

The word for **establish** suggests the beginning of something which continues to the writer's time. This applies strictly only to the Passover, not to the sprinkling of blood on the doors.

Passover has a glossary note in some translations, including TEV fourth edition.

The initial statement of this verse, namely, **It was faith that made him establish the Passover,** may need to be somewhat restructured and amplified; for example, "because Moses trusted God, he instituted the Passover festival," or ". . . he caused the people to celebrate the festival for remembering the angel's passing over," or ". . . the festival called 'the passing over of the angel.' "

If it is necessary to expand the reference to **the Passover,** it may be best to end the sentence after the reference to the Passover festival and to begin a new sentence as "He also ordered blood to be sprinkled on the doors" or "He also ordered the people to sprinkle blood on their doors." In this way the purpose of sprinkling the doors, namely, to avoid death from the angel, is made quite specific.

The Angel of Death (NEB and NAB "destroying angel") is literally "**the Destroyer**" (RSV). The first readers would know from Exodus 12 that it was an angel, but some modern readers will need to be given this information. The phrase **the Angel of Death** may be rendered as "the angel who brings death," or "the angel who causes people to die," or "the angel who kills." The fundamental difficulty is that people's ideas about supernatural beings vary so much from one culture to another. The main elements in "the Destroyer," here as in Exodus 12, are (a) a supernatural power, (b) sent by God, (c) to destroy God's enemies (in this case the Egyptians). There is also (d) a suggestion of military activity. To convey this in translation raises problems. In Western cultures, angels are often thought of as sweet, peaceful, and usually feminine. Non-Western cultures may lack the idea of a secondary supernatural power completely under the control of the one God. It may be better to avoid the traditional term for "angel," which in any case is not in the Greek text, and expand "the Destroyer" to something like "a spirit sent by God to destroy his enemies." The Greek has "the destroyer," which assumes that this figure was well known to the original readers. "A destroyer," expanded if necessary, may be better for modern readers.

On the doors is made explicit on the basis of Exodus 12, and **of the Israelites** expands the Greek "of them," for the sake of clarity. RSV's literal translation does not make it clear that "**the first-born**" and "**them**" are the same group of people. TEV makes the meaning plain.

The first-born sons of the Israelites may be expressed as "the first sons in the families of the Israelites," or more specifically "the first-born son in each of the families of the Israelites."

11.29   **It was faith that made the Israelites able to cross the Red Sea as if on dry land; when the Egyptians tried to do it, the water swallowed them up.**

See Exodus 14.16,17. A comparison of TEV with RSV will show which parts of TEV are not expressed in the Greek text, but there is no doubt that they are implied.

A literal rendering of **to cross the Red Sea** may be misleading, since it might imply "crossing the surface of the Red Sea." It may therefore be necessary to translate **to cross the Red Sea as if on dry land** as "to cross on dry land where the Red Sea had been" or "to cross on dry land through the Red Sea."

KJV shows how the two halves of the sentence are linked in the Greek text: "which the Egyptians assaying to do were drowned." Most translations, especially those in common language, leave the contrast between the Egyptians and the Israelites implicit. A few insert some such conjunction as "whereas" (Knox) or "while" (JB).

Tried suggests making a test or trial.

The figurative expression **the water swallowed them up** may need to be translated "they drowned in the water," or "the water covered them up and drowned them," or "the water covered them over, and they died."

11.30   **It was faith that made the walls of Jericho fall down after the Israelites had marched around them for seven days.**

See Joshua 6.1-20. This verse contains the first reference to **faith** which does not indicate precisely who has the faith. If the actor is not made explicit, the sentence may seem to say that it is the walls which have faith—an error found in some translations. The implied reference is to the faith or confidence which the people of Israel had, and therefore the first part of verse 30 may be translated as "Because the Israelites trusted God, the walls of Jericho collapsed" or ". . . the wall of the city of Jericho collapsed." It is important to avoid the suggestion that the walls had faith!

In the choice of a verb to translate **fall down,** it is important to make a clear distinction between (1) the falling of an object from one level to another and (2) the collapsing of some object to the level of its base. It is the second meaning which must be employed in this verse.

Translators sometimes create unnecessary problems in dealing with this essentially simple verse. TEV's and RSV's **for seven days** is quite adequate; the phrase means "over a period of seven days." It need not mean that the entire seven days were spent in marching round the walls, as Knox suggests; Joshua 6 makes it clear that this did not happen. Unlike Joshua 6, the rest of Hebrews does not say that the Israelites marched around the walls "each day for seven days" (Brc). DuCL's "that happened when they had gone round seven times, once each day" goes beyond the text of Hebrews and actually contradicts Joshua 6.15.

The verb translated **marched around** can mean either "stood around in a circle" (RSV and NEB **"encircled"**; Phps and Mft "surrounded") or "marched around them," that is, the walls (CLTs, Brc, TNT). The first meaning is the more common, but the second is suggested by Joshua 6.

It may be clearer in some languages to speak of the Israelites "marching around Jericho" rather than "marching around the walls."

11.31   **It was faith that kept the prostitute Rahab from being killed with those who disobeyed God, for she gave the Israelite spies a friendly welcome.**

See Joshua 2.1-21, particularly verses 11,12; also 6.22-25. The precise way in which Rahab showed her faith is not stated. JB suggests that it was by her friendly welcome of the spies: "It was by faith that Rahab the prostitute welcomed the spies." More probably, here "welcome" was thought to be obedience to Israel's God, and her confidence in the future of Israel as a nation. GeCL implies this: "Because the prostitute Rahab trusted God, she gave the Israelite spies a friendly welcome." This translation has the advantage of making it clear that the faith was Rahab's. It may, however, be better to follow the order of the Greek text as reflected in TEV; for example, "Because the prostitute Rahab trusted God, she was not killed with those who disobeyed God, for she welcomed into her home the Israelite spies," or ". . . those Israelites who were spying out the land," or ". . . those Israelites who had come to see what the land was like."

God is implied. The Greek phrase for **those who disobeyed (God)** is used also in 3.18, though there the reference is to a different group.

Gave a friendly welcome is literally "receiving with peace" and may imply the "kiss of peace." However, this latter expression is best avoided in this context, unless the custom is common in the receptor culture and has no sexual connotations.

The meaning of the words for **spies** needs careful analysis, if the right expression is to be chosen in translation. The main element is someone sent out to reconnoiter, especially in foreign territory. Secrecy is also implied in Joshua 2. In some languages "spy" is a despised term, and in such cases an alternative should be found, such as Phps "the Israelites sent out to reconnoiter."

	TEV	**11.32-38**	RSV

32 Should I go on? There isn't enough time for me to speak of Gideon, Barak, Samson, Jephthah, David, Samuel, and the prophets. 33 Through faith they fought whole countries and won. They did what was right and received what God had promised. They shut the mouths of lions, 34 put out fierce fires,

32 And what more shall I say? For time would fail me to tell of Gideon, Barak, Samson, Jephthah, of David and Samuel and the prophets—33 who through faith conquered kingdoms, enforced justice, received promises, stopped the mouths of lions, 34 quenched raging fire, escaped the

escaped being killed by the sword. They were weak, but became strong; they were mighty in battle and defeated the armies of foreigners. 35 Through faith women received their dead relatives raised back to life.

Others, refusing to accept freedom, died under torture in order to be raised to a better life. 36 Some were mocked and whipped, and others were put in chains and taken off to prison. 37 They were stoned, they were sawn in two, they were killed by the sword. They went around clothed in skins of sheep or goats—poor, persecuted, and mistreated. 38 The world was not good enough for them! They wandered like refugees in the deserts and hills, living in caves and holes in the ground.

edge of the sword, won strength out of weakness, became mighty in war, put foreign armies to flight. 35 Women received their dead by resurrection. Some were tortured, refusing to accept release, that they might rise again to a better life. 36 Others suffered mocking and scourging, and even chains and imprisonment. 37 They were stoned, they were sawn in two,ʸ they were killed with the sword; they went about in skins of sheep and goats, destitute, afflicted, ill-treated—38 of whom the world was not worthy—wandering over deserts and mountains, and in dens and caves of the earth.

ʸ Other manuscripts add *they were tempted*

Verses 32-38 are a single sentence in the Greek. It is the climax of this chapter and reaches a high emotional level. Each language has its own ways of communicating emotion, and it is difficult to lay down rules. However, the translator should pay even greater attention than usual to style, and should avoid heavy or prosaic expressions. The sentence will almost certainly have to be divided, as even KJV and Lu do at verse 35. This may involve repeating **through faith** as TEV does in verses 33,35.

11.32   **Should I go on? There isn't enough time for me to speak of Gideon, Barak, Samson, Jephthah, David, Samuel, and the prophets.**

The translator has to make two decisions: first, he must decide whether it is natural in his language to use a rhetorical question, or whether a strong negative statement such as "There is no need for me to say any more" is better. Or else, "I could go on and on, but there isn't enough time for me. For I haven't yet mentioned . . . ." Second, if a rhetorical question is used, the translator must decide what form it should take: (i) "What more need I say?" TNT; Brc "And what other examples should I give?"; or (ii) "Need I say more?" NEB; similarly TEV. Form (i) fits in better with the references to Gideon and the others; form (ii) fits in better with **There isn't enough time.** The difference in meaning is slight, and the translator should choose whichever sounds more natural in his own language.

Speak does not mean "talk" in general; it means "tell the stories" (NEB), with the suggestion of a series or list. **To speak of** or "to mention" may need to be rendered as "to write about," since this is a written text.

On **prophets**, see comments on 1.1.

<u>11.33-34</u>   Through faith they fought whole countries and won. They
did what was right and received what God had promised. They
shut the mouths of lions, 34 put out fierce fires, escaped being
killed by the sword. They were weak, but became strong; they
were mighty in battle and defeated the armies of foreigners.

In translating verse 33 it is important to avoid the implication that all of
the persons just mentioned in verse 32 did everything listed in verses 33 and 34.
To avoid this, the first sentence may be translated as "Because men like this
trusted God, they were able to fight against the armies of entire countries and to
defeat them" or ". . . against the population of entire countries and conquer
them."

Verses 33-34 in Greek consist of nine short, rhythmic clauses, perhaps
arranged in three groups of three.

They fought: the ones who fought are not only or primarily the prophets,
but generally the people mentioned in verse 32. The translator does not need to
know which phrases refer to which Old Testament characters, since this does not
usually affect the meaning. **They fought whole countries and won** suggests that
individuals won victories over entire armies. This is probably not the intention of
the text, and TEV's **whole** is not followed by other CLTs. If a literal translation
such as TEV is unclear or sounds stylistically weak, the words may be translated
"they fought foreign nations and won." In some languages **fought** can be made
implicit, since the word for **won,** or "victorious over," already implies the idea of
fighting.

Received translates a word which implies some activity, not mere passive
receiving. Many translations have "obtained," but JB's "earned" is too strong; BJ
has "obtained the fulfillment of the promises."

They did what was right and received what God had promised (see comments on 11.13) may be a general statement, of which the rest of verses 33-34
gives examples. In this case, DuCL is justified in putting it at the beginning of the
verse. The two parts of the statement in any case fit well together. One might
translate "they did what God required and received what God promised." This
seems on the whole to give better sense than to paraphrase following the order of
the Greek, "they conquered kingdoms; having conquered them, they maintained
justice in them; and (therefore) God gave them the blessings he had promised,"
similarly Phps "conquered kingdoms, ruled in justice and proved the truth of God's
promises." **What God had promised:** the Greek suggests "promises" in general, not
"the promises," as in verse 13. Because they trusted God, his promises to help
them were fulfilled.

They shut the mouths of lions may be rendered as "They caused lions to
keep their mouths shut," or "They forced shut the mouths of lions," or "They would
not let lions open their mouths."

Escaped being killed by the sword is literally "fled mouths of the sword,"
the plural for "mouths" suggesting repeated escapes from death. This may be
rendered as "they escaped from people who were trying to kill them with swords"
or ". . . who kept on trying to kill them with swords." In some languages,

especially those where swords are not known, it may be better to translate
". . . who were trying to kill them violently" or "kill them in war."

They were weak, but became strong could suggest recovery from illness,
but more probably it means that God turned weak people like Gideon and David
into powerful men of war. If so, **they were mighty in battle and defeated the
armies of foreigners** shows in greater detail in what way **they were weak, but
became strong.**

The statement **They were weak, but became strong** may be expressed by a
concessive clause, followed by a result clause; for example, "Even though they
were weak, they became strong."

They were mighty in battle may be expressed as "they were great fighters"
or "they were strong soldiers."

The phrase translated **defeated the armies** usually means "caused fortified
camps to fall," but translations agree with TEV in using the term **armies.** There is
no **the** before **armies** in the Greek text. There is no suggestion that Israel fought
only in self-defence, though ItCL speaks of "invaders."

11.35   Through faith women received their dead relatives raised back
to life.
            Others, refusing to accept freedom, died under torture in
order to be raised to a better life.

The translator has to decide whether verse 35a belongs with 32-34 (TEV and
GeCL), with 35b-38 (ItCL), or on its own. By beginning a new paragraph at 35b,
TEV links 35a with what goes before. The structure of the Greek sentence implies, on the contrary, that the women are the first examples in a new series,
which is continued by **Others** in verse 35b, and by **Some** and **others** in verse 36. It
is therefore probably better not to begin a new paragraph at verse 35b.

Through faith is repeated from verse 33, since the long Greek sentence is
divided.

Received is a grammatically active verb with a passive meaning. It makes
the transition from action in the previous examples to suffering in the examples
that follow. Similarly, **raised back to life** makes a transition from active to
passive signs of faith, from what people achieved (verses 32-34) to what they
suffered (verses 35b-38) because they trusted God.

Relatives is implied. **Received their dead relatives raised back to life** is a
more complex statement than might appear. It may need to be translated as
"women welcomed back those relatives who had died but who were then brought
back to life again" or ". . . caused to live again."

The three statements of 35b are closely connected: they **died under torture**
because they refused to accept freedom, since freedom was offered on condition
that they give up their Jewish faith; see 2 Maccabees 7.1,24.

It is good to make clear the relation between the three statements **refusing
to accept freedom, died under torture,** and **be raised to a better life.** The most
natural sequence is: they refused **to accept freedom;** as a result, they **died under**

torture; but they did this in order to **be raised to a better life**. The second statement is one of result, the third is one of purpose, and there is an implied contrast between them.

In a number of languages a verb meaning "to refuse" introduces direct discourse, and accordingly **Others, refusing to accept freedom** may be rendered as "Other people said, 'We will not accept freedom' " or ". . . 'We do not wish to be free.' " The following statement, **died under torture**, may then be rendered as "And so they died, because they were tortured to death."

The precise meaning of the verb translated **died under torture** is uncertain; Mft has "broken on the wheel"; Knox and GeCL have "the rack." **Died under torture** probably refers to being tied to a frame or block and beaten to death.

They refused **to accept freedom** on such a condition **in order to be raised to a better life**. The last phrase is literally "that they might obtain a better resurrection," as in KJV. The "better resurrection" is either resurrection **to a better life** than this one, as implied in TEV and RSV, or resurrection to a better state than their enemies. The second is more probable in view of 2 Maccabees 7.14; compare Daniel 12.2. The verb for "obtain" (KJV) is related to the verb used in verse 33 (received) and shows that the contrast between active and passive signs of faith is not complete.

11.36   Some were mocked and whipped, and others were put in chains
          and taken off to prison.

Most translations except TEV and perhaps FrCL make this verse refer to a single group of people who suffer two types of punishment: (a) mocking and whipping, which last for a short time; and (b) being chained and imprisoned, which are worse because they last for a longer period. Brc makes this explicit: "Some had to face mockery and the lash, and the even worse fate of chains and imprisonment"; NEB "Others, again, had to face jeers and flogging, even fetters and prison bars." However, the noun translated **mocked** may itself suggest torture, as in 2 Maccabees 7.7, where NEB has "brutality." If this is so, the verse as a whole will mean "Others, again, were tortured and whipped, and tied up and put in prison as well."

Put in chains and taken off to prison should not be taken to mean that they were chained only while on their way to prison. It was common to chain people while in prison (for example, Acts 28.20 and Col 4.18) or on trial (Acts 26.29).

The passive expressions in this verse may be readily changed into active ones, "People mocked and whipped some of those who trusted God, and others they put in chains and kept in prison."

11.37   They were stoned, they were sawn in two, they were killed by
          the sword. They went around clothed in skins of sheep or goats
          —poor, persecuted, and mistreated.

[281]

The speed of the sentence increases with a series of short phrases or single words. This effect should be kept in translation if possible.

Stoned implies that these victims were killed by stoning, not that they merely had a few stones thrown at them. Stoning was a recognized form of execution, and as in Acts 7.58-60, mobs sometimes took the law into their own hands. In order to indicate clearly that stoning resulted in death, it may be necessary to translate **They were stoned** as "They died because people hurled stones at them" or "Stones were thrown at them until they died."

Many manuscripts add "they were tempted" (or "tested") before or after **they were sawn in two**; there are other variants. These words are omitted by the UBS Greek New Testament and the text of most modern translations. It is difficult to say whether "they were tempted" was omitted because it is similar in Greek to the expression for **they were sawn in two**, or whether it was added by a scribe who misread the same word a second time. NEB's footnote "they were put to the question" is an old way of saying "they were tortured to make them confess."

They went around may be translated "they wandered about," indicating the nature of their persecution. The point is that they had no clothes in the usual sense of the word.

Clothed in skins of sheep or goats may be rendered as "their only clothes were the skins of sheep or goats." The reference here is to skin with the hair on it and probably untanned.

Poor: Brc's "they had not even the bare necessities of life" is too long and heavy but gives the exact meaning of the word used. "They were desperately poor" may be an appropriate equivalent.

Persecuted translates a word which suggests oppression, the opposite of freedom of action, or living in a confined space. "Under constraint" is an English equivalent, though not in common language.

The word for **mistreated** is a general term, but since it is an unusual word in the Bible (13.3; compare 11.25) and occurs here near the climax of the sentence, a stronger translation such as "tormented" would be possible. The word is common in this sense in ancient writings outside the New Testament.

11.38 **The world was not good enough for them! They wandered like refugees in the deserts and hills, living in caves and holes in the ground.**

At this tremendous climax the writer throws in a quiet aside, literally translated in RSV, which is easy to translate in itself, but difficult to relate to the rest of the passage. CLTs and other modern translations (NEB, NAB, Brc, TNT) make it a separate sentence and are thus in danger of making the rest of verse 38 an anticlimax. To link the first part of this verse with the rest is worse: JB "They were too good for the world and they went out to live in deserts and mountains and in caves and ravines." On the other hand, a common language translation must keep its sentences as short and light as possible. In some languages the best solution may be to link 38a with 37: ". . . poor, persecuted, tormented—people who were too good for this world." Though the Greek text says literally "the world was not worthy of them" or ". . . was not good enough for them," the meaning may often be expressed more effectively as "These people were too good for this world," or "These people were so good that the world was not worthy of them" or ". . . the world did not deserve to have such people."

Like refugees is not expressed in the Greek text but fits better here than does refugees in verse 13. This phrase is intended to summarize the wandering of such people and their living in caves and holes.

Rather than saying **They wandered like refugees in the deserts and hills**, it may be better to say "Like refugees they wandered about in desert regions and hilly country." The basic difference between **caves** and **holes** is that a cave would normally be entered horizontally, while a hole would be entered vertically. In other words, a hole would be below the surface of the ground, and a cave might simply be an opening in the hillside or cliff.

TEV	**11.39-40**	RSV

39 What a record all of these have won by their faith! Yet they did not receive what God had promised, 40 because God had decided on an even better plan for us. His purpose was that only in company with us would they be made perfect.

39 And all these, though well attested by their faith, did not receive what was promised, 40 since God had foreseen something better for us, that apart from us they should not be made perfect.

These verses typically combine a summary of earlier statements with an introduction of the next main theme. Verse 39 and part of verse 40 consist of a summary of earlier statements.

11.39   **What a record all of these have won by their faith! Yet they did not receive what God had promised,**

All of these renders a phrase used in verse 13, all these persons. Here it probably refers to the entire list of "heroes of faith," less probably to those mentioned in verses 32-38 only.

What a record . . . have won translates the verb used in verse 2 (see the comments) where TEV translated won God's approval. The verb probably has the same meaning in verse 39; FrCL "all these men were approved by God because of their faith"; so Brc and TNT. (TEV fourth edition's persons, verse 2, recognizes that women are included.) Other translations either (1) leave "God" implicit; NAB "all of these were approved because of their faith"; (2) refer to the witness or record of scripture; NEB "These also . . . are commemorated for their faith"; or (3) use a general phrase which could refer to the witness either of God or of scripture; Phps "won a glowing testimony to their faith"; so RSV and GeCL.

[283]

Verses 2 and 39 are closely linked, occurring at the beginning and end of the list of believers. The same meaning should therefore be given to the word for "witness" in both verses, either "approval of God," or more specifically, "the witness of God in scripture."

The reference in TEV to **a record** is intended to refer to the witness of scripture. The exclamation is effective in English, but it may be better in some languages to use a strong declarative statement, "Because they trusted God they certainly won his approval."

Did not receive what God had promised recalls verse 13 (see the comments). Here the writer uses a singular form, "the promise," and in verse 13 the plural, but the meaning is the same.

11.40   **because God had decided on an even better plan for us. His purpose was that only in company with us would they be made perfect.**

Verses 39-40 introduce the main theme of chapters 12 and 13. These chapters apply all that has been said to the situation of the readers and make a final appeal to them to stand firm and not abandon their faith. Verse 40 raises a number of related questions.

(a) What is the **"something better"** (RSV)? TEV, GeCL, and other translations add **plan,** which overlaps in meaning with "foreseen" (RSV), so TEV rightly uses the verb **decided on. Better** is a key word in this letter, which is often concerned with comparisons between the situations before and after the coming of Jesus to earth. It sometimes has the general meaning "greater, more important," as in 1.4 and 7.7. More often it refers to the "better covenant" (7.22 and 8.6; compare 12.24), or to the "better hope" (7.19), "sacrifices" (9.23), "possessions" (10.34), "country" (11.16), and "resurrection" (11.35), which are associated with this "better covenant" of 7.22 and 8.6. Here the writer is thinking generally of these better gifts. It would therefore be too general to translate "something better" as "better covenant"; the "something better" is "being made perfect."

(b) How are these gifts "better"? Better than what? Some people have thought that the religious experience of Christians is "better" than that of people who lived before Christ. This, though perhaps true in itself, does not seem to make the best sense of this verse. What God has "prepared" **for us,** and in the end for Old Testament believers also (verse 40b), is better than the gifts or blessings which people received in Old Testament times. The new covenant is better than the old because the actual fulfillment of God's purpose is something greater or better than the promise that it would be fulfilled. In other words, what Christians and Old Testament believers receive through Christ is what Israel was promised in Old Testament times but never received.

(c) By starting a new sentence with **his purpose was,** TEV makes the text not only clearer but also more precise. God's deciding on **an even better plan for us** is only part of the means of achieving **his purpose . . . that only in company with us would they be made perfect.** In other words, what happens to **us** is one condition, but not the only one, for the fulfillment of God's **purpose.**

Verse 40b is logically related to verse 39b rather than to verse 40a. The sequence of thought may be set out as follows:

    (a) God promised something to Old Testament believers. (39b)

    (b) They did not receive it then. (39b)

    (c) God had decided on something better (than promises not yet fulfilled). (40a)

    (d) This "something better" is for both Old Testament believers and "us." (40a, b)

    (e) This "something better" is the fulfillment of God's promises by making them and us perfect together. (40b)

    (f) All this is God's purpose. (40a)

The verse can thus be restructured as follows: "Yet they did not receive what God had promised (or, God did not give to them what he had promised) because God has a better plan not only for them, but also for us."

Even better recalls verse 16. **Plan** is implicit. The two statements in verses 39 and 40 are the converse of one another: the "better thing" which the Old Testament heroes longed for is intended for "us" to enjoy "together with them."[1]

God had decided on an even better plan for us may be rendered as "God decided that he would plan something which would be even better for us."

In some languages it may be difficult to speak of **His purpose,** and then immediately after, of the content of what he purposed. This final statement may be rendered as "What God desired was that they should be made perfect, but only in company with us," or ". . . but only along with us," or ". . . only when we also are made perfect."

On **made perfect,** see comments on 2.10. This is the writer's favorite word for describing the final aim or end of salvation. It is generally related to "the Kingdom of God" in Mark and Luke, "the Kingdom of heaven" in Matthew, and "eternal life" in John. **Perfect** may be expressed as "to be as one should be" or "to be completely what God wants us to be."

---

[1] Michel writes on this passage: " 'something better' is neither something better than the men of old obtained, nor something better than the Christian community has yet received. 'Something better' is much more, absolutely, the expression of what goes beyond earthly well-being." In other words, the expression is comparative in grammatical form but not in meaning. If so, translators may choose some such absolute expression as "a perfect plan" or "God's own plan."

Chapter 12

God Our Father

1 As for us, we have this large crowd of witnesses around us. So then, let us rid ourselves of everything that gets in the way, and of the sin which holds on to us so tightly, and let us run with determination the race that lies before us. 2 Let us keep our eyes fixed on Jesus, on whom our faith depends from beginning to end. He did not give up because of the cross! On the contrary, because of the joy that was waiting for him, he thought nothing of the disgrace of dying on the cross, and he is now seated at the right side of God's throne.

3 Think of what he went through; how he put up with so much hatred from sinners! So do not let yourselves become discouraged and give up. 4 For in your struggle against sin you have not yet had to resist to the point of being killed. 5 Have you forgotten the encouraging words which God speaks to you as his sons?

"My son, pay attention when the
    Lord corrects you,
and do not be discouraged when
    he rebukes you.
6   Because the Lord corrects
      everyone he loves,
and punishes everyone he
      accepts as a son."

7 Endure what you suffer as being a father's punishment; your suffering shows that God is treating you as his sons. Was there ever a son who was not punished by his father? 8 If you are not

1 Therefore, since we are surrounded by so great a cloud of witnesses, let us also lay aside every weight, and sin which clings so closely, and let us run with perseverance the race that is set before us, 2 looking to Jesus the pioneer and perfecter of our faith, who for the joy that was set before him endured the cross, despising the shame, and is seated at the right hand of the throne of God.

3 Consider him who endured from sinners such hostility against himself, so that you may not grow weary or fainthearted. 4 In your struggle against sin you have not yet resisted to the point of shedding your blood. 5 And have you forgotten the exhortation which addresses you as sons?—

"My son, do not regard lightly the
    discipline of the Lord,
nor lose courage when you are
    punished by him.
6   For the Lord disciplines him whom
      he loves,
and chastises every son whom he
      receives."

7 It is for discipline that you have to endure. God is treating you as sons; for what son is there whom his father does not discipline? 8 If you are left without discipline, in which all have participated, then you are illegitimate children and not sons. 9 Besides this, we have had earthly fathers to discipline us and we respected them. Shall we not much more be subject to the Father of spirits

punished, as all his sons are, it means you are not real sons, but bastards. 9 In the case of our human fathers, they punished us and we respected them. How much more, then, should we submit to our spiritual Father and live! 10 Our human fathers punished us for a short time, as it seemed right to them; but God does it for our own good, so that we may share his holiness. 11 When we are punished, it seems to us at the time something to make us sad, not glad. Later, however, those who have been disciplined by such punishment reap the peaceful reward of a righteous life.

and live? 10 For they disciplined us for a short time at their pleasure, but he disciplines us for our good, that we may share his holiness. 11 For the moment all discipline seems painful rather than pleasant; later it yields the peaceful fruit of righteousness to those who have been trained by it.

Some links with this section were mentioned in the comments on 10.19-39; others are mentioned in the comments that follow this section. The writer begins to turn from Old Testament history to his readers' situation. In this section he refers to parental discipline in order to illustrate one aspect of Christians' life as "God's children."

The section heading in TEV, **God Our Father**, picks up a theme of verses 7-11 and seems to be a fitting heading for this section.

<u>12.1</u>   **As for us, we have this large crowd of witnesses around us. So then, let us rid ourselves of everything that gets in the way, and of the sin which holds on to us so tightly, and let us run with determination the race that lies before us.**

Verses 1-2 form a single sentence in the Greek. Grammatically, the main verb is the verb for **let us run.** In addition there are three dependent clauses, the verbs of which are rendered (1) **we have**, literally "having," (2) **rid ourselves of**, literally "ridding ourselves of" or "laying aside," and (3) **let us keep our eyes fixed**, literally "looking steadily at."

As for us translates an emphatic "We also," meaning we as well as the Old Testament characters mentioned in chapter 11.

"**Cloud**" (RSV and others) renders a common metaphor for "a large number of people." Many modern translations either turn it into a simile, "like a cloud" (GeCL, NEB), or use a nonfigurative expression (TEV, **crowd**; DuCL "so many"; Mft "host"; Phps "serried ranks").

Witnesses: a "witness," at least in the Bible, is not just a passive "spectator" (Brc) but an active "witness to faith" (DuCL, NEB, TNT), more specifically "people who have demonstrated their faith" (SpCL). The thought is that the Old Testament heroes are watching how the writer of Hebrews and his readers "run their race" in the Christian life, since their own salvation is linked with that of Christians (11.40). This **large crowd of witnesses** consists of the heroes of faith recorded in chapter 11.

We have this large crowd of witnesses around us may be expressed as "this large crowd of those who have witnessed to their faith are around us" or ". . . are, as it were, close by around us."

The central part of this verse, from **So then** to **so tightly**, has been understood in rather different ways by translators and commentators. It is best to look first at the individual Greek words, and then at the relations between them:

> RSV's "**Therefore**" is a strong word which TEV fourth edition translates as **So then**.
>
> **Rid ourselves** may have either the general meaning "throw off, get rid of," or the narrower idea of "taking off clothes."
>
> **Everything that gets in the way** is literally "every impediment" or "encumbrance." This is an unusual Greek word which partly overlaps in meaning with the more common biblical metaphor of the "stumbling-block." The idea of "**weight**" (RSV) does not seem prominent here, though in some texts outside the Bible the Greek word is used of flesh "weighing down" the spirit.
>
> **Sin** translates the common word used in 1.3 and many other places. In Hebrews, "sin" is often thought of as a burden of guilt which can only be removed by sacrifice. DuCL translates "burden of sin." Despite the article **the**, nothing in the context suggests that the writer is thinking of any particular kind of sin or sinful act. Some English translations therefore omit **the**: Mft "strip off sin"; NAB "every encumbrance of sin"; so NEB and TNT. Knox's "the sinful habit that clings so closely" is too narrow. In many languages there will be no separate word corresponding to **the** in English, but there will be other ways of indicating old information.
>
> In the phrase **which holds on to us so tightly**, **to us** is implied. A few manuscripts have "which so easily distracts us"; see NEB note. Most translations agree generally with TEV. Brc makes the metaphor more explicit by turning it into a simile: "We must therefore, as an athlete strips for action, strip off every encumbrance and the sin which clings to us . . . ." NEB's text, "every sin to which we cling," is grammatically possible but perhaps does not fit the context so well.

What is the relation between the rare word meaning "impediment," translated **that gets in the way**, and the common word for **sin**? The writer may be thinking of things which, though not sinful in themselves, can "get in our way" by preventing us from "keeping our eyes fixed on Jesus." However, it seems better not to contrast "impediment" and **sin**, but to take **sin** as explaining or widening the meaning of "impediment." If so, it is better to restructure these phrases within the clause, as in DuCL "get rid of every burden of sin which so easily hinders us"; NAB "every encumbrance of sin which clings to us." GeCL distinguishes "impediment" and **sin,** but shows that they are connected: "free ourselves from everything which weighs us down, especially from sin, which so easily clings to us." **Sin** renders a more general word than "impediment," but the meaning of "impediment" is widened in Greek by the addition of "every."

A literal rendering of **let us rid ourselves of everything that gets in the way** causes problems. It might suggest that one is justified in eliminating anything which hinders a person's drive for success or which might limit a person's ambition. This exhortation is not an excuse for aggression, and therefore it may be better to indicate clearly the relationship between **everything that gets in the way** and **the sin which holds on to us so tightly.** In fact, it may be better to render **everything that gets in the way** as "everything that keeps us from doing what we should." One may translate the central part of verse 1 as "Therefore let us get rid of everything which keeps us from doing what we should, that is, the sin which clings so tightly to us." In some languages, however, it may be impossible to speak of sin clinging to a person. One can often speak of "the sin which we love so much."

The words for **run** (verse 1) and paths (verse 13) are related in Greek. **With determination** is emphasized in the Greek by its position, and in TEV by the choice of words. In Romans 8.25 the same expression is somewhat undertranslated as with patience; similarly in Hebrews 10.36. In 10.32 the related verb is expanded to were not defeated. The idea is that of enduring to the end.

The word translated **race** may also mean "struggle," but the meaning **race** is required here because of **run**; see comment on verse 4. The idea of life as an athletic contest is quite common, both in and outside the Bible (see 10.32). Some translations emphasize the metaphor implied in the words **that lies before us,** as in Knox, NEB, DuCL "the race for which we are entered." Phps' "the race that we have to run," like TEV, gives the figure in a more simple form. **Before** refers to future time rather than to a place ahead of us.

It may be necessary to mark the final part of this verse as being figurative. This may be done by adding an expression which indicates that this is a simile; for example, "let us, as it were, run with determination."

With determination can sometimes be expressed as "let us decide in our hearts" or "let us tell our hearts." Instead of "running the race," it is often necessary to say "to run the path" or "to run the course." Accordingly, **the race that lies before us** may be "the course ahead of us which we must take" or "the path which we must follow in the future." Or it may be necessary to avoid the figure of speech and to say "let us be determined to act as we should in the life that we now will have."

The idea that God has set us to run the race is not emphasized here. Verses 3-4 speak of human elements in the "struggle."

12.2   **Let us keep our eyes fixed on Jesus, on whom our faith depends from beginning to end. He did not give up because of the cross! On the contrary, because of the joy that was waiting for him, he thought nothing of the disgrace of dying on the cross, and he is now seated at the right side of God's throne.**

Let us keep our eyes fixed on Jesus may be expressed as "Let us keep looking at Jesus," or in a figurative sense "Let us keep looking at Jesus, so to speak." However, it may not be possible to use this type of figure, since Jesus was not in actual view, and therefore one must often translate "Let us keep constantly thinking about Jesus."

On whom our faith depends from beginning to end is literally "the pioneer and perfecter of the faith." Translations vary in their understanding of the Greek for "pioneer and perfecter." For the thought, compare Colossians 1.18 and Revelation 1.17; 2.8; 22.13. On "pioneer," see comments on For Jesus is the one . . . in 2.10. The word "perfecter" is related to words used in 11.40 (perfect) and many other places, but the writer seems to have invented this particular Greek term. The meaning is best seen in contrast to 4.8; Jesus, unlike Joshua, has the power to bring his people to the end of their journey. It may be necessary in translation to add **our** before **faith,** but **our** is not expressed here in the Greek text, which may have a wider meaning for **faith,** as in 11.1. If "pioneer" and "perfecter" are primarily expressions of time ("beginner" and "ender"), Jesus is thought of here as the supreme *example* of faith in God. On the other hand, "pioneer" and "perfecter" may refer to Jesus as the *source* of other people's faith in God, and as the one who brings that faith to full maturity. "Our" may be implied if Jesus is the source but not if he is the example. In the rest of the verse it is Jesus's example which is emphasized, but verse 3b makes a link between what Jesus suffered and the readers' need to hold on to their faith. Most translations except RSV and Mft ("the pioneer and perfection of faith") choose the second meaning, Jesus as the source of faith. FrCL follows TEV, and NEB is similar. GeCL has "he has opened to us the way of trust and also brings us to the goal." An additional argument in favor of the second meaning is that it includes the first.

For many translators it is easier to follow the somewhat figurative expressions of "pioneer and perfecter of the faith," since this may be expressed as "the one who goes ahead of us and causes our faith in God to be what it should be" or ". . . and makes perfect our confidence in God," or "the one who makes it possible for us to trust in God, and also to keep on trusting in him." The rendering in TEV, **on whom our faith depends from beginning to end,** is somewhat more abstract in meaning and therefore more difficult to reproduce in other languages. One can, however, translate **on whom our faith depends from beginning to end** as "our confidence in God has always been and will always be because of Jesus," or "Jesus is the one who causes us to have confidence in God. This is always true, even from the very beginning of the time when we began to trust God." There is always some difficulty in the use of **end,** since this might imply that faith would come to an end sometime during a person's life.

The rest of this verse recalls both 2.9 and 12.1. RSV's **set before him** renders the same verb as "set before us" in verse 1, and "endured" is related to "perseverance" in verse 1. These expressions should be translated similarly. JB misleadingly has "the race we have started" in verse 1, and "the joy which was still in the future" in verse 2. The implied message is that there are difficult times ahead for the readers, as there were for Jesus, but that if they hold on to their faith they will share the joy of his victory.

Because of the cross is implied. The meaning is that Jesus held on to his purpose despite the suffering of the cross. The sentence **He did not give up because of the cross** may be rendered as "He did not give up just because he had to die on a cross."

The phrase **On the contrary** may be expressed emphatically as "No, indeed."

Because of the joy that was waiting for him may be expressed as "because of the joy which he would later have" or ". . . which would later be his," or "because of the fact that later he would have joy." Some restructuring of the TEV rendering is often almost obligatory, since in many languages it is impossible to speak of joy "waiting" for anyone.

Thought nothing of or "disregarded" (so JB) is better here than "despised," since the Greek word is used here in a positive sense rather than in the usual negative sense. **He thought nothing of** may be best expressed as "he refused to think about." In some languages **he thought nothing of the disgrace of dying on the cross** may need to be radically restructured; for example, "people thought that dying on a cross was a terrible disgrace but Jesus didn't think so."

Disgrace includes not only the abuse which was directed against Jesus on the cross, but the disgrace of the punishment itself compared, for example, with the honorable death of being beheaded. Crucifixion was a Roman punishment. But Galatians 3.13 identifies it with hanging from a tree (Deut 21.23), which was the Old Testament form of execution and was believed to bring God's curse on the land. **Dying on the cross** brings out the implication of the text, which is literally "a cross." SpCL does so more strongly: "the shame of this kind of death."

On **seated at the right side of God's throne** see comments on 1.3; 8.1; 10.12. Here the tense of the verb, changed from Psalm 110.1, includes both past and present. TEV's **now seated** brings out the present element, leaving implicit the past event of sitting down on God's right side, which was expressed in 1.3 and elsewhere.

In some parts of the world it is necessary to have a footnote, here or on 1.3, to indicate that from the biblical viewpoint **the right side** was the side of honor. In some societies the left side is the preferred side.

12.3   **Think of what he went through; how he put up with so much hatred from sinners! So do not let yourselves become discouraged and give up.**

KJV's "For" translates a word which indicates that verse 3 partly repeats something already said, like the English "Yes, think of what he went through . . . ." This word is often omitted in translation.

Think of includes the idea of comparing, that is, comparing Christ's sufferings with the readers' own less severe persecutions. Brc brings this out precisely, if rather heavily: "The way to avoid the failure of your nerve and heart is to compare your situation with the situation of him who met the opposition of sinners with such constancy and courage."

What he went through and **put up with** translate a single verb, related to determination in verse 1 and not give up in verse 2. The repetition helps to make this passage the strongest call for action in Hebrews. FrCL is simpler here: "Think of him, of the way in which he put up with such opposition on the part of (from) sinners."

It is rare that one can translate literally **Think of what he went through,** since this might very well be interpreted as suggesting that Jesus passed through some kind of structure or dwelling. A more satisfactory rendering is often "Consider how much he suffered."

Hatred includes opposition both of word and deed, especially the latter in this context. It may be difficult to speak of "putting up with hatred," for what is endured is not so much the hatred as what people do who hate. Therefore, **how he put up with so much hatred from sinners** may be expressed as "consider how much he endured from sinners who hated him so much" or "think about how much those sinners who hated him caused him to suffer."[1]

Yourselves is an idiomatic translation of the Greek for "your souls" (see 4.12). KJV has "in your minds," but the whole personality is involved.

Give up renders the same verb, with the same meaning, which is translated be discouraged in verse 5. KJV has "faint" in both places.

So do not let yourselves become discouraged may be expressed as "Therefore, don't ever lose your courage" or "don't let yourselves feel like giving up." In some languages **give up** may be effectively rendered as "stop trusting God."

12.4 **For in your struggle against sin you have not yet had to resist to the point of being killed.**

Struggle renders a verb related to race in verse 1, but here the meaning is wider; a real battle, rather than an athletic competition, is probably now in the writer's mind.

Against sin does not simply mean "against evil impulses within your own hearts"; it means essentially the same as "sinful men" in verse 3. **Sin** is now almost personified. This could be brought out by some such translation as "your struggle against the forces of sin" or even ". . . forces of evil." However, it may not always be possible to speak of **sin** as a force which can initiate action or carry out some campaign of opposition. For many languages such happenings can only be attributed directly to people who sin. The struggle which is involved here is primarily a defensive struggle, as suggested by the rendering **resist**. Therefore **in your struggle against sin** may be expressed in some languages as "in defending yourself against sinners" or "in defending yourself when sinners attack you."

---

[1] The UBS Greek text ("D" rating) corresponds to RSV's "against himself," which is not especially emphasized, and which TEV and other CLTs omit. The weight of manuscript evidence is on the side of the difficult reading "against themselves," similar in meaning to "on their own account" in 6.6. This may be explained as an allusion to Numbers 16.38 (17.3 in the Septuagint), where Korah, Dathan, and Abiram are said to have sinned "in their own souls."

The word for **resist** is not used anywhere else in the New Testament; in secular writings it has the meaning of passive "holding out" rather than that of active aggression.

To the point of being killed gives the meaning of KJV's literal "unto blood." "Blood" in the Bible often has the meaning of violent death. In this verse there is no idea of sacrifice. In 2 Maccabees 13.14 NEB translates the same phrase "to the death." **You have not yet had to resist to the point of being killed** may be rendered as "you have not yet had to endure to the point where people killed you."

12.5-6   **Have you forgotten the encouraging words which God speaks to you as his sons?**
           "My son, pay attention when the Lord corrects you,
              and do not be discouraged when he rebukes you.
       6 Because the Lord corrects everyone he loves,
              and punishes everyone he accepts as a son."

See Proverbs 3.11-12. Hebrews as usual follows the Septuagint, which is different from the Hebrew.

RSV's **"And"** is omitted by most modern translations, since there is no close connection between verses 4 and 5. It probably has the meaning "What is more," introducing a new point.

Have you forgotten could be translated "You have forgotten" (NEB, NAB, TOB, and older translations). This would make good sense if verse 4 were blaming the readers, suggesting that if they had been faithful some of them would have suffered martyrdom. However, there seems to be no basis for this, so it is best to translate verse 5a as a question. **Forgotten** renders an unusual and strong word. In order to emphasize the significance of the term **forgotten,** it may be possible to use some such expression as "Have you disregarded?" or "Have you set aside in your thinking?" If **Have you forgotten** is understood as a rhetorical question, it may be translated, "Don't forget . . ." or "I am sure you have not forgotten . . . ."

The moral of these verses is the need to endure God's discipline even when it is painful. TNT's "comfort," and perhaps even TEV's **encouraging,** are probably too weak. The Greek includes the idea of a call to action (3.13; 6.18; and especially 13.22), which Brc conveys by "Have you forgotten that challenging passage of scripture . . . ?" The word for **encouraging** is not related to the word translated become discouraged in verse 3 and **be discouraged** here. **The encouraging words** may be rendered as "words which give you courage." But a more satisfactory equivalent may be "words which cause you to have confidence" or "words which fill your hearts with confidence."

As a comparison with RSV shows, **God** is implied. The meaning may also be "scripture encourages you" or ". . . challenges you."[2]

RSV's **"the exhortation which addresses you . . ."** implies that there is someone who makes the exhortation. Most modern translations make it explicit that the encouraging words come either from God (TEV and most CLTs, Knox), from scripture (NEB, Brc, TNT, JB), or from both (SpCL "Have you forgotten what God advises you as his sons? He says thus in Scripture . . ."). The writer did not distinguish sharply between a word of God and a word of scripture. However, it is stylistically better to make "scripture" the subject of "encourage," since God is referred to in the third person in the quotation.

The Old Testament setting is that of an older man addressing a younger man as his **son.** The following verses in Hebrew suggest that the writer understands the passage in the same way. That is, he understands the quotation as being a message from God in a broad sense, like the rest of the Old Testament, but does not think that God is the speaker in the quotation. If so, it becomes easier to understand why God should be spoken of in the third person as **the Lord.** If this interpretation is followed, certain translation problems are legitimately avoided. Otherwise, if God is understood as the speaker in the quotation, it may be necessary in translation to change third person references to the first person; for example, "when I correct you" for **when the Lord corrects you.**

In the introduction to the quotation, **as his sons,** the writer indicates what for his purpose is its key word, namely **sons.** He will comment on this word in verses 7-11. The word **sons** is taken from **son** in the quotation, but there is no emphasis on maleness, and it may be translated "children." **As** is often ambiguous in English. Here it means "in your capacity as sons," or more simply "because you are sons," not "like sons."

The quotation is in poetry form, and there is therefore some parallelism, even in the Septuagint, between the two halves of each couplet.

Pay attention is a positive equivalent of RSV's more literal "**do not regard lightly.**" There is a clear parallel between **corrects** and **rebukes.**

The Greek noun translated **corrects** has a range of meanings which includes "upbringing," "training," "instruction," "discipline," and "punishment." It includes practically everything involved in bringing up a child. "Punishment" is no doubt included, but "punishes" here could misleadingly suggest that the readers were suffering because God was punishing them for their sins, and this idea is not supported by the context. GeCL has "accept it, my son, when the Lord treats you hard" and continues in verse 6 "for whom the Lord loves, he brings up with strictness."

Pay attention when the Lord corrects you may be rendered as "pay close attention when the Lord shows you that you are wrong" or ". . . makes you realize that you have done wrong."

It is sometimes possible to render **corrects** as "makes you recognize when you have done wrong." This may imply some degree of punishment. In fact, it may be possible to translate "punishes you in order to make you realize that you have done wrong."

---

[2] In this and similar places (for example, verse 12) ItCL has "the *Bible says," the asterisk referring to a glossary note which explains that in the New Testament, the word refers to the Old Testament. This avoids the church-language term "scripture" but goes against current Christian usage, in which "the Bible" usually includes both Testaments. Jews, however, commonly use the expression "the Bible" in speaking of the Old Testament.

Some commentators think **corrects** has the meaning of "educate" in verse 5, and "discipline" or "punish" in verse 6, but this is unlikely. Problems of translation will arise in cultures which have a different idea of what is involved in bringing up a child. This is to some extent the case in modern Western society, which would perhaps give a less prominent place to "punishment" within the family. This, however, is part of the cultural strangeness of any ancient text, which the translator should not try to remove.

The word for **rebukes** sometimes includes the idea of "correction" or even "punishment"; compare Revelation 3.19.

And do not be discouraged when he rebukes you may be translated as "and do not feel like giving up when he criticizes you" or even ". . . scolds you."

Corrects in verse 6 renders the verbal equivalent of the Greek noun translated corrects in verse 5 (see the comments).

Everyone in verse 6a is implied; NEB "those whom he loves"; **everyone** in verse 6b, on the other hand, is literally "every son."

Punishes is literally "whips" (TNT); Phps has "scourgeth"; NEB "lays the rod on." The writer of Hebrews probably understood the word in this harsh, literal meaning, since he avoids repeating it in his comments.

TEV brings out better than RSV the connection between **accepts** and **as a son.**

12.7   **Endure what you suffer as being a father's punishment; your suffering shows that God is treating you as his sons. Was there ever a son who was not punished by his father?**

This verse consists of three short statements: **Endure . . . your suffering shows . . . Was there ever . . . ?** The second statement expands part of the meaning of the first, and the third draws a conclusion from the second. Earlier editions of TEV had "because your suffering . . . ," understanding the second statement as giving a reason for the first, but this is not necessary. The third statement has the form of a rhetorical question, which Phps turns into a strong negative statement: "No true son ever grows up uncorrected by his father." TEV fourth edition, which changed "punishes" into **corrects** in verses 5 and 6a, did not do the same in verses 7-10, where the same Greek words are used.

On **Endure,** see verses 1-3. The indicative "You endure" is a possible but unlikely translation.

What you suffer is implied. **As being** is stronger than FrCL's "bear your sufferings as if they were the punishment of a father." Both the discipline and God's fatherhood are real, as the next part of the verse shows. Other CLTs bring out the same meaning in different words: DuCL "That is part of your upbringing: bear it in that way . . ."; GeCL: "Bear the blows (patiently). God is treating you as his sons." KJV's "If ye endure chastening" is based on inferior manuscripts.

A father's is not in the Greek text but is added in order to soften **punishment** and to bring out the wider idea of upbringing by a parent.

The statement **Endure what you suffer as being a father's punishment** leaves implicit the son's reaction to the father's action, or his understanding of its nature and purpose. Therefore it may be necessary to translate the first part of verse 7 as "Consider the suffering that you endure as being like the way in which a son suffers because of the way his father punishes him" or ". . . like the way in which a father punishes his son to show him that he has done wrong."

In the statement **your suffering shows that God is treating you as his sons,** it is implied that the readers should draw a certain conclusion from the way in which God is treating them. The statement may therefore be translated as "if you suffer, then you know that God is treating you as his sons." But it would be more satisfactory to translate "the fact that you are suffering shows that God is treating you as his sons" or ". . . is dealing with you just as though you are his sons."

The connection between the two sentences of verse 7 in TEV is shown by the repetition **sons . . . son;** RSV's **"for"** is therefore omitted. **Was there ever a son** may also be translated "Who, having the status of a son . . . ?" The difference of meaning is slight. In either case, the rhetorical question is equivalent to a strong double negative statement, "There is no son whose father does not punish him," which ItCL simplifies to the positive: "In fact, it is normal that a son be corrected by his father." Other possible forms of the statement are "there never was a son who was not punished by his father" or "There never were sons who were not corrected by their fathers."

12.8 **If you are not punished, as all his sons are, it means you are not real sons, but bastards.**

This verse brings out a further implication of the last sentence and confirms that TEV was right to translate <u>accepts as a son</u> in verse 6.

The introduction of the comparative clause **as all his sons are** between the conditional clause and the main clause of this verse may pose problems in translation. It may be better to separate the comparative clause **as all his sons are** and make it an independent and initial statement; for example, "God punishes all his sons. Therefore, if you are not punished it means you are not his sons but someone else's sons." It is also possible to use "children" in place of **sons,** as mentioned in the comments on verse 5.

But bastards: the Greek puts this positive statement first, before the negative **not real sons,** and this may be more natural in some other languages too. **Real** and **it means** are implied. The repeated **are** suggests that the writer is thinking of real cases, perhaps of some of his readers who are now suffering the correction of which he speaks. However, the verse is introduced by a Greek word for **If,** so GeCL's translation is possible: "God has brought up all his children in this way. If it were different with you, then you would not be his legitimate children."

It may be necessary to indicate that **bastards** is to be understood in a figurative sense. Otherwise a reader might assume that all persons who are not sons of God are literally **bastards,** that is to say, "born out of wedlock." Therefore **but bastards** may be expressed as a simile instead of a metaphor; for example, "but, on the contrary, you are like bastards."

12.9 **In the case of our human fathers, they punished us and we respected them. How much more, then, should we submit to our spiritual Father and live!**

The writer now moves on to speak of human fathers in verses 9-10, coming back to the main theme in verse 11. Verses 9-10 consist of two "how much more" comparisons, as, for example, in 9.14.

RSV's **"Besides this"** marks the transition; NEB and Brc "Again"; Phps "After all"; other CLTs and TNT omit. Human or "earthly" **fathers** gives the meaning of KJV and Mft's literal "fathers of our flesh." On "flesh," see comments on 2.14. There is a clear contrast with God as **spiritual Father**, so **human** or its equivalent should not be omitted, as Phps does.

It may be possible to render **In the case of our human fathers** as "Think about our human fathers." But in some languages it may seem strange to talk about "human fathers." One can talk about "our fathers here on earth," but it may be more satisfactory to say "Consider what our own fathers did to us; they punished us and we honored them" or ". . . respected them."

Respected translates a word which includes also the meaning of **submit.** Two different words are used, more for the sake of variety than to express different ideas. However, the word for submit is stronger.

Our spiritual Father is also the translation of NEB, JB, TNT. Brc "a spiritual Father"; FrCL and SpCl "our heavenly Father"; GeCL "our divine Father"; DuCL "God who is our Father in a higher sense." The phrase is literally "**the Father of spirits,**" as in RSV. "Our" is expressed in the previous phrase, literally "fathers of our flesh," meaning human fathers, and is probably implied in "the Father of spirits" also, as reflected in TEV and also Mft, "Father of our spirits." Translators should make sure that the difference between **father** and **Father** is clear even when the passage is read aloud. The simplest way of doing this is by using adjectives such as "human" and "spiritual." It may be difficult in translation to speak of **our spiritual Father**, since this might turn out to mean nothing more than "our Father who is a spirit." In that case "our Father in heaven" or even "God who is our Father in heaven" may be used instead.

How much more . . . !: it may be convenient to use an emphatic statement rather than an exclamation, since the exclamation suggests a comparison which may require expansion. Accordingly, the first part of the second sentence of this verse may be rendered as "Therefore we should certainly submit to the punishment that our Father in heaven gives us" or ". . . causes us to experience."

And live implies "and therefore live"; NEB "and so attain life"; Knox and TOB "and draw life from him"; ItCL "have life." Phps (similarly Brc) has "and learn how to live," which fits in well with the idea of bringing up children. However, the writer may be thinking of Exodus 20.12 . . . that you may live a long time in the land; therefore he may be concerned, not only with the initial training of children, but with a whole way of life which God can bless with prosperity. Alternatively, the meaning may be that if the readers do what the writer recommends, they will survive the final test and receive the gift of eternal life. Verses 10 and 11b suggest that the writer is more concerned about a good relationship with God than with rules of behavior.

[297]

12.10   Our human fathers punished us for a short time, as it seemed
right to them; but God does it for our own good, so that we
may share his holiness.

The contrast betwen human fathers and the heavenly Father is now expanded a little.

Our human fathers may be expressed as "Our own fathers" or "Our fathers on earth," as in verse 9.

Punished is once more the word translated corrects in verse 6.

For a short time in the Greek is literally an understatement, "for a few days," as in KJV and ItCL; Phps, unnecessarily, "during the brief days of childhood." This is a usual expression of time, found also in James 4.14. It is also possible but less likely that purpose may be implied, as in NAB's "to prepare us for the short span of mortal life," see Genesis 47.9 and Psalm 109.8. **For a short time** may be rendered as "for the short time that we were children" or "for the limited time while we were still children."

As it seemed right to them: RSV's "at their pleasure" modifies KJV's "after their own pleasure," which sounds cruel to a speaker of modern English. The writer and his readers knew that the father, especially under Roman law, had almost absolute power over his children, and was therefore considered to be the final judge of how best to bring them up. **As it seemed right to them** may be rendered "as they thought it was best" or "as they thought they should punish us."

But God does it: RSV's "he" is **God,** and most modern translations say so. The statement **but God does it for our own good** may be rendered as "but when God punishes us, it is for our own good" or ". . . it is in order to help us."

So that we may share his holiness expands **for our own good** and makes it more specific. **Holiness,** rather surprisingly, translates a Greek word not used anywhere else in the New Testament, except in some manuscripts of 2 Corinthians 1.12. It means primarily, not good conduct, but what makes God different from human beings. **Share his holiness** therefore means practically the same as share the divine nature in 2 Peter 1.4, though the Greek is different. ItCL and SpCL bring this out by "to make us holy as he is holy"; GeCL, more precisely, "that we may participate in his perfection." In some languages, however, the term "holy," when it is applied to individuals, means "dedicated to God" or "consecrated to God." In such cases it would be difficult to use the same term for "holy" in reference both to people and to God himself. An equivalent might be "so that we might be like God" or ". . . be in a measure like God."

12.11   When we are punished, it seems to us at the time something to
make us sad, not glad. Later, however, those who have been
disciplined by such punishment reap the peaceful reward of a
righteous life.

This verse contains another contrast. The first part of it was a common saying, almost a proverb, in popular moral teaching of New Testament times.

The structure of this verse emphasizes the contrast between **at the time** and **Later**. **Later** may also mean "Last of all," or "In the end," as in Matthew 21.37. This sense is suggested by references to the "last times" at the end of this verse and in the wider context.

The phrase rendered **sad, not glad** sounds a little heavy in the original as well as in translation. The writer is thinking back to the joy mentioned in verse 2 and uses the same Greek word here.

As RSV shows, the verse is a contrast between the effect of discipline **at the time** and **later**. TEV expands the first part of the contrast, expressing "**all discipline**" (RSV) as **When we are punished.** "Whenever" would have been closer to the meaning of the Greek. If TEV is taken as base for renderings in other languages, there may be some repetition in the reference to time. If so, the first sentence may be translated as "Whenever we are punished it seems to us to be something to make us glad," deleting **at the time.**

Since the expression **it seems to us** involves some kind of reasoning or thought, it may be better to restructure the statement as "When we are punished, we regard it as making us sad and certainly not glad" or ". . . happy."

The second half of this verse (from **Later, however**) is written in a particularly impressive Greek literary style. This suggests that it is intended as a summary and conclusion of the section. This is confirmed by "Therefore" in verse 12 (RSV) and by the change from argument to direct imperatives. CLTs (but not the UBS Greek New Testament or TOB) therefore begin a new section at verse 12 rather than at verse 14.

Disciplined in 5.14 was translated through practice are able (see the comments). The idea of athletic training may be carried over from the beginning of the chapter; several translations have "trained."

Those who have been disciplined by such punishment may be expressed as "those whom God has punished in order to show them what they have done wrong" or "those who have been corrected by the way in which God has punished them." It may be essential to indicate that this is punishment which comes from God, especially in view of the explicit reference to God in verse 10.

RSV suggests some confusion in this verse between the metaphors of athletic training and harvesting. The Greek for **reap** is in fact a dead metaphor meaning "to receive something in return" and may be translated in a nonfigurative way.

Peaceful reward is a rather strange expression. Several translations separate "peace" from **reward** and link it with **a righteous life**, literally "righteousness," as in 1.9: DuCL "the peace which comes from a righteous life"; FrCL "peace associated with a just life"; TNT "lives of peace and goodness." These translations present a rather static view of the "good life" as one in which relationships with God and other people are what they should be. It is true that "peace" in the Bible implies total well-being; see 7.2; 13.21. However, in biblical thought, "peace," like "righteousness," involves action, and this aspect is brought out by GeCL: "But later it appears, to all who have been brought up by this punishment, that it was good, and that they have become people who do what is right, and spread peace (around them)."

[299]

Reward is literally "**fruit**" (RSV), meaning "the effect it produces" (FrCL). It is not the word used for reward in 11.26, but the meaning is the same, that is, the fulfillment in men of God's purposes (compare 11.40).

The expression **a righteous life** (in Greek literally "righteousness") is in apposition to **the peaceful reward.** In other words this peaceful reward consists of a righteous life. But **peaceful** is actually a qualification of the life more than it is of the reward itself. Accordingly, one may render **reap the peaceful reward of a righteous life** as "obtain a reward which is a peaceful and righteous life" or "obtain the reward of living peacefully and righteously." **Righteous** may be rendered as "in accordance with what God wants a person to do."

TEV	**12.12-17**	RSV

Instructions and Warnings

12 Lift up your tired hands, then, and strengthen your trembling knees! 13 Keep walking on straight paths, so that the lame foot may not be disabled, but instead be healed.

14 Try to be at peace with everyone, and try to live a holy life, because no one will see the Lord without it. 15 Guard against turning back from the grace of God. Let no one become like a bitter plant that grows up and causes many troubles with its poison. 16 Let no one become immoral or unspiritual like Esau, who for a single meal sold his rights as the older son. 17 Afterward, you know, he wanted to receive his father's blessing; but he was turned back, because he could not find any way to change what he had done, even though in tears he looked for it. [h]

12 Therefore lift your drooping hands and strengthen your weak knees, 13 and make straight paths for your feet, so that what is lame may not be put out of joint but rather be healed. 14 Strive for peace with all men, and for the holiness without which no one will see the Lord. 15 See to it that no one fail to obtain the grace of God; that no "root of bitterness" spring up and cause trouble, and by it the many become defiled; 16 that no one be immoral or irreligious like Esau, who sold his birthright for a single meal. 17 For you know that afterward, when he desired to inherit the blessing, he was rejected, for he found no chance to repent, though he sought it with tears.

[h] he looked for it; or he tried to get the blessing.

The TEV section heading may be rendered as "How people must live" or "Believers are warned and told what they must do."

12.12-13   Lift up your tired hands, then, and strengthen your trembling knees! 13 Keep walking on straight paths, so that the lame foot may not be disabled, but instead be healed.

These verses form a transition between verses 1-11 and 14-29. It is therefore not surprising that some editions, such as the UBS Greek New Testament, put them at the end of the previous section, while others, like TEV, put them at the beginning of a new section. Languages vary in the ways in which they deal with transitional material, and each group of translators should do what is most natural in its own language.

Most of verse 12 consists of a free quotation from Isaiah 35.3 or Sirach 25.23 (in Greek). Verse 13a, and perhaps **strengthen** in verse 12, are based on Proverbs 4.26. Since several Old Testament texts are involved, it is probably unnecessary to use quotation marks, but footnote references may be given. **Then** in verse 12 is not part of the quotation. It is added to emphasize the following words. It may also help to mark the beginning of a new section.

The translator needs to decide whether the metaphors of **tired** or "drooping" **hands** and **trembling knees** are natural in the receptor language. Phps skillfully adapts the first metaphor with "tighten your loosening grip"; Brc "fill the listless hands with energy." **Your,** in both places, is literally "the." There is no doubt about whom the parts of the body belong to, but **your** is natural in English. Alternatively, the definite article "the" could be omitted, since **tired hands** have not been mentioned before. Most translations have either "weak" (TEV third edition) or **trembling knees,** and this is no doubt the meaning of the passage quoted. However, the Greek can also mean "disabled" or even "paralyzed." In the light of verse 13b, perhaps that is how the writer of Hebrews understood this word in the quotation. If so, **strengthen** could mean straighten, as in Luke 13.13.

It is in fact rare that one can reproduce the metaphors in verse 12. For example, a literal translation of **Lift up your tired hands** might only suggest demanding more work from people who are already tired out from labor. One may translate this figurative expression as "Be strong and be encouraged" or ". . . take heart."

Verse 13 falls into three parts, the first two of which raise distinct problems.

(a) **Keep walking on straight paths:** the quotation from Proverbs may be translated "make smooth (or, straight) paths for your feet." The word which TEV and RSV translate **straight** includes the ideas of a "path" being neither crooked nor rough. The underlying nonfigurative meaning may be either (i) behave in a just way, or (ii) take special care of the weak. CLTs choose or suggest (i). This choice is supported by **your** in verse 12 (not part of the quotation) and by the tense of the verb for "make," which is the basis for TEV's **keep walking.** There is no clear evidence in this passage that the writer is distinguishing between the "strong" and the "weak" as, for example, Paul does in Romans 14 and 1 Corinthians 8. All members of the Christian community are in danger of losing heart and giving up their faith, and the writer's message of encouragement (13.22) is addressed to them all. For this reason he adds "**your**" to the second quotation (verse 13a, see RSV), and TEV is justified in adding **your** in two places to the first quotation (verse 12).

It is possible to express the metaphor **keep walking on straight paths** as a simile; for example, "keep walking, as it were, on straight paths." But this may still be almost meaningless, since **walking on straight paths** may have nothing to do with proper behavior. If one adopts a nonfigurative translation of **keep walking on straight paths**, for example, "behave in a just way," the rest of the sentence must also be modified, and this may be far more difficult. One alternative may be "so that you might not be weakened in your lives but rather become strong."

(b) **So that the lame foot may not be disabled** is difficult. **Foot** is implied (compare RSV), and the writer may equally well be referring back to **knees** in verse 12.

The more common meaning of the verb translated **be disabled** is "turn away" (BJ, but not JB), but this does not fit the context here. Most modern translations, including TEV and RSV, suggest some abnormal physical condition such as "lameness," which the writer hopes will not get worse, for example, by dislocation of the limb, but instead will be cured. This reflects the pattern of the argument in such passages as 6.1-12 and 10.19-39. There, positive statements both precede and follow stern warnings that the readers' spiritual condition cannot remain as it is, but will get worse if it does not improve.[3]

12.14   **Try to be at peace with everyone, and try to live a holy life, because no one will see the Lord without it.**

This verse, like verse 13, contains three statements. The first and second are introduced by **try** and the third by **because**, giving a reason for the previous instructions. **Peace** and **holy life** are both to be understood in a broad sense. **Peace** is total well-being, as in 7.2 and 11.31, but here there is a special emphasis on good human relationships. "Holiness" (**holy life**) is total dedication to God, as in verse 10, where a different but related Greek word is used. The relation between **peace** and **holy life** is understood differently by translators, and also by the punctuation added by different editors of the Greek text. Is it (a) only "holiness," or (b) both "peace and holiness," without which **no one will see the Lord**? (a) Most translations link "holiness" but not "peace" with the words "**without which no one will see the Lord**" (RSV); for example, FrCL "for, without a holy life, no one will be able to see the Lord"; NAB "that holiness without which no one can see the Lord." (b) GeCL, on the other hand, appears to link both "peace" and "holiness" with "see the Lord": "Be concerned for peace with all men and for a perfect life. Who(ever) misses that will not see the Lord"; so DuCL and probably NEB. The punctuation of the UBS Greek text favors (a), but it is impossible to be certain. The matter cannot be settled by appeal to the Old Testament texts. **Try to be at peace with everyone** echoes Psalm 34.14, but this text says nothing about seeing God. Phps puts "without which no man shall see the Lord" in quotation marks, but if this is a quotation, its source has not been found.

Some commentators think that **with everyone** means "with all the members of the Christian community," as in 13.24. However, this is not what the Greek

---

[3] See diagram at the beginning of the comments on chapter 6.

means, and there is no convincing evidence to show that the letter is addressed to a divided community. The deeper, positive meaning of **peace** is in the writer's mind, not just the absence of quarrelling.

Try to be at peace with everyone may be translated by an idiom; for example, "try to have a quiet heart in your relationships with everyone" or "as you live with others, be sure to try to always sit down in your hearts." In some languages **to be at peace with everyone** must be expressed as a negative; for example, "try to live with everyone without quarrelling," or ". . . without bickering," or ". . . without harsh words."

Some translations, including BJ and TOB, have "consecration" or "sanctification" instead of "holiness." This emphasizes God's role in making people "holy," rather than the human effort **to live a holy life.** The two aspects are involved, both in "holiness" and "peace." However, since the sentence begins with an imperative, **try to be at peace** (literally, "follow peace"), TEV is perhaps right to conclude that here the writer is thinking primarily of something which his readers must do.

It may be possible to translate **a holy life** as "a life which is dedicated to God." Or it may be necessary to render **try to live a holy life** as "try to live like a person who is dedicated to God" or ". . . who is completely dedicated to God."

In translating **no one will see the Lord** it is best to employ an expression for **the Lord** which is capable of referring either to God or to Christ. If this is not possible, a reference to God is slightly more probable.

If **try to live a holy life** is rendered as "try to live like one who is completely dedicated to God," then the phrase **without it** must often be restructured as a clause; for example, "unless you do." Therefore the final clause of this verse may be rendered as "because no one will see the Lord unless he lives such a life" or "because you will not see the Lord unless you live that way."

12.15   **Guard against turning back from the grace of God. Let no one become like a bitter plant that grows up and causes many troubles with its poison.**

As TEV's **Guard against. . . . Let no one. . . . Let no one** shows, verses 15-16 consist of three warnings expressed in a similar form. The introductory words of each warning are the same in Greek, literally "lest anyone." A continual effort is suggested.

See Deuteronomy 29.17-18; also 1 Maccabees 1.10, where a pagan ruler is called a "sinful root." The verb which TEV fourth edition translates **Guard against** (TEV third edition "Be careful"), and which introduces the three warnings of verses 15-16, is used in 1 Peter 5.2 of the activity of church leaders; it is related to the word for "bishop." Here, however, there is no suggestion that the writer of Hebrews is addressing only church leaders, and in fact, 13.7,17 implies the opposite.

Guard against may often be rendered as "Be sure you do not" or "Make certain that you do not," or even "By all means do not."

12.15

The word translated **turning back** may mean "be deprived of" (JB), or more precisely "deprive himself of" (Brc). This is the likely meaning of a related verb, for example, in Romans 3.23 (NEB "all . . . are deprived of the divine splendour"). However, in the present verse there is an additional word meaning "(away) from," so **turning back from**; NAB, TNT "falls away from" is more likely. The wider context (including 6.4; 10.39; 12.25) supports the idea of receiving God's grace and then letting it go rather than that of missing it altogether (RSV).

In place of **turning back**, many languages employ an expression such as "turning away from" or "departing from," or even "leaving." But it may be difficult, if not impossible, to speak of "turning away from the grace of God." One can, however, "turn away from God who shows grace," or ". . . who shows loving kindness," or ". . . who is so good to us."

The whole of this verse, especially the second half, recalls Deuteronomy 29.18. However, there is no need for quotation marks, since this is not a direct quotation. Translations of the Hebrew text of Deuteronomy 29.18 vary: RSV "a root bearing poisonous and bitter fruit"; NEB "a root from which springs gall and wormwood"; TEV a root that grows to be a bitter and poisonous plant. Some Greek manuscripts of Deuteronomy contain the word for "gall," but there is nothing in Hebrews 12.15 about either "gall" or "poison" in the literal sense. The Greek words for "in gall" (*en cholē*) and troubles (*enochlē*) are easily confused. "Root of bitterness" (Acts 8.23 RSV), applied to a person, means a bad influence, and figuratively a "poisonous" influence.

Let no one become like a bitter plant may be understood as "See to it that no one becomes like a bitter plant." In other words, this could be an admonition for people to prevent someone in the Christian community from becoming like a bitter plant. On the other hand, it may also be understood as "No one among you should become like a bitter plant."

The word for **causes . . . troubles** sometimes describes the activity of people who disturb the peace of a country by stirring up a revolt against the government (1 Esdras 2.29). Instead of modifying **troubles** as in TEV, the Greek for **many** may mean "everyone," that is, "people in general," or more specifically "the Christian community as a whole"; Brc "to make trouble for you and to contaminate the whole community"; similarly TOB; TNT "spoil everybody's life."

12.16   Let no one become immoral or unspiritual like Esau, who for a
single meal sold his rights as the older son.

Let no one does not mean "Do not permit anyone to become" but "No one should become."

Immoral means "sexually immoral," KJV "fornicator," probably in the literal sense, rather than "unfaithful to God." In a number of languages sexual immorality is described as "sleeping with a woman who is not your wife." But such immorality is frequently spoken of by means of idioms, for example "to live like a dog," or "to chase after women," or "to be always looking for vulvas."

Unspiritual means "having no respect for holy things"; FrCL; similarly ItCL. GeCL links this with the rest of the sentence: "Because he did not honor God, he sold his privilege as elder son . . . ."

A single meal is emphatic, but KJV's "one morsel of meat" (that is, "food") goes too far; see Genesis 25.33-34.

The use of a term such as **sold** may suggest some kind of monetary payment. But since only an exchange was involved, it may be necessary to translate **who for a single meal sold his rights as the older son** as "who in exchange for just one meal gave up what was coming to him as the older son" or ". . . the older brother."

12.17 **Afterward, you know, he wanted to receive his father's blessing; but he was turned back, because he could not find any way to change what he had done, even though in tears he looked for it.**[h]

[h] he looked for it; *or* he tried to get the blessing.

See Genesis 27.30-40, especially verse 38. On **receive,** see 1.4 and 6.12.

There are two main problems in translating this verse. First, what is the meaning of the word which RSV translates "to repent," and TEV **to change what he had done?** Second, what did Esau **look for . . . in tears?**

The first problem is the more complicated one. The Greek is literally "a place of repentance." "Place" often has the meaning "opportunity," for example, in Acts 25.16, and this is likely here. "Repentance" means a change of mind or heart which results in a change of behavior and life (see comments on 6.1,6). The translator has first to decide whether the change is in Esau himself, as most people think, or in his father, Isaac (Seg text "he found no means of bringing his father to change his mind"; Syn and JB). It seems unlikely that Isaac would be introduced without this being shown more clearly; in the first part of the sentence, **his father's** is not in the Greek but is implied. If the reference is to Esau himself, the translator has next to decide whether the writer is concerned (i) with a change in Esau's mind, as in DuCL "he got no more chance to show sorrow"; RSV and Mft **"no chance to repent"**; Phps "He never afterward found the way of repentance"; or (ii) with Esau's desire to change the results of his decision to sell his birthright, as in most CLTs; TNT "undoing what he had done"; ItCL "change his situation." Some translations, for example NAB, "alter his choice," leave the matter rather vague; Brc makes both possibilities explicit with "There was no possibility for him to think again, although he tried with tears to undo what he had done." There is evidence that the phrase translated **way to change what he had done** may have the legal sense of "opportunity to change a former decision," almost "leave to appeal" against a judgment. This fits Genesis 27.30-40 very well and would suggest that Esau was looking for a way of changing his own decision, or more probably Isaac's decision. But since a word, once given, was thought of as taking on a life of its own (see Isa 55.11), the situation could not be reversed. Meaning (ii) is therefore to be preferred.

The second problem is simpler. (i) Knox, NAB, TNT think that what Esau **looked for . . . in tears** was **his father's blessing**. This interpretation fits in better with Genesis 27. Note that **way** or **"chance"** (RSV) can not grammatically be what he **looked for** in Greek. (ii) TEV and other translations think it was "repentance" that he sought, in one or another of the senses discussed earlier. In favor of this interpretation is the fact that the writer is accustomed to drawing from Old Testament stories a moral different from the main message or intention of the original story. Also, in Greek, "repentance" is closer than **blessing** to the phrase **looked for it with tears**. Note also that the writer is concerned in other places with the impossibility of repentance after certain particularly serious sins (note 6.4, and "repentance" in 6.6). Finally, if it is the **blessing** he sought, the clause "he found no chance to repent" would be an awkward parenthetical expression, spoiling the contrast between "found" and "sought." The weight of evidence seems to support (ii), but (i) may be mentioned in a footnote.

Though in English the separation of **Afterward** from the rest of the clause by inserting the parenthetical expression **you know** seems perfectly natural and satisfactory, in many languages this would lead to misunderstanding. Therefore in some languages the order must be changed to "You know that later he wanted."

He wanted to receive his father's blessing may be rendered as "he wanted his father to bless him."

But he was turned back may be rendered as "but he was refused." An even more general expression may be employed; for example, "but this was impossible."

The clause which introduces cause, namely, **because he could not find any way to change what he had done,** may be expressed in some languages as "because he could not find a way to undo what he had done," or ". . . to make invalid what he had done," or ". . . to reverse what he had done," or ". . . to make what he had done seem as though he had never done it."

Looked for may have its usual meaning of "tried to find," but in this context it more probably means "tried to obtain."

In tears: see Genesis 27.34,38. **Even though in tears he looked for it** may be expressed as "even though he cried as he was trying to find a way to change what he had done" or "even though in trying to change what he did he cried" or ". . . wept."

TEV   **12.18-24**   RSV

18 You have not come, as the people of Israel came, to what you can feel, to Mount Sinai with its blazing fire, the darkness and the gloom, the storm, 19 the blast of a trumpet, and the sound of a voice. When the people heard the voice, they begged not to hear another word, 20 because they could not bear the order which said, "If even an animal touches the mountain, it

18 For you have not come to what may be touched, a blazing fire, and darkness, and gloom, and a tempest, 19 and the sound of a trumpet, and a voice whose words made the hearers entreat that no further messages be spoken to them. 20 For they could not endure the order that was given, "If even a beast touches the mountain, it shall be stoned." 21 Indeed, so

must be stoned to death." 21 The sight was so terrifying that Moses said, "I am trembling and afraid."

22 Instead, you have come to Mount Zion and to the city of the living God, the heavenly Jerusalem, with its thousands of angels. 23 You have come to the joyful gathering of God's first-born sons, whose names are written in heaven. You have come to God, who is the judge of all mankind, and to the spirits of good people made perfect. 24 You have come to Jesus, who arranged the new covenant, and to the sprinkled blood that promises much better things than does the blood of Abel.

terrifying was the sight that Moses said, "I tremble with fear." 22 But you have come to Mount Zion and to the city of the living God, the heavenly Jerusalem, and to innumerable angels in festal gathering, 23 and to the assembly^z of the first-born who are enrolled in heaven, and to a judge who is God of all, and to the spirits of just men made perfect, 24 and to Jesus, the mediator of a new covenant, and to the sprinkled blood that speaks more graciously than the blood of Abel.

^{z} Or angels, and to the festal gathering and assembly

Verses 18-24 gather up many strands in the author's teaching and appeals for action, and may be considered the climax of the entire letter. It consists in Greek of two sentences (18-21 and 22-24) which belong so closely together, as the two halves of a contrast, that for practical purposes they must be considered as one. As is usual in such long sentences, the emotional level is high, as the accumulation of details shows. There is some symbolic or pictorial language which will present problems in translation. These verses especially recall and summarize teaching on the related subjects of sacrifice, the covenant, and "coming" or "drawing near" to God, discussed in detail in 9.11—10.22. Verses 25-29 recall the warning of 10.26-31.

12.18 You have not come, as the people of Israel came, to what you can feel, to Mount Sinai with its blazing fire, the darkness and the gloom, the storm,

The translator must first decide how to translate the verb rendered **come to** in verses 18 and 22. The verb consists of the common verb for **come** and a prefix meaning "toward." In some contexts, for example, Matthew 5.1, it means "come to," not merely "come near to" or "approach." The question here is whether Christians are thought of as already fully part of the city of the living God (verse 22), with its joyful gathering of God's first-born sons (verse 23), or whether they have only "approached" it. KJV and GeCL agree with TEV's you have come to; ItCL and some other CLTs have "you have approached"; NEB "you stand before." The meaning of such picture language is difficult to define precisely, but the wider context, especially verse 25, suggests that the readers are not yet completely part of the heavenly city and can still turn away. Indeed, turn away from is a natural opposite to "draw near to" or "approach." The Greek verb is commonly used of approaching God in "worship" (Heb 4.16; 7.25; 10.1,22; 11.6). In verses 18.21 the Israelites come near to Mount Sinai but are forbidden to set foot on it.

As the people of Israel came is added, as in other CLTs and TNT, because the modern non-Jewish reader might not realize that the writer is referring to such passages as Exodus 10.21-22; 19.12-22; 20.18-21; Deuteronomy 4.11-12; 5.22-27.

The name **Sinai** is certainly not part of the Greek text; the word translated **Mount** is not found in some manuscripts either, nor is it in the UBS Greek text.[4] However, it correctly represents the meaning, and it should be made explicit in translation, to make clearer the contrast with Mount Zion in verse 22, where both words are expressed in the Greek. Other possibilities are (a) something other than only the mountain which can be "sensed," "touched," or "felt"; not RSV's **"may be touched,"** since "may" appears to contradict verse 20, which recalls the command not to approach; or (b) with NEB to take "palpable," that is, "which can be touched," with "fire." Choice (a) is attractive; it involves taking "which can be touched" as a general term, "which can be sensed," referring to all the details mentioned in verses 18-19, details which could be perceived by various senses. In any case, TEV's **you** before **can feel** has the more general meaning "one can feel"; it does not refer only to the readers, like the **You** with which the sentence begins. A translation taking these points into account would be "You have not come, as the people of Israel came, to things that can be perceived with the senses: to a blazing fire . . . ."

Verse 18 and what follows through verse 21 pose serious problems for the translator in contrasting the experience of the Christian believers with the experience which the people of Israel had at Mount Sinai. The problem is particularly acute with the first part of verse 18, which combines a negative **You have not come** with a positive **to what you can feel.** A more satisfactory way of showing the contrast may be to begin verse 18 as "You are not like the people of Israel who came to what they could feel—to Mount Sinai with its blazing fire . . . ." The contrast may then be introduced at verse 22 by translating "You are not like those people of Israel, for you have come to Mount Zion . . . ."

It may be better to translate **to Mount Sinai with its blazing fire . . .**" as "to Mount Sinai, where there was the blazing fire, the darkness, and the gloom . . . ."

Deuteronomy 4.11 refers to "darkness and cloud," and Exodus 19.16 to "thunder and lightning." The Greek word for **storm** usually means an intense windstorm. It may be difficult to distinguish between **the darkness** and **the gloom.** The two terms in Greek may, in fact, be designed to reinforce the intensity of the darkness, and so one may be able to employ "the intense darkness." For **storm**, one may use "windstorm."

12.19   **the blast of a trumpet, and the sound of a voice. When the people heard the voice, they begged not to hear another word,**

---

[4] The first two editions of the UBS Greek New Testament included it in square brackets, with a "D" rating, the lowest possible. The third edition gives a "C" rating to the text which omits it.

The writer is not concerned with the function of the **trumpet** or "ram's horn" (Exo 19.13 NEB), which is not entirely clear even in Exodus. In this verse it is a sign of God's activity, like the **storm** and the **voice**. There is no difference of meaning between the words translated **blast** and **sound**. A single **blast** is mentioned in Exodus 19.13,16. Similarly, **voice**, literally "spoken words," as in 1.3, and **word**, as in 2.2, are probably used for the sake of variety rather than to emphasize the singular **another word** as in Exodus 20.19.

The blast of a trumpet may be "the loud noise made by a trumpet." There may be a problem in translating **the sound of a voice**, since "voice" is generally related to someone speaking. But it would be wrong to translate **the sound of a voice** as "the sound of someone speaking," since this would raise the question "Who is that someone?" Because the declaration referred to is uttered by God, it may be necessary to translate **the sound of a voice** as "the sound of God speaking." This means that the temporal clause **When the people heard the voice** must be rendered as "When the people heard God speaking" or ". . . heard God's voice."

If one introduces a term such as **begged**, it may be necessary to indicate to whom the petition was addressed. But this may create complications, and therefore it may be better to translate **they begged not to hear another word** as "they strongly said they did not want to hear another word."

12.20 **because they could not bear the order which said, "If even an animal touches the mountain, it must be stoned to death."**

The quotation is from Exodus 19.12-13; compare Deuteronomy 5.23-25. **The order which said** it is clearly implied that the order was given by God, and it may be better to say so in translation. Brc turns the sentence into indirect speech, and this may be more natural in some languages: "they were appalled by the order that, if even a beast touched the mountain, it should be stoned to death."

Because they could not bear the order which said may be rendered as "because they could not bear what God had ordered" or ". . . what God had commanded." In some instances **they could not bear** may be expressed as "they could not accept," or "they refused to accept," or "they did not want to accept."

The writer of Hebrews increases the emphasis of the Old Testament verse he quotes. The differences may be expressed as follows:

Exodus 19.12-13 "Whoever touches the mountain . . . whether beast or man, shall be put to death."

Hebrews "Not even a wild animal is allowed to touch the mountain, however lightly." **Even** is important; Hebrews condenses the Old Testament passage, but the writer knows that human beings are also threatened with death.

To death is implied; see comment on 11.37. KJV's "or thrust through with a dart" is not part of the original text of Hebrews. It may be too easy for the reader to understand **even** as applying to touching the mountain rather than as applying to an animal. Therefore it may be better to make the meaning explicit; for example, "If anyone, even an animal, touches the mountain." Accordingly the final part of the command may be rendered as "you must stone to death that person or animal."

12.21   The sight was so terrifying that Moses said, "I am trembling and afraid"

Sight translates an unusual word which may include reference to other senses, as in verses 18-19. **The sight was so terrifying** may be expressed as "What the people experienced frightened them so much" or "What happened there at Mount Sinai frightened people so much" or ". . . caused them to be so terrified."

I am trembling is quoted out of context from Deuteronomy 9.19; the writer adds **and afraid** for emphasis. The addition is intended as part of the quotation, not as in JB, "Moses said: 'I am afraid,' and was trembling with fright." It is doubtful whether the addition of a synonym really increases the impact; in English, at least, it may produce an anticlimax. GeCL and TNT have simply "I tremble with fear." Brc puts the quotation into indirect speech: "The sight was so terrible that Moses said that it left him trembling and afraid," but this sentence is too long and complicated to make a strong impact on the average reader.

Something of the impact of **I am trembling and afraid** may be expressed as "I am so afraid as to tremble."

12.22   Instead, you have come to Mount Zion and to the city of the living God, the heavenly Jerusalem, with its thousands of angels.

RSV's **"But"** is too weak to introduce the second half of a major contrast with verse 18. The structure and content of verses 18-24 require something like **Instead,** "No!" (Brc), or "On the contrary" (SpCL and Seg). ItCL has "You, on the contrary."

The series of eight items which follows recalls the list of 11.37, but here each item is introduced in the Greek by "and." The use or omission of "and" in translation depends on what is most natural and forceful in the receptor language.

Mount Zion stands on its own as the first item in the list; a contrast with Mount Sinai is implied. **Mount Zion** is probably distinguished from the city of Jerusalem which is built on it. The words which follow show that both **Zion** and **Jerusalem** are understood in a symbolic sense. In some languages a title such as **Mount Zion** must be expressed as "mountain called Zion" or "mountain named Zion."

The city of the living God is the second item. In some contexts **the living God** means "the God who gives life," and this makes a good contrast with the reference to <u>death</u> in verse 20. **The city of the living God** and **the heavenly Jerusalem** are the same. SpCL has "the city of the living God, that is, the heavenly Jerusalem"; and ItCL repeats "but" in "but the city of the living God, but Jerusalem of Heaven." It may be better to put **the heavenly Jerusalem** first, in order to make it clear as early as possible in the sentence that symbolic language is being used. As in the phrase <u>heavenly country</u> in 11.16, it may be wise to translate **the heavenly Jerusalem** as "the Jerusalem which is in heaven." If one introduces only a qualitative adjective such as **heavenly,** a reader might think that the earthly Jerusalem is to be regarded as like heaven.

The third item is the **thousands of angels. Thousands** is literally "ten thousands." NEB and TOB use the literary equivalent "myriads"; JB "millions"; and GeCL has "with its many thousand angels." In any case the number is not intended to be precise. In order to relate the phrase **with its thousands of angels** to the previous statement about the heavenly Jerusalem, it may be best to translate "the Jerusalem in heaven, where there are the thousands of angels." In some languages a literal rendering of **with** suggests only accompaniment, and of course the angels are not accompanying Jerusalem.

12.23   **You have come to the joyful gathering of God's first-born sons, whose names are written in heaven. You have come to God, who is the judge of all mankind, and to the spirits of good people made perfect.**

The fourth item in the list is **the joyful gathering,** the "**assembly of the first-born who are enrolled in heaven**" (RSV). RSV and TEV show the two possibilities for translating "in festal gathering" (see RSV footnote) or **joyful gathering.** The choice is related to problems of punctuation, and even of the division between verses 22 and 23. The UBS Greek text makes the word translated **joyful gathering** part of verse 22, but punctuates the sentence in such a way as to link it with verse 23. Most CLTs make the word part of verse 23 and translate accordingly. ItCL, however, agrees with RSV in translating "You have come near to the festal meeting, to the assembly of God's first-born sons." The structure of the sentence, in particular the position of the word "and," supports this. TEV and other CLTs are probably right, however, to take "festal meeting" and "assembly" as two phrases in apposition, referring to the same object. If this is so, it is better to omit RSV's "**and**" at the beginning of the verse, or any similar expression which leads the reader to expect additional information.

Joyful gathering is a single word in Greek. **Joyful** may be implied, but the context also suggests "solemn." **The joyful gathering** may be rendered as "the gathering of happy people" or "the gathering of those who are joyful."

In the phrase **God's first-born sons, God's** and **sons** are strongly implied. However, neither the plural nor the metaphor must be pressed too far, as in JB "the whole Church in which everyone is a 'first-born son.' " The meaning is close to Exodus 4.22: "Thus says the LORD, 'Israel is my first-born son' " (RSV), implying special choice and privilege, as in verse 16. Neither **sons** (implied) nor **all mankind** (TEV fourth edition) excludes women; here both sons and daughters who are adults are intended.

Since the phrase **God's first-born sons** is a figurative reference to the followers of Christ, it may be important to mark this by translating as a simile.

Accordingly the first part of verse 23 may be rendered as "You have come to a gathering of those who are, as it were, God's first-born sons, and they are joyful." With this rendering it may be necessary to make a separate sentence out of the clause **whose names are written in heaven;** for example, "These persons have their names written in heaven." At this point it may be useful to have some note to explain the significance of this figurative statement about **names . . . written in heaven,** since this indicates that such persons "are destined to occupy heaven."

The fifth item is **God, who is the judge of all mankind.** RSV follows the order of the Greek, somewhat emphasizing **judge,** but most translations link "of all" with **judge,** not with **God;** Brc "God who is judge of all." JB's "the supreme judge" is slightly misleading; there is no reference, even implicit, to other judges at this point. In this context it is important to use a term for **judge** which will not suggest only "to condemn." **Judge** here indicates impartial evaluation of what people have done during their lives.

The sixth item is **the spirits of good people made perfect.** **Spirits** are human spirits. On **made perfect,** see 5.14. The **good people made perfect** no doubt include the Old Testament believers listed in chapter 11, as well as Christians (compare 11.40).

There is a serious problem in the rendering **You have come . . . to the spirits of good people made perfect,** since this might suggest approaching the disembodied spirits of those perfect individuals who have passed on to the next world; in other words, "You have come in contact with the spirits of the saints." To avoid such a misinterpretation it may be best to translate "You have come to those good people who have been made perfect," or ". . . who have been made to be just what God wants them to be," or ". . . to be in every respect just as they should be." To retain the idea that they have died, it may be necessary to say "those good people from the past" or ". . . from long ago," or "those good people who died but who have been made perfect."

12.24 **You have come to Jesus, who arranged the new covenant, and to the sprinkled blood that promises much better things than does the blood of Abel.**

The seventh item in the list is **Jesus. Jesus,** as in 2.9 and other places, is emphatic. On **who arranged,** literally "mediator" (RSV), see 8.6 and 9.15. **New** renders a different word from that used in 8.8 and elsewhere, but the meaning in this context is the same.

As both RSV and TEV show, the **sprinkled blood** is a separate item in the list, the eighth item. However, several translations show the close relation between **Jesus** and **the sprinkled blood:** FrCL "Jesus, the intermediary of the new covenant, and his shed blood . . ." and TNT "and whose shed blood . . . ." As 9.13-14 shows, the nonfigurative meaning of **sprinkle** is "make holy" or "purify." DuCL combines the last three items in the list, since they are related in meaning, even if they are separated grammatically: "Jesus, through whose mediation a new covenant is concluded, and whose shed blood speaks more powerfully than that of

Abel." As for example in 1.4 and 11.40, the Greek combines the meaning of "better" and "greater"; Mft has "nobler." As in 9.13,19,21, **sprinkled** makes it necessary to keep the word **blood**, rather than to use some more general expression like "(violent) death" or "sacrifice." But the blood of Old Testament sacrifices was **sprinkled** in order to make things ritually clean, and Phps makes this clear by "cleansing of blood"; JB "blood for purification."

It may be difficult to speak of "coming" **to the sprinkled blood**. Since **the sprinkled blood** relates to **Jesus**, it is often better to render verse 24 as "You have come to Jesus, who was the means of producing the new covenent and whose blood, which was shed, promises for us that which is better than what the blood of Abel stands for" or ". . . represents."

Than does the blood of Abel is literally "than Abel," but most translations add **blood**, following Genesis 4.10. A few manuscripts have "than that of Abel," implying "than Abel's blood." In this case the meaning would be that Abel's blood cried for vengeance, and Christ's blood speaks of salvation. The idea of blood speaking may be difficult to express in translation. JB tries to avoid the problem by using a more specific expression, "pleads more insistently"; similarly TNT, "far better things to say to us than Abel's"; more smoothly, ItCL has "sprinkled blood, which has a more powerful voice than that (meaning, than the voice) of Abel."

This very brief reference to Abel's blood may require an Old Testament reference or a marginal note to give the historical background. It is, however, quite possible to make sense of **than . . . Abel** without adding **blood**, since Abel was earlier presented as the first true worshiper, not as the first murder victim (see notes on 11.4). In this case the main reference would be to Abel's sacrifice, offered in faith, though his murder, considered as a "sacrifice" of himself, would not be excluded.

	12.25-29	
TEV		RSV

25 Be careful, then, and do not refuse to hear him who speaks. Those who refused to hear the one who gave the divine message on earth did not escape. How much less shall we escape, then, if we turn away from the one who speaks from heaven! 26 His voice shook the earth at that time, but now he has promised, "I will once more shake not only the earth but heaven as well." 27 The words "once more" plainly show that the created things will be shaken and removed, so that the things that cannot be shaken will remain.

28 Let us be thankful, then, because we receive a kingdom that cannot be shaken. Let us be grateful and

25 See that you do not refuse him who is speaking. For if they did not escape when they refused him who warned them on earth, much less shall we escape if we reject him who warns from heaven. 26 His voice then shook the earth; but now he has promised, "Yet once more I will shake not only the earth but also the heaven." 27 This phrase, "Yet once more," indicates the removal of what is shaken, as of what has been made, in order that what cannot be shaken may remain. 28 Therefore let us be grateful for receiving a kingdom that cannot be shaken, and thus let us offer to God acceptable worship, with reverence and awe; 29 for our God is a consuming fire.

[313]

worship God in a way that will please
him, with reverence and awe; 29 because our God is indeed a destroying
fire.

The writer now applies to his readers' situation the contrast between God's message through Moses on <u>Mount Sinai</u> (verses 18-21) and his message through Jesus in the heavenly <u>Mount Zion</u> (verses 22-24).

<u>12.25</u> **Be careful, then, and do not refuse to hear him who speaks. Those who refused to hear the one who gave the divine message on earth did not escape. How much less shall we escape, then, if we turn away from the one who speaks from heaven!**

Be careful and **do not refuse** are closely linked; Phps "be sure you do not refuse"; similarly NEB. **Refuse to hear** is the immediate meaning in this context of a word which can mean to "reject" someone or something. The author probably did not distinguish sharply between rejecting God or Christ, and rejecting what they say; but the latter is in focus here.

For many languages **do not refuse to hear** is a double negative, since **refuse to hear** implies not hearing or not paying attention. Such double negatives must often be translated as positive expressions. If so, **do not refuse to hear him who speaks** must be rendered as "pay close attention to the one who speaks."

Those who refused to hear may be expressed idiomatically; for example, "those who stopped their ears," or "those who put their hands over their ears," or "those who made themselves deaf to what was said."

It is uncertain who is meant by the phrases (a) **him who speaks,** (b) **the one who gave the divine message on earth,** and (c) **the one who speaks from heaven.** **Gave the divine message** renders a single verb, which sometimes means "warns" (RSV), but can be used of any divine oracle (see 8.5 and 11.7). **Speaks** in (c) is implicit; one could equally well understand **gave the divine message.** (a) and (c) may be God or Christ; (b) may be God or Moses; if (c) is Christ, (b) may also be Christ. Most commentators think of God as the speaker referred to throughout the verse, but verse 19 does not specify that the one who spoke was God, and verse 24 has just mentioned the blood of Jesus as "speaking" (phrase (a) has the same Greek verb). If it is clearer in translation to state who the speaker is, it is probably safest to make it God, at least in (a). The Greek suggests that the speaker is the same throughout. It may be helpful to make some of these identifications explicit in translation. The TNT text, for example, takes **him who speaks** as Jesus. Brc and TNT identify **the one who gave the divine message on earth** as Moses, and Brc identifies **the one who speaks from heaven** as Christ but translates "the one who comes from heaven," recalling 10.37. However, "comes" adds something not in the text.

[314]

For most languages the phrase **the divine message** must be expressed as "the message that comes from God." But this rendering may cause complications, if God is specifically mentioned as the one who gives this message on earth.

The rest of the verse introduces a "how much more" type of comparison, on which see the comments on 2.1, **all the more firmly**, and 9.14, and see also Matthew 6.30. This is a negative comparison, implying "How much more shall we not escape?" which TEV rightly simplifies into **How much less shall we escape ...!** In some languages this may cause a problem, since one either escapes or does not. In this case "How much more certain is it that we shall not escape?" is an alternative. ItCL has "All the more shall we be condemned," avoiding the rhetorical question. RSV's "**if**" does not imply any doubt or condition; it means "if, as was the case, they did not escape . . . ." TEV turns this into a separate statement, linked with what follows by **then,** and meaning "therefore."

In a high percentage of languages, conditional clauses tend to precede the main clause, and therefore the order of the final sentence may need to be changed; for example, "If we reject the one who speaks from heaven, we certainly shall not escape." Such a positive statement is often clearer than an exclamation involving some degree of probability (for example, **how much less**).

12.26   **His voice shook the earth at that time, but now he has promised, "I will once more shake not only the earth but heaven as well."**

The translator must decide at this point how to handle the language in which verses 26-29 describe the "shaking." Four main terms are involved: (a) the word for **shake** used in the quotation itself (verse 26b), which suggests an earthquake; (b) another word for shake used in the writer's comments on the quotation (verses 26a,27), and the related adjective for "unshakable" (verse 28); (c) the noun which TEV rightly translates removed (verse 27) but which may also mean "change," as in 7.12; and (d) the word for destroying (verse 29). See the detailed comments below.

In some languages, what appears to be the closest equivalent of **shake** is a transitive verb which could be used in speaking of one person shaking another person or shaking a basket. But the kind of shaking which would be characteristic of an earthquake may be expressed with a term which essentially means "to tremble." If so, **I will once more shake not only the earth but heaven as well** must be rendered as "Again I will cause not only the earth to tremble but also heaven."

The writer introduces another contrast between **that time** (that is, the time of Moses) and **now. His voice** is most probably "God's" voice, as in verse 25a, and SpCL and TNT make this explicit. Brc seems to think it is Christ's voice, which fits in well with the end of verse 25, but less well with the wider context. It is therefore probably best to translate "God's voice shook the earth at that time" or ". . . caused the earth to shake then."

Has promised implies "in scripture." The tense of the Greek suggests a past event with present consequences.

[315]

The RSV text should strictly speaking be punctuated " 'Yet once more I will shake' not only 'the earth' but 'also the heavens,' " to show which words are actually quoted (Hag 2.6; compare 2.21), but this punctuation is unnecessarily complicated in practice. The result of the writer's selective use of Haggai is to give greater emphasis (**not only . . . but . . . as well**) and to widen its meaning. **Earth** and **heaven** mean "the universe" and may be translated as such here, though in Haggai they have a narrower meaning.[5]

12.27   **The words "once more" plainly show that the created things will be shaken and removed, so that the things that cannot be shaken will remain.**

Plainly is implied. The word translated **show** does not by itself suggest supernatural revelation; the writer is simply explaining what he thinks the words **"once more"** imply. **The words "once more" plainly show** may be rendered as "Those words 'once more' indicate clearly" or ". . . surely mean."

The created things may be rendered as "that which has been created" or "what God has created." **The created things will be shaken and removed** is literally "(the) removal of things-shaken as having-been-made." TEV gives the meaning. The word translated **removed** was adequately translated changed in 7.12, but in the present context that would be too weak. Here the meaning is "set aside," or "carried away," or "be replaced by something else." The text implies that earthly things can be shaken and removed because they are "made"; the same idea was expressed in an Old Testament quotation in 1.10-12. On the other hand, things which belong to heaven, not to the visible world, **cannot be shaken** (literally, "are not shaken," but TEV is clearer).

12.28   **Let us be thankful, then, because we receive a kingdom that cannot be shaken. Let us be grateful and worship God in a way that will please him, with reverence and awe;**

Let us be thankful may be rendered as "We should be thankful" or "We should thank God."[6] The Greek phrase is common both in the New Testament (see 1 Tim 1.12; 2 Tim 1.3; Rom 7.25) and in non-Christian Greek literature of the same period.

---

[5] Most manuscript evidence supports I will . . . shake (so, probably, the Septuagint, also most translations), but many manuscripts have "I shake" (so the Septuagint in Hag 2.21, KJV). Even if "I shake" is the correct text, it probably means "I am about to shake" and should be translated as such. See comments on cannot be shaken in 12.28.

[6] Manuscripts vary between "we are" and "let us be grateful," and "we worship" and "let us worship." TEV and most other translations follow the UBS Greek text.

The meaning of **receive a kingdom** is uncertain. On the meaning of **kingdom,** see comments on 1.8. Most commonly in the New Testament it refers to God's rule over believers, and some older commentators have understood **receive a kingdom** to mean (a) "accept God's rule over us in faith." However, this seems both rather weak in itself and also difficult to fit in with the context (especially **that cannot be shaken**). It is therefore probably better to understand **receive a kingdom** as (b) "receive from God the right to rule with him," as in Daniel 7.14,18, and Gospel texts such as Matthew 19.28; 25.34; Luke 12.32; 22.30. (c) Elsewhere in Hebrews the writer speaks of Christians as being like Israel on the way to the promised land (3.7—4.12), and of believers looking for a permanent place to live (11.13-16). GeCL accordingly translates "We want to be grateful, because we receive a homeland which cannot be taken away from us." In support of this use of "homeland" it may be noted that Deuteronomy 4.24, quoted in the next verse, occurs in a passage about the promised land.

The passages from Daniel and the gospels mentioned in the last paragraph suggest that **receive a kingdom** in this verse may include also the meaning "receive from God a heavenly 'place' in which to rule with him." If so, an alternative translation would be "because we have been given the privilege of ruling, and this will never change."

"**Thus**" (RSV), omitted by TEV, is literally "through which," referring back either to "thanks" or to "kingdom." If it is taken with "thanks," RSV's "**thus**" and NEB's "and so" are adequate.

Let us be grateful and worship God may be rendered as "We should be grateful to God and worship him."

In a way that will please him may be expressed as "in a manner with which he will be pleased" or ". . . which will cause him to be glad."

Reverence and **awe** overlap considerably in meaning. In 5.7 TEV translates the same Greek word for **reverence** as humble and devoted. **Awe** is literally "fear." One or two translations use "godly fear" (Mft) or "holy fear," to avoid suggesting an unworthy, nonbiblical idea of being afraid of God. A single term may be used for **reverence** and **awe** if this is natural in the receptor language. Since in a number of languages the usual equivalents of **reverence** and "fear" are almost contradictory in meaning, it may be best to combine the meanings as "with great reverence" or "by showing great honor."

12.29   **because our God is indeed a destroying fire.**

This verse quotes Deuteronomy 4.24; compare Deuteronomy 9.3; Isaiah 33.14. **Our** is not part of the quotation. It is not especially emphasized, as if a contrast with some other god were intended. The author rather suggests that what was said about God in the Old Testament is still true for Christians.

There is a danger in linking the clause **because our God is indeed a destroying fire** too closely with the preceding clause, for it might seem strange and even contradictory to "be grateful to God because he is a destroying fire." The underlying thought may be either (a) "let us hold on to God's promises, because he will destroy us if we are unfaithful to him"; or (b) "let us be grateful that God, who is able to destroy, has kept a permanent home for us in heaven." Choice (a) is the meaning in the Old Testament context, and also fits in well with the writer of Hebrews' tendency to give alternately hopeful and warning messages.

There is also a problem in the statement **because our God is indeed a destroying fire**, since it could be interpreted as completely identifying God with fire. This is not what is intended by the writer, and therefore it may be necessary to translate **our God is indeed a destroying fire** as "our God is indeed like a destroying fire" or ". . . a fire which destroys completely." **Destroying** renders a stronger form of the verb used in its literal sense in Luke 9.54, of fire "consuming" or "destroying." There is no suggestion here or in 10.27 of fire as a means of "refining" or "purifying."

Chapter 13

This chapter, sometimes described as a postscript, has a looser structure than the rest of the letter. It also includes more personal messages, though such passages as 5.11,12 and 10.32,33 have already shown the writer's concern for his first readers. Echoes of earlier chapters will be mentioned in the notes on individual verses.

TEV   **13.1-6**   RSV

How to Please God

1 Keep on loving one another as Christian brothers. 2 Remember to welcome strangers in your homes. There were some who did that and welcomed angels without knowing it. 3 Remember those who are in prison, as though you were in prison with them. Remember those who are suffering, as though you were suffering as they are.

4 Marriage is to be honored by all, and husbands and wives must be faithful to each other. God will judge those who are immoral and those who commit adultery.

5 Keep your lives free from the love of money, and be satisfied with what you have. For God has said, "I will never leave you; I will never abandon you." 6 Let us be bold, then, and say,
"The Lord is my helper,
 I will not be afraid.
What can anyone do to me?"

1 Let brotherly love continue. 2 Do not neglect to show hospitality to strangers, for thereby some have entertained angels unawares. 3 Remember those who are in prison, as though in prison with them; and those who are illtreated, since you also are in the body. 4 Let marriage be held in honor among all, and let the marriage bed be undefiled; for God will judge the immoral and adulterous. 5 Keep your life free from love of money, and be content with what you have; for he has said, "I will never fail you nor forsake you." 6 Hence we can confidently say,
"The Lord is my helper,
 I will not be afraid;
 what can man do to me?"

The TEV section heading **How to Please God** may need to be rendered as "How we should please God" or "How to make God happy with us."

13.1   **Keep on loving one another as Christian brothers.**

For other reminders of Christian love, see 10.24,32-34. It is interesting to compare TEV with RSV's more literal translation. TEV is much longer than RSV, but much closer to the meaning of the text. It uses a verb instead of the noun **"brotherly love,"** since action by the readers is involved. The tense of the Greek verb for "remain" (RSV **"continue"**) shows that continuous action is called for, hence **keep on loving.**

As Christian brothers: the traditional translation **"brotherly love"** (RSV) does not show what was new and special about relationships within the first Christian communities. At that time it was rare for the word "brother" to be used in speaking of those who were not members of the same family, or at least of the same ethnic group. In the Old Testament, "brother" in its widest sense meant "fellow-Israelite" (Lev 19.17-18; Acts 13.26). Christians thought of themselves as members of the same family, whether or not they were physically related. So **"brotherly love"** is not love which is merely *like* the love of brothers (ItCL), but the love of those who were truly, though not physically, related in the Christian "brotherhood" (1 Peter 2.17; 5.9). In modern English, "brother" is used so loosely in a weak figurative sense that some translations even avoid the word completely; Brc "Christians must never stop loving their fellow-Christians." **As Christian brothers** may be misinterpreted to mean "as though they were Christian brothers." The phrase may need to be made more specific in the form of a clause; for example, "as Christian brothers should love one another."

13.2 **Remember to welcome strangers in your homes. There were some who did that and welcomed angels without knowing it.**

Compare 11.31. There are three sound effects in the Greek of this verse which are almost plays on words. The translator should note them, but he should not worry if he cannot reproduce them, since they do not affect the meaning of the text. (a) The words for "brotherly love" (verse 1) and **"hospitality"** (RSV, verse 2) begin in the same way, suggesting "friendship" both for brothers and for **strangers** or "guests." There is, however, no contrast between the two; the "guest" was often a fellow-Christian. (b) The words for **"neglect"** and **"unawares"** (RSV) are related in Greek; and (c) so are the words for **"hospitality"** and **"entertained"** (RSV).

Remember to welcome strangers in your homes is a positive rendering of what is essentially a double negative statement in the Greek, namely, "Do not cease to be hospitable to strangers." "Hospitable-to-strangers" is a single word in Greek, which in some contexts simply means "hospitable." The positive expression is often more satisfactory, and it may also be rendered as "Be sure to welcome strangers in your homes," or "Be certain that you receive strangers into your homes," or ". . . receive people from far away . . . ," or "Be sure to be hospitable."

Some is quite general; commentaries refer to various stories of visits by **angels,** both in the Old Testament and in ancient pagan writings.

Welcomed angels without knowing it means "they welcomed angels without knowing that the persons involved were angels." In some languages it may be necessary to specify this fact.

13.3 **Remember those who are in prison, as though you were in prison with them. Remember those who are suffering, as though you were suffering as they are.**

NEB starts a new paragraph here, to mark the change of subject, though **Remember** links verses 2 and 3, at least in form. **Remember** may imply that the writer wants his readers to give practical help to those who are in prison. The tense of the verb suggests duration; Phps has "Think constantly of." **As though** rightly excludes the suggestion that the writer is writing directly to people in prison.

Remember those who are in prison may be more satisfactorily rendered as "Be concerned for those who are in prison" or "Be concerned for and give help to those who are in prison."

Some languages do not have a convenient way of expressing a condition contrary to fact, such as **as though you were in prison with them**. An equivalent may be "think what it would be to be in prison with them" or "imagine yourself to be in prison with them."

"In (the) body" (see RSV) has been understood in various ways:

(1) "Members of the Christian fellowship," understanding "body" in the figurative sense used by Paul (JB "since you too are in the one body"), is most unlikely. There is no similar text in Hebrews; there is no definite article for "the" in the Greek, and this explanation does not fit in with verse 3a, which in other ways is parallel to 3b.

(2) Many translators think "in (the) body" means "in this mortal life" (compare 2 Cor 5.6 and Rom 7.24); Knox "since you are still in the world"; similarly Phps.

(3) Other CLTs, and some other translations, suggest either:

(a) that the readers should identify themselves in sympathy with those who are ill-treated: TEV **as though you were suffering as they are** (similarly GeCL); TNT "as if you too shared their lot"; or

(b) that the readers may suffer in the same way in the future: DuCL "for the same can happen to you"; NAB "for you may yet suffer as they do." This is not necessarily implied by the text, though it is perhaps included in (a), which also makes a good parallel with verse 3a, **as though.**

Brc combines (2) and (3-a): "you have not yet left this life, and the same fate can happen to you." This is not very likely. Where distinct meanings are involved, with no suggestion of deliberate ambiguity or play on words, the translator should choose the meaning which, after having considered all the possibilities, he thinks most likely. An alternative translation may, if necessary, be put in a footnote.

In accordance with the structure which is necessary in the rendering of verse 3a, one may translate verse 3b as "Be concerned for those who are suffering; consider what it is to suffer" or ". . . for you yourself to suffer."

13.4   **Marriage is to be honored by all, and husbands and wives must be faithful to each other. God will judge those who are immoral and those who commit adultery.**

Is to be honored is literally "marriage is honourable" (see NEB and Phps). However, there is no verb such as "should be" or "is" in the Greek text, and it fits in better with the context to make this verse a recommendation (**is to be**) rather than a statement ("is"), as in CLTs and many other translations. The two halves of the verse are joined by "**for**" (RSV), showing that verse 4b gives the reason for the statements in verse 4a. TEV leaves this connection to be implied.

In place of the passive expression **be honored**, it may be better to use an active statement: "All persons should honor marriage" or "All persons should consider marriage to be something good."

The two statements, **marriage is to be honored by all** and **husbands and wives must be faithful to each other**, mean essentially the same, so the first **and** may be omitted in languages where it leads the reader to expect new information. In some languages it may be replaced by a word meaning "indeed."

Modern translations often replace the reference to "**the marriage bed**" (RSV) by a nonfigurative expression; for example, DuCL "faithfulness in marriage must remain inviolate." RSV's "**undefiled**" here renders a word used in the same sense of Jesus in 7.26. In place of the positive statement **husbands and wives must be faithful to each other**, it may be more natural to express this negatively as "a husband and a wife must not go about looking for someone else to sleep with."

The statement **God will judge** implies a negative judgment, and therefore must be rendered in some languages as "God will condemn."

Those who are immoral means those who, whether married or not, are sexually immoral. **Those who commit adultery** refers only to those who are married. ItCL reverses the two phrases and translates "adultery or other immorality."

In some languages no distinction is made between fornication and adultery. But both are included in such phrases as "sexual relations apart from being married" or "sexual relations with someone who is not one's own spouse." In some languages fornication is described as "sex with a prostitute," while adultery involves "sex with another person's spouse."

13.5   **Keep your lives free from the love of money, and be satisfied with what you have. For God has said, "I will never leave you; I will never abandon you."**

Compare 10.34. The source of this quotation is not quite certain; Deuteronomy 31.6,8; Genesis 28.15; Joshua 1.5; and 1 Chronicles 28.20 are all possible. This verse brings another change of theme, as the new paragraph in CLTs, Mft, and NEB shows. However, sexual immorality and the love of money are often linked, as in 1 Corinthians 5.10-11, as different kinds of selfishness. Other translations do not begin a new paragraph here, but in common language translations shorter paragraphs are generally better.

The word translated **lives** is singular and means the way of life of each reader, considered collectively. Whether singular or plural is used depends on how the receptor language deals with objects in the possession of each member of a group; ItCL has the singular "life." The thought of verse 5a (though not the language) is found also in Luke 3.14.

Keep your lives free from the love of money may seem to be a rather roundabout way of rendering "Do not love money" or "Do not desire to have a lot of money." The Greek contains no suggestion of freedom as opposed to slavery, but the context suggests a continuing process.

For **and,** it may be more natural to use a word meaning "but" or "on the contrary." **What you have** renders a plural expression in the Greek text, "the things you have." **Be satisfied with what you have** may be rendered as "be happy that you have what you have."

God is clearly implied; in the Greek, "himself" (RSV "**he**") is emphatic and cannot mean "scripture."

Never in both cases gives the meaning of what is in Greek an emphatic "not."

It is important in rendering **I will never leave you; I will never abandon you** to employ two expressions which will not seem to be merely repetitive. This can usually be done by making the second term stronger than the first; for example, "I will not go away from you; I will not leave you without anything" or even ". . . leave you to be harmed by others"—which would be the implication of a term such as **abandon** or "desert." Alternatively, a single strong expression may be used.

13.6   Let us be bold, then, and say,
        "The Lord is my helper,
        I will not be afraid.
        What can anyone do to me?"

Then means "therefore." It does not refer to time, but indicates a conclusion drawn from verse 5b: "Because God has said that he will never abandon us, we can say with confidence, 'I will not be afraid.' "

It may be necessary to indicate to whom a particular statement is made. Accordingly, the first part of verse 6 may be rendered as "Therefore we should have confidence in God and say to people."

The quotation is from Psalm 118.6. The result of the confidence is given in line 2 of the quotation, as GeCL makes clear by putting it first: "We can say with confidence: 'I will have no fear, for the Lord helps me.' " This is effective in itself, but takes some of the emphasis away from **The Lord is my helper,** which FrCL expresses more strongly by "The Lord is the one who comes to my help." The word for **helper,** surprisingly, is not used anywhere else in the New Testament, but it is common in the Septuagint. It suggests "someone who responds to a call for help" rather than "an assistant."

13.6

Modern translations omit KJV's "and" before "I will not fear." This is more effective in translation, and the word is bracketed as doubtful in the UBS Greek text.

The writer of Hebrews probably changes the punctuation of the Septuagint text, which means "I will not fear what man will do to me." The change to a rhetorical question, **What can anyone** (RSV "man") **do to me?** is more vivid.

"**Man**" (RSV) renders a quite general Greek term, which refers to human beings in contrast with **Lord.** GeCL has "a human being" and ItCL "men," with the same meaning. SpCL restructures to read "I will not fear what any man can do to me." Women are not excluded.

TEV	13.7-16	RSV

7 Remember your former leaders, who spoke God's message to you. Think back on how they lived and died, and imitate their faith. 8 Jesus Christ is the same yesterday, today, and forever. 9 Do not let all kinds of strange teachings lead you from the right way. It is good to receive inner strength from God's grace, and not by obeying rules about foods; those who obey these rules have not been helped by them.

10 The priests who serve in the Jewish place of worship have no right to eat any of the sacrifice on our altar. 11 The Jewish High Priest brings the blood of the animals into the Most Holy Place to offer it as a sacrifice for sins; but the bodies of the animals are burned outside the camp. 12 For this reason Jesus also died outside the city, in order to purify the people from sin with his own blood. 13 Let us, then, go to him outside the camp and share his shame. 14 For there is no permanent city for us here on earth; we are looking for the city which is to come. 15 Let us, then, always offer praise to God as our sacrifice through Jesus, which is the offering presented by lips that confess him as Lord. 16 Do not forget to do good and to help one another, because these are the sacrifices that please God.

7 Remember your leaders, those who spoke to you the word of God; consider the outcome of their life, and imitate their faith. 8 Jesus Christ is the same yesterday and today and for ever. 9 Do not be led away by diverse and strange teachings; for it is well that the heart be strengthened by grace, not by foods, which have not benefited their adherents. 10 We have an altar from which those who serve the tent[a] have no right to eat. 11 For the bodies of those animals whose blood is brought into the sanctuary by the high priest as a sacrifice for sin are burned outside the camp. 12 So Jesus also suffered outside the gate in order to sanctify the people through his own blood. 13 Therefore let us go forth to him outside the camp, and bear the abuse he endured. 14 For here we have no lasting city, but we seek the city which is to come. 15 Through him then let us continually offer up a sacrifice of praise to God, that is, the fruit of lips that acknowledge his name. 16 Do not neglect to do good and to share what you have, for such sacrifices are pleasing to God.

[a] Or *tabernacle*

13.7 **Remember your former leaders, who spoke God's message to you. Think back on how they lived and died, and imitate their faith.**

Remember renders a different word from that used in verse 3, but the meaning is the same; GeCL has "do not forget," as in verse 2 (see RSV), for the sake of variety. In a number of languages a literal rendering of **Remember** is somewhat misleading. The Greek term may often be more satisfactorily translated as "Consider" or "Think about." There is no suggestion that people had literally forgotten who their former leaders were.

Former is implied. We do not know the names or precise functions of the leaders, and therefore specific titles such as "bishop" should be avoided.

On **God's message** see 4.12, where TEV translates literally The word of God. This phrase may also mean "the message about God."

Who spoke God's message to you may be expressed as "who spoke to you about God's message concerning Christ," or ". . . what God has announced concerning Christ," or ". . . the message that has come from God."

Think back on may be expressed as "Consider carefully" or "Meditate on."

TEV's simple translation **how they lived and died** is the result of careful analysis and a rather complicated restructuring of the original text. This is literally "looking-back-on the going-out of their way-of-life." "Looking-back-on" is an implied imperative. The text may be understood in two main ways. (a) "Going-out" means "end," and "way-of-life" in this context means simply "life." This is the interpretation of GeCL, "Remember how they died." (b) "Going-out" means "outcome"; Phps "result"; compare SpCL "what resulted from their life."

The main argument in favor of (a) is that the writer is constantly concerned that his readers shall hold on to their faith "to the end" (3.6,14; 6.11). The main argument in favor of (b) is that it gives the word for "way-of-life" its usual meaning. **How they lived and died** combines the strongest parts of both interpretations, showing that although the writer is concerned with the quality of the former leaders' life, he also has a special interest in **how they . . . died,** that is, still holding on to their faith. **Lived and died** are thus closely connected.

Imitate their faith may be expressed as "have the same kind of confidence in God that they had" or "show the same kind of trust in God which they showed."

13.8   **Jesus Christ is the same yesterday, today, and forever.**

Though at first sight this verse seems to stand on its own, in fact, connections are implied and some translations express them. **Jesus Christ** is the content of **God's message** in verse 7, and **yesterday** (with the extended meaning "in the past"), like **today** (compare 3.15), points back to your former leaders, perhaps even to the "heroes of faith" in chapter 11. The same (compare 1.12) contrasts with all kinds of strange teachings in verse 9, as NEB suggests by beginning verse 9 "So do not be swept off your course."

The same is emphasized in the Greek by being in an unusual position. A possible alternative translation would be "Jesus Christ is yesterday and today the same, and (also the same) forever." The simpler translation of TEV and RSV, in which the three main parts of the sentence are given equal weight, is probably better.

[325]

There are a number of problems involved in translating **Jesus Christ is the same yesterday, today, and forever.** In the first place the statement that **Jesus Christ is the same** may be regarded as simply a truism. Therefore it may be necessary to translate "Jesus Christ never changes." In the second place **yesterday** may not be a figurative symbol for past events or past time, and a literal rendering of **today** may suggest only a particular day rather than present time. Therefore **yesterday, today, and forever** may need to be rendered as "in the past, now, and in the future." To communicate this information clearly may require considerable expansion; for example, "Jesus Christ never changes. He has not changed in the past, he does not change now, and he will never change in the future."

13.9   **Do not let all kinds of strange teachings lead you from the right way. It is good to receive inner strength from God's grace, and not by obeying rules about foods; those who obey these rules have not been helped by them.**

All kinds of need not have a bad sense; see 2.4. It is the word **strange** which shows that the teachings are dangerous. **Strange** means "alien to the Gospel," not merely "odd." The plural **teachings** may refer to different kinds of false teaching, and should be kept in translation if possible. **All kinds of strange teachings** may be most effectively expressed as "all kinds of different teachings" or "all kinds of teachings that are different from the Good News."

Lead you from the right way means "be carried along" (as in Jude 12), or in this context, more precisely, "be swept away" (Brc). The rest of the verse shows that the contrast is with "standing firm" rather than "staying on a fixed course" (see NEB). The thought, though not the language, is similar to 2.1. In some languages **lead you from the right way** may be expressed idiomatically as "cause you to go down the wrong road," or "cause you to be turned aside from the truth," or "lead you off from the right road."

The word for **good** includes the idea of beauty or attractiveness. It has been called "that kind of goodness which is at once seen to be good." **To receive inner strength** is literally "for the heart to be strengthened" (see RSV). Thus **inner** is literally "the heart." It can be understood as "our heart," as the next verse shows (see RSV), but since verse 8 is an imperative, "your heart" fits the context better. A translation may therefore be something like "It is good for you to be strengthened inwardly by God's grace." **God's** is strongly implied. If "inwardly" is chosen to translate "the heart," meaning "what is deepest in man" as a whole, then "outwardly" may be used later in the sentence, to point out the contrast.

See comments on **grace** in 4.16.

Earlier editions of TEV had for our souls after **It is good.** TEV fourth edition omits these words, probably because soul was thought to be little used outside religious circles, and because the meaning is better conveyed by adding **inner** before **strength.**

The statement **It is good to receive inner strength from God's grace** may need considerable restructuring. One may need to employ a rendering such as "The fact that our hearts are made strong because of God's loving kindness to us is good." It may be important to render the first part of the second sentence in such a way as to anticipate the statement about obeying rules about foods. Therefore one may translate "God's kindness to us causes our hearts to have strength. This helps us, but obeying rules about food doesn't help us."

Most modern translations, like TEV, understand "by foods" to refer to **rules about foods,** not literally to the strengthening of the body by what is eaten. The phrase **right to eat** in the next verse confirms that this is correct, as does **obey** (literally "walk in") **these rules** in this verse. RSV's "by foods" and "their adherents" is unclear. Brc expresses the meaning strongly with a little expansion, as "The best thing to fortify your souls is the grace of God, not regulations about what we may eat and not eat, which have never been of the slightest use to those who use them as rules of life." TEV brings out the meaning of **by them,** which may also mean "in them": "those who walk in them," that is, **obey these rules, have not been helped by them.** The last part of this verse may also be rendered as "to obey rules about what to eat or not to eat doesn't help them" or ". . . doesn't do people any good."

13.10   **The priests who serve in the Jewish place of worship have no right to eat any of the sacrifice on our altar.**

This verse, like verse 8, points both backward and forward. This is one of the reasons why it is difficult to understand, and therefore difficult to translate. Two contrasts are involved, one of which is expressed and the other only implied. The expressed contrast is between the **Jewish place of worship** (**Jewish** is not explicit in the Greek) and **our altar.** The implied contrast, which has not always been noticed, is between the rules about foods and the Christian sacrifices of **praise to God** (verse 15) and doing **good** (verse 16). The writer is thinking particularly of the rule mentioned in verses 10-11, that the Old Testament priests are not allowed to eat the sacrifice for sins.

It is in this setting that the question "Does this verse refer to the Lord's Supper?" may be answered. The view of most Roman Catholics until recent years was that it did, and Knox's translation reflects this: "We have an altar of our own, and it is not those who carry out the worship of the tabernacle that are qualified to eat its sacrifices" (implying "but Christians do so in the Mass"). More recently, scholars of various churches have come to agree that **our altar** is "not the table used for the Eucharist, but either the cross on which Christ was sacrificed, or Christ himself through whom we offer the sacrifice of prayer to God" (JB note; similarly TOB).

How is this to be made clear in translation? In the clause, literally, "**We have an altar**" (RSV), SpCL replaces "altar" by "sacrifice" and so points more clearly to verses 15-16, "We have a different sacrifice, from which the priests of the old sanctuary have no right to eat," but even this could be misunderstood to refer to the Lord's Supper. TEV adds **the sacrifice on,** in order to avoid the idea of eating the altar itself. More important, the sentence is restructured so that **our altar** is deliberately given a less emphatic place than it has in the Greek text. This also makes a better link between **The priests** as the grammatical subject of verse 10, and the Jewish High Priest as the subject of verse 11. **Jewish,** as always in Hebrews, is implied; see comment on 10.1. **Priests** also fits the context better than Mft's "worshippers," which is another possible meaning of the Greek.

This makes it clearer that the elements of the comparison, with implied items in square brackets, are:

1. our altar (verse 10)	1. The [Old Testament] place of worship (verse 10)
2. [our sacrifice:] praise to God and doing good (verses 15,16)	2. the [Old Testament] sacrifice for sins: animals (verse 11)
3. the [Old Testament] priests do not eat our [sacrifice], [and neither do we] (verse 10)	3. the [Old Testament] priests burn this sacrifice, [and do not eat it] (verse 11)
4. Jesus died outside the city gate (verse 12)	4. the bodies of the animals offered in the [Old Testament] sacrifice for sins are burned outside the camp (verse 11)

In the Jewish place of worship may be expressed as "in the Jewish Temple." But to speak about the priest having **no right to eat any of the sacrifice on our altar** may wrongly suggest that Christians made sacrifices on altars. It is only after the reader comes to verse 15 that he realizes that the sacrifice is one of praise to God. It may therefore be necessary to introduce a marginal note referring the reader to verse 15. It may be possible to anticipate part of the content of verse 15 by translating this verse "The priests who serve in the Jewish place of worship have no right to share in any of the sacrifice of praise which we offer on our altar" or ". . . in our place of worship."

13.11   **The Jewish High Priest brings the blood of the animals into the Most Holy Place to offer it as a sacrifice for sins; but the bodies of the animals are burned outside the camp.**

Compare Leviticus 16.27 and, for the significance of being **outside the camp,** see Numbers 12.14-15. It is clear from the above summary that the Old Testament "sacrifice" for sin is partly contrasted and partly compared with the "sacrifice" of Christ. In verses 11-12 the two are compared rather than contrasted. On **High Priest**, see 2.17.

The Greek verbs in this verse, like the verb for serve in verse 10, are in the present. This is probably not because the writer thinks of the Old Testament sacrifices as still being offered in Jerusalem, but because the Old Testament itself is still available. In order to make clear the meaning of the present tenses **brings** and **are burned**, it may be necessary in some languages to specify that the action of bringing the blood of animals into the Most Holy Place was a yearly event. Therefore the first part of the verse may have "The Jewish High Priest each year brought the blood of animals into the Most Holy Place in order to offer it as a sacrifice for people's sins."

Most is implied; see comment on 8.2.

Bodies here clearly implies "dead bodies." The use of the word for **camp** takes the readers back to the time of the exodus from Egypt (for example, Exo 29.14; Lev 4.12).

The bodies are **burned** in this case to destroy impurity, not as part of the sacrifice. **Outside the camp** may be rendered as "outside the area where people lived" or "away from the dwellings of the people." There is no suggestion of a military camp.

13.12   **For this reason Jesus also died outside the city, in order to purify the people from sin with his own blood.**

For this reason points back to verse 11; Brc "That is why Jesus had to suffer outside the city . . . ." JB "and so Jesus too suffered outside the gate . . ." (so GeCL). **City** is literally "gate" (RSV). The picture is that of a walled town, such as was usual at that time (compare Acts 9.25). For the Old Testament background, see Leviticus 24.14 and Numbers 15.35. "**Suffered**" (RSV) here implies **died**, as, for example, in Luke 22.15. The meaning of RSV's "**sanctify the people**" is expressed negatively by TEV **purify the people from sin**, and positively by Brc "make the people fit to enter the presence of God." Both aspects are involved, but the second includes the first and may therefore be better. On **purify**, see 2.11 and 9.13. **The people** (see comments on 2.17) implies "God's people," as in 4.9. The Christian community is still thought of as being in continuity with Israel. **His own blood** is emphatic, in contrast with the blood of the animals in verse 11; see 9.25-26.

The purpose clause **in order to purify the people from sin with his own blood** may be rendered as "in order to take away from people their guilt by means of his blood which flowed out when he died."

13.13   **Let us, then, go to him outside the camp and share his shame.**

Then ("**Therefore**," RSV) renders a strong word in an unusual and therefore emphatic position, like the different Greek word for "therefore" in verse 12.1. It marks a transition from history to an appeal for action by the writer together with his readers. On **camp**, see verse 11. On **shame**, see comment on insulted in 10.33, and see especially 11.26, suffer scorn for the Messiah. These verses recall Psalm 89.50-51. Here **his shame** means "the shame which Jesus suffered because of the way in which he was killed."

It may be necessary to indicate clearly the figurative nature of this admonition to **go to him outside the camp and share his shame**. In order to mark that this is a figure, one may translate "Therefore we should, as it were, go to him outside the place where people are dwelling and share with him the shame he suffered," or ". . . be put to shame in the same way that he was put to shame," or ". . . be despised with him."

13.14 **For there is no permanent city for us here on earth; we are looking for the city which is to come.**

This verse contrasts **the city which is to come** with a **city for us here on earth**. As often in Hebrews, the language of time and space is intertwined. This verse recalls 11.10,16. The difference between the **city which is to come** and the **heavenly country** of 11.16a is one of language, not of meaning. They are both pictures of the state of being made perfect (11.40), which even for Christians still lies in the future. DuCL perhaps rightly emphasizes the permanence at the expense of other aspects of the **city**, such as size: "we have here no permanent place to live"; ItCL "a city in which we remain forever." GeCL throws the emphasis on the changing state of human life: "On earth there is no city in which we can stay," but in view of 12.26-27, and also 1.11-12, this does not seem to give the whole meaning, which should include the idea that no city is permanent. Another possible restructuring of the first half of this verse would be "For here on earth we have no place to dwell which will always be ours."

Looking for renders the verb used in 11.14. It is a strong Greek word which implies, not usually looking for something which is lost, but longing and striving to obtain something which is out of reach and out of sight. **To come** does not imply movement but means "in the future."

We are looking for the city which is to come may be expressed as "we are looking for a future city" or ". . . for a city which will exist in the future." A literal rendering of **we are looking for** might mean only "going around seeking to discover." If so, it may be better to employ an expression such as "we strongly desire to have a city which will be ours in the future."

13.15 **Let us, then, always offer praise to God as our sacrifice through Jesus, which is the offering presented by lips that confess him as Lord.**

It is very uncertain whether **then** is part of the original text. The UBS Greek New Testament includes it in square brackets. GeCL indicates only a loose relationship with earlier verses by beginning a new paragraph at this point. However, verses 15-16 are linked with verses 10-11 by the theme of sacrifice. **Sacrifice** even in the Old Testament could include **praise to God**, for example, in Psalm 50.14,23; 54.6. In translation a general term like "offering" may be needed, and the meaning of the term chosen needs to be carefully analyzed. In **praise to God** and "doing good" (verse 16), for example, there is clearly no thought of a sacrificial victim dying. The central idea is that of "giving something" to God. In verse 15 this involves response to his grace (verse 9); in verse 16 it involves action in the form of practical help.

Let us, then, always offer praise to God may need to be changed from an exhortation to a statement of obligation; for example, "Therefore, we should always praise God." In a few languages the concept of "praising God" must be expressed as direct discourse, since it involves verbalization; for example, "Therefore, we must always say, 'God is wonderful.' " The Greek for **"sacrifice of praise"** (RSV) is found in the Septuagint of Psalm 50.14, where the RSV footnote has "make thanksgiving your sacrifice to God."

Always is not emphasized but may suggest some contrast with the Old Testament sacrifices which were offered at set times.

Through Jesus is emphasized by being placed at the beginning of the Greek sentence. It is linked with the whole of the first part of the sentence, not just with **sacrifice**. It is a common phrase which is usually translated literally without its meaning being analyzed. GeCL first edition suggested "as we call upon Jesus." These words link verse 15 more closely with verse 12 than with verse 14. It may be difficult to link the phrase **as our sacrifice through Jesus** with what precedes. In fact it may be better to have an entirely new sentence, "This is our sacrifice to God which is made possible through Jesus" or ". . . made possible because of what Jesus did." **As our sacrifice** may also be expressed as "This is the way in which we sacrifice to God."

The offering presented . . . : RSV's **"fruit of lips that acknowledge his name"** explains "sacrifice of praise." **Which is the offering presented by lips** may be rendered as "what we say is our offering" or "our words are our offering."

Confess renders the usual meaning of the Greek word, and this is followed here by Brc "lips which publicly affirm their faith in him"; GeCL "we want to confess (our faith) in him with our singing and praying." Other translations choose the meaning "praise," which is more commonly that of a related compound verb; FrCL "let us praise his name continually with our mouths"; Mft "celebrate."

Him as Lord: God's "name" (RSV; see comments on 1.4) is the same as his "nature," thus referring to God himself; in 6.10, where KJV has "toward his name," RSV has "for him."

That confess him as Lord may be rendered as "when we confess him as our Lord" or "when we say, 'He is our Lord.' "

13.16 Do not forget to do good and to help one another, because these are the sacrifices that please God.

[331]

Do not forget renders the same Greek word used in verse 2 (TEV Remember) and in 6.10. **Do not forget** may sometimes be better expressed as "Make certain to" or "Be sure that you."

To do good renders a quite general expression, but the writer immediately makes it clear that he is thinking of practical **help** or "sharing," which were associated with **sacrifices** both in Jewish tradition and in the New Testament. **To do good and to help one another** may be more satisfactorily expressed as "to do good by helping one another." These are not two different kinds of coordinate activities; **to help one another** is a manner in which one does good.

These are the sacrifices is stronger than RSV's "**such sacrifices,**" and fits in better with the writer's generally negative judgment on other types of "sacrifice," for example, in 10.4. **These are the sacrifices that please God** may be rendered as "God is pleased with these kinds of sacrifices" or "when we offer these kinds of sacrifices God is pleased." In some languages it may seem strange to speak of doing good as a sacrifice. If so, one may translate "Your good deeds will please God and will be like a sacrifice (or, offering) given to him."

TEV	13.17-19	RSV

17 Obey your leaders and follow their orders. They watch over your souls without resting, since they must give to God an account of their service. If you obey them, they will do their work gladly; if not, they will do it with sadness, and that would be of no help to you.

18 Keep on praying for us. We are sure we have a clear conscience, because we want to do the right thing at all times. 19 And I beg you even more earnestly to pray that God will send me back to you soon.

17 Obey your leaders and submit to them; for they are keeping watch over your souls, as men who will have to give account. Let them do this joyfully, and not sadly, for that would be of no advantage to you.

18 Pray for us, for we are sure that we have a clear conscience, desiring to act honorably in all things. 19 I urge you the more earnestly to do this in order that I may be restored to you the sooner.

13.17   **Obey your leaders and follow their orders. They watch over your souls without resting, since they must give to God an account of their service. If you obey them, they will do their work gladly; if not, they will do it with sadness, and that would be of no help to you.**

This verse is more closely related to verses 8-16 than to verse 7, which speaks of _former leaders_. The present **leaders** of the Christian community are those especially responsible for seeing that its members are not "led astray" (verse 9). However, most translations, like the UBS Greek text, begin a new paragraph here.

Obey your leaders and follow their orders is not a statement of two different activities but of closely related ones, the first being general and the second more specific. Therefore it may be better in some languages to translate the first sentence of verse 17 as "Obey your leaders by following their orders" or ". . . by doing what they tell you to do."

On **souls**, see 4.12; Brc "Their care for you"; DuCL and GeCL "they watch over you." A strictly literal translation of **They watch over your souls without resting** may be misunderstood as being the activity of a sorcerer on the lookout for people's souls which he can control. It may therefore be better to translate **They watch over your souls without resting** as "They constantly care for you" or "They never rest in their concern to take care of you."

To God and **of their service** are implied. **Since they must give to God an account of their service** may be rendered as "because they must explain to God how they have carried out their responsibility" or ". . . how they have done their work," or even ". . . how they have cared for you."

Translations of the rest of the verse differ more in style and language than in meaning. RSV (see also NEB) would have been improved by omitting "**and**" before "**not sadly**," since the second phrase does not add any new information.

The elliptical clause **if not** may require some expansion; for example, "but if you do not obey them."

They will do it with sadness does not mean that they will go about their task with sad faces, but "they will do what they must do, but it will make them sad."

And that would be of no help to you may be expressed as "and that will not help you" or "and you will not benefit from that."

13.18   Keep on praying for us. We are sure we have a clear con-
          science, because we want to do the right thing at all times.

So little is known about the circumstances in which this letter was written that it is impossible to be sure whether **we** in this verse refers to the author alone, as Mft thinks, or to a number of people, as other translators believe. The fact that I is used in the next verse (for the first time, see verse 22) can be used as evidence on both sides. On the one hand, it can be argued that if the writer is talking of himself in verse 19, he is likely to be doing so in verse 18 too. On the other hand, if he is already talking about himself in verse 18, why should he change from **we** to I in verse 19? A stronger argument in favor of "I" in verse 18 is that the writer speaks of conscience, which almost by definition is something inward and therefore individual.

In some languages the positive statement **Keep on praying for us** may be more effectively stated in a negative form, "Do not cease to pray for us" or "Do not ever stop praying on our behalf" or ". . . speaking to God for our benefit."

We are sure we have a clear conscience may be expressed as "We are certain that our heart has no guilt."

[333]

Most modern translations omit RSV's **"for."** It seems here to act as a rather weak and general connecting link, rather than marking a logical relation between the two parts of the verse.

The right thing renders an adverb related to the word for good used in verse 9 (see the comment). There is, of course, no reference to any particular **thing;** Brc "to live a good life"; GeCL "to do what is right."

At all times is literally "in all (things)" or "in all (people)"; there is no explicit reference to time. "In all you do" would be a possible paraphrase; alternatively, but less probably, "in each of you." It is also possible to translate **at all times** as "in all circumstances."

13.19 **And I beg you even more earnestly to pray that God will send me back to you soon.**

This verse is closely linked in meaning with verse 18, though it is a separate sentence grammatically. **I beg you even more earnestly** is a strong expression and may be rendered idiomatically as "with all my heart I ask you" or "with all the strength I have I plead with you."

RSV's literal **"do this"** is made explicit as **to pray** in TEV and other translations. A comparison with RSV also shows that the reference to God is implied. Some CLTs and most other translations have **"the sooner"** (so RSV), implying "sooner than if you did not pray." It may , however, simply mean "very soon" (NAB), "soon" (ItCL and SpCL), or "as soon as possible" (GeCL).

TEV	**13.20-25**	RSV

Closing Prayer

20-21 God has raised from death our Lord Jesus, who is the Great Shepherd of the sheep as the result of his sacrificial death, by which the eternal covenant is sealed. May the God of peace provide you with every good thing you need in order to do his will, and may he, through Jesus Christ, do in us what pleases him. And to Christ be the glory forever and ever! Amen.

Final Words

22 I beg you, my brothers, to listen patiently to this message of encouragement; for this letter I have written you is not very long. 23 I want you to know that our brother Timothy has been

20 Now may the God of peace who brought again from the dead our Lord Jesus, the great shepherd of the sheep, by the blood of the eternal covenant, 21 equip you with everything good that you may do his will, working in you[b] that which is pleasing in his sight, through Jesus Christ; to whom be glory for ever and ever. Amen.

22 I appeal to you, brethren, bear with my word of exhortation, for I have written to you briefly. 23 You should understand that our brother Timothy has been released, with whom I shall see you if he comes soon. 24 Greet all your leaders and all the saints. Those who come from Italy send you

let out of prison. If he comes soon
enough, I will have him with me when I
see you.

24 Give our greetings to all your
leaders and to all God's people. The
brothers from Italy send you their
greetings.

25 May God's grace be with you all.

greetings.   25 Grace be with all of
you. Amen.

^b Other ancient authorities read *us*

The TEV section heading **Closing Prayer** may be rendered as "A prayer at
the end of the epistle" or "The writer ends with a prayer."

13.20-21   God has raised from death our Lord Jesus, who is the
                Great Shepherd of the sheep as the result of his sacrificial
                death, by which the eternal covenant is sealed. May the God
                of peace provide you with every good thing you need in order
                to do his will, and may he, through Jesus Christ, do in us what
                pleases him. And to Christ be the glory forever and ever!
                Amen.

Verses 20-21 are combined in TEV, since **the God of peace** belongs to verse
20 in the Greek, but has been moved to the beginning of verse 21, the second
sentence in TEV. Verse 20 recalls Isaiah 63.11.

It was common for Christians to end their letters with prayer, praise, and
blessing; see, for example, 1 Thessalonians 5.23 and 1 Peter 5.11. But these
closing words are not merely a formality; the writer weaves into this long sentence some of the most important key words of the letter, including "blood"
(**sacrificial death**) and **covenant.**

The main difficulty in this long sentence is to decide on the relation between **raised, the Great Shepherd of the sheep,** and **his death, by which the eternal
covenant is sealed.** The third phrase is literally "**by the blood of the eternal
covenant**" (RSV). The two possibilities are (a) God raised Jesus by means of "the
blood of the eternal covenant"; (b) Jesus became **the Great Shepherd of the sheep**
by means of **his sacrificial death, by which the eternal covenant is sealed.** Choice
(a) is the basis for Mft's translation "May the God of peace who brought up from
the dead our Lord Jesus, the great shepherd of the sheep, with the blood of the
eternal covenant . . . ." NEB has "who brought up from the dead our Lord
Jesus . . . by the blood of the eternal covenant," but the idea of Christ's "blood"
(**sacrificial death**) being the means of his "resurrection" is difficult, especially
since "God" is the subject of the sentence. Most modern translations choose (b).

Raised means literally "brought up"; this is not a common way of speaking
of the resurrection, but the meaning is nonetheless clear.

God has raised from death our Lord Jesus may be expressed as "God has
caused our Lord Jesus to live again."

In this sentence the writer uses the language of Isaiah 63.11 (**Shepherd of
the sheep;** for **Great,** compare 4.14); Zechariah 9.11 ("with the blood of the

covenant," RSV); and Isaiah 55.3 (**eternal covenant**). **Who is the Great Shepherd of the sheep** may require marking as a figurative expression; for example, "who is like a Wonderful Shepherd for the sheep." Otherwise some readers might think that Jesus has now become a chief shepherd over a flock of sheep.

As the result of his sacrificial death may be expressed as "because he died as a sacrifice."

By which the eternal covenant is sealed may be expressed as "by his death he established the covenant which will last forever."

The last part of this passage is a prayer directed to God. Therefore it may be necessary to introduce the prayer by a statement such as "I pray that." The translators of GeCL first edition felt that prayers in the subjunctive, corresponding to the English May . . . God, are no longer part of common language. They therefore restructured the text to say:

> I pray to God, who gives us peace. . . . I ask him to help you to
> do all the good he wants to be done. He himself will do in us
> what pleases him. He does it through Jesus Christ, to whom be
> praise for all times. Amen.

The text of verse 21, the second sentence in TEV, is doubtful at several points: (a) After **every good thing** (**thing** is implied) most manuscripts add "work," but this is not included in some of the best manuscripts. Among modern translations it is included only in JB as "good action" (not in BJ).

(b) After RSV's "**working**," some good manuscripts add a word meaning "to him" (unintelligible in this context), which is omitted in translation.

(c) In place of RSV's "**working in you**," the UBS Greek text has "working in us."

(d) The UBS Greek text has "forever [and ever]," indicating doubt as to whether the last two words are part of the original text. The difference is one of emphasis rather than meaning.

RSV's "**in his sight**" is literally "before him"; TEV's **what pleases him** gives the meaning.

The term **peace** in the expression **the God of peace** may be understood as a causative; for example, "the God who causes peace." In this context, in which the reference is to the **covenant, peace** may be understood in terms of reconciliation; for example, "the God who causes reconciliation."

Provide or "equip" **you with every good thing you need in order to do his will** recalls Philippians 2.13; see also Hebrews 11.5-6; 13.16. The writer speaks of "doing God's will" in terms of an active task, not just passive acceptance of one's fate. Earlier he has shown that for Jesus (10.7,9), as for Christians (10.36), "suffering" formed part of "doing God's will," but now he is emphasizing the positive achievement and victory of Christ.

Provide you with every good thing you need in order to do his will may also be rendered as "give to you all that is good which you need in order to do what he wants you to do" or ". . . all that is good and necessary in order to do what he desires you to do."

The first part of the prayer to **the God of peace** relates to what the believer himself should be doing in order to accomplish God's will, while the second part relates to what the believer himself should become. This second part may then be rendered as "may he make of us what he would have us to be." With this type of statement the phrase **through Jesus Christ** may be made a separate clause; for example, "this he will do through Jesus Christ" or "he will do this by causing Jesus Christ to accomplish it."

The closest equivalent to the statement **to Christ be the glory forever and ever** may be an admonition for praise or honor; for example, "Christ is the one to be praised forever and ever" or "let us honor Christ forever and ever."

In this context **Amen** fits well because this is the end of a prayer to God.

13.22   **I beg you, my brothers, to listen patiently to this message of encouragement; for this letter I have written you is not very long.**

Verses 22-25 may be a covering note, sent with the rest of the letter to another congregation. The TEV section heading **Final Words** may be rendered as "The last words of this letter."

Verse 22 contains the writer's second personal appeal. He now uses the first person singular, translated **I**.

Listen patiently could be misunderstood: (a) if the text is read aloud, as referring to a message of encouragement still to come; and (b) if the text is read silently, as making the reader ask "Why did the writer not ask his readers at the beginning of his letter to **listen patiently**?" The problem is solved if two things are kept in mind:

(1) **Listen patiently** need not refer to the danger of being bored; it refers more often to the danger of being angry or annoyed.

(2) **Encouragement** is only one part of the meaning of a flexible word, which in 12.5 has more the meaning of "challenge" (see comments there).

These two considerations lead to a translation similar to that of JB: "I do ask you, brothers, to take these words of advice kindly; that is why I have written to you so briefly." It is also possible to render the first part of this verse as "My fellow Christians, I urge you to listen willingly to this message in which I have encouraged you" or ". . . in which I have exhorted you." The final part of the verse may also be rendered as "That is why I have written to you such a short letter" or "since what I have written to you is very short."

13.23   **I want you to know that our brother Timothy has been let out of prison. If he comes soon enough, I will have him with me when I see you.**

"You know" is a grammatically possible translation of the first word in Greek, but "Know!" or **I want you to know** is more likely. **Brother** has the special Christian sense of "fellow Christian," implied by 13.1. **Let out of prison: of prison** is not expressed in the Greek text and is not absolutely necessary in translation (literally, simply **"released,"** RSV), but it seems the most likely meaning. TEV, GeCL, Brc make **out of prison** explicit, but most translations do not.

The most likely explanation of the second part of the verse is that as soon as Timothy joins the writer, the writer will take Timothy with him to see the readers of this letter (compare verse 19). "As soon as" is a well-attested meaning of the Greek words translated **soon enough,** but has not been chosen by translators. ItCL has simply "quickly."

For **I will have him with me,** FrCL has "I will take him with me"; TNT and GeCL have "I will bring him with me." FrCL takes as the point of reference the place where the writer is; TNT takes it as the place where the readers are. The translator must decide which is more natural in his own language. In English, as well as in this context, both are possible, and also TEV's neutral **I will have him with me.** However, the use of "bring" rather than "take" suggests a warmer identification with the readers' point of view.

13.24   Give our greetings to all your leaders and to all God's people. The brothers from Italy send you their greetings.

Give our greetings to is literally "Greet." As in verse 18, no one can be sure whether the writer is speaking in his own name alone or on behalf of a group. Here most translations avoid adding either **our** or "my" to **greetings;** Brc and TNT have "my." **Give our greetings to all your leaders** may be expressed as "Greet all your leaders with words as coming from us" or "Greet all your leaders as though we were greeting them."

All God's people: RSV "all the saints" does not mean "all the outstandingly religious members of the church," but "all the members of the Christian community," that is, "all who have been set apart as Christians to belong to God in a special way"; see comments on 3.1.

Brothers is not expressed in the Greek text, but it is natural to assume that "**those who come from Italy**" (RSV) are fellow-Christians, as in the previous verse. JB thinks "saints" is implied, but this view is not shared even by BJ.

The Greek is literally "those of Italy" or "those from Italy." (a) "Of Italy" would mean that the writer is in Italy and sends greetings from the church. (b) "From Italy" would mean that the writer is somewhere else and sends greetings from a group of expatriate Italians in the same place. Most translations either leave the matter open (Mft "The Italians salute you") or choose (b), like TEV and RSV. Phps ("The Christians of Italy") and JB choose (a). No one really knows whether the writer was in Italy or not.

13.25   May God's grace be with you all.

This is the final blessing. TEV translates the most likely text. Some manuscripts, followed by SpCL, Mft, Knox, and older translations, add "Amen." Others replace **you** with "the saints." On **grace**, see comments on 4.16. **God's** is implied. **May God's grace be with you all** may be rendered as "May God be good to you all." Or, as in the form of a prayer, "I pray that God may be good to you all," or ". . . show you his loving kindness," or ". . . demonstrate to you his love and kindness."

Appendix A

The Literary Structure of Hebrews

Section divisions in this Handbook follow TEV for the convenience of translators using TEV as a model. A detailed outline of the structure of Hebrews is given in A. Vanhoye's La structure littéraire de l'épître aux Hébreux, details of which are given in the bibliography. The main conclusions of this book are presented in English in A Structured Translation of the Epistle to the Hebrews (Rome: Pontifical Biblical Institute, 1964). This is a deliberately literal translation, designed for the special purpose of showing the structure of the original Greek. It is not intended as a model for any translation for general use, and should therefore not be used for that purpose.

Vanhoye suggests that Hebrews uses six main devices to show the structure of the text.

1. New subjects are announced in an introductory statement; see, for example, 1.4; 2.17-18; 5.9-10; 10.36-39; 12.11.

2. The same word or phrase is often used at the beginning and at the end of the development of a subject; for example, "to what angel" in 1.5 and 1.13 (RSV). This device is known as "inclusion."

3. "Hook words" are used to make a smooth transition from one paragraph to another; for example, the word "angels" is used in 1.4 at the end of the introduction, and is then repeated in 1.5 at the beginning of division 1.

4. Characteristic terms are sometimes repeated throughout a section, thereby giving it a certain unity; for example, "angel" in 1.5—2.18, and "faith" in chapter 11.

5. The text alternates between sections of teaching and appeals for action (exhortations); for example, the appeal of 2.1-4 is preceded (in 1.5-14) and followed (in 2.5-18) by two sections of teaching.

6. Vanhoye sees throughout the letter a symmetrical arrangement in which the first section is balanced by the last, the second by the section just prior to the last, and so inward to the center. This is called "chiasmus"; it is found in many parts of the Bible and elsewhere. The resulting pattern is as follows:

Appendix A

The Structure of the Letter to the Hebrews

Section	Subject	Dominant genre	Ref.
Introduction			1.1-4
1	The name above that of angels	d	1.5—2.18
2.1	Jesus, the faithful one	p	3.1—4.14
2.2	Jesus, the compassionate high priest	d	4.15—5.10
3.1	Preliminary exhortation	p	5.11—6.20
3.2	Jesus and Melchizedek	d	7.1-28
3.3	Jesus attained fulfillment	d	8.1—9.28
3.4	Jesus, cause of salvation	d	10.1-18
3.5	Final exhortation	p	10.19-39
4.1	The faith of men of old	d	11.1-40
4.2	Endurance is necessary	p	12.1-13
5	The fruit of righteousness	p	12.14—13.19
Conclusion			13.20f.

d = doctrinal teaching
p = paraenesis (exhortation, calls for action)

Vanhoye's presentation has been widely discussed, and particular aspects of it have been criticized. Not every detail of the letter need be pressed into this mold, and it is not always the case that the development of the thought of Hebrews (its "theological structure") follows precisely the same pattern as the literary structure of the letter with which Vanhoye is concerned. However, the broad outline of his proposals have been generally accepted. They are, for example, the basis on which the material in G.W. Buchanan's commentary is arranged (see bibliography).

Appendix B

The Translation of "Covenant"

Elements in the problem are as follows:
1. From the side of the biblical text and culture:
1.1 The "covenant" has been called "the most central theological concept in the Old Testament." In Hebrews and other parts of the New Testament, it defines the new relationship between God and men which has been set up by the life, and especially by the death, of Christ. There is continuity between Old and New Testaments as well as difference. This is shown, for example, not only by the use of the word "Testament" to describe two divisions of the Bible ("testament" comes from a Latin mistranslation of the Greek word for "covenant"), but also by the repetition, through the Bible, of statements describing the way in which God and his people (Israel or the Church) belong together. Exodus 29.45 is typical: "I will dwell among the people of Israel, and will be their God" (RSV; compare Exo 6.7; Lev 26.12; Ezek 37.27; 2 Cor 6.16; Rev 21.3).
1.2 The "covenant" between God and Israel was probably unique, even in its various Old Testament forms, and even more in the New Testament. The closest parallels in Old Testament times may be treaties between an important ruler and the less important, only partly independent, chiefs who depended on him for protection. In such a situation one of the conditions of the biblical "covenant" was partly fulfilled: the more powerful ruler could more or less dictate terms to the others; that is to say, there was no question of a bargain or agreement between equals. But the biblical covenant remains very different: (a) the initiative comes, not mainly, but entirely from God; (b) the founder of the covenant is not a human ruler, but the distinctive "living God" of Israelite belief; (c) all the advantage is on the side of Israel, none on the side of God, though God expects a response from his people.
1.3 There are special problems with the Greek word for "covenant," since it also means "will" and is almost certainly used in this sense in Hebrews 9.16-17 (see comments on these verses).
2. From the side of present-day language and culture:
2.1 It is unusual to find a culture in which both the following conditions are met:

- national life based on the idea of an "agreement" between God and the people.
- the initiative wholly from God's side, and the advantages wholly on the side of the people.

2.2 It is even difficult to find parallels in secular (for example, political) life to an "agreement" in which all the conditions are determined by one party, but without any overtones of tyranny or dictatorship.

2.3 In languages with a long history of Bible translation, there is therefore a strong tendency to keep traditional words for "covenant" even in modern common language translations.

2.3.1 In English, KJV used "covenant" and "testament" almost interchangeably in the New Testament, especially in Hebrews. Both TEV and RSV use "covenant" throughout Hebrews, except in 9.16,17, where they use "will," the modern equivalent of "testament." However, "covenant" in present-day English is used exclusively in legal and church language. Its older use in common language to mean "agreement" has almost disappeared. The use of "covenant" in TEV indicates an unsolved problem. Phps uses "agreement," which does not sufficiently show the distinctive features of the biblical covenant. Brc has "a better relationship between God and man" in 7.22, but afterward "covenant." Another possibility would be "the special contract between God and man" the first time the word for "covenant" is used in a passage, and "this contract," or "the contract" afterward.

2.3.2 In French and German, for example, the problem is similar in that the traditional words for "covenant," respectively *alliance* and *Bund*, are kept in modern translations (Zür even has "*Testament*," like the earlier editions of Lu). It is, however, different in that the French and German words are still used in non-church and even common language, but with other meanings; the French word *alliance*, for example, may mean a political or military alliance, a marriage (in literary language), or a wedding ring; and the German *Bund* may mean a federation (as in "German Federal Republic"), band, bandage, etc.

2.4 The dilemma illustrated by these European languages recurs in many parts of the world. If a familiar expression is used to describe this central and unique institution of the "covenant," it may be misunderstood, but on the other hand, if an unfamiliar expression is used, it may not be understood at all.

Appendix C

It is difficult to make good sense either of a completely objective or of a completely subjective definition of faith. Hebrews 11.1 almost certainly does not mean either "faith gives an objective basis to hopes which would not otherwise have any such basis," or "faith is feeling sure that we shall get what we hope for." A choice between the three translations mentioned in the text of this Handbook must take into account a number of other factors.

(a) A similar problem arises in the second half of the verse, with the word which RSV translates "conviction" (most translations agree, or use equivalent verbal expressions like to be certain), but KJV translates "evidence," and BJ "proof," which is the more common meaning of the word.

(b) Faith is clearly "faith in God" or "in Christ"; it is therefore a personal relationship rather than something which can be neatly defined as either subjective or objective. It is a human response to a call or initiative from God, and therefore in a good sense subjective.

(c) This verse is not necessarily a definition of faith. Its underlying meaning may be, as Knox and NEB text suggest, that faith is the cause, and our "conviction" is an effect.

(d) There is nothing explicitly in this verse about "us" (despite TEV, NEB, TNT and other translations); the rest of the chapter shows that the reference is much wider. Other translations have "one" or "you" in the sense of "someone."

Bibliography

BIBLE TEXTS AND VERSIONS CITED

Texts

The Greek New Testament. Third edition, 1975. K. Aland, M. Black, C.M. Martini, B.M. Metzger, and A. Wikgren, eds. Stuttgart: United Bible Societies. (Cited as UBS Greek New Testament.)

Novum Testamentum Graece. 26th edition, 1979. Kurt Aland and others, eds. Stuttgart: Deutsche Bibelstiftung.

Versions

Die Bibel in heutigem Deutsch: Die Gute Nachricht des Alten und Neuen Testaments. 1982. Stuttgart: Deutsche Bibelgesellschaft. (Cited as GeCL.)

Die Bibel: Nach der Übersetzung Martin Luthers, Revidierter Text. 1975, 1978. Stuttgart: Deutsche Bibelstiftung. (Cited as Lu.)

The Bible: A New Translation. James Moffatt. 1922. New York: Harper and Row; London: Hodder and Stoughton. (Cited as Mft.)

La Bible de Jérusalem. 1973. Paris: Les Éditions du Cerf. (Cited as BJ.)

La Bible en français courant. 1982. Paris: Alliance Biblique Universelle. (Cited as FrCL.)

Dios Llega Al Hombre. El Nuevo Testamento de Nuestro Señor Jesucristo: Versión Popular. First edition, 1966; Second edition, 1970. Asunción: Sociedades Bíblicas Unidas. European edition, 1971. Madrid: Sociedad Bíblica. (Cited as SpCL.)

Good News Bible: The Bible in Today's English Version. 1976, 1979. New York: American Bible Society. (Cited as TEV.)

Bibliography

Groot Nieuws Bijbel: vertaling in omgangstaal. 1983. Boxtel: Katholieke Bijbelstichting; Haarlem: Nederlands Bijbelgenootschap. (Cited as DuCL.)

Die Gute Nachricht: Das Neue Testament in heutigem Deutsch. 1971. Stuttgart: Württembergische Bibelanstalt. (Cited as GeCL first edition.)

Die Heilige Schrift des Alten und des Neuen Testaments. 1935. Zürich: Zwingli-Bibel. (Cited as Zür.)

The Holy Bible (Authorized or King James Version). 1611. (Cited as KJV.)

The Holy Bible: New International Version. 1978. Grand Rapids, Michigan: Zondervan Bible Publishers; London: Hodder and Stoughton. (Cited as NIV.)

The Holy Bible: Revised Standard Version. 1952, 1971, 1973. New York: Division of Christian Education of the National Council of the Churches of Christ in the United States of America. (Cited as RSV.)

The Jerusalem Bible. 1966. London: Darton, Longman & Todd. (Cited as JB.)

The New American Bible. 1970. Camden, New Jersey: Thomas Nelson, Inc. (Cited as NAB.)

The New English Bible. First edition of the New Testament, 1961; Second edition, 1970. London: Oxford University Press and Cambridge University Press. (Cited as NEB.)

The New Testament: A new translation by William Barclay. Volume 2: The Letters and the Revelation. 1969. London: Collins. (Cited as Brc.)

The New Testament of Our Lord and Saviour Jesus Christ: A New Translation. 1952. Ronald P. Knox. New York: Sheed and Ward, Inc. (Cited as Knox.)

The New Testament in Modern English. 1962. J.B. Phillips. New York: Macmillan (Cited as Phps.)

Le Nouveau Testament. Version Synodale. 1949. Paris: Alliance Biblique Française. (Cited as Syn.)

O Novo Testamento: a Boa Nova para toda gente. 1978. Lisbon: Sociedade Bíblica. (Cited as PoCL.)

Parola Del Signore: Il Nuovo Testamento: Traduzione interconfessionale dal testo greco in lingua corrente. 1976. Leumann: Elle Di Ci; Rome: Alleanza Biblica Universale. (Cited as ItCL.)

La Sainte Bible, traduite d'après les textes originaux hébreu et grec. Louis Segond, éd. revue. 1959. Paris. (Cited as Seg.)

Septuaginta (editio quarta). 1950. Alfred Rahlfs, ed. Stuttgart: Württembergische Bibelanstalt. (Cited as Septuagint.)

Traduction Oecuménique de la Bible: Nouveau Testament. 1974. Paris: Sociétés Bibliques/Les Éditions du Cerf. (Cited as TOB.)

The Translator's New Testament. 1973. London: British & Foreign Bible Society. (Cited as TNT.)

GENERAL BIBLIOGRAPHY

Grammars

Blass, F., and A. Debrunner. 1961. A Greek Grammar of the New Testament and Other Early Christian Literature. Translated by Robert W. Funk. Chicago: University of Chicago Press.

A Grammar of New Testament Greek. Vol. 1: J.H. Moulton. 1908. Prolegomena. Vol. 2: J.H. Moulton and W.F. Howard. 1919. Accidence and Word Formation. Vol. 3: N. Turner. 1963. Syntax. Vol. 4: N. Turner. 1976. Style. Edinburgh: T. & T. Clark.

Lexicons

Arndt, W.F., and F.W. Gingrich. 1979. A Greek-English Lexicon of the New Testament and Other Early Christian Literature. Second edition, revised by F.W. Gingrich and F.W. Danker. Chicago: University of Chicago Press.

Moulton, J.H., and G. Milligan. 1914-1929. The Vocabulary of the Greek Testament Illustrated from the Papyri and Other Non-Literary Sources. London: Hodder and Stoughton.

Commentaries

Bleek, F. 1828-1840. Der Brief an die Hebräer. 3 volumes. Berlin: F. Dummler.

The first great modern commentary. Particularly useful for examples of how words which occur in Hebrews are used by other authors. Based on the Greek text.

Bibliography

Bruce, F.F. 1965. Commentary on the Epistle to the Hebrews. London: Marshall, Morgan & Scott.

Probably the best all-round commentary on Hebrews in English.

Buchanan, G.W. 1972. To the Hebrews (Anchor Bible). New York: Doubleday.

Readable and original; sometimes exaggerates the relevance of Qumran.

Calvin, John. 1853. Commentaries on the Epistle of Paul the Apostle to the Hebrews. Translated by John Owen. Edinburgh: Calvin Translation Society.

A theological commentary which also pays careful attention to different possible interpretations of the text.

Héring, Jean. 1970. The Epistle to the Hebrews. London: Epworth Press.

Concise, original, helpful on details of the text.

Hughes, Graham. 1979. Hebrews and Hermeneutics: The Epistle to the Hebrews as an Example of Biblical Interpretation. Cambridge: Cambridge University Press.

More important for interpretation in the wider sense than for translation. Unfortunately no index of texts.

Hughes, P.E. 1977. A Commentary on the Epistle to the Hebrews. Grand Rapids, Michigan: Eerdmans.

Useful information on how Hebrews was understood in earlier times; too wordy for most translators.

Jewett, R. 1981. Letter to Pilgrims: A Commentary on the Epistle to the Hebrews. New York: The Pilgrim Press.

The author believes that Hebrews and Colossians were written to the same general group. Many incidental comments of use to translators.

Michel, Otto. 13th edition, 1975. Der Brief an die Hebräer. Göttingen: Vandenhoeck & Ruprecht.

Perhaps the greatest current commentary on Hebrews; particularly valuable on the Jewish background. Based on the Greek text.

Moffatt, James. 1924. A Critical and Exegetical Commentary on the Epistle to the Hebrews (International Critical Commentary). Edinburgh: T. & T. Clark.

Valuable information on classical and other non-biblical Greek usage. Based on the Greek text.

Montefiore, Hugh. 1964. A Commentary on the Epistle to the Hebrews. London: A. & C. Black.

Sometimes controversial on background issues, but always interesting.

Riggenbach, E. 1913; second edition, 1922. Der Brief an die Hebräer. Leipzig: Deichert.

Keeps close to the Greek text, and lets nothing through the net.

Spicq, C. 1952. L'Épître aux Hébreux. Two volumes. Paris: Gabalda.

Combines study of the original meaning of the text with the history of its interpretation. Based on the Greek text.

————. 1977. L'Épître aux Hébreux (Sources Bibliques). Paris: Librairie Lecoffre et Gabalda.

Often more useful to translators than his two-volume commentary. Excellent updated bibliography.

Vanhoye, Albert. 1963; second revised edition, 1976. La structure littéraire de l'épître aux Hébreux. Bruges and Paris: Desclée de Brouwer.

See Appendix A.

————. 1969. Situation du Christ. Paris: Éditions du Cerf.

Very detailed but sensitive and readable commentary on Hebrews 1--2.

Westcott, B.F. Second edition 1892. The Epistle to the Hebrews. London: Macmillan. Reprinted 1970. Grand Rapids, Michigan: Eerdmans.

A classic theological commentary; sometimes exaggerates differences between synonyms. Based on the Greek text.

Windisch, H. 1913; second, greatly revised edition, 1931. Der Hebräerbrief. Tübingen: Mohr.

Concise, factual, always to the point. Based on the Greek text.

Bibliography

Other Works

Dussaut, Louis. 1981. Synopse structurelle de l'Épître aux Hébreux. Paris: Éditions du Cerf.

    Not a commentary, but discusses the structure of each section of Hebrews in relation to the whole. Not always convincing in detail.

Ellingworth, P. 1977. Just like Melchizedek. The Bible Translator 28.236-239.

——————. 1975. Like the Son of God: Form and content in Hebrews 7.1-10. Biblica 64(2).255-262.

Fauna and Flora of the Bible (Helps for Translators). 1972; second edition, 1980. New York: United Bible Societies.

Hollander, Harm. Hebrews 7.11 and 8.6: A suggestion for the translation of nenomothetētai epi. The Bible Translator 30.244-247.

Metzger, Bruce M. 1975. A Textual Commentary on the Greek New Testament. New York: United Bible Societies.

Nida, E.A., and Charles R. Taber. 1974. The Theory and Practice of Translation. Leiden: E.J. Brill.

de Waard, J. 1973. Biblical metaphors and their translation. The Bible Translator 25.107-116.

Williamson, Ronald. 1970. Philo and the Epistle to the Hebrews. Leiden: Brill.

    Analyzes differences between Philo and Hebrews, even where they use similar language. Not a commentary.

Glossary

This Glossary contains terms which are technical from an exegetical or a linguistic viewpoint. Other terms not defined here may be referred to in a Bible dictionary.

active. See voice.

adjective is a word which limits, describes, or qualifies a noun. In English, "red," "tall," "beautiful," and "important" are adjectives.

adverb is a word which limits, describes, or qualifies a verb, an adjective, or another adverb. In English, "quickly," "soon," "primarily," and "very" are adverbs.

adversative describes something opposed to or in contrast with something already stated. "But" and "however" are adversative conjunctions.

affix is a part of a word which cannot stand alone and which is added to a root or stem, for example, "im- (in impossible)," "-ly (in friendly)," "-est (in largest)."

agent is that which accomplishes the action in a sentence or clause, regardless of whether the grammatical construction is active or passive. In "John struck Bill" (active) and "Bill was struck by John" (passive), the agent in either case is John.

ambiguity is the quality of being ambiguous in meaning. See ambiguous.

ambiguous describes a word or phrase which in a specific context may have two or more different meanings. For example, "Bill did not leave because John came" could mean either (1) "the coming of John prevented Bill from leaving" or (2) "the coming of John was not the cause of Bill's leaving." It is often the case that what is ambiguous in written form is not ambiguous when actually spoken, since features of intonation and slight pauses usually make clear which of two or more meanings is intended. Furthermore, even in written discourse, the entire context normally serves to indicate which meaning is intended by the writer.

anachronism is an expression which is incorrectly used because it is historically or chronologically misplaced. For example, to refer to Jonah buying a ticket for his sea voyage would be an anachronism because it introduces a modern custom into an ancient setting.

analogy is a comparison between two items that have some features which are
similar.

antecedent designates an object or event which precedes or exists prior to something or someone else. In the grammatical sense, an antecedent is an object
or event referred to by a term which occurs later in the discourse. In "When
John came, he greeted me," "John" is the antecedant of "he."

anticipatory refers to the use of a pronoun prior to a noun identified by a relative
clause, in order to emphasize the identity of the noun. An anticipatory pronoun such as "it" may be employed in such a way as to put the new information into the predicate part of the sentence. For example, in "It was the big
dog that barked," "It" anticipates which dog barked and emphasizes its
identity.

anticlimax is any part of a story, speech, or other form of discourse which is less
important or less striking than expected, or is less important than the real
climax. See climax.

apposition (appositional) is the placing of two expressions together so that they
both refer to the same object, event, or concept; for example, "my friend,
Mr. Smith." The one expression is said to be the appositive of the other.

article is a grammatical class of words, usually obligatory, which indicate whether
the accompanying word is definite or indefinite. In English the definite
article is "the," and the indefinite article is "a" (or "an").

aspect is a grammatical category which specifies the nature of an action; for
example, whether the action is completed, uncompleted, repeated, begun,
continuing, increasing in intensity, decreasing in intensity, etc. "Was built"
indicates completed aspect, while "was running" indicates continuing aspect.

attributive is a term which limits or describes another term. In "The big man ran
slowly," the adjective "big" is an attributive of "man." See adjective, adverb.

auxiliary is a word which combines closely with another word and which serves to
specify certain important aspects of meaning. The term auxiliary is normally employed in referring to auxiliaries to verbs; for example, "shall,"
"will," "may," or "ought."

causative relates to events and indicates that someone or something caused something to happen, rather than that the person or thing did it directly. In "John
ran the horse," the verb "ran" is a causative, since it was not John who ran,
but rather it was John who caused the horse to run.

chiasmus is a reversal of the order of words or phrases in an otherwise parallel
construction. For example: "I (1)/was shapen (2) in iniquity (3)//in sin (3)/did
my mother conceive (2)/me (1)."

clause is a grammatical construction, normally consisting of a subject and a
predicate. The main clause is that clause in a sentence which could stand

[354]

alone as a complete sentence, but which has one or more dependent or subordinate clauses related to it. A <u>subordinate clause</u> is dependent on the main clause, but it does not form a complete sentence.

<u>climax</u> is the point in a discourse, such as a story or speech, which is the most important, or the turning point, or the point of decision. See also <u>anticlimax</u>.

<u>collective</u> refers to a number of things (or persons) considered as a whole. In English, a collective noun is considered to be singular or plural, more or less on the basis of traditional usage; for example, "The crowd is (the people are) becoming angry."

<u>common language translation</u> is one that uses only that portion of the total resources of a language that is understood and accepted by all native speakers as good usage. Excluded are features peculiar to a dialect, substandard or vulgar language, and technical or highly literary language not understood by all.

<u>comparative</u> refers to the form of an adjective or adverb that indicates that the object or event described possesses a certain quality to a greater degree than does another object or event. "Richer" and "smaller" are adjectives in the comparative degree, while "sooner" and "more quickly" are adverbs in the comparative degree.

<u>complement</u> is a word or phrase which grammatically completes another word or phrase. The term is used particularly of expressions which specify time, place, manner, means, etc.

<u>concessive</u> means expressing a <u>concession</u>, that is, the allowance or admission of something which is at variance with the principal thing stated. Concession is usually expressed in English by "though" ("even though," "although"). For example, "Though the current was swift, James was able to cross the stream."

<u>condition</u> is that which shows the circumstance under which something may be true. In English, a <u>conditional</u> phrase or clause is usually introduced by "if."

<u>conjunctions</u> are words which serve as connectors between words, phrases, clauses, and sentences. "And," "but," "if," and "because" are typical conjunctions in English.

<u>connotation</u> involves the emotional attitude of a speaker (or writer) to an expression he uses, and the emotional response of the hearers (or readers). Connotations may be good or bad, strong or weak, and they are often described in such terms as "colloquial," "taboo," "vulgar," "old-fashioned," and "intimate."

<u>construction</u>. See <u>structure</u>.

<u>context</u> is that which precedes and/or follows any part of a discourse. For example, the context of a word or phrase in Scripture would be the other words

and phrases associated with it in the sentence, paragraph, section, and even the entire book in which it occurs. The context of a term often affects its meaning, so that a word does not mean exactly the same thing in one context that it does in another context.

culture (cultural) is the sum total of the beliefs, patterns of behavior, and sets of interpersonal relations of any group of people. A culture is passed on from one generation to another, but undergoes development or gradual change.

definite article. See article.

direct discourse. See discourse.

direct object is the goal of an event or action specified by a verb. In "John hit the ball," the direct object of "hit" is "ball."

discourse is the connected and continuous communication of thought by means of language, whether spoken or written. The way in which the elements of a discourse are arranged is called discourse structure. Direct discourse is the reproduction of the actual words of one person quoted and included in the discourse of another person; for example, "He declared *'I will have nothing to do with this man.'* " Indirect discourse is the reporting of the words of one person within the discourse of another person, but in an altered grammatical form rather than as an exact quotation; for example, "He said *he would have nothing to do with that man.*"

distributive refers not to the group as a whole, but to the members of the group.

double negative is a grammatical construction in which two negative words are used in the same clause. In English two negatives usually produce a positive meaning ("He did not say nothing" means "He did say something"). In many languages, however, a double negative is often an emphatic negative (as in Greek, where "no not" means "*definitely* not").

dynamic equivalence is a type of translation in which the message of the original text is so conveyed in the receptor language that the response of the receptors is (or, can be) essentially like that of the original receptors, or that the receptors can in large measure comprehend the response of the original receptors, if, as in certain instances, the differences between the two cultures are extremely great.

elliptical refers to words or phrases normally omitted in a discourse when the sense is perfectly clear without them. In the following sentence, the words within brackets are elliptical: "If [it is] necessary [for me to do so], I will wait up all night."

emphasis (emphatic) is the special importance given to an element in a discourse, sometimes indicated by the choice of words or by position in the sentence. For example, in "Never will I eat pork again," "Never" is given emphasis by placing it at the beginning of the sentence.

event is a semantic category of meanings referring to actions, processes, etc., in which objects can participate. In English, most events are grammatically classified as verbs ("run," "grow," "think," etc.), but many nouns also may refer to events, as for example, "baptism," "song," "game," "prayer."

exclusive first person plural excludes the person(s) addressed. That is, a speaker may use "we" to refer to himself and his companions, while specifically excluding the person(s) to whom he is speaking. See inclusive.

expletive, as a grammatical term, is a word or phrase which appears in the place of the subject or object in the normal word order, anticipating a subsequent word or phrase which will complete the meaning. For example, in the statement "It is difficult to sing the high notes," the word "it" is an expletive which anticipates the real subject, "to sing the high notes."

explicit refers to information which is expressed in the words of a discourse. This is in contrast to implicit information. See implicit.

figure, figurative expression, or figure of speech involves the use of words in other than their literal or ordinary sense, in order to bring out some aspect of meaning by means of comparison or association. For example, "raindrops dancing on the street," or "his speech was like thunder." Metaphors and similes are figures of speech.

first person. See person.

full stop, or period, is a marker indicating the end of a sentence.

future tense. See tense.

generic has reference to a general class or kind of objects, events, or abstracts; it is the opposite of specific. For example, the term "animal" is generic in relation to "dog," which is a specific kind of animal. However, "dog" is generic in relation to the more specific term "poodle."

goal is the object which receives or undergoes the action of a verb. Grammatically, the goal may be the subject of a passive construction ("John was hit," in which "John" is the goal of "hit"), or of certain intransitives ("the door shut"), or it may be the direct object of a transitive verb ("[something] hit John").

hyperbole is a figure of speech that makes use of exaggeration. That is, a deliberate overstatement is made to create a special effect. For example, "John ate tons of rice for dinner."

idiom (idiomatic) is a combination of terms whose meanings cannot be understood by adding up the meanings of the parts. "To hang one's head" and "to have a green thumb" are English idioms. Idioms almost always lose their meaning or convey a wrong meaning when translated literally from one language to another.

imperative refers to forms of a verb which indicate commands or requests. In "Go and do likewise," the verbs "Go" and "do" are imperatives. In many languages, imperatives are confined to the grammatical second person; but some languages have corresponding forms for the first and third persons. These are usually expressed in English by the use of "may" or "let"; for example, "May we not have to beg!" "Let them work harder!"

implicit (implied) refers to information that is not formally represented in a discourse, since it is assumed that it is already known to the receptor, or evident from the meaning of the words in question. For example, the phrase "the other son" carries with it the implicit information that there is a son in addition to the one mentioned. This is in contrast to explicit information, which is expressly stated in a discourse. See explicit.

inclusive first person plural includes both the speaker and the one(s) to whom that person is speaking. See exclusive.

indefinite article. See article.

indicative refers to forms of a verb in which an act or conditon is stated as an actual fact rather than as a potentiality, a hope, or an unrealized condition. The verb "won" in "The king won the battle" is in the indicative form. See subjunctive.

indirect speech, indirect discourse. See discourse.

infinitive is a verb form which indicates an action or state without specifying such factors as agent or time; for example, "to mark," "to sing," or "to go." It is in contrast to finite verb form, which often distinguishes person, number, tense, mode, or aspect; for example, "marked," "sung," or "will go."

interrogative pronoun is a pronoun which indicates that a question is being asked. "Who," "whose," "whom," "which," and "what" are interrogative pronouns.

literal means the ordinary or primary meaning of a term or expression, in contrast with a figurative meaning. A literal translation is one which represents the exact words and word order of the source language; such a translation is frequently unnatural or awkward in the receptor language.

manuscripts are books, documents, or letters written by hand. Thousands of manuscript copies of various Old and New Testament books still exist, but none of the original manuscripts. See text.

metaphor is likening one object, event, or state to another by speaking of it as if it were the other; for example, "flowers dancing in the breeze." Metaphors are so commonly used and so well established in all languages that speakers and writers often use them without being conscious of the fact that they are using figurative language. See simile.

modal refers to forms of verbs in certain languages which indicate the attitude of a speaker to what he is saying; for example, wish, hesitancy, command, etc. The various categories of modal verb forms are called modes or moods. In

English they are expressed by such auxiliary verbs as "can," "do," "may," "shall," etc.

nonrestrictive clauses. See restrictive clauses.

object. See direct object.

paragraph is a distinct segment of discourse dealing with a particular idea, and usually marked with an indentation on a new line.

parallel, parallelism, generally refers to some similarity in the content and/or form of a construction; for example, "Hear this, all peoples! Give ear, all inhabitants of the world." The structures that correspond to each other in the two statements are said to be parallel. Parallels, or parallel passages, refers to two or more portions of biblical text that resemble each other, often by using a series of words that are identical. For example, the Lord's Prayer as recorded in Matthew 6.9-13 has as its parallel Luke 11.2-4.

parenthetical statement is a statement that interrupts a discourse by departing from its main theme. It is frequently set off by marks of parenthesis ( ).

participial indicates that the phrase, clause, construction, or other expression described is governed by a participle.

participle is a verbal adjective, that is, a word which retains some of the characteristics of a verb while functioning as an adjective. In "singing children" and "painted house," "singing" and "painted" are participles.

passive. See voice.

past tense. See tense.

perfective aspect of the verb involves an event or state which takes place prior to the time of the discourse, but the implication or effect of such an event or state continues until the time of the discourse. For example, in "What I have written, I have written," the effect or implication of the event of writing continues to the time when Pontius Pilate speaks these words.

person , as a grammatical term, refers to the speaker, the person spoken to, or the person or thing spoken about. First person is the person(s) speaking (such as "I," "me," "my," "mine," "we," "us," "our," or "ours"). Second person is the person(s) or thing(s) spoken to (such as "thou," "thee," "thy," "thine," "ye," "you," "your," or "yours"). Third person is the person(s) or thing(s) spoken about (such as "he," "she," "it," "his," "her," "them," or "their,"). The examples here given are all pronouns, but in many languages the verb forms have affixes which indicate first, second, or third person and also indicate whether they are singular or plural.

play on words is the use of the similarity in the sounds of two words to produce a special effect.

plural refers to the form of a word which indicates more than one. See singular.

possessive pronouns are pronouns such as "my," "our," "your," or "his," which indicate possession.

predicate is the part of a clause which complements the subject. The subject is the topic of the clause, and the predicate is what is said about the subject. For example, in "The small boy ran swiftly," the subject is "The small boy," and the predicate is "ran swiftly." See subject.

preposition is a word (usually a particle) whose function is to indicate the relation of a noun or pronoun to another noun, pronoun, verb, or adjective. Some English prepositions are "for," "from," "in," "to," and "with."

present tense. See tense.

pronouns are words which are used in place of nouns, such as "he," "him," "his," "she," "we," "them," "who," "which," "this," or "these."

purpose clause designates a construction which states the purpose involved in some other action; for example, "John came in order to help him," or "John mentioned the problem to his colleagues, so that they would know how to help out."

qualifier is a term which limits the meaning of another term. See qualify.

qualify is to limit the meaning of a term by means of another term. For example, in "old man," the term "old" qualifies the term "man."

receptor is the person receiving a message. The receptor language is the language into which a translation is made. For example, in a translation from Hebrew into German, Hebrew is the source language and German is the receptor language.

relative clause is a dependent clause which describes the object to which it refers. In "the man whom you saw," the clause "whom you saw" is relative because it relates to and describes "man."

restrictive clauses are so called because they restrict the reference of the objects which they qualify, while nonrestrictive clauses do not. In the expression "the soldiers who were retreating were commanded to halt and regroup" (no commas), the clause "who were retreating" indicates that the command was restricted to a particular class of soldiers, namely, those who were retreating. But in the expression "the soldiers, who were retreating, were commanded to halt and regroup," the same clause (this time set off by commas) refers to the same soldiers but does not define them; it simply provides supplementary information about them. In the latter case, the clause is nonrestrictive.

restructure. See structure.

rhetorical question is an expression which is put in the form of a question but which is not intended to ask for information. Rhetorical questions are usually employed for the sake of emphasis.

sentence is a grammatical construction composed of one or more clauses and capable of standing alone.

Septuagint is a translation of the Hebrew Old Testament into Greek, made some two hundred years before Christ. It is often abbreviated as LXX.

simile (pronounced SIM-i-lee) is a figure of speech which describes one event or object by comparing it to another, using "like," "as," or some other word to mark or signal the comparison. For example, "She runs like a deer," "He is as straight as an arrow." Similes are less subtle than metaphors in that metaphors do not mark the comparison with words such as "like" or "as." See metaphor.

singular refers to the form of a word which indicates one thing or person in contrast to plural, which indicates more than one. See plural.

specific is the opposite of generic. See generic.

structure is the systematic arrangement of the elements of language, including the ways in which words combine into phrases, phrases into clauses, and clauses into sentences. Because this process may be compared to the building of a house or bridge, such words as structure and construction are used in reference to it. To separate and rearrange the various components of a sentence or other unit of discourse in the translation process is to restructure it.

style is a particular or a characteristic manner in discourse. Each language has certain distinctive stylistic features which cannot be reproduced literally in another language. Within any language, certain groups of speakers may have their characteristic discourse styles, and among individual speakers and writers, each has his own style.

subject is one of the major divisions of a clause, the other being the predicate. In "The small boy walked to school," "The small boy" is the subject. Typically the subject is a noun phrase. It should not be confused with the semantic "agent," or actor. See predicate.

subjunctive refers to certain forms of verbs that are used to express an act or state as being contingent, possible, or probable (sometimes also as wish or desire), rather than as actual fact. For example, in "If John were here, he would help us," the verbs are traditionally called subjunctive. See indicative.

subordinate clause. See clause.

taboo refers to something set apart as sacred by religious custom and is therefore forbidden to all but certain persons or uses (positive taboo), or something which is regarded as evil and therefore forbidden to all by tradition or social usage (negative taboo).

temporal refers to time. A temporal abverb indicates the time of the verb it modifies.

tense is usually a form of a verb which indicates time relative to a discourse or
some event in a discourse. The most common forms of tense are past,
present, and future.

text, textual, refers to the various Greek and Hebrew manuscripts of the Scriptures. Textual variants are forms of the same passage that differ in one or
more details in some manuscripts. Textual problems arise when it is difficult to reconcile or to account for conflicting forms of the same text in two
or more manuscripts.

third person. See person.

Torah refers to the first five books of the Old Testament. It is a Hebrew word
meaning "teaching" or "law."

transitive is a predicate construction in which the verb has a direct object; for
example, "hit the man." By contrast, in an intransitive construction the verb
does not have or need a direct object to complete its meaning; for example,
"he lives."

transitionals are words or phrases which mark the connections between related
events. Some typical transitionals are "next," "then," "later," "after this,"
"when he arrived."

translation is the reproduction in a receptor language of the closest natural equivalent of a message in the source language, first, in terms of meaning, and
second, in terms of style.

variants, textual. See text, textual.

verbs are a grammatical class of words which express existence, action, or occur-
rence, such as "be," "become," "run," or "think."

vocative indicates that a word or phrase is used for referring to a person or persons spoken to. In "Brother, please come here," the word "Brother" is a
vocative.

voice in grammar is the relation of the action expressed by a verb to the partici-
pants in the action. In English and many other languages, the active voice
indicates that the subject performs the action ("John hit the man"), while the
passive voice indicates that the subject is being acted upon ("The man was
hit").

Index

This index includes concepts, key words, and terms for which the Handbook contains a discussion useful for translators.

[363]

Index

Printed in the United States of America